Principles of Land Law

Fourth Edition

Cavendish
Publishing
Limited

London • Sydney

Principles of Land Law

Fourth Edition

Martin Dixon, MA
Fellow and University Senior Lecturer in Law
Queens' College, University of Cambridge

Cavendish
Publishing
Limited

London • Sydney

Fourth edition first published in Great Britain 2002 by Cavendish Publishing Limited, The Glass House, Wharton Street, London WC1X 9PX, United Kingdom

Telephone: +44 (0)20 7278 8000   Facsimile: +44 (0)20 7278 8080

Email: info@cavendishpublishing.com

Website: www.cavendishpublishing.com

Dixon, Martin

Principles of land law – 4th ed – (Principles of law series)

1 Land tenure – Law and legislation – England 2 Land tenure – Law and legislation – Wales

I Title

346.4'2'043

ISBN 1 85941 472 9

Printed and bound in Great Britain

To Cornflake

PREFACE

Approaching land law can seem a daunting prospect. One major aim of this text is to dispel fears and to explain land law in an understandable and logical way. No attempt has been made to minimise the complexities of the subject simply to make it attractive or readable – for that benefits no one. Yet, the text is designed to explode the myths and mysteries of land law and substitute instead a picture that is both detailed and comprehensible. There is no denying that land law is different from other subjects, not least because its language is at first unfamiliar. But different does not mean difficult. Similarly, there is a common belief that land law is boring, not as sexy or apparently relevant as other legal disciplines! This too is misplaced, for land law remains at the heart of the legal system and is the vehicle for so much that concerns our everyday lives, both at home and work. Seen in context, the issues raised in land law can be as challenging and as relevant as any that any other law course has to offer.

Land law is also a subject based on principle: so *Principles of Land Law* is both a convenient and accurate title. The subject is like a jigsaw and this book aims to explain the principles and how they fit together to form a coherent whole. The arrangement of the chapters is intended to facilitate the growth of a steady understanding of each topic and its place within the jigsaw. There has been much important case law in recent years and important legislation reforming some of the core concepts in land law is now in place. The Land Registration Act 2002 received Royal Assent on 26 February 2002 and although it is not yet in force (that being a gradual process over the next five years), the Act changes the way we think and analyse modern land law. As it is, the subject has developed rapidly to meet the challenges of modern society and this has been reflected in the book.

Necessarily, while the author collects the criticisms that might be cast his or her way, there are many concerned with a book that deserve a share of any credit. Cavendish Publishing have been especially forgiving while the text was in preparation although I plead the Land Registration Act 2002. My wife has now given up pretending to be interested in land law but still ensures that I remain as sane as I ever was. My own students continue to be free with their advice about what they want from a text and I regard them as my most important audience.

Martin Dixon

Queens' College, Cambridge

April 2002

CONTENTS

Contents

Contents

TABLE OF CASES

TABLE OF STATUTES

TABLE OF ABBREVIATIONS

Terms

AGA	authorised guarantee agreement
AJA	Administration of Justice Act

Legislation

FLA	Family Law Act
LCA	Land Charges Act
LPA	Law of Property Act
LP (Misc Prov) A	Law of Property (Miscellaneous Provisions) Act
LRA	Land Registration Act
LTCA	Landlord and Tenants (Covenants) Act
SLA	Settled Land Act
TOLATA	Trusts of Land and Appointment of Trustees Act

Journals

CLJ	Cambridge Law Journal
Conv	The Conveyancer and Property Lawyer
CLP	Current Legal Problems
LQR	Law Quarterly Review
LS	Legal Studies
LTCA	Landlord and Tenant (Covenants) Act
MLR	Modern Law Review
SLR	Student Law Review
SLRYB	Student Law Review Yearbook

CHAPTER 1

AN INTRODUCTION TO MODERN LAND LAW

Land law is a subject steeped in history. It has its origins in the feudal reforms imposed on England by William the Conqueror after 1066 and many of the most fundamental concepts and principles of land law spring from the economic and social changes that began then. However, while these concepts and the feudal origins of land law should not, and cannot, be ignored, we must remember that we are about to examine a system of law that is alive and well in the 21st century. It would be easy to embark on an historical survey of land law, but not necessarily entirely profitable. Of course, the concepts and principles that were codified and refined in the years leading up to 1925 – the date of the great legislative reforms – are the products of decades of development, and every student of the subject must come to grips with the unfamiliar terminology and substance of the common law. Yet, the purpose of this book is to present land law as it is today without obscuring the concepts and principles it is built upon. Moreover, as we move speedily in our electronic age, there is no doubt that the 'modern' system of land law which came into effect on 1 January 1926 is beginning to creak with the strain of absorbing all that has happened to society since then. The Law Commission's proposals for reform of the land registration system have now come to fruition in the Land Registration Act (LRA) 2002 and much will be said of this critical legislation throughout this book.

Those reforms, found in detail in Law Commission Report No 271, *Land Registration for the 21st Century: A Conveyancing Revolution*, produced a draft Bill that, as noted, received Royal Assent on 26 February 2002. Although not all of the reforms will take effect immediately, this Act promises a new and genuinely modern mechanism for the regulation of land of registered title. Many of the reforms are controversial – at least for some – but they are the product of much labour and, on the whole, are greatly to be welcomed. Not least among them is the prospective introduction of a system of electronic conveyancing. This system – paperless, swift and hopefully efficient – will do much more than revolutionise the way in which land is sold or transferred. It marks the end of much ancient law (and lore) and is the clean break with the feudal past that has been too long coming. Indeed, it is not too grand to say that the consequences of the reform of the system of land registration and the gradual introduction of electronic conveyancing will be felt across the whole spectrum of land law. There is little that will be untouched. The early years of the 21st century will witness as radical a change to the way we use and enjoy this precious resource called 'land' as did those who first grappled with the 1925 legislation. For a property lawyer, these are interesting times.

1.1 The nature and scope of the law of real property

The law of real property (or land law) is, obviously, concerned with land, rights in or over land and the processes whereby those rights and interests are created and transferred. One starting point might be to consider the meaning of 'land' itself or, more properly, the legal definition of 'land' as found in the Law of Property Act (LPA) 1925. According to s 205(1)(ix) of the LPA 1925:

> Land includes land of any tenure, and mines and minerals ... buildings or parts of buildings and other corporeal hereditaments; also a manor, an advowson, and a rent and other incorporeal hereditaments, and an easement, right, privilege, or benefit in, over, or derived from land; but not an undivided share in land.

Clearly, this is complicated and this statutory definition assumes that the reader already has a working knowledge of the basic concepts of land law, such as 'incorporeal hereditaments', 'easements' or 'an undivided share in land'. In essence, what this statutory definition seeks to convey and what is at the heart of land law, is the idea that 'land' includes not only tangible, physical property like fields, houses or soil, but also intangible rights in the land, such as the right to walk across a neighbour's driveway (an example of an 'easement'), the right to control the use to which a neighbour may put his land (a 'restrictive covenant'), or the right to take something from another's land, such as fish (being a 'profit' and an example of an 'incorporeal hereditament'). As a matter of legal definition, 'land' is both the physical asset and the rights which the owner or others may enjoy in or over it. Consequently, 'land law' is the study of the creation, transfer, operation and termination of these rights, and the manner in which they affect the use and enjoyment of the physical asset.

It is also important to appreciate why land law is fundamentally different from other legal disciplines, such as contract law or the law of tort. As we shall see, very many transactions concerning land or rights in land take place through the medium of a contract. Thus, land is sold through a contract and the right to enjoy the exclusive possession of another's land for a defined period of time (a 'lease') may be given by a contract between the owner of the land (technically, the owner of an 'estate' in the land) and the person who is to enjoy the right. Obviously, the conclusion of the contract binds the parties to it and, pending the introduction of electronic, paperless conveyancing, usually requires them to 'complete' the transaction by executing a deed which formally 'grants' the right. In such cases, the contract is said to 'merge with the grant', and the contract ceases to have any separate existence. Indeed, in practice, the parties to a transaction may choose to proceed directly by grant (that is, by deed) without first formally concluding a separate contract. Clearly, however, whether the parties are bound by a 'mere' contract, or by the more formal deed, they may enforce the contract/deed against each other: in the former case, by an action for damages or specific performance, and in the latter by relying on the covenants (that is, promises) contained in the deed. Even if it comes about that property rights may be created electronically – that is without a paper deed or written contract – it will remain true that the parties to the electronic creation will be bound to each other. Yet, the thing that is so special about 'land law rights', whether created only by contract or by grant, is that they are capable of affecting other people, not simply the parties that originally created the right. To put it another way, 'land law rights' are capable of *attaching* to the land itself so that any person who comes into ownership or possession of the land may be entitled to enjoy the benefits that now come with the land (such as the right to possess the land exclusively, or the right to fix a television aerial to a neighbour's property), or may be subject to the burdens imposed on the land (such as the obligation to permit the exclusive possession of another person, or the fixing of the television aerial). This is the 'proprietary' nature of land law rights and it is very different from the merely 'personal' obligations which an ordinary contractual relationship establishes. In fact, another way of describing what land law is about is to say that it is the study of the creation and operation of proprietary rights, being rights which become part of the land and are not personal to the parties that created them.

This can be represented diagrammatically in the following ways:

Figure 1
Where A and B have entered into a contract for the creation of a proprietary right in favour of B, over A's land, the contract is enforceable between A and B like any other contract:

A – land owner: the grantor of the right

B – a person to whom A has granted a lease, easement or some other proprietary
right in A's land: the grantee of the right

Figure 2
Where A sells his land to X (or, more accurately, his right of ownership of the land), the proprietary nature of B's right means that it is *capable* of 'binding' X. The proprietary right is enforceable beyond the original parties to the contract: B's right may be enforceable against X, even though X had no part in the creation of the right:

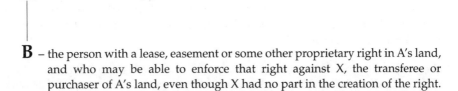

A————————▶**X**

B – the person with a lease, easement or some other proprietary right in A's land,
and who may be able to enforce that right against X, the transferee or
purchaser of A's land, even though X had no part in the creation of the right.

The intrinsic ability of proprietary rights to affect persons – in their capacity as owners or occupiers of land – other than the people who originally created those rights, means that the proper identification of what amounts to a 'proprietary right' is of particular importance. The categories of proprietary rights must be defined with some care, as not every right that has *something* to do with land can be proprietary. If that were the case, then the practical use and enjoyment of land by the owner would become extremely difficult, if not impossible. For example, in Chapter 9, we examine whether licences over land (being permissions given by the owner to another allowing use of the land for a specific purpose, such as the temporary erection of a marquee) are proprietary or merely personal. This is especially important given that licences may arise in a huge variety of circumstances. If licences are proprietary, the owner might find his land so overburdened by other peoples' rights that it becomes difficult to use for his own purposes and consequently less valuable on sale because the purchaser could also be bound to permit the licence holder to use the land. Necessarily, then, it is not all rights merely connected with land that are 'proprietary', and reference should be made to the *a priori* definition of 'an interest in land' (that is, a proprietary right) put forward by Lord Wilberforce in *National Provincial Bank v Ainsworth* (1965). In that case, the essential qualities of a proprietary right were said to be that it should be definable, identifiable by third parties, and capable of transferring to third parties. While this definition is open to the criticism that it is circular (for only if a right is already proprietary is it *capable* of transferring to third parties), it has the merit of emphasising the essentially durable nature of proprietary rights. It tells us that proprietary rights have a certain quality other than merely being connected with the use or enjoyment of land.

1.2 Types of proprietary rights

Generally, and with some necessary simplification for the purposes of exposition, 'proprietary rights' fall into two categories.

1.2.1 Estates in land

The 'doctrine of estates' forms one of the cornerstones of the law of real property, and this is as true today as it was in feudal times. Theoretically, all land in England and Wales is actually owned by the Crown and all other persons will own an estate in the land, rather than the land itself. In this sense, an estate confers a right to use and control land, being tantamount to ownership, but with the important difference that the estate will define the time for which the ownership lasts. An estate is equivalent to ownership of the land for a 'slice of time'.

- **The fee simple or freehold**

  When people say that they own land, they usually mean that they own this estate in the land: the fee simple. A fee simple comprises the right to use and enjoy the land for the duration of the life of the grantee and that of his heirs and successors. Furthermore, the fee simple estate is freely transferable ('alienable') during the life of the estate owner (that is, by gift, sale or loss through adverse possession – 'squatting') or on his death, by will or under the rules of intestate succession (when there is no will and the property passes to the next of kin), and each new estate owner is then entitled to enjoy the land for the duration of *his* life and that of *his* heirs and successors. Consequently, although the fee simple is, at its legal root, a description of ownership for a limited duration – as are all estates – the way in which the duration of the estate is defined and its free alienability means that, in most respects, the fee simple is equivalent to permanent ownership of the land and the paramount ownership of the Crown is irrelevant. Each fee simple owner has it within his own power to transfer the estate to another, and because the duration of the estate continues beyond the life of the current owner, it can survive through generations. However, in one situation, the true nature of the fee simple estate is revealed and the land will revert to the Crown as true absolute owner. If the current fee simple estate owner has not transferred the land during his life (and has not lost it through adverse possession), and then dies leaving no will and no next of kin to inherit under the rules of intestate succession, the estate has run its course and the land reverts to the Crown. This is uncommon, but it does illustrate the inherent nature of the fee simple as ownership for a slice of time. As we shall see, a fee simple may be either 'legal' or 'equitable', although the former is more common and the latter will arise only in special circumstances (for example, see Chapter 4 on co-ownership).

- **The leasehold**

  The leasehold estate comprises a right to use and enjoy the land as owner for a stated period of time. This may be one day, one year, one month, 99 years, or any defined period at all. Somewhat misleadingly, the leasehold estate (however long it is stated to last) is frequently referred to as a 'term of years'. The owner of a leasehold may be referred to as a 'leaseholder', 'lessee' or 'tenant' (sometimes 'underlessee' or 'subtenant'). The leasehold estate is carved out of any other estate (including itself), provided that its duration is fixed at less than the estate out of which it is carved. For example, a leasehold of any duration (say 999 years) may be carved out of a fee simple, the latter being of greater duration because of the principles discussed above. However, in the very unlikely event that the fee simple should actually terminate before the end of the leasehold period that is carved out of it, then the lease also terminates. Again, a leasehold can be carved out of a leasehold of longer duration: Y, who holds a lease of, say, seven years from the fee simple owner, may grant a lease of, say, three years to X. In fact, as will be discussed in Chapter 6, the fact that a lease can be carved from any estate of longer duration means that a plot of land may have several different 'owners', each enjoying specific rights in relation to the land; for example, a fee simple owner, a lessee, a sublessee, a sub-sublessee and so on. A leasehold may also be 'legal' or 'equitable', and both are common.

- **The fee tail**

  Although originally an estate, the fee tail is more properly regarded, since 1926, as an 'interest' in another's land. However, it is considered here because of its feudal origins as a true estate. The fee tail is an interest permitting its 'owner' the use of land for the duration of his life and that of his lineal descendants (not *all* heirs). A lineal descendant is a person who can show a parental, grandparental, great grandparental, etc, link. As with the fee simple, a fee tail (or 'entail') may turn out to be of very long duration indeed, save that an 'entail' may be curtailed in practice by restricting the qualifying successors to either male or female lineal descendants. At the death of the last lineal descendant (for example, the current interest holder has no sons or daughters), the land will revert either to the person entitled to the estate in fee simple or to the Crown if there is none. More importantly, although existing entails are unaffected, from 1 January 1997 it has become impossible to create any new interest in fee tail (Sched 1 to the Trusts of Land and Appointment of Trustees Act 1996). This, coupled with the fact that it has been, and still is, possible to turn an existing entail into a fee simple (by a process known as 'barring the entail') means that the interest in fee tail rarely survives as a feature of modern land law. Where it does exist, it may do so only as an 'equitable' interest (s 1 of the LPA 1925).

- **The life interest**

  Once again, the life interest was once an estate proper (that is, prior to the LPA 1925), and is considered here because of that history. A life interest gives the holder the right to use and enjoy the land for the duration of his life. On death, the life interest comes to an end and the land reverts to the superior estate owner, who is usually the fee simple owner. Somewhat confusingly, the owner of a life interest is frequently referred to as a 'life tenant', although this has nothing to do with the leasehold estate. As with the interest in fee tail, the life interest may exist only as an 'equitable' interest (s 1 of the LPA 1925).

All of this may seem complicated, but the important point to remember is that an estate effectively means ownership of the land: either of virtually permanent duration (fee simple), or limited by agreement to a defined period (the leasehold). The other two interests represent ownership for different slices of time, but are relatively unimportant. They will be discussed in the text where appropriate. All four estates/interests are 'proprietary' in that they are capable of being sold or transferred. In common parlance, the land (the fee simple) or the lease (leasehold) may be sold or transferred by the current owner at any time, provided that the estate/interest has not terminated. A may sell his freehold to B; C may sell his 999 year lease to D, provided that there is still time to run.

1.2.2   Interests in land

The above section considered those rights in land which give the holder a right of ownership for a defined period of time. By way of contrast, 'interests in land' may be used to denote those proprietary rights which one person enjoys in the land (technically, the 'estate') of another. As above, according to s 1 of the LPA 1925, the only true estates are the legal fee simple and the legal term of years (lease), because all other estates and interests 'take effect as equitable interests' (s 1(3) of the LPA 1925), but for ease of understanding an 'interest' can be regarded not as a right in one's own land, but in the 'estate' of another person. Good examples are the right of way over someone else's land (an easement) or the right to prevent an owner carrying on some specific activity on his own land (no trade or business: a restrictive covenant). These are proprietary interests in another person's land. As such, the right to enjoy the interest may be transferred or sold to another (usually, but not always, along with land benefitted by the right) and may be binding against a new owner of the 'estate' over which they exist, as illustrated by Figure 2, above.

1.3   The legal or equitable quality of proprietary rights

In the discussion of estates in land in the previous section, reference was made to whether the estate could be 'legal', or 'equitable', or both. In fact, it is important to determine of all proprietary rights (both estates and interests) whether they *may* exist as a legal or equitable right, and whether they do *in fact* exist as a legal or equitable right in any given case. To discuss whether a proprietary right is legal or equitable is to consider its quality as opposed to its content: the question is *not*, 'what does the right entitle a person to do on the land?' (content), but 'what is the nature of the right?' (that is, is it legal or equitable?). Moreover, even though the distinction between 'legal' and 'equitable' proprietary rights has become less important because of the changes brought about by the 1925 property legislation, it is impossible to come to grips with the modern law of real property without an understanding of (a) how the distinction between legal and equitable proprietary rights is to be made, and (b) the significance of the distinction. For the future, it may well be that the introduction of electronic, paperless conveyancing will make the distinction between legal and equitable rights largely redundant. Under s 93 of the LRA 2002, certain proprietary rights (estates or interests) will not actually exist unless created electronically by entry on the Register (or rather the 'virtual register') and so there will be no scope for the distinction between a 'legal' and 'equitable' version of these rights. They will either exist, or they will not. How this will work in practice and whether the courts will invent a 'default' status for rights not created electronically (when they should have been, for example, through proprietary estoppel (Chapter 9)) remains to be seen.

1.3.1 The origins of the distinction between legal and equitable rights

Historically, the distinction between legal and equitable rights was based on the type of court in which a claimant might obtain a remedy against a defendant for the unlawful denial of the claimant's right over the defendant's land. Thus, the King's Court (or court of common law) would grant a remedy to a claimant who could establish a case 'at law', usually on proof of certain formalities and on pleading a specified 'form of action'. The court of common law was, however, fairly inflexible in its approach to legal problems and would often deny a remedy to a deserving claimant simply because the proper formalities had not been observed. Consequently, the Chancellor's Court (or Court of Chancery) began to mitigate the harshness of the common law by giving an equitable remedy to a deserving claimant, even in the absence of the proper formalities. This led to many clashes of jurisdiction where a claimant was denied a remedy 'at law' in one court, but was able to secure a remedy 'in equity' in a different court, but it was the Court of Chancery, administering the rules of equity, which was to prevail. Consequently, what started out as different procedures for the administration of justice eventually developed into two different sets of substantive legal principles: the common law and equity administering 'legal' and 'equitable' rights respectively. Since the Judicature Act 1875, all courts are empowered to apply rules of 'law' or rules of 'equity', but, for the present, the distinction still remains in modern law. In the particular context of real property, this diversity of procedure led to the development of legal and equitable rights, initially being rights which either a court of law or a court of equity would recognise and enforce respectively. Today, the distinction between legal and equitable rights rests on other grounds but, as we shall see, it still has a flavour of the old distinction between the formality of the common law and the fairness of equity.

1.3.2 Making the distinction between legal and equitable rights today

In order to determine today (that is, prior to the introduction in full of electronic conveyancing) whether any given proprietary right is legal or equitable, two issues need to be addressed. First, is the right *capable* of existing as either a legal or equitable right? Secondly, if it is, has the right come into existence in the manner recognised as creating either a legal or equitable right? It follows from this that there are certain rights which may be only equitable (there are none which may be only legal), and some which may be of either quality, depending on how they have been created.

1.3.3   Section 1 of the Law of Property Act 1925: is the right capable of being either legal or equitable?

The starting point must be s 1 of the LPA 1925. This defines conclusively those rights which *may* be legal. Necessarily, therefore, any rights not within this statutory definition can only be equitable. According to s 1:

1   (1)   The only estates in land which are capable of subsisting or of being conveyed or created at law are –

(a)   an estate in fee simple absolute in possession;

(b)   a term of years absolute.

(2)   The only interests or charges in or over land which are capable of subsisting or of being conveyed or created at law are –

(a)   an easement, right or privilege in or over land [held as an adjunct to a fee simple or leasehold absolute in possession];

(b)   a rentcharge;

(c)   a charge by way of legal mortgage;

(d)   [not relevant for present purposes];

(e)   rights of entry [annexed to a legal lease or legal rentcharge].

(3)   All other estates, interests and charges in or over land take effect as equitable interests.

In simple terms, this means that, in the language of the distinction between *estates* and *interests*, the only *estates* which may be legal are the fee simple (the 'freehold'), provided it gives an immediate right to possession of the land ('absolute in possession') and the leasehold (whether giving possession immediately or on the termination of a prior right, that is, in 'possession' or 'reversion'); and the only *interests* capable of being legal are easements (and associated rights to enter another's land and take something from it, such as fish: *profits à prendre*), mortgages, rights of entry contained in a legal lease, and the (now, largely redundant) rentcharge. Given, therefore, that in the words of s 1(3), 'all other estates [and] interests ... take effect as equitable interests', such rights as the life interest and fee tail and such other interests as the restrictive covenant will always be equitable.

1.3.4   The manner of creation of the right

Section 1 of the LPA 1925 tells us only what rights *may* be legal; it does not say that they *always will* be legal. In other words, even the estates and interests specified in s 1 may be equitable in certain circumstances. If a proprietary right may, in principle, be either legal or equitable, then its final quality depends on the manner in which it has been created and whether the formality requirements established by statute have been observed. Generally, full formality is required for the creation of legal rights, and more informality permitted for the creation of equitable rights. Here lies the heart of the pre-electronic legal/equitable distinction, especially if we remember that the historical division between law and equity originated in a dispute between two sets of courts, one of which was prepared to enforce rights only if they were accompanied with the proper formality, the other that was prepared to enforce rights when it was equitable to do so, notwithstanding the lack of proper formality:

- **When is a proprietary right legal?**

  Assuming it falls within s 1 of the LPA 1925, a right will be 'legal' if it is created with proper formality, which at present generally means the use of a deed. A deed is a written document of a special kind which, according to s 1 of the Law of Property (Miscellaneous Provisions) Act (LP (Misc Prov) A) 1989, is expressed to be a deed on its face or by the person signing it. A deed must be witnessed by some person other than the persons who are parties to it. Usually, a document intended to be a deed will state that it is 'executed as a deed by X and Y'. Note, however, that, in special circumstances, certain proprietary rights may be legal without the execution of a deed, such as with certain leases for three years or less (Chapter 6) or an easement by 'prescription' (or long use: see Chapter 7). These special cases will be considered where appropriate. Also, it is important to appreciate at this stage that the Land Registration Act (LRA) 1925 – the statute that currently establishes a nationwide register of land ownership (see Chapter 2) – has affected the position. So, even if an estate that is capable of being legal has, in fact, been created by a deed (that is, the fee simple absolute in possession and leasehold), it will not take effect as a legal right until it is registered on the register of title as required by the LRA 1925. This is simply the consequence of the land registration system, which guarantees a person's estate (and its legal quality) when, but only when, it has been properly registered.

- **When is a proprietary right equitable?**

  A proprietary right will be equitable either because it is excluded from the definition of a legal estate/interest found in s 1 of the LPA 1925 and is created in the manner appropriate for the creation of equitable rights, or because it is a right which could have been legal or equitable, but is equitable because it is created only in the manner appropriate for the creation of equitable rights. In either case, the lesser formalities for the creation of equitable rights must be observed. In the majority of cases, this means that the equitable right must be created by a comprehensive written contract signed by, or on behalf of, the parties creating the right as required by s 2 of the LP (Misc Prov) A 1989 or by a written instrument within s 53 of the LPA 1925. Failing this, the proprietary right does not exist at all: it is 'void', although it may be possible to save part of a written instrument by severing a valid clause from an invalid one (*Murray v Guinness* (1998)). Of course, a written contract or instrument is relatively formal, but there is a clear distinction between these and a deed, not least that the latter must be witnessed. Note, however, that in exceptional circumstances, equity will recognise the existence of an equitable right arising from an oral contract or promise, providing the conditions for proprietary estoppel or constructive trust have been fulfilled (Chapters 4 and 9). As will be seen in Chapters 4 and 9, the creation of equitable rights by purely verbal dealings between the parties is not particularly uncommon, because it serves the needs of fairness – or equity – between the parties. It is an anathema to the law that a person should be able to deny that they have granted a proprietary right to another by pleading non-compliance with statutory formalities if this is their own fault. Nevertheless, the creation of equitable rights by proprietary estoppel or constructive trust (that is, verbally) are in the nature of exceptions to the rule that equitable rights usually should be created in writing, and, consequently, the relevant principles may not be so widely interpreted as to destroy the basic rule. For completeness, it should also be noted that rights arising before the 1989 Act can be equitable if created by an oral contract without the need to plead proprietary estoppel or constructive trust, provided that that oral contract was supported by some act of part performance in pursuit of the right, as in *Thatcher v Douglas* (1996), applying s 40 of the LPA 1925 (now repealed for rights arising post the 1989 Act).

1.3.5 The proposed system of electronic conveyancing

The picture presented above can, at its simplest, be stated thus: such rights as may be legal usually must be created or transferred by a deed in order actually to be legal (with some limited exceptions such as short leases and easements by 'prescription'); such rights as may be equitable (including 'failed' legal rights) usually must be created or transferred by a written instrument in order actually to exist in equity. In the absence of these 'formalities', the relevant right simply will not exist, unless rescued by some exceptional principle such as proprietary estoppel or constructive/resulting trusts. Necessarily, electronic or paperless conveyancing will change this. Under the proposed scheme – which although authorised by the LRA 2002 is lacking in detail pending the development of suitable Land Registration Rules – certain rights will not be able to be created unless they are entered electronically on the register of title of the relevant land: s 93 of the LRA 2002. So, it will matter not that a freehold or leasehold has been transferred or created by deed. If it (the freehold or leasehold) is in that class of 'disposition' that is required to be made by electronic entry on the register, it will not exist at all (legally or equitably) until it is so registered. Clearly, such a 'formality' requirement necessarily removes any meaningful distinction between legal and equitable rights. In reality, these rights (those required to be created by electronic registration) will either exist, or they will not.

In fact, this is rather a simple picture, because not all proprietary rights will be required to be transferred or created by electronic entry on the register. We do not yet know what rights will be subject to this new electronic regime or whether it will be mandatory in all circumstances. However, it is clear that some proprietary rights still will be capable of creation by deed or in writing (at least initially) possibly with a choice of either a paper deed/writing or electronic deed/writing, and so (presumably) the old legal/equitable distinction will have some relevance in these cases.

1.3.6   The division of ownership and the 'trust'

Although the distinction between legal and equitable rights turns, primarily, on the definition in s 1 of the LPA 1925 and the manner in which the right is created, there is a third way by which the distinction can arise. This is where enjoyment of the land is regulated by use of the 'trust'. In English law and systems derived from it, it is perfectly possible for a single piece of property (*any* property) to be owned by two or more people at the same time. This is not simply that two people may share ownership; it is, rather, that two or more people may have a different quality of ownership over the same property at the same time. In other words, one person may have the legal title to the property, and another may have the equitable title. Of course, in the normal course of events, when a person owns land (or any other property), this legal and equitable title is not separated, and the person is regarded simply as 'the owner'. However, it is the ability to split ownership that is so unique to the English legal system and other systems derived from it. So, for land, it is possible to have a legal owner and an equitable owner, one with legal rights of ownership, the other with equitable rights. Necessarily, these two owners must stand in a relationship to each other and this relationship is known as a 'trust'. This is what is meant when it is said that A holds land on trust for B: A is the legal owner (and trustee), and B is the equitable owner:

Figure 3

| Legal owner | Equitable owner |
| (trustee) | (beneficiary) |

Land, or rights in land, are held by A on trust for B.

The trust that exists between A and B can take many forms and different rights and duties can be imposed on A (the trustee) for the benefit of B (the beneficiary) depending on how the trust was established and any relevant statutory provisions (for example, the Trust of Land and Appointment of Trustees Act 1996 – see Chapter 4). In some circumstances, a trust will be imposed on a landowner without a deliberate act of trust creation, thus creating by force of law a distinction between the legal and equitable titles (see Chapter 4). Finally, it is also important to appreciate that the creation of legal and equitable proprietary rights through the use of a trust requires compliance with a different but complementary set of formality rules: that is, rules similar to (but not identical with) those required for the simple creation of proprietary rights. Unless there is a 'constructive trust', 'resulting trust' (see Chapter 4), or a successful claim of proprietary estoppel (Chapter 9), a trust concerning land or any right therein must be 'manifested and proved by some writing' (s 53(1)(b) of the LPA 1925). This means that the existence of the legal and equitable interests under a trust concerning land depends on the trust being created in the proper manner, although the requirement here is that the trust of land must be evidenced by some written document, rather than actually be in writing itself.

1.4   The consequences of the legal/equitable distinction

It is apparent from the above that whether a proprietary right is legal or equitable may tell us many things; for example, how the right was created and whether there is any possibility of the existence of a trust. However, one of the most important consequences of the distinction, albeit much modified by statute, is the different way in which legal or equitable rights can affect the new owners or occupiers of the land over which such rights exist. As noted at the outset of this chapter, the peculiar quality of proprietary rights is that they attach to the land, and thus the right to enforce them, or the obligation to honour them, is *capable* of passing to new owners of the benefitted or burdened land. This is the situation represented by Figure 2, above. So, in practice, the precise effect of a proprietary right on a third party (in the sense of their obligation to honour it) can sometimes depend on whether it is 'legal' or 'equitable'. Necessarily this is a simple picture because the situation is much modified by the 1925 legislation. But even now it is impossible to understand modern land law without an appreciation of this issue.

1.4.1   Legal status before the 1925 legislation

Prior to 1 January 1926, if a proprietary right was *legal*, it would always bind every person who came to own or occupy the land over which it existed. As was commonly said, 'legal rights bind the whole world', and the person entitled to enforce the legal proprietary right could exercise it against any purchasers, squatters, donees of gifts and all others. So, for example, the person entitled to a legal right of way (an easement) would have been able to enjoy that right no matter who came to own or occupy the land over which it existed.

1.4.2   Equitable status before the 1925 legislation

Prior to 1 January 1926, if the right was *equitable*, it would bind every transferee of the land *except* a *bona fide* purchaser for value of a legal estate in the land who had no notice of the equitable right. This appears to be a complicated rule, but it can be broken down into its constituent parts. Thus, an equitable right *would* be binding on a transferee of the land in all the following cases:

(a) where the transferee was not a purchaser for value, as where he received the land by will, or as a gift, or under the rules of adverse possession (squatting);

(b) where the transferee did not purchase a legal estate in the land, as where he occupied the land under an equitable lease;

(c) where the transferee was not *bona fide*, as where he acted in bad faith;

(d) where the transferee had notice of the equitable right, as where he either knew of its existence (actual notice) or knew of circumstances from which a reasonable person would have been aware of its existence (constructive notice) (*Hunt v Luck* (1902); *Kingsnorth v Tizard* (1986)), or the transferee's agent had actual or constructive notice (so called imputed notice, when, for example, the transferee's solicitor had notice).

In all these cases, the equitable right would have been binding on a transferee of the land. However, it is important to realise that, in the great majority of cases, the transferee of the land would easily fulfil the first three requirements of the *'bona fide* purchaser' rule and so hope to escape being bound by the equitable right. In practice, the only real question would be whether he had notice of the equitable right. Consequently, the rule about equitable interests became known as the 'doctrine of notice', because it was usually the transferee's 'notice' of the equitable interest (therefore, bound by it) or lack of notice (not bound) that was the live issue. Unfortunately, such were (and are) the vagaries of the doctrine of notice that both the transferee of the land and the owner of the equitable right could never be sure whether his land or his right (as the case may have been) was secure. In many cases, the 'owner' of an equitable right over land could do little to ensure its survival should the burdened land be sold, and, conversely, a purchaser might find that the land they had just purchased was encumbered by an equitable right of which they were deemed to have constructive notice. In short, the operation of the doctrine of notice was so uncertain that the 1925 property legislation modified the rule in a radical way and thereby substantially reduced the importance of the legal/equitable distinction.

1.5   The 1925 property legislation

All that we have considered so far forms the basis of the modern law of real property. However, the start of the 20th century brought with it fundamental social and economic changes, and when these were allied to the defects, mysteries, vagaries and plain injustices of the law before 1925, it was clear that wholesale reform was necessary. The detail of the legislative changes that came into effect on 1 January 1926 are considered later, in the appropriate chapters, especially Chapters 2, 3 and 4, but for now it is important to realise that both substantive and structural changes were made in 1925, particularly regarding the question of ownership of land and the way in which proprietary rights could affect 'third parties', being persons who came to the land after the proprietary right had been created. The main legislative enactments are noted below.

1.5.1 The Law of Property Act 1925

The LPA 1925 made substantive changes in the law of real property, including, as we have seen, a redefinition of what rights could be legal or equitable. It also has much to say about joint ownership of land, the creation of proprietary rights, the nature of the fee simple and leasehold, and much more. Although amended in parts, it remains the governing statute for modern land law.

1.5.2 The Settled Land Act 1925

The Settled Land Act 1925 is a complicated statute, designed to regulate the creation and operation of successive interests in land, as where a house is given to A for his life, and then to B. It is considered in Chapter 5. Its importance is much diminished by the abolition of settled land for dispositions taking effect on or after 1 January 1997: see s 2 of the Trusts of Land and Appointment of Trustees Act 1996.

1.5.3 The Land Registration Act 1925

The machinery established by the LRA 1925 is examined in detail in Chapter 2. Currently, this statute is fundamental to the modern law of real property. It creates a system whereby title to land (being the estates of legal fee simple or legal leasehold) and many other rights in that land are recorded by the Land Registry in a register of land held by district offices. In essence, each title will be assigned a 'title number' linked to a plot of land, under which the ownership and many other rights will be recorded. The purpose is to replace the haphazard system of conveyancing that existed before 1 January 1926 and, especially, to bring certainty and stability to the difficulties surrounding the effect of proprietary rights on third parties. As such, the LRA 1925 applies to what is loosely called 'registered land'. As indicated already, the system introduced by the LRA 1925 was ripe for reform and that reform has now found shape in the LRA 2002. The detail of this will be discussed in Chapter 2 and although most of the central principles of land registration will remain the same (albeit 'tidied up' to reflect modern circumstances) there is much that will be different. The 2002 Act will not take effect all at once, but gradually as circumstances determine. It is anticipated that no significant provision will be brought into force before early 2003.

1.5.4 The Land Charges Act 1972

The Land Charges Act (LCA) 1972 (originally, the Land Charges Act 1925) is also examined in detail later (Chapter 3). Once again, it establishes a system to regulate the transfer of land and is also designed to bring certainty to dealings with land affected by another's equitable interest in that land. Importantly, land that is covered by the LCA 1972 is not 'registered land' and it falls outside the scope of the LRA 1925 and the LRA 2002. Thus, the LCA 1972 governs what is called 'unregistered land', this being land to which the title is not entered on a register but proved by the title deeds and related documents.

1.6 The distinction between registered and unregistered land

The fundamental distinction which every student and practitioner must draw since 1 January 1926 is between registered and unregistered land. The former is governed by the LPA 1925, the common law and currently the LRA 1925 (as amended). The latter is governed by the LPA 1925, the common law and the LCA 1972. Most importantly of all, registered and unregistered land are mutually exclusive. Land either falls into one system or the other, but never both at the same time. Gradually (as explained in Chapter 2), virtually all land will become of registered title but, until then, two systems of land conveyancing are in operation in this country side by side. What follows is an outline of the two systems and the detail is provided later in Chapters 2 and 3. Particular attention should be paid to the way in which both systems deal with the question of the effect of proprietary interests on third parties, that is, the issue that was once governed, principally, by the distinction between legal and equitable rights and the doctrine of notice.

1.6.1 Registered land

(a) Registered land is land to which *the title* is registered in a register. Every title is given a title number and details of the current owners are registered against it. Once a person is registered as title owner, that ownership is guaranteed by the State and prospective purchasers may buy the land in the certainty that the title has been thoroughly investigated and approved before it was first registered (for example, as in *Habenec v Harris* (1998)). The essence of this scheme will be preserved under the LRA 2002.

(b) A second category of right in registered land is the *registered charge*. These are essentially mortgages, used to raise money for the estate owner by offering the land as security. They are also entered against the title. Corresponding provision is made under the LRA 2002.

(c) There is another category of proprietary right in registered land, defined in the LRA 1925, called *overriding interests*. Overriding interests are automatically binding on any transferee or occupier of the land, without the need for any kind of registration or notice. Note that overriding interests are not only comprised of legal rights, but include a number of equitable rights. This is because overriding interests currently are statutorily defined in the LRA 1925 (see s 70(1)) and this definition is conclusive. In fact, it is a right's status as an 'overriding interest' that is important (not its legal or equitable quality) and it is this statutory status that makes such rights binding on a third party. The concept of interests which override is preserved by the LRA 2002, albeit in much modified form.

(d) A fourth category of right in registered land is the *minor interest*. Minor interests include all other proprietary rights not included in the above categories, although nearly all will be equitable. The fundamental point about minor interests is that they will only bind a purchaser of the land *if* they registered against the registered title. If they are not registered, they are void against a purchaser of the affected land, meaning that they cannot be enforced against him and are destroyed (for example, as in *Petrou v Petrou* (1998)). Similar provisions exist under the LRA 2002.

To conclude, three points about registered land bear repetition:

First, in registered land, currently the effect of a proprietary right on a transferee of the land is determined by its status under the LRA 1925, especially whether it is an overriding or minor interest. Its legal or equitable quality is relevant, but not crucial.

Secondly, under the system of the LRA 1925, the 'doctrine of notice' is entirely irrelevant.

Thirdly, the concept of overreaching (see Chapters 2 and 4) may allow a purchaser of registered land to defeat *certain* equitable rights, even if they are technically overriding or are properly registered as minor interests. So, a purchaser who pays the purchase price to the co-owners of a legal estate will 'overreach' any equitable owners, meaning that the equitable ownership rights cannot bind that purchaser, whether or not the rights fall within the definition of overriding interests or registered minor interests. The equitable owner's rights are, in fact, transferred to the purchase money that has been paid. Overreaching is a limited, but powerful, 'trump card' and is explained in greater detail later – see Chapters 3 and 4.

1.6.2 Unregistered land

Unregistered land is land to which *the title is not registered*. The title is located in the title deeds, and a prospective purchaser must investigate 'root of title' through examination of the title deeds in order to be confident of obtaining an unimpeachable right to the land. Further, in unregistered land, it remains true that 'legal rights bind the whole world'. This aspect of the pre-1926 common law remains important and an understanding of how 'legal' rights come into existence is therefore crucial. However, equitable rights in unregistered land fall into three distinct and separate categories:

(a) most equitable rights are 'land charges' within the LCA 1972. As such, they must be registered against the owner of the land over which they take effect (*not* the land itself) in order to bind a purchaser of it. If they are not registered, they are not binding (void) and the doctrine of notice is irrelevant. It should be noted that this is an *entirely separate* system of registration from that which exists in registered land. The two different systems of registration are mutually exclusive, and operate under different statutes. The equitable rights that are land charges for the purposes of registration under the LCA 1972 are defined in the LCA 1972 itself. They are generally rights of a commercial nature (for example, an equitable mortgage);

(b) there are a number of equitable rights which do not fall within the statutory definition of land charges. Consequently, they are *not* registrable under the LCA 1972 and are not 'land charges'. Their effectiveness against a purchaser is decided by the application of the old doctrine of notice. This is a very limited class of right;

(c) there are certain special equitable rights which are neither land charges nor always subject to the doctrine of notice. These are the rights that are overreachable (see Chapter 4). They are equitable rights of a special character, being rights capable of easy quantification in money (for example, equitable ownership of a proportion of a house). They may be 'overreached' so as not to be binding on a new purchaser of the land, meaning that the equitable owner may be required to take the monetary value of the right rather than enjoy the right over the land itself. This is explained more fully in Chapter 3, but its relevance here is to signpost the existence of equitable rights in unregistered land that are neither land charges under the LCA 1972, nor subject to the old doctrine of notice.

So, to reiterate with respect to unregistered land:

First, in unregistered land, the distinction between legal and equitable rights is still of fundamental importance.

Secondly, in unregistered land, the doctrine of notice is largely irrelevant, but may still play a part for those equitable rights which fall outside of the LCA 1972 and which are not overreached.

Thirdly, the concept of overreaching (see Chapters 3 and 4) also applies to unregistered land, and may allow a purchaser of unregistered land to defeat *certain* equitable rights.

Fourthly, over 85% of all titles are registered land and unregistered land is slowly but surely disappearing from the map. Land that is currently unregistered becomes registered on the occasion of certain dealings with it. These 'triggers' for compulsory registration are discussed in Chapter 2. There are also procedures by which an estate owner may apply for voluntary registration of title. The entry into force of the LRA 2002 is likely to encourage greater voluntary registration. However, the point is simply that unregistered land is a fading system and soon will barely trouble practitioners and students alike.

1.7 A diagrammatic representation of the 1925 property legislation

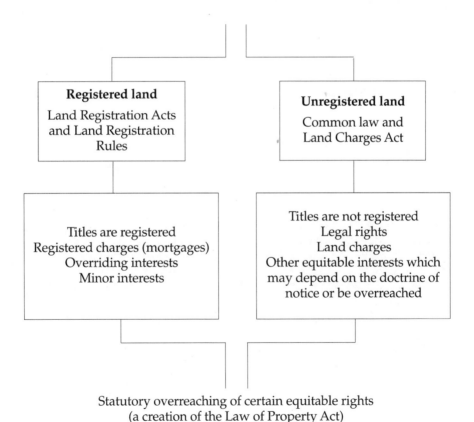

LAW OF PROPERTY ACT 1925

introducing substantive change to land law
effective 1 January 1926

Registered land

Land Registration Acts
and Land Registration
Rules

Unregistered land

Common law and
Land Charges Act

Titles are registered
Registered charges (mortgages)
Overriding interests
Minor interests

Titles are not registered
Legal rights
Land charges
Other equitable interests which
may depend on the doctrine of
notice or be overreached

Statutory overreaching of certain equitable rights
(a creation of the Law of Property Act)
applicable to both registered and unregistered land

AN INTRODUCTION TO MODERN LAND LAW

The nature and scope of the law of real property

The law of real property (or land law) is concerned with land, rights in or over land and the processes whereby those rights and interests are created and transferred. Rights in or over land are different from 'mere' contractual rights, in that 'land law rights' are capable of affecting persons other than the parties who created the rights. This is the 'proprietary' nature of land law rights and it is completely different from the merely 'personal' obligations which an ordinary contractual relationship establishes. Proprietary rights can 'run' with the land and can confer benefits and burdens on whomsoever comes to own the land.

Types of proprietary rights

Proprietary rights are either 'estates' or 'interests'. An 'estate' is a right to use and control land, being tantamount to ownership, but with the important difference that the 'estate' will define the time for which their 'ownership' lasts. An 'estate' is equivalent to ownership of the land for a slice of time. The two estates proper are:

(a) the fee simple (or freehold); and

(b) the leasehold (or term of years or tenancy).

An 'interest' is generally a right which one person enjoys over land belonging to someone else; technically, an interest is a right in the estate of another person. These include two former estates (the fee tail and life interest), but also more limited rights such as the easement (for example, a right of way) and restrictive covenant (a right to control a neighbour's use of land).

The legal or equitable quality of proprietary rights

Section 1 of the LPA 1925 defines which proprietary rights may be legal. These include the fee simple absolute in possession, the term of years absolute (both 'estates'), the easement, mortgage and right of re-entry (all 'interests'). An estate or interest not falling within this section must necessarily be equitable. For estates and interests that *do* fall within the section, their legal or equitable status will be determined by the manner of their creation. Assuming the estate or interest falls within s 1 of the LPA 1925:

- a right will be 'legal' if it is created with proper formality, which usually means by deed. Note that, in special circumstances, certain proprietary rights may be legal without the execution of a deed, such as where there is a lease for three years or less, or an easement is generated by prescription;

- a right will be 'equitable' if it is created by written contract or instrument within s 2 of the LP (Misc Prov) A 1989. In exceptional circumstances, equity will recognise the existence of a right arising from an oral contract or promise, providing the conditions for proprietary estoppel or constructive trust have been fulfilled;

- it will be possible (and later mandatory) to create proprietary rights electronically under the LRA 2002;

- for proprietary rights falling outside s 1 of the LPA 1925 (and which can, therefore, only ever be equitable) the right must also be created according to s 2 of the LP (Misc Prov) A 1989 in order to exist as an equitable right. Without such written instrument (or the exception of estoppel/constructive trust), the right will not exist at all;

- the distinction between legal and equitable proprietary rights also can arise through the use of the 'trust'. One person may have the 'legal' title to property and another may have the 'equitable' title. This is common in co-ownership situations.

The original significance of the 'legal'/'equitable' distinction prior to 1926

As well as indicating how a proprietary right came into existence and whether any trust is involved, a significant reason for distinguishing between legal and equitable proprietary rights before the 1925 property legislation was that this could determine their effect on third parties:

(a) if the right were legal, it would always bind every transferee of the land over which it existed;

(b) if the right were equitable, it would bind every transferee of the land except a *bona fide* purchaser for value of a legal estate in the land who had no notice of the equitable right.

These principles have been replaced to a very considerable extent by requirements of registration.

The 1925 property legislation

The LPA 1925 made substantive changes in the law of real property, including, as we have seen, a redefinition of what rights may be 'legal' or 'equitable'. It applies in equal measure to registered and unregistered land.

The LRA 1925 establishes a system whereby title to land is recorded in a Register held at district offices. Provision is made for the registration of other rights affecting the land. 'Registered land' now counts for over 85% of all titles. The land registration system will be thoroughly overhauled on entry into force of the LRA 2002.

The LCA 1972 (replacing the LCA 1925) establishes a system of registration of equitable interests in unregistered land, being land where title is not entered on a register. Land covered by the LCA falls outside of 'registered land'. So called unregistered land is now much less important, given that most titles fall under the LRA 1925. Unregistered conveyancing will largely disappear as more titles become registered.

The SLA 1925 controls dealings with 'successive' interests in land, but only in respect of settlements in existence before 1 January 1997. Thereafter, any new successive interests are controlled by the Trusts of Land and Appointment of Trustees Act 1996.

The distinction between 'registered' and 'unregistered land'

- **Registered land**

  Registered land is land to which the title is registered, for example, the legal freehold or currently the legal lease of over 21 years' duration (this changes under the LRA 2002). Other categories of right in registered land are: registered charges (for example, mortgages); overriding interests (being rights that are automatically binding on a transferee of the land without the need for any kind of registration or notice); and minor interests (being rights requiring registration to bind a purchaser of the land).

- **Unregistered land**

  Unregistered land is land to which the title is not registered. The title is located in the title deeds and a prospective purchaser must investigate 'root of title'. In unregistered land, it remains true that 'legal rights bind the whole world', although the validity of equitable rights against a purchaser depends on their status as land charges (requiring registration under the LCA 1972), overreachable rights, or rights dependant on the doctrine of notice.

CHAPTER 2

REGISTERED LAND

2.1 Introduction

The system of registered land was perhaps the greatest of the reforms that came out of the wholesale restructuring of English property law in 1925. Simply put, to describe land as 'registered' means that the *title* to it (which for convenience can be thought of as a right of ownership) is recorded in a register maintained by the Land Registry at a number of District Land Registries around the country. In addition to information about the title itself (for example, quality of title, identity of estate owner), other rights and interests affecting the title may be entered on the Register against the title number. Moreover, while it is convenient to talk of registration of 'land', in fact, the system turns on registration of title and is not undertaken plot by plot, although the land to which each title is assigned is recorded in the Register. It is perfectly possible, therefore, for one plot of land to have more than one type of title registered in respect of it and where this occurs (for example, a registered fee simple and a registered long lease) this will be identified clearly on the Register. As things currently stand, not every 'estate' may be a 'registered title' and, in fact, a 'registered title' is either a *legal freehold* (being the fee simple absolute in possession) or a *legal leasehold* of over 21 years duration (or with over 21 years left to run). All other estates cannot be registered in their own right but, as discussed in the previous chapter, these two 'qualifying' titles are for all intents and purposes the most important indicia of land ownership in modern land law. The Land Register is thus intended to provide a comprehensive picture of land ownership in England and Wales and registration of title is intended to replace deeds of title as the proof of that ownership. So while the mechanics of the system are complicated, the central idea is simple enough. There should exist an accurate and reasonably comprehensive record of title to land and of third party interests in that land so that dealings with the land can be accomplished safely and quickly. In pursuit of this, on 1 December 1990, all land in England and Wales became subject to compulsory first registration of title, although, at that time, there were already some 13 million registered titles. Today, the Land Registry estimates that over 80% of titles are registered.

The consequence of the introduction of nationwide compulsory first registration of title on 1 December 1990 is that certain transactions concerning what is currently unregistered land will trigger the requirement that the new owner seeks registration by application to the relevant District Land Registry. On such application, the Land Registry will investigate the title and will register it by assigning a unique title number. In order to speed up the process of registration, the Land Registration Act 1997 has increased the number of transactions that will trigger a compulsory first registration of a qualifying title. As specified in s 123 of the Land Registration Act (LRA) 1925, as amended by s 1 of the LRA 1997, the 'triggers' for compulsory first registration of the two registrable titles now are:

- the transfer ('conveyance') on sale of the freehold (that is, the fee simple absolute in possession);

- the creation ('grant') of the long lease (that is, over 21 years duration);

- the transfer ('assignment') of an existing lease to a new lessee, provided the lease has over 21 years to run;

- the transfer by gift of the qualifying titles (new);

- the transfer of the qualifying titles pursuant to a court order (new);

- the creation of a first legal mortgage over the qualifying titles (new);

- assents in respect of the qualifying titles, an assent being the document necessary to transfer the title to a person entitled on the death of the former owner (new);

- vesting deeds in respect of the qualifying titles. A vesting deed is the document necessary to vest title in the person entitled to the life estate under a settlement (see Chapter 5).

The great majority of transactions concerning unregistered land will be caught by these triggers with the consequence that, as the Land Registry estimates, over 90% of all qualifying titles will be registered by the year 2004. Some land will, however, remain of unregistered title under these provisions (for example, land owned by an incorporated charity where retention of the land is essential to furtherance of the charitable purpose) unless the triggers for compulsory first registration are extended (as they may be under s 1(4) of the LRA 1997), or if incentives for *voluntary* first registration become effective.

It is a common misconception that land registration in England and Wales is a relatively modern phenomenon. In fact, the first legislation occurred in 1862, with further statutes in 1875 and 1897, although admittedly it was not until the entry into force of the Land Registration Act 1925 on 1 January 1926 that giant steps were taken toward a nationwide system of title registration. This primary piece of legislation still governs registered land today, albeit that it has been amended on a number of occasions since. However, it is a creaking statute and, in parts, it is not well drafted. In other areas its provisions sit ill at ease with modern conceptions of 'property' and it often fails to reflect the reality of the many uses of land in a modern economy. It makes no provision for the technological age in which we live. Consequently, the recent past has witnessed a joint effort by the Land Registry and the Law Commission to produce new legislation that will take land registration into the 21st century. In July 1998, the Law Commission published its Report No 271 entitled *Land Registration for the 21st Century: A Conveyancing Revolution*. This contained a Draft Bill designed to replace the LRA 1925 in its entirety while, of course, re-enacting many of its provisions. On 26 February 2002, the Land Registration Act (LRA) 2002 received Royal Assent. The LRA 2002 is not yet in force and no major part of it is expected to be so until early 2003. Even then, the LRA 2002 will be brought into force piecemeal and it may be many years before some of its more radical provisions – for example, those concerned with electronic conveyancing – start to govern registered land. What this means for a student of the subject is that he or she will have to become familiar with two systems governing land of registered title, albeit that those systems will share very many common features. The law of the LRA 1925 is, at present, the governing law. The law of the LRA 2002 will become the law governing registered land in due course, but not all in one go. Consequently, this chapter will analyse the law in force in 2002: the law of the LRA 1925. However, appropriate reference will be made to any changes made by the LRA 2002 to the LRA 1925 system and, for ease of reference, the chapter will conclude with an overview of the principal features of the new legislation.

2.2 The nature and purpose of the system of registered land

The LRA 1925 (as amended) and the Land Registration Rules made thereunder contain the detail of the current system of registered land. Together they provide a statutory code that seeks to regulate the transfer, use and enjoyment of registered land. Undoubtedly, the system of registered land is not perfect and it is not always logical, but an understanding of it is indispensable for a proper understanding of modern land law. As we shall see, many of the concepts and traditions of the pre-1926 law have been retained and one way of approaching registered land is to see it as a mechanism in which pre-1926 concepts are given a new direction. However, we must remember that the 1925 LRA represents an attempt to impose a structure on an area of law that had hitherto developed organically and spasmodically as social and economic circumstances dictated. Of course, that does not mean that the system of registered land itself has not developed organically within the confines of the legislative scheme that surrounds it, and it would be disastrous had it been otherwise, but that should not obscure the fundamental change that came into effect on 1 January 1926. We now have a legal system for the control and management of land, and interests in land, that was intended to operate as an integrated whole. Thus, students must be familiar with the *mechanics* of registered land before attempting to deal with the substantive proprietary rights which that system regulates.

Indeed, the advantage in seeing 'registered land' as separate system distinct from unregistered land (and not merely as a gloss on unregistered land) will become a necessity under the LRA 2002. One of the philosophical foundations of the 2002 Act is that registered land should not be hindered in its development or operation by concepts drawn from land of unregistered title. Thus, in many areas, the LRA 2002 departs from the ancient principles of unregistered conveyancing. As the Law Commission pointed out in its Report No 271, there is neither need nor profit in tying the law of registered land to the dictates of unregistered land. Perhaps the most obvious example of this is provided by the provisions of the LRA 2002 relating to adverse possession of registered land. These have departed in a radical way from the principles applicable to land of unregistered title (see Chapter 11).

Moreover, it should not be thought that this change of approach – to a legislatively confined, rather than totally organic system – was undertaken lightly. The 1925 reforms were necessary in order to meet the economic and social demands of the modern era just as the 2002 reforms are necessary to take the system forward in the 21st century. Land is one of the most important economic assets of any nation, but it is also used for a variety of social and domestic purposes that many would argue are at the foundation of a civilised society. Land law has to reflect the needs of commerce, families, financial institutions, neighbours, purchasers and occupiers. It is in this context that the system of registered land must operate, for it is these masters that land law has to serve.

Consequently, it is difficult to draw up a complete list of the aims and purposes of the land registration system of England and Wales, not least because the LRA 1925 was just one component of the widespread and co-ordinated legislative reforms of 1925. In this respect, it must also be remembered that many of these structural changes in the mechanics of land law would not have been possible without the complimentary changes in the substantive law of estates and interests that were brought about by the Law of Property Act 1925. These were discussed in Chapter 1 and are an important step in the achievement of the objectives outlined below. With that in mind, we may note that the system of registered land is dedicated:

• to reducing the expense and effort of purchasing land by eliminating the lengthy and formalistic process of investigating root of title. If title is registered, the owners of land should be easily discoverable and the possibility of fraud reduced. Thus, land becomes much more saleable and alienable;

• to reducing the dangers facing a purchaser who is buying land from a person whose title is unsafe, unclear or difficult to establish. The purchaser can rely on the register of title if title to that land has been recorded after investigation by the Land Registrar;

- to ensuring that a purchaser of land knows of the rights and interests of other persons over that land, thereby ensuring that the price paid reflects the true economic and social value of the land. The purchase can be abandoned if the purchaser is unable to use the land for the purpose intended;

- to enabling the purchaser to buy land completely free of certain types of interest over that land, those interests then taking effect in the money paid to the seller (overreaching);

- to providing a mechanism whereby certain third party rights in land can be protected and so survive a sale of that land to a new owner. For this reason, the old doctrine of notice plays no part in the system of registered land, having been superseded by the operation of the Register, in particular by overriding interests and minor interests.

As well as these important aims which – as we shall see – have been implemented with varying degrees of success by the 1925 Act, registration of title has brought other benefits: accurate plans are provided, simple forms and procedures have replaced bulky title deeds, disputes can usually be resolved more easily and confidence has been brought to the conveyancing process.

2.2.1   Under the Land Registration Act 2002

The aims and achievements of the LRA 1925 are used as the foundations for the LRA 2002 and, indeed, a primary purpose of the new Act is to enhance even further the security of title offered by registered land and to quicken the conveyancing process. In this sense, the scheme of the LRA 2002 reduces the extent to which any interest not on the register can affect a purchaser of registered land (see, for example, the discussion of 'overriding interests') and establishes mechanisms to make 'title by registration' a reality instead of 'registration of title' as it stands under the LRA 1925. Of particular importance in this regard are the provisions relating to adverse possession and electronic conveyancing. The role of the former is severely curtailed in registered land, thus improving the security offered by the register, and the latter will do much to ensure that the land is burdened only by those rights actually noted on the register. It will also, in time, speed up the conveyancing process because most transactions concerning registered land will be required to be undertaken electronically so that dealings with the land occur simultaneously with an entry being made on the register (not, as now, by paper dealings which are later sent for registration). In consequence, the register will become more clearly a true record of all rights and interests over the registered title with a reduction in the need to make additional enquiries or numerous physical inspections of the property. As the Law Commission commented in Report No 271, the 'fundamental objective' of the Act is that 'the register should be a complete and accurate reflection of the state of the title of the land at any given time, so that it is possible to investigate title to land on line, with the absolute minimum of additional enquiries and inspections' (Report No 271, para 1.5).

2.3 The so called 'three principles' of registered land

It is sometimes said that there are three principles underlying the system of registered land against which we should judge the reality of the LRA 1925. These are the mirror principle, the curtain principle and the insurance principle.

2.3.1 The mirror principle

The *mirror principle* encapsulates the idea that the Land Register should reflect the totality of the rights and interests concerning a title of registered land. Thus, inspection of the Register should reveal the identity of the owner, the nature of his ownership, any limitations on his ownership and any rights enjoyed by other persons over the land which are adverse to the owner. The point is simply that if the Register reflects the full character of the land, any purchaser and any third party can rest assured that they are fully protected: the purchaser knows what he is buying and the person with an interest in the land knows that it will be protected. Yet, as we shall see, the mirror principle does not operate fully in the system of registered land in England and Wales under the LRA 1925, not least because of the existence of a large category of rights which affect the land and which bind any purchaser of it without ever being entered on any register (overriding interests: s 70(1) of the LRA 1925). However, before we criticise the draughtsmen of the LRA 1925 too severely, it is important to remember that overriding interests were not a mistake: the Register was never intended under the 1925 system to be a perfect mirror, nor was it ever intended to replace physical inspection of the land by the purchaser as a way of discovering whether there were any adverse rights over that land. The original intention was that overriding interests should be largely discoverable by physical inspection of the land and should not derogate in any practical way from the sanctity of the Register.

Consequently, although the image reflected by the Register under the LRA 1925 is imperfect, the imperfection will not necessarily cause loss to a diligent purchaser. Title registration exists to ease the purchaser's path, not to exclude his participation in the conveyancing process. However, if there are circumstances where these unrecorded, overriding interests are not in fact discoverable by a prudent purchaser, then the mirror principle is seriously compromised.

This possibility – the possibility of undiscoverable binding rights – is one of the issues addressed in the LRA 2002. Necessarily, the register will never be a truly perfect mirror, as not everything can be expected to be entered on a register (for example, informally created rights where no property professional has been involved), but the changes made by the LRA 2002 will do much to improve the reflection. As noted already, many more interests will be brought on to the register through the dictates of the electronic conveyancing process (as where the right will not exist at all unless it is electronically registered: see s 93 of the LRA 2002) and the extent to which unregistered interests (called 'overriding interests' under the LRA 1925, but called 'interests that override' within Scheds 1 and 3 under the LRA 2002) can affect a purchaser of registered land will be reduced. Similarly, it will be very difficult for a registered proprietor to lose title through adverse possession and many more short term titles (for example, legal leases over seven years) will be required to be registered in their own right. All in all, if only a few of the reforms instigated by the LRA 2002 are effective (and there is every reason to suppose that the Act will be a major success), the mirror principle will become more like the mirror fact.

2.3.2   The curtain principle

The *curtain principle* encapsulates the idea that certain equitable interests in land should be hidden behind the 'curtain' of special types of trust. Thus, if a person wishes to buy registered land which is subject to a trust of land, the purchaser need be concerned only with the legal title to the land which is held by the trustees. He need not look behind the curtain of the trust or worry about any equitable rights of ownership that might exist. The reason is that any such equitable rights will be overreached if the proper formalities of the purchase are observed (s 2 of the LPA 1925 and see below, 2.8). Consequently, these equitable rights will not affect the purchaser in his enjoyment of the land. Moreover, although the interests of the equitable owners cannot affect the purchaser because of overreaching, they are not completely destroyed because the process of overreaching operates to transfer the rights of the equitable owner from the land itself to the money which the purchaser has just paid for it. Thereafter, the trustees (the legal owners) hold the purchase money on trust for the equitable owners. This doctrine of overreaching (which also operates in unregistered land) is discussed more fully in Chapter 4 on co-ownership, but for now the important point is that once again the aim is to facilitate the alienability of land by freeing the purchaser from the effort and worry of dealing with equitable owners. As we shall see, the 'curtain' principle operates effectively in the majority of cases, but when it fails (usually because the preconditions for statutory overreaching cannot be met), the purchaser is faced with considerable difficulties. It may then become necessary for the purchaser to look behind the curtain: see, for example, *Williams and Glyn's Bank v Boland* (1981). It is not clear at this stage whether the LRA 2002 will have a major impact in this area. The LRA 2002 does not alter the fundamentals of overreaching and so does not resolve most of the problems that arise when overreaching does not occur: that is, when the purchaser has to look behind the curtain. The 2002 Act does confirm that legal owners of land have all the powers of an absolute owner, subject only to restrictions on their powers placed on the register (s 23 of the LRA 2002), and this will support the overreaching mechanism where there are the required minimum of two legal owners. It may well be that more equitable interests that currently exist behind the curtain of the trust (for example, a wife's equitable share of ownership of the family home) come on to the register because of the duty on the registered proprietor to disclose such rights if he knows of them (s 71 of the LRA 2002), and this will serve to alert the purchaser that he must either overreach or take some other action to obtain priority (for example, extract a consent from the equitable owner). However, this does suppose that the registered proprietor is aware of the rights of the claimants and is aware of the duty under s 71 of the LRA 2002.

2.3.3 The insurance principle

The *insurance principle* was one of the most ambitious of the motives underlying the LRA 1925. It encapsulates the idea that if a title is duly registered, it is guaranteed by the State. This guarantee is supported by a system of statutory indemnity (that is, monetary compensation) for any purchaser who suffers loss by reason of the conclusive nature of the Register.

The original scheme of indemnity provided by the LRA 1925 was quite narrow. The details of the original indemnity provisions, and their subsequent amendment by s 2 of the LRA 1997 are considered later in this chapter (below, 2.10). The point to be grasped here is that any registration system that guarantees title effectively will need to provide a system of compensation for those persons who suffer loss by reason of the application of the system. A register of land titles, especially one that is designed to be absolutely conclusive for most purposes, will always generate cases where loss is caused to innocent parties simply because of the way the system works. If A is the 'true' freehold owner of land, but B is registered with the title by innocent mistake, and then C buys the land from B on the basis of his registered title as guaranteed by the LRA 1925, it is obvious that either A or C will suffer loss by reason of the application of the registration system. The 'insurance' principle stipulates that a registration system must compensate in such cases. As we shall see, the indemnity provisions of the amended LRA 1925 remain open to criticism but they do go a long way to make the insurance principle a reality. Necessarily, the indemnity provisions are carried forward to the LRA 2002 (see Sched 8) and it may well be that the more stringent registration requirements of the new Act lead to more claims of indemnity. However, given that the rules were modified in 1997, the LRA 2002 makes little change to the operation of the 'insurance principle' as it works under the LRA 1925 (as amended).

2.4 An overview of the registered land system under the Land Registration Act 1925

Land is registered land when title to it is recorded in the Land Register, provided that the title is either the legal fee simple absolute in possession (freehold) or the legal leasehold of over 21 years duration (or with over 21 years left to run). These are the two important titles in current land law which, when registered, are known as 'registered estates' and the owner is the registered proprietor. Title is registered usually because of some dealing with the land (for example, a sale or mortgage) and after an official of the Land Registry has checked the validity of the title from the documents supplied by the person asking to be entered as the registered proprietor. The Register is housed in District Land Registries throughout England and Wales and the Register itself is now an open public document (LRA 1988). Each registered title is given a unique title number and its entry is divided into three parts:

(a) the property register, which describes the land itself, usually by reference to a plan, and which notes the type of title (that is, the estate) which the registered proprietor has;

(b) the proprietorship register, which gives the name, etc, of the proprietor and describes the *grade* of their title. The grade of the title varies according to the extent to which the Land Registry is satisfied that the title has been established (below, 2.5); and

(c) the charges register, which gives details of all third party rights over the land (except overriding interests) that detract from the registered proprietor's full use and enjoyment of the land.

An important feature of the land registration system is that it largely discards the old distinction between legal and equitable interests as a method of regulating dealings with land. It also completely abandons the doctrine of notice as a method of assessing whether any third party rights over land bind a purchaser of it. In fact, the LRA 1925 establishes four categories of proprietary rights (below, 2.4.1, 2.4.2, 2.4.3 and 2.4.4) and the crucial issue in any given case is to identify the category into which a person's right falls and not to ask whether that right is legal or equitable. Not surprisingly, the 1925 Act utilises the legal/equitable distinction as a method of assigning specific rights to one of these different categories, but it is not the nature of the right that is ultimately important, it is the category into which it falls.

Under the LRA 2002

In general terms, this pattern is replicated in the LRA 2002, although in matters of detail there are some differences. Two points in particular are worthy of note. First, under the LRA 2002, legal leaseholds of over seven years (or with more than seven years left to run) are registrable in their own right. There is also a power to reduce this threshold further and ultimately the trigger for registration will be for leases over three years, so corresponding to the period for which legal leases may be created without a deed (see Chapter 6). The reasons are to ensure that the register is a more accurate mirror of all rights concerned with the land and in recognition of the fact that in practice commercial leases are rarely longer than 10 years. Secondly, the LRA 2002 does not specifically refer to all the categories of right about to be discussed, although the categories still exist in substance. Thus, 'minor interests' are not specifically singled out but in substance are those rights which should be protected by a 'notice' against the registered title (see Pt IV of the Act and ss 28–30). Likewise, the LRA 2002 does not carry forward the name 'overriding interests', although in substance these are rights which may override a first registration or a registered disposition under Scheds 1 and 3 of the LRA 2002 respectively.

2.4.1 Registrable interests (including titles) under the Land Registration Act 1925

Registrable interests are those estates and interests that are capable of existing at law (that is, as legal rights: s 1 of the LPA 1925 and s 2(1) of the LRA 1925) and which may be registered in their own right with a unique title number. Two of the registrable interests are the legal estates already discussed and these are what are commonly referred to as registered titles or registered estates. These form the very great majority of registrable interests, viz:

• legal freeholds (legal fee simple absolute taking effect in possession); and

• legal leaseholds granted for more than 21 years and, on the occasion of a 'trigger' (see above, 2.1), legal leaseholds with more than 21 years to run.

The third registrable interest is the 'legal rentcharge'. A rentcharge is a periodic payment charged on land, paid by the owner, to another person, where the payee has no superior title to the land: as where A sells the freehold to B (A therefore keeping no interest in the land), but B promises to pay A an annual sum charged against the land. Clearly, this is an interest in another person's land (so is not commonly referred to as a 'title') but exceptionally may be registered in its own right with a title number. The registration of rentcharges in their own right is very rare and most take effect as 'minor interests', registered against the land against which they are charged (that is, against *its* title number). In essence then, and putting aside rentcharges, the category of 'registrable interests' under the LRA 1925 is where title, or ownership, is registered. Indeed, if the freehold or long leasehold is to take effect as a legal estate at all, it must be registered in this category, otherwise it operates in equity as a *minor* or *overriding interest*.

Under the LRA 2002

Once again, the pattern is familiar under the LRA 2002, although with some changes. Under s 3 of the LRA 2002, five legal estates may be registered with their own titles, although the first two categories will remain the most important. They are the freehold (as before), legal leases of over seven years (or with more than seven years left to run consequent upon a 'trigger' for registration), a rentcharge (as before), a franchise (being a right granted by the Crown to hold a fair, collect tolls etc) and a *profit á prendre* in gross (being a right independent of the ownership of any land which enables the right holder to enter another's land and take something from it, such as fish, game, wood, pasture, turf). It is also important to appreciate that legal titles will be the type of right most affected by principles of electronic conveyancing. There are two points here. First, that it will be possible in the future to execute a deed electronically (s 91 of the LRA 2002). Given that deeds are the principal way in which legal estates are created and conveyed, a legal title holder will have the choice of either executing a paper deed (as now) or an electronic version. The electronic version will not actually be a deed, but it 'is to be regarded for the purposes of any enactment as a deed' (s 91(5) of the LRA 2002). Secondly, in due course no creation or transfer of a registrable title will be effective at all unless it is entered on the register and this will be required to be done electronically (s 93 of the LRA 2002). Consequently, it will not be a case of creation/ transfer by deed followed by registration (as now): electronic registration will be the act of creation or transfer of the legal estate. Any attempt to create or transfer a legal estate that is specified in the Rules by other means will be void both at law and in equity.

2.4.2 Registered charges

Registered charges derive from the power of the registered proprietor to mortgage the land in order to release its capital value. These are legal mortgages of registered land. The easiest way to execute a mortgage of registered land is by 'a charge expressed to be by way of legal mortgage' and the category of registered charges refers to this. Mortgages are considered in depth in Chapter 10. For now it is enough to note that legal mortgages must be registered as registered charges against the relevant title if they are to retain the character of legal interests with the priority that this entails (see, for example, *Barclays Bank v Zaroovabli* (1997)).

Under the LRA 2002

The LRA 2002 makes some changes to the way in which registered charges will work, although there is nothing that is truly fundamental. After the Act enters force, it will no longer be possible to create a mortgage of registered land by the 'long lease' method (see Chapter 10). Mortgages of registered land will have to be executed by 'the charge' and there is a power to stipulate a standard form of charge. In addition, the 'charge certificate', currently the mortgagee's evidence of title, will be abolished, as the Register itself will provide full protection for the mortgagee. Finally, the creation of registered charges will be subject to the same principles of electronic conveyancing as other registrable dispositions of registered land: for example, electronic deeds and simultaneous creation/registration of legal estates and interests.

2.4.3 Overriding interests

Overriding interests are interests which are statutorily defined in s 70(1) of the LRA 1925. As noted previously, they do not have to be entered on the Land Register at all in order to bind a purchaser of registered land – s 20(1) and s 23(1) of the LRA 1925. In fact, if they are so registered, they lose their overriding character and become a registered interest or a minor interest as appropriate. Moreover, it is immaterial whether such interests are legal or equitable, so long as they fall within one of the classes defined in s 70(1) of the LRA 1925. Originally, such rights would have been obvious to a careful purchaser who undertook a physical inspection of the land and this is one of the reasons why their registration is not required. The purchaser would see the interest on inspection and could act accordingly – perhaps abandoning the transaction or offering a lower price. To a considerable extent, however, this is no longer true and the 'undiscoverable' overriding interest is one of the problems of the 1925 system. Again, for the moment, the crucial point is that an overriding interest is not actually registered on the Register against the title but nevertheless remains binding on the land irrespective of who purchases it. As with all registered land, the doctrine of notice is irrelevant.

Under the LRA 2002

The LRA 2002 adopts a similar policy to the 1925 legislation in that there is a class of right that will bind a future owner of registered land (that is, the registered proprietor of an estate or a registered chargee (mortgagee)) without that right being entered on the register. However, there are significant changes. First, the LRA 2002 does not actually refer to 'overriding interests' and there is no exact equivalent of s 70(1) of the LRA 1925. Instead, the LRA 2002 talks of interests which 'override' a first registration of title or a registered disposition. The effect is the same, but the style is different. Secondly, 'interests that override' (and perhaps we will still call them overriding interests) are dealt with in two ways. There are, in Sched 1 to the LRA 2002, interests that override a first registration of title. These are those rights that will bind a registered proprietor or registered chargee of the land when it is registered for the first time, the land having previously been of unregistered title. Schedule 1 rights are generally wider in scope than Sched 3 rights, the latter being rights that will override a registered disposition of registered land. That is, Sched 3 rights are those that will bind a new registered proprietor or registered chargee following a disposition of land that is already registered. This divergence is in part intended to reflect the fact that many rights that override a first registration will actually come on to the register (or should come on to it) by the time the land is transferred again. Thirdly, the definitions of the existing classes of overriding interests of s 70(1) of the LRA 1925 are changed, primarily to narrow their scope so that fewer rights (or fewer examples of rights) bind without being entered on the register. In other words, some of the existing categories of overriding interest are abolished or reduced in scope. Fourthly, some classes of rights will cease to override dispositions after a set period of time: in other words, a right that once overrode a registered proprietor will cease to have this status simply by effluxion of time and will either have to be entered on the register or will become void.

2.4.4 Minor interests

Minor interests are those proprietary rights (legal or equitable) that are not within any of the other categories considered above – s 3(xv) of the LRA 1925. Essentially, they form a residuary category of rights (see the negative definition in s 3) and as such there is no exhaustive statutory list. In practice, many of the rights that qualify as minor interests could have been overriding interests had the facts of the particular case been different. The essence of minor interests is that they are either protectable by entry in the charges section of the Land Register or subject to statutory overreaching under the curtain principle. Again, the doctrine of notice is irrelevant.

Under the LRA 2002

The role played by minor interests in the scheme of the LRA 1925 is carried forward to the system of the LRA 2002. There will remain a class of right that will need to be entered on the register in order to be binding against an owner of the registered land or an interest in it. Necessarily, given that the definition of 'interests that override' is narrower than its counterpart in the 1925 scheme, more interests will have to be entered on the register under the LRA 2002 if they are to continue to affect the registered land. It is, of course, an aim of the LRA 2002 that as many interests as possible should be so entered. In addition, the method by which these interests can be protected is going to change (see below), although in essence this is driven by the need to simplify the process rather than any major change in policy. Again, we should note that in due course, many of these third party rights will be capable of creation either on paper or electronically. More importantly, there will come a time when we will not be able to speak of rights being created and then entered on the register. Under s 93 of the LRA 2002, certain specified rights will not exist at all until they are electronically registered.

This reclassification of proprietary rights into four different statutory classes is fundamental to the land registration system under the LRA 1925. It enables owners, purchasers and third parties to know in advance how to protect their rights and what will happen to those rights if the land over which they exist should be sold, mortgaged or transferred. Such a radical shift away from the old legal/equitable distinction and the abandonment of the doctrine of notice was designed to eliminate the conveyancing dangers for purchasers that were so prevalent pre-1926. It also brings certainty and stability for persons who have rights in land which is owned by someone else. The categorisation and the philosophy are continued under the LRA 2002, with perhaps even more emphasis on providing purchasers of land with certainty about the land they are acquiring. The intended introduction of electronic conveyancing will also reduce even further the old legal/equitable distinction. It will still be important to know whether certain rights would have been legal or equitable (for example, we can register as titles only legal estates), but of more importance will be the status of a right as an entry on the electronic register or as an interest that overrides a registered proprietor or chargee.

2.5   The operation of registered land: titles

The registration of titles is the heart of registered land and this is what distinguishes it from unregistered land where title is found in the title deeds. Under s 69(1) of the LRA 1925, the registered proprietor 'shall be deemed' to have been vested with the legal estate (that is, the freehold or long leasehold) as it is noted on the Register. This is irrespective of whether there has actually been any conveyance to him. So, a person registered as the result of fraud or mistake has a good title (*Argyle Building Society v Hammond* (1984)) and is able to rely on the provisions of the LRA 1925 as to the conclusiveness of their interest, albeit that they may be subject to a claim to have the register rectified against them. Any suggestions to the contrary, as in *Malory Enterprises Ltd v Cheshire Homes and Chief Land Registrar* (2002) where Arden LJ implies both that a registration following fraud is not conclusive as to the proprietor's title and, if title is innocently acquired from a fraudster, is not a 'disposition' to them within s 20 of the LRA 2002, must be viewed with suspicion and as *per incuriam*. Any other view, such as that of the learned Lord Justice in *Malory* that such transfers are not in law of any effect, is to import principles of unregistered conveyancing into registered land and would wholly contradict the system of registration of title which sees such registration as a guarantee of title. Indeed, the *raison d'être* of the registration system is that title to land depends on a person being registered as the estate owner and on no other proof of ownership. On registration under the LRA 1925, the registered proprietor is entitled to a land certificate which effectively summarises the entry in the Register and constitutes evidence of title. The exception is where the land is subject to a registered mortgage, in which case the mortgagee (the lender) is currently issued with a 'charge certificate', being very similar to a land certificate save only that the mortgage document is attached. In any event, the registered proprietor is able to keep watch on the status of his property by requesting an official copy of the Register. As we shall see, the registered title may be subject to other rights as regulated by the land registration system (s 69 of the LRA 1925), and there may be an opportunity for rectification of the Register, but the importance of the Register is typified by the presumed conclusiveness of it as proof of ownership.

For example, under s 123A of the LRA 1925 (as inserted by s 1 of the LRA 1997), the new estate owner is required to apply for first registration of title (having purchased or otherwise dealt with unregistered land: see above, 2.1), and failure to apply within the 'applicable period' (currently two months from completion of the transaction) means that the purchase, etc, becomes void as regards the transfer or creation of the legal estate. This means that in the case of an outright transfer to the new owner, the legal title actually remains in the transferor, who will hold on trust for the new owner (s 123A(5)(a) of the LRA 1925, illustrated by *Pinkerry Ltd v Needs (Kenneth) (Contractors) Ltd* (1992), and in the case of the creation of a legal long leasehold or legal mortgage, the new mortgagee or lessee obtains only equitable title to the lease or mortgagee (s 123A(5)(a), illustrated by *Leeman v Mohammed* (2001)). In either case, if no proper registration of the estate is undertaken subsequently, the new owner will have to rely on the other mechanisms of the LRA 1925 to protect his interest, such as relying on the category of overriding or minor interests. Failing this, the estate could be lost if the land is then transferred to another. Similar penalties of nullity apply where an estate in land that is already registered is conveyed. This is well illustrated by *Brown and Root Technology Ltd v Sun Alliance and London Assurance Co Ltd* (1998), where the assignment of a long lease of registered land was not itself registered by the new tenant and the Court of Appeal held that the assignee had not acquired legal title. This had the consequence that the assignee had no power to give notice to end the lease and that power remained with the assignor (the original tenant) who still held legal title.

As indicated above, when land is presented for first registration, an official of the Land Registry will investigate the root of title and check the validity of the application. Obviously, this is vital given that registration has such a conclusive effect. There are, however, four possible grades of title with which a person may be registered and these reflect the fact that in some cases it may be difficult to establish a conclusive title due to the absence of relevant documents or other similar factual difficulties.

2.5.1 Absolute title

Absolute title is the highest grade of title possible and amounts to full recognition of the rights of the proprietor. It is available for freeholds and leaseholds, although only rarely in the latter case because the Registrar is not usually in a position to validate the landlord's title (as required by s 8(1)(i) of the LRA 1925) as well as that of the leaseholder who actually applies for registration. Registration with absolute title to freehold land invests the proprietor with the full fee simple, subject only to overriding interests and registered minor interests (s 5 of the LRA 1925). The only exception to this is where the registered proprietor is a trustee of the legal estate, in which case they are also bound by those beneficial (equitable) interests of which they have notice at the time of first registration. However, it should be noted that this is simply to ensure that subsisting equitable rights are not lost on first registration and, after that, notice of these rights ceases to be important and the matter is governed by the overreaching provisions of the LRA 1925 and LPA 1925. A person registered with absolute leasehold title is in the same position, save only that they are also bound by all express and implied covenants (promises to do, or not to do, certain things in relation to the land) that are incidental to the leasehold estate (ss 9, 23 of the LRA 1925; and see Chapter 6).

2.5.2 Good leasehold title

As noted above, it is rare for a leasehold owner to be registered with absolute title on first registration simply because this requires the landlord's title to have been verified and itself registered as absolute (s 8 of the LRA 1925). Thus, many proprietors of long leaseholds will be registered with good leasehold title. This invests the proprietor with the same quality of title as absolute title except that it is subject to any interests affecting the landlord's freehold or other superior title (s 10 of the LRA 1925). In other words, the proprietor with good leasehold title has a strong title, every bit as marketable as an absolute title, save only that the validity of the freehold (or superior leasehold) out of which it is carved is not admitted. Should that freehold or superior title become registered with absolute title or should the Registrar become convinced of the quality of the freehold or superior title, the good leasehold owner may apply for upgrading to absolute under s 77(1) of the LRA 1925.

2.5.3 Possessory title

If an owner cannot produce sufficient evidence of title (freehold or leasehold) on an application for first registration, he may be registered with possessory title. This is effectively the position of someone who relies on adverse possession as the basis of his title or a person who is unable to prove their title formally because of some disaster with the title deeds. The possessory title is, however, subject to *all* adverse interests that exist at the date of registration, not merely those which are overriding or protected minor interests (ss 6 and 11 of the LRA 1925). This appears, then, to be a rather unattractive title with which to be registered for the proprietor may find the land burdened by undisclosed interests, even perhaps a superior title. However, the Registrar must upgrade the possessory title if he is satisfied as to the validity of the proprietor's title or (under the LRA 1925) if the land has been registered with possessory title for more than 12 years and the proprietor is in possession, s 77(2) of the LRA 1925. Moreover, an owner registered with possessory title because of some mishap with the title deeds usually takes out title insurance whereby the title is privately guaranteed. This should suffice for a purchaser interested in buying the land from a person registered with possessory title.

2.5.4 Qualified title

Persons whose title is subject to fundamental defects may be invested with a qualified title. However, qualified title is subject to all interests which existed at the date of registration, ss 7 and 12 of the LRA 1925. It is, therefore, of limited comfort to an estate owner and rarely does the Land Registry agree to a request for such registration. They will do so where there is some prospect of the qualified title being converted into an absolute or good leasehold title under s 77 of the LRA 1925.

Of course, once a person is registered as proprietor with one of the titles noted above, any subsequent dealings with that land will take place within the registered land system. The land is now registered. So, on a sale, mortgage or transfer of the land two issues arise, viz: what is the position of the transferee (for example, new owner or mortgagee) and what is the position of any other person with an interest in that land?

2.5.5 The new owner or mortgagee (the purchaser)

According to ss 19 and 22 of the LRA 1925, a transfer of a registered freehold or leasehold of a legal estate is not completed until the new owner is entered on the Register as registered proprietor. For convenience, this is taken to be when an application to register title is made. The penalty for failure to register is that the legal estate remains in the transferor (that is, the seller) and the new owner receives an equitable estate only, even if all the other formalities necessary for a transfer of land have been observed (as illustrated by *Mascall v Mascall* (1984)). This means that the new owner who fails to register their ownership is theoretically vulnerable to a subsequent sale of the land by the person from whom he bought (even though, of course, this would be in breach of contract). In practice, however, the purchaser may well find their interest protected as an overriding interest under s 70(1)(g) of the LRA 1925 if they are in actual occupation of the property (below, 2.6.4). As we can see, then, this is a good example of how the LRA 1925 has superseded traditional property law concepts because under its system the validity or otherwise of legal title depends crucially on the existence of registration, not on the method or manner in which that title was conveyed.

2.5.6 The third party

It is inherent in what we have been considering so far that a major purpose of the LRA 1925 is to ensure that land may be sold freely. Necessarily, this means that other persons' rights over that land must be readily identifiable and their effect on the land must be known in advance in order to protect a prospective purchaser. As we have seen when considering absolute title, when freehold registered land is sold and a new proprietor is registered as owner, that proprietor obtains a fee simple subject only to overriding interests and registered minor interests (s 20 of the LRA 1925) and discounting contrary *dicta* in *Malory v Cheshire Homes* (2002). Any other rights are either void or subject to statutory overreaching. Likewise, a registered purchaser of an absolute or good leasehold title obtains the land subject only to overriding interests, registered minor interests and leasehold covenants which run with the land (s 23 of the LRA 1925). Importantly, the doctrine of notice plays no part in determining whether any third party rights bind the purchaser and the matter is dealt with according to the statutory scheme established by the LRA 1925 and LPA 1925.

Under the LRA 2002 as to titles

As might now be anticipated, the scheme of the LRA 2002 follows the same general principles with respect to the provisions relating to titles as the scheme under the LRA 1925. It will remain the case that a person registered as first proprietor obtains full title with all the benefits associated with the land, but subject to rights entered on the register and any interests which override first registration (ss 11 and 12 of the LRA 2002: equivalent ss 5 and 9 of the LRA 1925), plus a new provision which makes the first registered proprietor subject to rights acquired by another person as a result of adverse possession of which the new registered proprietor has notice. The latter is designed to meet the very specific case (and close a loophole under the LRA 1925) of an adverse possessor who has completed the required period of possession but who goes out of possession before the new owner is registered as proprietor. Significantly, s 23 of the LRA 2002 confirms that a registered proprietor has all the powers of an absolute owner of the land (subject to entries on the register) and ss 28–30 of the LRA 2002 confirm that dispositions of the registered title confer full title on the new registered proprietor subject only to interests that override and interests protected by entry on the register (equivalent ss 20 and 23 of the LRA 1925). This is supported by s 58 of the LRA 2002, confirming the conclusiveness of registered title as found currently in s 69 of the LRA 1925. Once again, it is not appropriate to import unregistered land concepts into land registration, so any argument suggesting that in some way a registered proprietor's title can be impeached on the ground that they obtained it from someone not entitled to transfer it (see the fallacious argument in *Malory*) must be rejected. As before, the remedy lies in the provisions relating to the power to rectify or alter the register. It also remains the case that failure to register a registrable title by a purchaser means that the vendor remains as proprietor, but as before that the vendor holds the land as trustee for the purchaser (s 7 of the LRA 2002: equivalent s 123A of the LRA 1925).

Other provisions of the new scheme are also similar to those found in the 1925 legislation. Under the LRA 2002, the proprietor may be registered with the same grades of title as under the LRA 1925 and with the same general effect. As noted, the purchaser from an existing registered proprietor will take the land subject to rights noted on the register and interest that override and third parties will have the opportunity to gain protection for their rights by registration or through Sched 1 and 3 (interests that override). Significantly, the reduction in the number and types of interests that override (compared to the 1925 overriding interests) and the rules about electronic conveyancing will mean that more rights will be on the register under the LRA 2002 than under the LRA 1925. Finally, of course, we should not forget that transfers of registered titles (and other registrable estates) will eventually take effect electronically and that the entry on the register of a title, a charge or a third party right will also constitute the act of creation of that right (s 93 of the LRA 2002).

2.6 The operation of registered land: overriding interests

Much of the criticism of the operation of the system of registered land under the LRA 1925 has been directed at the effect that overriding interests have on the land of a registered proprietor. The basic principle is, as we have seen, that a purchaser takes the land subject to any existing overriding interests (ss 20 and 23 of the LRA 1925). Crucially, these overriding interests are not registered on the Land Register. It is sometimes said that they 'bind automatically', meaning that a purchaser takes the land subject to such rights whether or not he knew about them and irrespective of registration. Of course, this does distort the pure 'mirror' principle, but it must be remembered that the rights which fall into the category of overriding interests are, for the most part, rights which *should* be obvious to a purchaser of land on inspection of the property, or which are in the nature of public rights that do not seriously affect the registered proprietor's use of the land. It is only with the emergence of the 'undiscoverable' overriding interest (for example, as a result of *Pettitt v Pettitt* (1970); *Williams and Glyn's Bank v Boland* (1981); see Chapter 4) that the purchaser faces the very serious risk that he may buy land subject to a paramount right about which he did not know and which he may not have been able to discover by even the most diligent enquiries and inspections.

Overriding interests are defined in s 70(1) of the LRA 1925 and they may be either legal or equitable. Importantly, no interest which appears on the Register either as a registrable interest or a minor interest is capable of constituting an overriding interest (s 3(xvi) of the LRA 1925). In this sense, the categories of rights and interests found in the LRA 1925 are mutually exclusive even though originally a person may well have had the choice whether to register or rely on s 70(1) for protection of his rights. Some rights are, in addition, excluded by other statutes from being overriding interests: interests arising under the Settled Land Act 1925, s 86(2) of the LRA 1925 (see Chapter

5); matrimonial homes rights under s 31(10)(b) of the Family Law Act 1996; tenants' rights under s 5(5) of the Leasehold Reform Act 1967; a tenant's notice under the Leasehold Reform Act; s 97(1) of the Housing and Urban Development Act 1993; rights under an access order granted under s 5(5) of the Access to Neighbouring Land Act 1992; and the right to claim an overriding lease under s 20(b) of the Landlord and Tenant (Covenants) Act 1995.

The various categories of overriding interests under the LRA 1925 are discussed below. As a preliminary point it must be remembered that to some extent the statutory definition found in s 70 of the LRA 1925 is open-ended. Although there are very many examples of rights which have been held to be overriding interests, new factual situations may give rise to new examples of overriding interests *provided* they fall within the statute. Moreover, in working out the solution to practical problems in registered land, it is not always enough to determine whether a right falls within the definition of overriding interests as a matter of principle. Further matters relating to the enforcement or 'bindingness' of the overriding interest also may be in issue. Consequently, there are two questions to be examined. First, is the right in question capable of being an overriding interest within s 70(1) of the LRA? Secondly, in what circumstances will the normal rule that overriding interests bind automatically be displaced by the special facts of a case?

2.6.1 Easements and profits: s 70(1)(a) of the Land Registration Act 1925

Section 70(1)(a) covers legal and equitable *profits à prendre,* 'easements not being equitable easements required to be protected by notice on the register' and certain other public rights (s 70(1)(a)).

This first category of overriding interest concerns rights which one person enjoys over the land of another for the purpose of some limited activity. Typical examples of 'easements' include a right of way over a neighbour's land or a right to run water pipes under the land, while *'profits à prendre'* are rights to enter another's land and take some produce ('profit') of it, such as fish, wood or turf. They are rights which, while being exercised, are generally of limited inconvenience to the registered proprietor, although they may well reduce the value of the land over which they exist.

Section 70(1)(a) clearly includes all profits, whether legal or equitable and this is a good example of how the land registration system has modified the old legal/equitable distinction: all are presumptively binding on the land without the need for registration. The definition also includes legal easements, being those easements created over unregistered land in accordance with the rules for the creation of legal interests. This is discussed in the previous chapter. These too are automatically presumptively binding, although in reality nearly all legal easements will, in fact, have been noted on the title register of the land they affect (and be binding for this reason), having been created on the occasion of a transfer of registered land. For example, if unregistered land over which there exists a legal right of way is sold to a new owner, the opportunity will be taken to note the legal easement on the title of the land when the new owner applies for first registration. Note also that if it is intended to create a legal easement over land that is already registered, the easement will not in any event exist as a legal interest until 'completed' by registration and, as above, it will be binding because of such registration (ss 18, 19, 21 of the LRA 1925). Failure to complete the creation of the easement in this way means that it takes effect as a (unregistered) minor interest. In consequence, legal easements falling within s 70(1)(a) are in practice those legal easements created before title to the land was registered and which have not been noted on the title of the affected land.

The general protection given to legal easements (and all *profits à prendre*) means that the real difficulty here is whether any *equitable* easements can qualify as overriding interests under s 70(1)(a). The statute appears to suggest not, for 'equitable easements required to be protected by notice on the register' are excluded. However, in *Celsteel Ltd v Alton House Holdings Ltd* (1985), Scott J held that equitable easements which were openly exercised and enjoyed with the land could be regarded as overriding interests because they did not need (were not 'required') to be registered due to the effect of r 258 of the Land Registration Rules. This rule provides that 'rights, privileges and appurtenances appertaining or reputed to appertain to land ... occupied or enjoyed therewith ... which adversely affect registered land' shall be overriding interests over it. Taken literally, this rule might support the conclusion reached in *Celsteel* and has the consequence that very many more rights slip into the category of overriding interests, binding the land automatically and in further distortion of the mirror principle.

In fact, there is evidence to suggest that equitable easements were never intended to be overriding interests within s 70(1)(a) (see Law Commission, *Third Report on Land Registration*, Report No 158, para 2.33) and that r 258 was intended to operate in a much more limited way in conjunction with the creation of legal easements under s 62 of the LPA 1925 (see Chapter 7). If this is true, then all equitable easements would be 'minor interests' needing registration to be effective against a purchaser of the land. Nevertheless, in *Thatcher v Douglas* (1996), the Court of Appeal (without much analysis) confirmed that equitable easements could be overriding interests within s 70(1)(a) because of the effect of r 258. The position currently is that an equitable easement, openly exercised or enjoyed and not needed (that is, 'required') to be protected by entry on the Register can be overriding. Given that most equitable easements will be openly exercised or enjoyed, the door is wide open to the inclusion of all such easements within s 70(1)(a). This has been addressed in the LRA 2002 (see below).

Finally, note also that s 70(1)(a) includes a number of anomalous easement-type rights which are also overriding interests. These 'rights of common, drainage rights, customary rights ... public rights [and] rights of sheepwalk' may actually amount to true easements or profits and the intention seems to be to catch those that are not and give them overriding status.

2.6.2 Rights in the nature of public or residual feudal obligations: s 70(1)(b), (c), (d), (e) of the Land Registration Act 1925

Section 70(1)(b) to (e) of the LRA 1925 lists a number of rights with varying degrees of practical importance. They include liability to repair highways and other feudal dues (s 70(1)(b)), liability to repair the chancel of a church (s 70(1)(c) but see *Parochial Church Council of Aston Cantlow and Wilmcote v Wallbank* (2001) where the overriding status of such a right was effectively destroyed because of a determination that its enforcement would be contrary to the Human rights Act 1998), liability in respect of sea and river walls or embankments (s 70(1)(d)) and certain tithe liabilities (s 70(1)(e)). Obviously, this is a miscellany of rights which impose burdens on land, many of them of ancient origin. They generally involve the expenditure of money by the estate owner and, as overriding interests, will pass on to successive registered proprietors automatically unless these are rendered impotent on other grounds, such as being incompatible with human rights legislation (*Wallbank*). Their existence (that is, their effect on the burdened land) is usually well known, either by reputation or by documents collected with the title.

2.6.3 Adverse possession: s 70(1)(f) of the Land Registration Act 1925

Section 70(1)(f) ensures that 'rights acquired or in the course of being acquired' by an adverse possessor are protected if the land over which they have accrued, or are accruing, is sold by the registered proprietor (the 'paper owner') to another. So, assume A is the registered proprietor of a field and B, the squatter, is in adverse possession of it, if A sells the land to X, X will be bound under s 70(1)(f) to recognise such rights as B has acquired. As discussed in Chapter 11, under the present law a person must usually be in adverse possession of the land for 12 years in order to extinguish the paper owner's title. Consequently, if the adverse possessor (B) has completed 12 years' adverse possession against the former owner (A) before the purchaser (X) is registered as the new estate owner, X will be bound to respect B's ownership of the land because the adverse possession will have extinguished A's title (as illustrated by *Bridges v Mees* (1957)). X, the purchaser, may have a remedy in contract against A, but X's title to the land is bound by B's superior ownership and B may apply for rectification of the Register in due course. If, however, B has not completed 12 years' adverse possession by the time X is registered as proprietor, X will be bound only by such time as has actually expired – this being the rights 'in the course of being acquired' under s 70(1)(f). Therefore, X can take steps to evict B anytime before B completes the necessary 12 years' possession.

2.6.4 Rights and actual occupation: s 70(1)(g) of the Land Registration Act 1925

The rights of every person in actual occupation of the land, or in receipt of rents and profits thereof, save where enquiry is made of such person and the rights are not disclosed: s 70(1)(g).

Section 70(1)(g) of the LRA 1925 is, without question, the most important category of overriding interests under the 1925 registration system. In practical terms, it is the category most likely to affect a purchaser of registered land because it does not identify individual, specific rights, but rather describes a factual situation. The section makes as overriding and therefore, in principle, binding automatically on the land, *any* proprietary right provided that the person entitled to enforce it is in 'actual occupation' of the affected land, or in receipt of 'rents and profits' from it, except if such rights are not disclosed on enquiry or are not otherwise excluded by statute. The various limbs of this definition will be discussed shortly, but it is important to emphasise at this stage that the category of s 70(1)(g) rights is potentially very destructive of the registered proprietor's title. There may be no difficulty if a purchaser is aware of the existence of the overriding interest before he purchases: the price can be adjusted to reflect the existence of the adverse right or the purchaser can walk away. However, while many of the rights falling within s 70(1)(g) will be known to a purchaser – either through documentation, reputation or physical inspection of the land – some may not. These so called 'undiscoverable' overriding interests still bind the purchaser even though they can seriously affect the intended use of the land. So, for example, if a bank (A) lends money to the registered proprietor by way of mortgage (that is, the bank purchases an estate in the land), the proprietary rights of any other person in actual occupation of the land (B) can affect the bank. If the bank did not know of the existence of this right, it will have lent more money than the land is worth: the rights of B will take priority to the bank, being binding on the bank as an overriding interest. In view of this situation, there is a premium of defining precisely what rights fall within s 70(1)(g). There are a number of factors to consider, some of which relate to all the categories of overriding interest under s 70(1), but which are more appropriately dealt with here given that they arise for consideration most frequently when dealing with s 70(1)(g):

(1) The right alleged to be an overriding interest must be a proprietary right in the land, legal or equitable. Section 70(1)(g) does not protect rights which are inherently personal, as explained in *National Provincial Bank v Ainsworth* (1965), where the House of Lords rejected the proprietary status of a wife's right to occupy the matrimonial home if that were owned exclusively by the husband. Further, as illustrated by *Habermann v Koehler* (1996), the question whether any right to use the land amounts to a proprietary or personal right is one to be determined before any other questions concerning the enforcement of the right can be addressed. This can be difficult, as there are many situations where a person is given a right to use another's land which are not proprietary – as with permission to enter and view a garden. Failure to be clear about this issue leads only to confusion. In *Saeed v Plustrade Ltd* (2001), one issue before the Court of Appeal was whether Mrs Saeed's right to park could be capable of being an easement or whether it was a contractual (personal) right. In a baffling concession (which the court did not challenge), counsel for Plustrade accepted that Mrs Saeed's right could be overriding under s 70(1)(g) of the LRA 1925 whether it was a 'merely contractual' personal right or a true easement. This is clearly wrong and contrary to *Ainsworth* which makes it absolutely clear that s 70(1)(g) confers overriding status only on those rights which are proprietary in nature. A non-exhaustive list of examples of rights typically falling within s 70(1)(g) are a person's equitable right of ownership where legal title is vested in another (*Williams and Glyn's Bank v Boland* (1981), now confirmed by s 3 of the Trusts of Land and Appointment of Trustees Act (TOLATA) 1996), an equitable freehold, an equitable lease (*Grace Rymer Investments Ltd v Waite* (1958)), a right to rectification of title (*Blacklocks v JB Developments (Godalming) Ltd* (1981); *Malory v Cheshire Homes* (2001)), including a right to rectify a lease (*Nurdin and Peacock v Ramsden* (1998)); an 'estate contract', being a contract to purchase a legal estate (*Webb v Pollmount* (1966)) and an 'unpaid vendor's lien', being the seller of land's right to charge any unpaid purchase price against the land itself (*Nationwide Building Society v Ahmed* (1995)). Moreover, while it is now reasonably certain that some rights are not proprietary and, therefore, not within s 70(1)(g) – such as a mere contractual licence (for example, see *Ashburn Anstalt v Arnold* (1989); *Lloyd v Dugdale* (2001)) the precise boundaries are not fixed. Thus, it now seems clear that rights generated by proprietary estoppel are proprietary (*Lloyd v Dugdale* (2001)) despite some uncertainties in the previous case law (see Chapter 9).

(2) The proprietary right must not be substantively registered elsewhere under the land registration system. In s 3(xvi) of the LRA 1925, overriding

interests are defined as all proprietary rights 'not entered on the register'. Consequently, if a person chooses to protect their proprietary right by means of registration as a minor interest (for example, an equitable lease) or the right is properly registered as an estate (registrable interest) with its own title number (for example, a legal long lease), then it cannot be an overriding interest within s 70(1)(g) or, indeed, any other category of s 70(1). This is a perfectly sensible position, particularly because the proprietary right will be protected adequately by its substantive registration and there is no need to fall back on the automatic effect of overriding interests.

(3) The proprietary right must not be excluded from the category of overriding interests by other statutes. Again, this applies to all categories of s 70(1), and details are given above, 2.6.

(4) The holder of the proprietary right must be in 'actual occupation' of the land or in receipt of rents and profits thereof at the time of the sale of the property to the new purchaser or mortgage to the bank (as the case may be), as explained by the House of Lords in *Abbey National Building Society v Cann* (1990). The need for 'actual occupation' or the receipt of rents and profits are genuine alternatives. However, in most cases, the claim will be that the holder of the proprietary right was in actual occupation and this is where the most difficulty lies.

Actual occupation is a question of fact in each case, to be determined by reference to the ordinary meaning of the term: it is not a term of art and the word 'actual' is not intended to convey any higher obstacle of proof: *Boland* and *Chhokar v Chhokar* (1984). Importantly, the right which is alleged to be overriding does not have to give a right of occupation itself and there is no need to prove that occupation is in pursuance of the right: it is enough if the right holder is simply in lawful and relevant 'occupation' (see *Pollmount* (1966)). However, the occupation may not be merely transient or temporary, even if this is preparatory to permanent occupation: there must be a degree of continuity and stability. Thus, in *Cann* it was very much doubted whether a person's presence on property for the purpose of laying carpets and other acts prior to permanent occupation was itself 'occupation' within s 70(1)(g). On the other hand, it is also true that the nature of the required occupation can vary according to the type of property under consideration. In *Malory v Cheshire Homes* (2001), the land was derelict and unusable in its present state. However, the claimant established 'actual occupation' through acts of minimal use, particularly the erection of a fence around the plot to keep out intruders. This might be thought to be an overly generous view of what constitutes actual occupation, but in reality it simply serves to highlight that each case really will depend on its own facts (*Leeman v Mohammed* (2001), following *Cann*).

In addition, although occupation can be achieved by the presence of the right holder's agents on the relevant land (for example, a housesitter or caretaker), it is doubtful whether every person present on the land at the request of the right holder can give the necessary degree of occupation. So, in *Lloyds Bank v Rosset* (1990), the House of Lords implied (contrary to the majority in the Court of Appeal in the same case) that the presence of builders on the land at the request of the right holder did not amount to her occupation and in *Strand Securities v Caswell* (1965) a relative of the right holder was held not to be in occupation on their behalf. So also the converse can be true. Thus in *Lloyd v Dugdale* (2001) Mr Dugdale could not rely on s 70(1)(g) of the LRA 1925 because although he held a proprietary right in the land, it was his company that was in actual occupation of the land and his presence there was indeed as agent of the company, not in his own right. Again, in *Hypo-Mortgage Services Ltd v Robinson* (1997), the Court of Appeal held that a child in occupation of premises with their parent could not be a person 'in actual occupation' within s 70(1)(g) so as to give an overriding interest against the purchaser. The child was there because the parent was there. Finally, we should also note that a right holder currently can enforce their right (as an overriding interest) against the entire property if the right inherently relates to all the property, even if they were only in actual occupation of part of it (*Ferrishurst v Wallcite* (1998)).

Clearly, what acts amount to 'actual occupation' and what persons may occupy on behalf of the right holder if the right holder is not personally present are questions of degree and will depend ultimately on the facts of each case. Certainly, however, mere temporary absences from the property by a person who is otherwise in 'actual occupation' does not detract from the existence of the overriding interest (*Chhokar*), and once the overriding interest is established – that is, that the actual occupation has acted on the proprietary right to protect it – there is no need to continue the occupation forever. Once the right under s 70(1)(g) has crystallised (on which important issue see below, 2.6.7), the occupier may leave the land, as with the right holder whose unpaid vendor's lien became an overriding interest in *London and Cheshire Insurance Co Ltd v Laplagrene Property Co* (1971), even though he later quit the property.

In the majority of cases, a person's presence on the land will be apparent to a prospective purchaser (for example, furniture, clothes) and this may lead him to make enquiries as to the existence of any adverse interests. If this happens, overriding interests established under s 70(1)(g) cause little hardship to a purchaser as he should be aware of their existence and can act accordingly: either to abort the purchase or obtain the consent of the person with the overriding interest to the proposed sale or mortgage (*Paddington Building Society v Mendelson* (1985), but see, now, *Woolwich Building Society v Dickman* (1996), below). However, it is in those cases where the presence of a person on the land (and hence their interest) is undiscoverable that cause concern, for the purchaser will still be bound by that interest according to the terms of s 70(1)(g) and s 20 of the LRA. The typical example is where the purely equitable owner of land is hidden from the purchaser or where such occupation is difficult or impossible to discover from physical inspection, as in *Chhokar*, where the equitable owner was in hospital at the relevant time and the legal owner had removed all evidence of her existence and possibly in *Malory* where it takes a degree of imagination to deduce that a fence amounts to the actual occupation of a third party (and is not merely the fence of the vendor!).

This problem of the undiscoverable but binding proprietary interest is most acute under s 70(1)(g) for the simple reason that a prospective purchaser when coming to inspect the land might be unaware that there are others in 'actual occupation' who have a proprietary right adverse to his proposed use of the land. This has led some commentators to suggest that a right should not qualify for protection under s 70(1)(g) unless it, or the actual occupation which supports it, is discoverable by a reasonably prudent purchaser. Not only would this inevitably introduce an element of 'notice' into registered land contrary to the rationale of the land registration system (for example, it would lead to the question 'what should the purchaser have discovered?'), it is contrary to the clear words of s 70(1)(g). This does *not* say 'the rights of every person in actual occupation, provided that this is discoverable by the purchaser'. Indeed, the 'absolutist' view (that it is immaterial whether the occupation or right was discoverable) holds good according to current authorities (as in *Skipton Building Society v Clayton* (1993); *Malory*), although there is the suspicion that it is being attacked indirectly by raising the hurdle of what amounts to actual occupation in the first place. As we shall see, the 'problem' has been tackled under the LRA 2002.

As an alternative to actual occupation, a person claiming an overriding interest under s 70(1)(g) currently can show that they are in receipt of the 'rents and profits' of the land. This will operate primarily to protect a person who has taken a lease from the freeholder but instead of occupying it himself (or registering it), leases the land to a subtenant. The subtenant will be protected if the freeholder sells the land, either under s 70(1)(k) (currently legal leases for 21 years or less: see below) or under s 70(1)(g), and the intermediate landlord will be protected as being in receipt of rents and profits (that is, receiving the subtenant's rent). This is illustrated by *Schwab (ES) & Co v McCarthy* (1975) which also suggests that the intermediate landlord must actually receive the rent to be protected rather than merely have a right to receive it. Once again, the LRA 2002 addresses this issue.

(5) The final condition for the existence of an overriding interest under s 70(1)(g) is that it bites only if the right holder has not denied the existence of his right after enquiry by the purchaser. If the purchaser does not ask the correct person (that is, the right holder, *Hodgson v Marks* (1971)) or if the right holder duly acknowledges his right, the overriding interest remains valid. It is only if the right is denied that the protection of s 70(1)(g) is lost. In addition, however, if a purchaser is buying a property

with the aid of a mortgage, and the purchaser makes enquiries of the right holder and the right *is* denied, it is not only the purchaser who takes free of the interest, but the mortgagee also. As explained in *UCB Bank v France* (1995), it is 'normal practice' for a purchaser to pass answers to such enquiries to his mortgagee and therefore the mortgagee is deemed to have made the enquiry of the right holder, and is entitled to rely on the answers. Of course, if it can be established that the answers to the purchaser's enquiries were not actually passed to the mortgagee, then the purchaser takes free, but his mortgagee does not. Finally, there is always the practical problem that the purchaser simply may not know who to ask (or may not know that there is *anyone* to ask) and may consequently fail to avail himself of this protection. In fact, examples of s 70(1)(g) rights deliberately concealed on enquiry (and therefore void) – as in *UCB v France* – are rare.

2.6.5 Legal leases for 21 years or less: s 70(1)(k) of the Land Registration Act 1925

Under s 70(1)(k), legal leases originally granted for 21 years or less enjoy the automatic protection of an overriding interest. These are the leases that are not currently registrable in their own right as titles, being of insufficient duration. The class does not include equitable leases (they are not 'granted': *City Permanent Building Society v Miller* (1952)) which in any event will usually fall within s 70(1)(g). Leases granted in pursuance of the Housing Act 1985 are also excluded: s 154(7) of the Housing Act 1985. The LRA 2002 modifies this provision.

2.6.6 Further overriding interests under s 70(1) of the Land Registration Act 1925

Further overriding interests are:

- s 70(1)(h): certain rights ancillary to possessory, qualified and good leasehold titles;

- s 70(1)(i): rights under local land charges until they are protected by entry on the Register;

- s 70(1)(j): rights of fishing and other feudal rights;

- s 70(1)(l): certain rights to mines and minerals in land registered before the LRA 1925 came into force;

- s 70(1)(m): certain rights under the Coal Industry Act 1994.

These remaining subsections of s 70(1) deal with a number of other rights that qualify as overriding interests and therefore for automatic protection when the land over which they exist is transferred to a new registered proprietor. They are relatively unimportant in the general scheme of the LRA 1925 although, of course, can seriously affect the use of the land over which they exist. This is particularly true of the very valuable coal rights of s 70(1)(m).

2.6.7 The bindingness of overriding interests under the Land Registration Act 1925

The existence of overriding interests is a vital element in the system of land registration under the 1925 Act. As the above sections illustrate, their definition is reasonably clear but certainly open to interpretation in some areas, particularly s 70(1)(a) and s 70(1)(g). However, we now come to the second important issue concerning overriding interests. If we are satisfied that a right falls within s 70(1) and qualifies in principle as an overriding interest, when precisely will it be binding against a purchaser? To put it another way, it cannot be true that a new registered proprietor will be bound by everything that could be an overriding interest whenever that interest came into existence or whatever the circumstances. It would be harsh indeed if, say, a new owner was bound by overriding interests that came into existence *after* he had purchased the land, or if the new owner was bound even if the right holder had promised expressly to waive the bindingness of his overriding interest. Consequently, the following principles determine the time at which the overriding interest must exist in order to bind a purchaser automatically and the circumstances in which agreement between the parties can remove their effect:

• For all categories of overriding interest apart from s 70(1)(g), the crucial date for determining whether the purchaser is bound by an overriding interest is the date on which the purchaser makes an application to register his title at the correct District Land Registry: the date of registration (s 20 of the LRA 1925).

This has been confirmed recently in *Barclays Bank v Zaroovabli* (1997), where Scott VC held that a lease falling within s 70(1)(k) would bind a purchaser (in that case, a bank as mortgagee) if the lease existed at the date the purchaser applied for registration. It mattered not, as in that case, that the overriding interest came into existence after the sale (mortgage) to the bank but before they registered their title. This period between completion of a purchase and the subsequent registration of the new proprietor is known as the 'registration gap' and it allows an interest in every category except s 70(1)(g) to bind a purchaser's land even though the binding right did not come into existence until after the purchase (but before registration of the title). This may seem unfair to the purchaser – after all, how can a purchaser walk away from burdened land or offer a lower price when it is not burdened at the time of sale – but until a new approach is found (see the LRA 2002) it will be something for a purchaser to be wary of. In fact, in *Zaroovabli* itself, the bank had waited over six years since completing the mortgage to apply for registration and it is hardly surprising that the court felt little sympathy when this plaintiff was caught by the registration gap. There would be more sympathy (but currently no different result) if, say, the bank had completed the mortgage in January, had applied to register in March, but an overriding interest under s 70(1)(k) had arisen in February. In such cases, however, it must be clear that the interest which is said to bind the purchaser really does exist as an overriding interest. So, in *Leeds Permanent Building Society v Famini* (1998), which appears to contradict *Zaroovabli* in holding that a right arising during the registration gap did not bind the purchaser, the lease which was alleged to fall within s 70(1)(k) of the LRA 1925 turned out on closer inspection to be an equitable lease whose claim to overriding interest status rested on s 70(1)(g) of the LRA 1925. As explained immediately below, rights reliant on s 70(1)(g) of the LRA 1925 for overriding interest status must satisfy a different timing test.

- For overriding interests established under s 70(1)(g) (being those rights that could seriously disrupt the new purchaser's enjoyment of the land because they presuppose someone else is in occupation), it is now clear that there is a two stage test. Although the overriding interest crystallises at the date of registration (as stated in s 20 of the LRA 1925), a person cannot claim the benefit of s 70(1)(g) unless they have a proprietary right and are in actual occupation of the land at the time the sale to the new owner was made or when the mortgage was granted (*Abbey National Building Society v Cann* (1991)). This pragmatic decision (also confirmed in *Zaroovabli*) effectively eliminates the 'registration gap' problem for s 70(1)(g) rights. This means that, in practice, a purchaser will not find the value or use of their land diminished by the emergence of a powerful adverse right in the interval between the purchase and application for registration as the new proprietor. The proprietary right, and the actual occupation that invests it with the status of an overriding interest, must exist prior to completion of the purchaser's transaction so increasing the chances that it will be discovered in time for the purchaser to react accordingly.

- As indicated above, the 'owner' of any overriding interest that would otherwise bind a new owner of the land may be able to waive voluntarily the priority given to their right by expressly consenting to the sale or mortgage of the land over which the right exists. Indeed, in some cases, this consent will be implied because of the conduct of the holder of the overriding interest (*Paddington Building Society v Mendelson* (1985); *Equity and Law Home Loans v Prestidge* (1992)). Indeed, a right holder who has consented to a particular purchaser (a mortgagee 'X'), may be taken to have consented to a different purchaser who steps into his shoes (a re-mortgagee 'Y' whose monies pay off the first mortgage), at least to the extent of the monies provided by the original mortgagee even if in reality the right holder did not know of the substitution (*Prestidge*; *TC v FC*

(2001)). Although the precise circumstances in which a right holder will be deemed to have consented to the sale or mortgage of the land over which the overriding interest takes effect are unclear, mere knowledge that a transaction concerning the land is proposed would not seem to be enough. Consequently, the person with the overriding interest need not volunteer information concerning their position and will not be taken to have consented simply because the transaction proceeds around them and they remain silent – having not been asked. The requirement is one of consent to the sale or mortgage, not simple knowledge of it: *Skipton Building Society v Clayton* (1993). However, active participation in organising the mortgage or encouraging a purchaser will be deemed to be consent. For example, an equitable owner in actual occupation who sits by while her husband arranges a mortgage will not thereby lose the priority which her overriding interest has over the mortgagee, but an equitable owner who participates by, say, explaining to the bank that the money is needed for an extension, will. Moreover, many purchasers (especially banks lending by way of mortgage) now require all occupiers to sign express consent forms waiving such rights as they might have in favour of the bank. This would seem to be perfectly adequate to protect the purchaser. However, in *Woolwich Building Society v Dickman* (1996), the ability of a holder of an overriding interest to waive their priority has been challenged. The case itself is explicable on other grounds, but the Court of Appeal does say that the express consent to a mortgage by a person with an overriding interest is *not* sufficient to waive priority unless such consent is itself entered on the Register. This is somewhat dubious. It is true that s 70(1) of the LRA 1925 says that overriding interests are effective against a purchaser 'unless … the contrary is expressed on the Register' (so suggesting that consents should themselves be registered), but this applies only to such interests that are 'for the time being subsisting' in reference to the land. Where a holder of what would otherwise be an overriding interest has consented to the priority of the purchaser/mortgagee, the right is no longer 'for the time being subsisting' in reference to the land and so whether the consent is entered on the Register or not is immaterial. The right does not exist vis à vis that purchaser. Moreover, not only does the decision in *Dickman* appear to rest on a misreading of s 70(1), most mortgagees have relied on 'unregistered' consent forms to escape the effect of overriding interests ever since *Paddington*. Many millions of pounds in loans have been lent on the basis that such consent forms are valid. Now is not the time to throw such a principle and practice into doubt and *Dickman* is best regarded as authority for the much more limited proposition that a right holder cannot consent away their overriding interest if that right is also protected by other statutory machinery – as with the protection given to the tenancy by the Rent Acts in *Dickman*. The Law Commission's view is that *Dickman* is incorrect. Indeed, in *Birmingham Midshires Building Society v Saberhawal* (2000), no objection was raised to the validity of a consent form and the court simply proceeded on the basis that it was effective to waive the rights of the claimant.

- Finally, for the sake of clarity, it is trite law that a right may qualify as an overriding interest only if it exists vis à vis the purchaser in question. This is not startling news, but it does mean, for example, that if it turns out that the alleged overriding interest is not a lease at all, but in reality is a licence (see Chapters 6 and 9), this licence can never be an overriding interest because licences are not capable of binding any third party, being merely personal rights (the contrary view expressed in *Saeed v Plustrade* (2001) should be regarded as *per incuriam*). Likewise, even if the alleged overriding interest does exist as a proprietary right, it may be ineffective against a particular purchaser because of circumstances wholly unrelated to the operation of overriding interests *per se*. One such case has been considered above, as where the purchaser gains the consent of the potential holder of the overriding interest so ensuring that that particular purchaser can never be bound. So also, if the alleged overriding interest is given by a landowner who had no power to give it: the right cannot bind the purchaser, because, vis à vis the purchaser, it does not exist. An example is *Famini* where the alleged overriding interest (a tenancy) was created by a landowner who had no power to create it, having promised the purchaser (the bank) that he would not do so.

Under the LRA 2002 as to interests that override

It is apparent from what has been said already about the LRA 2002 that its provisions relating to 'overriding interests' are some of the most important. The mere fact that there was (and will remain) a category of rights that bind a registered proprietor even though there is no entry on the register is an anathema to a system that hopes to provide title by registration instead of registration of title. In consequence, much of the LRA 2002 is about controlling and limiting the effects of 'overriding interests'.

The 2002 Act adopts many strategies to achieve this, but perhaps first we should note that the name (if not the concept) of overriding interests will disappear. After the LRA 2002 enters force, we will be referring to 'interests that override'. Indeed, we shall be thinking about two different types of 'interests that override': interests that override a first registration of title (Sched 1 to the LRA 2002) and interests that override a registered disposition of land that is already registered (Sched 3 to the LRA 2002). These two categories are, in fact, very similar and most of the concepts are the same, save that Sched 3 rights are more narrowly drawn because it is anticipated that many rights that override a first registration will subsequently be entered on the register or will expire before the title is transferred again.

Schedule 1 rights

Sections 11(4) and 12(4) of the LRA 2002, being rights which will bind a registered proprietor on first registration. These will be effective on the occasion that the land is first registered, either following a 'trigger' for registration or an application for voluntary registration. Some may eventually be entered on the register and hence cease to be overriding, especially as a duty is imposed on applicants under s 71 of the LRA 2002 to disclose such rights so that they may be so registered. The categories are:

- Paragraph 1 of Sched 1 of the LRA 2002, legal leases of seven years or less. This is the rough equivalent of s 70(1)(k) of the LRA 1925, save only that the duration threshold is lowered from 21 years or less to seven years or less. Legal leases over seven years will be registrable estates. Three types of lease are excluded from this status even if they are seven years or less, being the right to buy a lease, a lease taking effect more than three months after it was granted and leases by certain private sector landlords. (These 'short' leases will be registrable in their own right, as with legal leases over seven years.)

- Paragraph 2 of Sched 1, interests of persons in actual occupation. This is the new form of s 70(1)(g) of the LRA 1925 and the first point to note is that the rights of persons in receipt of rents and profits is now excluded from 'overriding' status. Also excluded are (as before) interests arising under settlements under the Settled Land Act 1925. In addition, it is now made clear that the interest that is said to override the first registration will do so only in relation to the land that is actually occupied by the claimant. That is, the decision in *Ferrishurst v Wallcite* (1998) is reversed. For the sake of clarity it should also be made clear that there is nothing in the 2002 Act to change the definition of what constitutes 'actual occupation', so the approach developed for the 1925 system remains valid. Likewise, the principles concerning the need for a proprietary right and concerning issues of waiver/consent remain unchanged. In so far as it will remain relevant, 'actual occupation' must be established as before at the time of transfer of the title, not the later date of first registration. However, we must remember that electronic conveyancing will in time remove this 'registration gap' because transfer and registration will occur simultaneously and electronically.

- Paragraph 3 of Sched 1, legal easements or profits. This will replace s 70(1)(a) of the LRA 1925, save that it is made clear that equitable easements will not override first registration. This effectively reverses *Celsteel v Alton* (1985). The point is quite simply that these equitable easements should have been registered as land charges under the Land Charges Act 1972 when the land was unregistered. If they were, they will be binding, being translated into notices on the register of title. If not, they would have been void under the unregistered system so should not now acquire overriding status simply because the land has become registered.

- Paragraphs 4 and 5 of Sched 1 ensure that 'a customary right' and 'a public right' respectively override first registration and para 6 confers the same status on local land charges. These reflect similar provisions under s 70(1) of the LRA 1925. Many of the rights within paras 4 and 5 will be entered on the title as they come to light and so this category is likely to diminish in importance.

- Paragraphs 7–9 of Sched 1 preserves the status of mineral rights under similar provisions in s 70(1) of the LRA 1925.

- Paragraphs 10–14 included a miscellany of rights (for example, franchises, liability in respect of sea walls) that were also in s 70(1) of the LRA 1925, although not a chancel repair liability following the decision in *Wallbank* that the enforcement of such an obligation violated the human rights (right to property) of the owners of the burdened land. Importantly, this category of right will be phased out over a maximum 10 year period. During that time, they should be entered on the register against the title of the land they bind. If they are not so entered, they will become unenforceable.

- Under s 90 of the LRA 2002, a Public Private Partnership (PPP) lease also enjoys the status of a right that overrides first registration. These are special statutory creations relating to the system of transport in London.

Schedule 3 rights

Sections 29(2)(a)(ii) and 29(4) of the LRA 2002, being rights that will bind a transferee for valuable consideration of a registered disposition. These rights will be effective against a purchaser of a legal estate in the land (for example, a new freeholder, leaseholder, mortgagee) when the land they have purchased is already registered. In other words, these are rights which bind a registered disposition and legal leases which do not need to be substantively registered (those of seven years or less: s 29(4) of the LRA 2002). In many respects, they are similar to those rights listed in Sched 1, but there are some important differences:

- Paragraph 1 of Sched 3, is similar to para 1 of Sched 1 (legal leases for seven years or less), save that the exceptions (that is, rights which do not override) includes the three exceptions under Sched 1 plus those leases which should be registered with their own titles even though they are seven years or less (for example, a discontinuous lease such as a timeshare).

- Paragraph 2 of Sched 3, being an interest belonging to a person in actual occupation. This raises similar issues as those arising in relation to parallel rights under para 2 of Sched 1, including questions about the meaning of 'actual occupation' and proprietary status, the reversal of *Ferrishurst*, the relevance of waiver/consent, the exclusion of the rights of persons in receipt of 'rent and profits' and Settled Land Act rights, and questions concerning the 'registration gap' and its eventual demise. However, most importantly, there are some additional exclusions, being cases where no 'overriding right' will arise under Sched 3 even though it would have done under Sched 1. Thus, also excluded are: first, the rights of a person of whom enquiry was made who failed to disclose the right when he reasonably should have done so; secondly a lease granted to take effect more than three months in advance but where the tenant has not actually entered possession; and thirdly, the rights of a person whose actual occupation would not have been obvious on a reasonably careful inspection of the land and about which the transferee did not know. Of these three additional exclusions, the 'enquiry' exclusion is already found in s 70(1)(g) of the LRA 1925 and denies overriding status to a person who hides his rights when asked, and the (new) lease exclusion prevents a person from claiming an interest that overrides when he should have registered that lease under its own title. The third exclusion is both new and far reaching. It is designed to prevent a purchaser being bound by the undiscoverable overriding interest that is (apparently) so problematic under s 70(1)(g) of the LRA 1925. Thus, if the actual occupation is not 'patent' (discoverable on a reasonably careful 'inspection') and the purchaser does not know of the right, the right cannot be overriding. The aim of this exclusion is clear. As noted, it is to protect purchasers from undiscoverable rights of which they were unaware. Although the provision in para 3 of Sched 3 may well achieve this, we can but hope that it does not import concepts of 'notice' into registered land. It may not, because after all it is the 'actual occupation' that must be obvious on a careful inspection, not the right which is said to be overriding and the Law Commission in its Report No 271 is clear that there is no reason to return to the fickle concept of notice. However, the fear is that this provision will generate much litigation before its meaning is clear and the temptation to return to the old unregistered land concept may prove too much for some courts.

- Paragraph 3 of Sched 3, legal easements and profits. Again, this is very similar to the provision in Sched 1 (for example equitable easements are again excluded). However, once again there are some additional exclusions not found in Sched 1 which effectively narrow its scope dramatically. In effect, the only legal easements and profits which will be overriding under this convoluted paragraph are: those registered under the Commons Registration Act 1965; or those about which the purchaser actually knows; or those that are 'patent' (obvious on a reasonably careful inspection of the land); or those which have been exercised (that is, used) within one year of the purchase. As noted, this dramatically reduces the scope of legal easements that will bind as interests that override a registrable disposition and, of course, equitable easements are excluded completely. These equitable easements must now be protected by an entry on the register. We should remember, however, that most legal easements over registered land will have been granted (and in the future must be so granted: s 93 of the LRA 2002) in such a way that they are actually entered against the title of the burdened land and so will be protected without reliance on this paragraph. In reality then, expressly granted legal easements will be binding as entered against the title and this paragraph will confer overriding status on impliedly granted legal easements (see Chapter 7).

The remaining paragraphs of Sched 3 are the same as their counterparts in Sched 1. Thus, the main differences between the Schedules occur in relation to easements and the rights of persons in actual occupation. The differences reflect the fact that relevant entries on the register of title either will be made or should be made concerning many rights that override a first registration so that protection is not needed when the land is transferred subsequently. In addition, of course, there is the policy of ensuring that a purchaser of land that is already registered should not be subject to rights which were not on the register nor discoverable by a reasonable inspection of the land. Overall, the differences between the Schedules on the one hand and the scheme of s 70(1) of the LRA 1925 on the other is a reflection of the aim of the LRA 2002 to produce a register of title that is as near complete as possible, with consequential benefits to purchasers and third parties alike. For example, the rights of persons in adverse possession will no longer be overriding interests in their own right (as they currently are under s 70(1)(f) of the LRA 1925). Such rights will override only if the adverse possessor is in actual occupation under the new definitions. Again, equitable easements are also excluded. Indeed, the reduction in the breadth and scope of 'overriding interests' has long been a goal and there is no doubt that, for good or ill, the LRA 2002 achieves it.

2.7 The operation of registered land: minor interests under the Land Registration Act 1925

Minor interests form a residual category of rights in the 1925 land registration system, being rights which are not protected by any of the methods outlined above. They are neither registrable titles or charges nor overriding interests. In practice, minor interests usually comprise the rights of a person other than the owner and are mostly equitable, although there is no *a priori* reason why this should be so. It is a basic tenet of the registration system that minor interests must be registered against the land (in the charges section of the Register) in order to bind a purchaser of it. The one exception to this is those rights which are 'overreachable' and therefore incapable of protection when an overreaching transaction occurs even if they are in fact registered (see below, 2.8). The mechanics of the registration process for minor interests can be complicated, but the crucial point to remember is that under the LRA 1925 there are *four* different ways to protect minor interests by registration. The position under the LRA 2002 is different.

2.7.1 Restriction: s 58 of the Land Registration Act 1925

The restriction is a form of protection which enables the proprietor of a registered title (or charge) or the Registrar (on the application of an interested person) to restrict any future dealings with the land. The restriction is entered in the proprietorship section of the Register and will ensure that no dealings with the registered title can occur until the conditions specified in the restriction are complied with. Entry of a restriction usually requires production of the land certificate (an exception is where the certificate is lost) and therefore occurs with the concurrence of the registered proprietor. For this reason, restrictions are rarely used to protect rights that are truly adverse to the registered proprietor – in the sense of being disputed by him – and, in such cases, registration by means of a 'caution' is normally more appropriate (see below).

Although a restriction can be used to protect most minor interests – by controlling how the registered proprietor may deal with the land – it is most commonly used to protect equitable interests existing behind trusts of land or strict settlements (see Chapters 4 and 5). In such cases, the restriction requires the registered proprietor to conduct a proper overreaching transaction (see below) and so ensures that the equitable interests are duly converted into their monetary value. Under the TOLATA 1996, dispositions of land subject to a 'trust of land' can be made dependent on the registered proprietor obtaining the consent of some other person (see Chapter 4) and a restriction may be appropriate to ensure that this requirement is observed. Restrictions may also be used to ensure that a purchaser of registered land undertakes direct liability for positive burdens affecting the land (such as an obligation to pay for the upkeep of a private road). So, a restriction can be entered preventing sale of the land unless the purchaser promises to undertake the burden.

2.7.2 Inhibition: s 57 of the Land Registration Act 1925

The inhibition is a powerful form of protection which inhibits any dealings with the registered land until an order of the court is obtained or a specified event occurs. Entry of an inhibition is made by either the Registrar or the court on the application of 'any person interested'. Its effect is usually to freeze all dealings with the land, as may be necessary, for example, where there is an allegation that the registered proprietor has obtained the title (or its registration) by fraud, or the registered proprietor is bankrupt and it is necessary to prevent the dissolution of his estate. It will be appreciated then, that entry of an inhibition is a drastic measure and indeed, it is rarely appropriate to enter an inhibition to protect 'normal' third party interests in land. The inhibition is, in reality, a method of preventing dealings with the registered title because of circumstances affecting the land or its owner, rather than because of the existence of the typical third party proprietary right. The court or Registrar has the power to substitute a 'restriction' or 'notice' if this is more appropriate: s 57(4) of the LRA 1925.

2.7.3 Notice: s 49 of the Land Registration Act 1925

A great many minor interests are capable of protection through the entry of a notice in the charges section of the Land Register, although as with the restriction this can prove problematic, given that the land certificate must be with the Registry before a successful registration can be made. The effect of an entry of a notice is that any person becoming registered as proprietor of the land to which the notice applies, takes that land subject to the rights protected by the notice. As stated, in most cases, entry of a notice may be made only on production of the land certificate and so with the concurrence of the registered proprietor, an important exception being the protection of matrimonial homes rights. Despite this limitation, entry of a notice is the most effective and appropriate form of registration for the protection of third party proprietary rights over the land. It typifies the way the registration system was supposed to work. Note, however, that entry of a notice has absolutely nothing to do with the pre-1925 'doctrine of notice'. As we shall see, the latter plays no part in the protection of minor interests when registered land is sold or transferred.

A notice is also the appropriate form of entry on the Register to protect certain non-proprietary rights affecting land. These are rights that are not inherently capable of binding land (that is, they are personal rights), but where Parliament has deemed that they should be raised to an equivalent status for social or economic purposes by means of the registration machinery. They are a special class and most fall outside the scope of land law. The most relevant right for our purposes is a spouse's matrimonial home right arising under ss 30(1) and 31(10)(a) of the Family Law Act 1996. This is the personal right to occupy land belonging to one's spouse and is enforceable against him or her. It is not proprietary but is given equivalent protection through the ability to enter a notice. This notice may be entered in the absence of the land certificate and so does not require the co-operation of the registered proprietor (by definition the other spouse). The entry of a notice will ensure that this non-proprietary right binds the purchaser of land over which it exists, as in *Wroth v Tyler* (1974), although it is now a statutorily implied term of a contract for sale with vacant possession that the vendor will procure cancellation of any such registration before completion of the sale (Sched 4, s 3 of the Family Law Act 1996).

2.7.4 Caution: ss 54, 55, 56 of the Land Registration Act 1925

The entry of a caution in the charges section of the Register is appropriate to trigger protection for nearly every possible type of minor interest. It is especially useful given that a caution may be registered in the absence of the land certificate and therefore can be done without the consent of the registered proprietor. However, it is now clear that entry of a caution gives only limited protection to a person seeking to protect a minor interest. A caution is really a warning against dealings with the land. Thus, in the event of any proposed dealing with the land (for example, a sale), the Land Registry is required to give the cautioner (the person entering the caution) 14 working days' warning during which time he may apply to protect his interest fully by the entry of (usually) a notice or a restriction. Failure to apply during this period, or a refusal by the Land Registry to 'upgrade' the caution, results in the caution being 'warned off'. If a caution is warned off, it ceases to protect the minor interest and a purchaser will take the land free of that interest (*Clark v Chief Land Registrar* (1993)).

Additionally, as is now made clear by *Clark v Chief Land Registrar* (1993) (following *Barclays Bank v Taylor* (1974)), failure by the Land Registry to give the required warning to a cautioner, resulting in a totally innocent failure to apply for and obtain a secure entry on the Register, still means that the interest is not protected and is void against a purchaser. The innocent cautioner would, in such circumstances, be able to claim an indemnity from the Land Registry, but it is not always the case that the loss of an interest in land can be compensated for by a cash payment. So, as *Clark* illustrates, the entry of a caution itself gives no priority to a minor interest, it is rather a transitional form of protection designed to trigger more permanent protection.

2.7.5 Enforcing minor interests

The whole purpose of the system of registration for minor interests is that such registration ensures that the protected right binds the land when the land is transferred to a new registered proprietor. This has two particular aspects: the 'validity rule' and the 'voidness rule' and these will be considered shortly. Before that, however, it is important to appreciate the precise purpose of the minor interest system. Registration of a minor interest can protect only that which is capable of protection. In other words, it must be clear that the right which is to be protected actually exists before the protection can take effect. Registration of a right which does not exist, or which is merely personal (such as a contractual licence) and not within the category of special non-proprietary minor interests, may not confer protection for the right. So, if I am in dispute with my neighbour over whether I enjoy an equitable right of way (an equitable easement) over his land, registration of the alleged easement by means of a caution does not necessarily confer protection. The right must exist first before it can be protected. In a similar vein, the priority of minor interests between themselves depends on the date of their creation, not the date of their registration as a minor interest (*Barclays Bank v Taylor* (1974)). So, if A has an equitable mortgage over X's land created on 1 January 1997 (registered as a minor interest in June 1997), and B has a second equitable mortgage created on 1 March 1997 (registered in April 1997), when the land is sold to Z, priority is given first to A's mortgage. It is only in exceptional circumstances that the 'first in time' rule for competing equitable interests can be waived, as in *Freeguard v Royal Bank of Scotland* (1998) where the first created equitable interest was wholly artificial.

- **The validity rule**

    If an interest is protected in the proper way by entry on the Register, it binds any subsequent purchaser or transferee of the registered land: ss 20 and 23 of the LRA 1925. To this end, an intending purchaser will usually request a search of the Register in order to discover whether there are any registered adverse interests. Following this search, the prospective purchaser will receive a 'search certificate' and this will give him a 30 day 'priority period' in which to apply for registration of his title. If an application to register title is made within this priority period, any newly registered minor interest (that is, registered after the search was made) will not be binding on the purchaser. Any minor interests properly registered at the date the new owner applies for registration and not excluded by the priority period will be binding. It must be remembered, however, that unlike unregistered land, it is the Register itself that is conclusive, not the search certificate. Thus, any registered minor interest that is not revealed because of an inaccurate search of the Register remains binding on the purchaser because it is still entered on the Register. Again, in such circumstances, a purchaser prejudiced by an inaccurate search may be entitled to an indemnity or may sue the Registry in negligence.

- **The voidness rule**

    The converse of the validity rule is that any minor interest which is not registered in the appropriate manner is void against a subsequent purchaser of the land who registers their title. It is vital to appreciate that this is the case whether or not the purchaser knew or should have known of the existence of that interest. In other words, the doctrine of notice is irrelevant because voidness is the penalty for lack of registration (ss 20, 23 and 59(6) of the LRA 1925; *Strand Securities v Caswell* (1965); *Petrou v Petrou* (1998)). This is a vital feature of the registration system. In the great majority of cases, the new owner of land will be a purchaser (as opposed to a donee of a gift or devisee under a will) and he will seek security in a search of the Register for registered minor interests. If any exist which are not appropriately registered, they are void against him and any subsequent transferee of the land. However, this is not the whole story and some exceptions to the voidness rule do exist, these being cases where an *unregistered* minor interest does in fact bind a new owner of the land. As explained below, these exceptions occur for specific rather than general reasons and consequently, whenever it is alleged that an unregistered minor interest binds a new registered proprietor, the facts of the case are likely to be crucial.

- An unregistered minor interest may nevertheless qualify as an overriding interest under s 70(1) of the LRA 1925, usually under s 70(1)(g). In such a case, it may well bind the new owner of the land but *only* because it now falls into this new category. A typical example is an equitable lease which could be registered as a minor interest, but which will usually bind a purchaser as an overriding interest under s 70(1)(g) of the LRA 1925 because the tenant will be a person in actual occupation of the land. This possibility will be much reduced under the LRA 2002 because of the reduction in the scope of overriding interests and because of the various techniques that encourage or require registration of these interests.

- An unregistered minor interest (not qualifying as an overriding interest) remains valid against a person who is *not* a purchaser for value of the land, for example, the recipient (donee) of a gift, the recipient (devisee) under a will or a squatter (adverse possessor). The voidness rule, as expressed in s 20 of the LRA 1925 (freeholds), s 23 of the LRA 1925 (leaseholds) and s 59(6) of the LRA 1925, is concerned with protecting purchasers of land, those who do give 'value'. Such donees, devisees and squatters acquire no greater right than their predecessor and if he was bound, so are they, irrespective of registration.

- An unregistered minor interest (not qualifying as an overriding interest) remains valid against a purchaser for value who does not register their title. In such cases, the new owner obtains an equitable title only and the unregistered minor interest takes priority over it being 'first in time'. This is another example of the *Barclays Bank v Taylor* principle, affirmed in *Mortgage Corp v Nationwide Credit Corp* (1993), and reinforces the policy of the LRA 1925 that as much as possible concerning registered land should be on the title. So, assume an equitable mortgagee fails to protect his mortgage by means of a notice, but the land over which the mortgage exists is sold to X. If X fails to register her estate, she has only an equitable title created after the equitable mortgage and thus ranking behind it. Of course, should X seek registration of her new estate, the equitable mortgage will cease to be effective against the land, unless it has by that time been registered or otherwise qualifies as an overriding interest. It is only in exceptional circumstances that an unregistered minor interest will become void against a purchaser who does not register his title. In *Freeguard*, for example, the plaintiff claimed to be able to enforce an unprotected minor interest against a later purchaser who had not registered their interest (the bank). This purchaser had only an equitable interest and the 'first in time' rule should have meant that the plaintiff's unprotected minor interest took priority. The court held, however, that the normal rule was displaced because the creation of the first equitable interest was a wholly artificial transaction. Hence, the 'later' right of the equitable purchaser had priority.

- An unregistered minor interest (not qualifying as an overriding interest) remains valid against a purchaser for value who has expressly promised to give effect to that interest and thereby gains some advantage, for example, a lower price. In such cases, if it would be unconscionable for the purchaser to deny the validity of the unregistered minor interest, that interest will be held binding on the purchaser by means of a personal constructive trust (*Lyus v Prowsa Developments* (1982); approved in *Lloyd v Dugdale* (2001)). It should be noted that this is an exceptional way in which an unregistered minor interest will be held binding and it depends entirely on the conduct of the particular purchaser against whom a remedy is sought. If, for example, that first purchaser were to sell the land on, the minor interest would then need to be registered in order to take effect against the second purchaser. In other words, this is a personal remedy against a particularly unconscionable purchaser. What amounts to 'unconscionable' conduct so as to deny a purchaser the benefit of the voidness rule necessarily will vary from case to case. As mentioned previously, a purchaser who promises the vendor that he will honour an unregistered minor interest and thereby obtains a lower price, will be held to his agreement (*Lloyd v Dugdale* (2001)). Again, however, it is important to emphasise that we are looking for 'unconscionability' on the part of the purchaser, not that he has old-style 'notice' of the minor interest (as explained in *Miles v Bull (No 2)* (1969)). So, a purchaser who knows of an adverse interest that is not registered and is keen to complete the purchase before it is registered, thereby securing a bargain, is not acting unconscionably simply because they have been able to take advantage of the provisions of the LRA 1925.

- An unregistered minor interest (not qualifying as an overriding interest) remains valid against a purchaser for value where the purchaser has knowledge of the interest *and* is relying on the voidness rule in order to perpetrate a fraud. This is similar to the situation outlined above and is an example of the old equitable rule that 'equity will not permit a statute to be used as an instrument of fraud' (*De Lusignan v Johnson* (1973)); viz, a person cannot plead the voidness rule established by the LRA 1925 as justification for their own fraudulent use of the land. Again, the emphasis is not on the purchaser's knowledge or notice of the existence of the unregistered minor interest, but that the purchaser is attempting to use the voidness rule to further a fraudulent design. Knowledge or notice of the unregistered minor interest *per se* does not make a purchaser fraudulent. In *Peffer v Rigg* (1978), Graham J commenting on s 59(6) of the LRA 1925, decided that a 'purchaser' could only plead the voidness rule if they were acting 'in good faith', as 'good faith' was part of the definition of a 'purchaser' in s 3(xxi) of the LRA. If correct, this undoubtedly introduces elements of the old doctrine of notice into the voidness rule and this extreme interpretation is now largely discounted (see the analysis in *De*

Lusignan (1973)). In short, 'fraud' means more than acting on one's rights under the LRA 1925. It appears to include schemes deliberately designed to defeat unregistered minor interests, as in *Jones v Lipman* (1962), where the new registered proprietor who claimed to be free from the unregistered interest was in fact a company controlled by the former proprietor who had been bound by that minor interest. Likewise, a promise given to the right holder to respect the right and therefore to discourage deliberately its protection by registration will amount to fraud.

Under the LRA 2002 as to 'minor interests'

The provisions of the LRA 2002 in relation to so called 'minor interests' generally concern matters of detail rather than groundbreaking questions of principle. The essential scheme of the LRA 1925 remains in place; that is, there is the validity rule and the voidness rule (ss 11(4), 12(4), 29(2)(a)(ii) and 29(4) of the LRA 2002). Thus it remains true that these third party rights (which are not identified as 'minor interests' by name in the LRA 2002) will bind if entered on the register and will be void against purchasers if they are not. Similarly, questions of priority continue to be determined by reference to the time of creation of the interest and an entry on the register cannot make valid that which is otherwise invalid (s 32(3) of the LRA 2002). However, there are some points of interest and change.

First, that there will no longer be four methods by which a 'minor interest' can be protected. There will be the 'restriction' combining the functions of the current restriction and inhibition (s 40 of the LRA 2002), and the 'notice' combining the functions of the current notice and caution (s 32 of the LRA 2002). Restrictions will record limits placed on a registered proprietor's ability to deal with the land (for example, in a co-ownership situation: see Chapters 4 and 5) and notices will record any third party rights over the land. Notices will either be consensual (as where the registered proprietor acknowledges the right) or unilateral (as where the right is disputed). There are provisions relating to the removal of notices and restrictions, but importantly both the consensual and unilateral notice give substantive protection to the right recorded (thus effectively reversing *Clarke v Chief Land Registrar* (1993) as regards cautions under the LRA 1925). Secondly, certain matters cannot be protected by notice (s 33 of the LRA 2002). These are an interest under a trust of land or settlement (for which a restriction should be used), leases for three years or less (being an interest that overrides), restrictive covenants between lessor and lessee relating to the property leased (these bind under special rules, but note that *Dartstone v Cleveland Petroleum* (1969) is reversed because such a covenant can be registered if it does not relate to the land leased), an interest capable of being registered under the Commons Registration Act 1965 (which is the proper form of protection) and certain mineral rights. Thirdly, the rule that such interests have priority from the moment of creation and not registration is preserved. This is because, under the full system of electronic conveyancing, creation and registration will occur simultaneously because registration of the right will be its creation. This will eliminate priority problems. Fourthly, given that in due course certain rights will not exist until they are electronically entered on the register (s 93 of the LRA 2002), only those third party rights that are so registered will bind the land and of course, the register will provide a very full picture of the state of the land at any given time. The possibility of the unregistered but valid 'minor interest' will all but disappear.

2.8   The operation of registered land: overreaching

Throughout the above analysis, especially when considering whether and how a third party right might be protected on a transfer of registered land, repeated reference has been made to the concept of overreaching. The following section will analyse the concept of overreaching and explain how it fits into the registration system. As will be seen, it is a process whereby rights which would otherwise be binding against a purchaser according to the rules of registered land, will not be so binding because of this 'statutory magic'. As a preliminary, it is also important to realise that 'overreaching' is not actually a creation of the LRA 1925: it operates in unregistered land also and in a similar fashion. It will continue to operate in much the same way under the LRA 2002. This is explained in the following sections.

Overreaching is a process whereby certain equitable rights in land which might otherwise have enjoyed protection in the system of registration on the occasion of a sale of that land to a purchaser for value, are 'swept off' the land and transferred to the purchase money which has just been paid. When this occurs, the equitable rights are said to be 'overreached' and no longer bind the purchaser, even though they might have fitted exactly into the category of overriding interests or protected minor interests. Overreaching is, in effect, a method of promoting the alienability of land by removing certain equitable rights from the land and recasting them as a monetary equivalent. Note, however, that not all equitable rights can be 'swept off' the land by overreaching. In fact, the rights which are capable of being overreached are those equitable rights which exist behind a trust of land: being those equitable ownership rights which exist when the land is co-owned (see Chapters 4 and 5) and which do have a readily identifiable monetary value. The crucial point is, then, that if overreaching occurs, a right which would have been protected against a purchaser ceases to be so protected, irrespective of whether it would have been an overriding interest or whether it was entered on the minor interests register (and equivalent under the LRA 2002). Overreaching is the purchaser's trump card.

It follows from the above that two essential conditions must be met before overreaching can occur.

2.8.1 The right must be capable of being overreached

The first condition is that the equitable right must be of the kind that is *capable* of being overreached. Not all equitable rights are 'overreachable' and so the trump card can be played only in defined circumstances. Overreachable equitable rights are defined in s 2 of the LPA 1925 and, in essence, are equitable co-ownership rights existing behind a trust of land (as in *City of London Building Society v Flegg* (1998); see Chapter 4) or equitable interests existing behind a strict settlement (see Chapter 5). Consequently, equitable interests such as the equitable easement and equitable lease can never be overreached and will bind a purchaser of the registered land (or not) according the rules of registered land just discussed.

2.8.2 The statutory conditions for overreaching must be fulfilled

The second condition is that the statutory conditions for overreaching must be fulfilled. This means that the sale must be made by those persons and in those circumstances that together constitute an overreaching transaction, s 2(1) of the LPA 1925. These are four in number, although the first is the one most frequently encountered, viz:

(1) the transaction is made by at least two trustees (or a trust corporation being a limited company of £250,000 capital) exercising valid powers under a trust of land, usually in a co-ownership situation. The trustees will be the legal owners of the land (see Chapter 4). The need for two trustees (legal owners) is a statutory requirement and has no relevance other than that this is the minimum number required. As we shall see, the maximum number of trustees of land are four, so that if there are four trustees, all four must concur in the transaction (and likewise if there are three, etc). The most common transaction effected by the trustees which will overreach any equitable co-owners is either the simple sale to a purchaser or the execution of a mortgage in return for funds. If there is a sale, the new registered proprietor will have overreached the equitable owners and may evict them; if there is a mortgage, the mortgagee's interest will have priority over that of the equitable owners and so in the event that the land is sold, the mortgagee will be paid first.

As noted, the sale/mortgage in a co-ownership situation is the most common type of overreaching transaction and it will be discussed at length in Chapter 4. At this stage, it is noteworthy that s 2 of the LPA 1925 appears to assume that overreaching occurs when the sale proceeds (either from sale proper or monies advanced by mortgage) are actually paid to the two (three or four) trustees. This is quite natural as the rationale for overreaching and its ability to release a purchaser from otherwise binding rights is that the equitable owners take a share of the money in 'compensation' for the loss of their right to the land. However, as became clear in the case of *State Bank of India v Sood* (1997), many trustees will take out a mortgage of registered land (that is, sell an interest to a purchaser) not in order to receive immediate monies, but to guarantee future borrowings from the bank: perhaps to finance a business venture. In these cases, no money is actually paid over even though there is an overreaching transaction by two or more trustees. Consequently, the question which arose in *Sood*, apparently for the first time, was whether this type of transaction is an overreaching transaction so as to give the bank priority over any equitable rights? The answer from *Sood* is that it is. The Court of Appeal decided that, under s 2(1)(ii) of the LPA 1925, if capital monies were to be paid as a result of a conveyance by the trustees, those monies actually have to be paid to two trustees to overreach. However, if capital monies did not arise on a transaction (as in the case of a mortgage to secure *future* borrowings), a conveyance by two trustees would overreach the equitable owners by mere execution of the conveyance. The court reached this conclusion through a generous interpretation of s 2(1)(ii) of the LPA 1925 – the overreaching section. Effectively, the court decided that, if money is *payable* on the transaction, it must be paid to two trustees; but, if money is not payable, overreaching occurs so long as the mortgage is properly executed. This interpretation was bolstered by two policy considerations. First, that the aim of the overreaching machinery is to encourage the free alienability of co-owned land and this should be protected. Secondly, that although the point in this case had not been decided before, many lenders had agreed to these types of mortgage and to have held in this case that they did not overreach because no capital monies changed hands would be most unfortunate. These are compelling reasons. The argument that existing commercial practice assumes the law to be as the court in *Sood* decided is not an attractive one, but it is realistic. On the other hand, apart from the absence of any authority for this decision, there are two real difficulties: first, that the words of s 2(1) of the LPA 1925 really do seem to contemplate the actual payment of money as a precondition for overreaching (even if they did not mean to); secondly, and more importantly, that overreaching can be justified as a matter of principle because the equitable owners' interests take effect in the money paid to the trustees. That is why the equitable interests can so easily be swept off the land. If overreaching can occur without the payment of such monies – because two trustees have charged the land for future debts – what protection/benefit is there for the equitable owners? Where do they get their *quid pro quo* for suffering overreaching? There is no capital money for them to take a share of, or if it was represented as credit at the bank it is likely to have been spent by the time the case comes to trial. In other words, *Sood* is almost certainly correct, but for reasons of practice not principle.

(2) The second circumstance where overreaching can occur is where the transaction is made under the provisions of the Settled Land Act 1925 relating to the operation of strict settlements (Chapter 5). As we shall see, a strict settlement is, in simple terms, a device for ensuring that land is given to X for life, thence to Y. There are 'trustees of the settlement' who will not be X or Y, but X (the life tenant) or the trustees may have power to deal with the land (for example, sell it) and this transaction can be an overreaching transaction, sweeping the interests of Y into the proceeds of sale. Settlements will become increasingly rare due to the inability to create new strict settlements after 31 December 1996 (s 2 of the TOLATA 1996).

(3) Thirdly, overreaching is possible if the transaction is made by a mortgagee (for example, bank, building society) or personal representative in exercise of their paramount powers to deal with the land.

(4) Fourthly, overreaching may occur if the transaction is made under order of the court, for example, s 14 of the TOLATA 1996. The court has wide powers to deal with land, particularly land subject to a trust. Any order of the court transferring the land to a third party, or directing that it should be sold, necessarily effects an overreaching transaction for the benefit of the transferee or purchaser.

2.8.3 The consequences of failing to overreach

It is only if both of the above conditions are satisfied that an overreaching transaction occurs. The existence of an overreachable right is simply a question of fact and rarely gives rise to problems. However, what is more common is failure to ensure that a proper overreaching transaction has occurred, thereby denying the purchaser the trump card and preventing the overreachable equitable interests from being swept off the title into the purchase money. Usually, this is a result of a failure to pay the purchase money to two trustees as required by the most common type of overreaching transaction, as in *Boland*. Should there be a failure to overreach, there are two possibilities to consider:

(1) if the equitable interest has been registered as a minor interest under the LRA 1925 (or equivalent under the LRA 2002) or if it constitutes an overriding interest (as most do because the equitable owner is usually in actual occupation, s 70(1)(g) – *Boland* and similarly under Scheds 1 and 3 to the LRA 2002), the purchaser will be bound by the interest and their use of land restricted accordingly; or

(2) if the equitable interest is not protected as either a minor interest or an overriding interest (or equivalent under the LRA 2002), the purchaser who registers his title takes the land free of that interest. This is not surprising, being simply an example of the voidness rule referred to above. Note here

that equitable rights under existing strict settlements (for example, life interests) are explicitly excluded from the category of overriding interests and must be registered as minor interests in such circumstances.

It sometimes causes surprise that even if a purchaser fails to overreach he may still take free of the relevant equitable interest. It is understood more clearly if it is remembered that overreaching is an exceptional process – like a trump card – that releases the purchaser from the normal rules of registered (or unregistered) conveyancing by providing an automatic release from some equitable interests. If the trump card fails, the normal rules of registered conveyancing come back into play. Hence, the equitable interest may still be void if not protected as an overriding or registered minor interest.

To sum up, overreaching is a special procedure and it can nullify the proprietary status of certain equitable interests in certain specified circumstances. When it works, these equitable interests are transferred to the purchase price of the land and cannot affect a purchaser. When it fails, the rules of registered land take effect in the normal way.

2.9 Rectification of the Register

It is a central tenet of the land registration system that the Register should be as accurate as possible so that it can be relied upon by all persons intending to deal with the land. Thus, the registration of persons as registered proprietors and the due entry of minor interests should be free from error. Of course, this is the ideal, but in practice faults in the registration process and registrations based on incomplete or inaccurate evidence do occur. Consequently, under s 82 of the LRA 1925, the Registrar (with an appeal to the court), or the court itself, has the power to order rectification of the Register in eight specified circumstances. The power is discretionary and rectification may be refused even if one of the statutory grounds are made out although it is not clear whether rectification when ordered is retrospective or merely regularises the title from the moment of the court order (*Kingsalton v Thames Water* (2001); and see the disagreement in *Malory v Cheshire Homes* (2002)). The statutory grounds are necessary for rectification, but they are not always sufficient. The Registrar or court may decide, for example, that the injury requiring rectification is *de minimus,* or that the harm caused by agreeing to rectification would far outweigh the harm caused by denying it. The specified grounds are:

- s 82(1)(a), where a court has decided that a person is entitled to an estate or interest in land and in consequence the Register is ordered or required to be rectified to reflect this, as in *Calgary and Edmonton Land Co Ltd v Discount Bank Overseas Ltd* (1971). For example, if there is a dispute, subsequently resolved by the court, as to the proper distribution of real property on death, perhaps because the will is contested. Likewise, the Register may be rectified under this head in order to place on the Register what is currently an overriding interest, as in *Chowood v Lyall (No 2)* (1930);

- s 82(1)(b), where a court orders rectification in order to place on the Register, or remove from it, an interest that was wrongly excluded or included as the case may be;

- s 82(1)(c), where the Registrar or the court orders rectification with the consent of all interested persons;

- s 82(1)(d), where the court or Registrar is satisfied that an entry has been obtained by fraud. This is a reasonably narrow ground for registration as it allows rectification where the entry on the Register has been obtained by fraud, rather than where the interest which is sought to be registered is obtained by fraud, as explained in *Norwich & Peterborough Building Society v Steed* (1992). So, if A obtains B's fee simple by falsifying B's signature to a conveyance, and then sells the estate to the innocent C, the Register cannot be rectified on this ground against C, because C's registration as proprietor was not obtained by fraud, even though the interest C purchased from A was obtained fraudulently by A. Similarly, this head is concerned with fraud perpetrated on the Register by the registered proprietor, so that if that person has not participated in the fraud, s 82(1)(d) is inappropriate;

- s 82(1)(e), where by mistake, two or more persons are registered as proprietors of either the estate or registered charge (mortgage). Note, this is not meant to imply that two or more people cannot own jointly such an interest, rather that 'double registrations' in error can be rectified;

- s 82(1)(f), where a mortgagee has been registered as proprietor of the land instead of the mortgage itself (the charge). This is applicable in those cases where the mortgagor (the borrower) still retains some interest in the property by way of the 'equity of redemption', and is thus holder of the paramount title to the land: that is, the freehold or leasehold over which the mortgage exists;

- s 82(1)(g), where a person has been registered as proprietor of a legal estate in circumstances that if the land had been of unregistered title, that person would have had no legal estate. This is an important ground of rectification in cases of adverse possession. So, if A sells registered land to B, who is then registered as proprietor, B would seem to have a valid title under the LRA 1925. If, however, X has successfully adversely possessed for 12 years prior to the sale to B, no title would have passed to B in unregistered land having been extinguished by adverse possession. Consequently, the Register can be rectified to reflect the 'true' owner, X (*Chowood v Lyall (No 2)* (1930)). The point is simply that the initial registration of B as proprietor gives title under the LRA 1925 (registration being everything), so provision must be made enabling rectification where title would not actually have passed to the new registered proprietor under substantive law. The same result would occur if A had sold to B under a conveyance whose validity was subsequently challenged successfully by A on the grounds of undue influence or fraud;

- s 82(1)(h), 'in any other case' where, because of 'any error or omission in the Register' or 'any entry made under a mistake', it is 'deemed just' to rectify the Register. This appears to be a very broad ground for rectification and in the past this residual power was interpreted very widely, as in *Argyle Building Society v Hammond* (1984). Not surprisingly, this generated fears that too liberal a use of s 82(1)(h) would undermine the integrity of the Register as the wider the power of rectification, the less certain the Register is as a reflection of title to land. However, in *Norwich & Peterborough Building Society v Steed* (1992), the Court of Appeal held that although there was a discretion to rectify the Register under s 82(1) of the LRA 1925, there was no general power to rectify merely because it was thought just and equitable to do so. Any particular claim for rectification had to fall squarely within one of the eight statutory grounds set out in the section. Moreover, as a general principle, s 82 was held not to create new grounds for challenging property rights that would not have existed prior to the advent of the land registration system. Rather, it was *interpreted* as a mechanism whereby the court could rectify the Register in order to recognise pre-existing proprietary rights or to remedy errors or omissions. In other words, no new substantive powers to challenge proprietary rights were created by the section. That does not mean that the court will always refuse rectification where nothing could be done in unregistered land, or that they will grant it where the dispute would have been settled differently in unregistered land (as in *London Borough of Hounslow v Hare* (1992) where the Register was not rectified against a registered proprietor even though the transfer to her would have been void in unregistered land), but it is a welcome statement of principle that upholds one of the central tenets of the land registration system.

Finally, we should note that although there is a discretionary power to rectify the Register if one of the statutory conditions is satisfied, it is not permissible rectification where this would affect the title of a registered proprietor in possession of the land, except in order to give effect to an overriding interest or an order of the court (*Kingsalton v Thames Water* (2001)), or where the proprietor has contributed to the error or mistake, or where it would be unjust not to do so, s 82(3) of the LRA 1925. This last provision has been considered in *London Borough of Hounslow v Hare* (1992). The plaintiffs were seeking rectification against a registered proprietor in possession who had purchased the property by virtue of a sale that was statutorily void. Rectification was refused because (following the normal rule) being registered as proprietor gave the defendant a title and it would have been 'unjust' to deny that title in the circumstances, even though in unregistered land the defendant would have no grounds for remaining an owner. The importance attached to a person in possession of land is a theme of the land registration system (see, for example, s 70(1)(g) of the LRA 1925) and it is appropriate that a registered proprietor should not be deprived of his interest when in possession save in exceptional cases.

Rectification was ordered against such a person in *Chowood v Lyall (No 2)* (1930) (to give effect to an overriding interest), but refused in *Kingsalton v Thames Water* (2001). Likewise, although rectification may be ordered where this would affect the interests of innocent third parties (s 82(3), as applied in *Hammond*, to rectify against an innocent mortgagee and rectification ordered against an innocent party in *Malory*), the court appears to be reluctant to do so if another course of action is available. So, in *Freer v Unwins* (1976), an assignee of a lease (A) had taken the lease aware that certain restrictive covenants had been mistakenly omitted from registration as minor interests against the superior title and so were not binding on him. On an application for rectification to register these covenants, the court decided that A had to be treated as if a disposition had been made to him under s 20(1) of the LRA 1925 and so acquired his lease free from unregistered minor interests. This was despite the fact that the Register was rectified against the superior title and so would affect future assignees of the lease: in essence, s 82(3), which gave the court authority to rectify to the discomfort of the innocent assignee, was ignored.

2.10 Indemnity under the Land Registration Act 1925

The authoritative status of the Register means that there will always be cases where a person suffers loss because of the workings of the registered land system. The power to rectify the Register is one response to this, although as we have seen there is no general discretion to rectify just because it is fair or just to do so. The power of the court to order an indemnity (that is, compensation) for a person who suffers loss by reason of some error or omission in the Register is another response. As originally conceived in the LRA 1925 (s 83), the entitlement to an indemnity was tied to the power to order rectification and they remain mutually supportive aspects of the system. However, s 2 of the LRA 1997 has substituted a new s 83 which more clearly identifies the payment of indemnity as a stand alone remedy for a person prejudiced by the land registration system.

The amended s 83 of the LRA 1925 provides that an indemnity shall be paid:

- to a person suffering loss by reason of the rectification of the Register (s 83(1)(a)). Usually, this will be the person who has 'lost' some estate or interest when the Register is rectified against them; for example, a landowner whose duly registered equitable easement is removed from the Register through rectification;

- to a person in whose favour the Register is rectified, but who still suffers loss (s 83(1)(b)). This is a change to the old law, recognising as it does that rectification in one's favour might not always be a sufficient compensation, as in *Freer v Unwins*. As the Law Commission has noted (*Transfer of Land: Land Registration*, Report No 235, para 4.2), it was never the intention to deny indemnity in such cases, rather, it was assumed that rectification would always compensate fully;

- to a person who suffers loss by reason of an error or omission in the Register, but the Register is not rectified (s 83(2)). This provision (also found in the original LRA) is in recognition that the power to order rectification is discretionary and that it may not be appropriate to rectify in all cases, even though loss will be caused. Such a person, for example, a person who fails to persuade the court or Registrar to rectify by entering a minor interest to protect their otherwise valid restrictive covenant, will receive an indemnity.

This is the basic indemnity scheme and a person falling within the above categories shall 'be entitled' to an indemnity subject to two further conditions. First, no indemnity is payable if the claimant has caused the loss wholly or partly by his or her own fraud or wholly by lack of proper care (s 83(5)(a) of the LRA 1925), although a partial indemnity is payable if the loss was caused partly by the claimant's lack of care (s 83(6) of the LRA 1925). Secondly, the person claiming indemnity must make a claim within the normal limitation period for the enforcement of contractual debts, usually being six years from the time he knew, or might have known but for his own default, of the existence of the claim (s 83(12)). A recent example of a successful claim for an indemnity in *Prestige Properties v Scottish Provident* (2002) where the claimant obtained indemnity for loss incurred as a result of relying on search certificates issued by the Registry.

Finally, however, despite the changes to s 83 of the LRA 1997, some difficulties remain with the indemnity provisions:

- no indemnity is payable for any costs or expenses incurred (for example, legal costs of fighting for the estate or interest in the land), without the consent of the Registrar, save where they are incurred as a matter of urgency and the Registrar approves them subsequently (s 83(5)(c));

- *Re Chowood's Registered Land* decides that no indemnity is payable if rectification is ordered to give effect to a pre-existing overriding interest, because the loss to the registered proprietor is not caused 'by reason of the rectification' within s 83(1)(a), but by the existence of the pre-existing right. The rectification merely recognises a loss that has already occurred. Although the Law Commission recommended previously the reversal of this rule (Report No 158, para 2.11), the current proposals recommend that the *Chowood* principle be retained;

- the amount of compensation may not always reflect the real loss to the person prejudiced. Thus, if indemnity is payable because of a refusal to rectify the Register even though an error has been made, the amount of compensation is assessed by reference to the value of the estate, interest or charge at the time the error was made, not the time rectification is refused.

This may have been many years earlier and may seriously prejudice an estate owner, although the Registrar's willingness to pay interest on the sum assessed may alleviate this. The Law Commission originally proposed amending this provision, but this was rejected in Law Commission Report No 235 and no change was made by the 1997 Act;

- no indemnity is payable on account of mines or minerals or the existence of any right to work such mines or minerals, unless it is noted on the title that mines or minerals are included in the estate (s 83(5)(b) of the LRA 1925);

- no amount of monetary compensation can compensate for some loses, for example, loss of a right of way, loss of title to a family home. This may be a ground for refusing rectification in the first place, for example, *Hare*.

Under the LRA 2002 as to rectification and indemnity

The provisions relating to rectification and indemnity have been recast by the LRA 2002, although it is only in relation to rectification that significant changes are made. Section 65 of the LRA 2002 contains new provisions relating to when 'alterations' may be made to the Register and these are detailed in Sched 4 to the Act. The key concept is to be one of 'alteration', with 'rectification' referring to a specific type of 'alteration'.

According to Sched 4, para 1, the register may be 'rectified' (using that term in its new sense) when an alteration involves correcting a mistake that prejudicially affects the title of a registered proprietor. This type of rectification may lead to an indemnity. Under para 2, the court (but not the Registrar) may order alteration of the Register to correct a mistake, to bring the Register up to date and to give effect to any estate or interest otherwise excepted from the effect of registration. Importantly, no rectification (in its new narrow sense) shall be ordered by the court against a proprietor in possession unless he consents or has by fraud of lack of proper care caused or substantially contributed to the mistake, or it would be unjust not to rectify. This is similar to (but not identical with) the existing law. The Registrar's powers to alter the Register for mistake are contained in para 5 (to correct a mistake, bring the Register up to date, give effect to a right etc, excepted from the effect of registration and to remove superfluous entries), but by para 6 any alteration which amounts to a rectification (that is, corrects a mistake that prejudicially affects the title of a registered proprietor) is subject to the same provisions as apply to the court under para 2.

The indemnity provisions are now triggered by s 103 of the LRA 2002 but the detail is found in Sched 8. As noted, they do not differ markedly form the current position under the LRA 1925. Thus, para 1 sets out the eight circumstances in which a person who suffers loss may be indemnified: rectification of the register; a mistake which would involve rectification; a mistake in an official search; a mistake in an official copy of a document; a mistake in a document kept by the Registry which is not original but which is referred to in the register; the loss or destruction of a document kept at the Registry; a mistake in the cautions register (cautions against first registration); and a failure by the Registrar to perform his duty. As currently, no indemnity is payable for any loss that is wholly or partly the result of the claimant's fraud or lack of proper care (para 5).

2.11   An overview of the Land Registration Act 2002

It will be apparent from the summary of the 2002 Act given in this chapter that it represents a fundamental shift in the way we think about registered land. It has been said many times, but the aim is to move to title by registration instead of registration of title. The introduction of electronic conveyancing is the driving force behind this and is the motivation for many of the reforms of the Act. The significant features of the 2002 Act are:

- The reclassification of overriding interests in to rights that override a first registration (Sched 1) and rights that override a subsequent registered disposition (Sched 3). The former is more extensive than the latter. The role of rights binding by actual occupation and easements is severely restricted for Sched 3 rights. Undiscoverable overriding interests will be eliminated in respect of Sched 3 rights.

- The new system of adverse possession as it applies to registered land. In essence, rarely will a registered proprietor lose title through adverse possession if he is prepared to take action to evict the adverse possessor. There will be no 'limitation period' *per se* for registered land.

- The provisions relating to the introduction of electronic conveyancing. Thus at first, it will be possible to create and transfer property rights by electronic 'written contracts' and 'deeds' (the intended s 2A of the LP (Misc Prov) A 1989 and s 91 of the LRA 2002 respectively). More importantly, in due course, the creation or transfer of most rights in or over registered land will be ineffective unless completed by registration. Rights not so electronically registered will not exist. Registration and creation will be simultaneous, the registration gap will disappear and the register will be a truer mirror. In time, and subject only to the limited rights in Scheds 1 and 3, rights not entered on the register will not exist at all.

- Rights arising by proprietary estoppel and 'mere equities' will be treated as proprietary (s 116 of the LRA 2002).

- Legal leases of over seven years' duration will be substantively registered with their own title number.

- The way in which so called 'minor interests' are protected will be rationalised.

- Mortgages of registered land may be created only by the 'charge' and the charge certificate will be abolished.

- The circumstances in which the register may be altered are clarified and the indemnity provisions are recast.

- The Crown will be able to register its land for the first time.

REGISTERED LAND

The nature and purpose of registered land

To ensure the *free alienability of land* by:

- easing the conveyancing process through the establishment of certainty;
- eliminating the vagaries of the doctrine of notice and thereby protecting the purchaser;
- enhancing the role of overreaching and thereby removing some obstacles to the sale of land which is subject to a trust of land.

To bring certainty to *land ownership* by:

- establishing a register of titles, held at local district offices, that is conclusive as to ownership and which is backed by a legislative and financial guarantee (registrable titles);
- establishing a defined list of rights that can bind the land automatically but which should be discoverable on physical inspection of the land (overriding interests);
- establishing a register of rights adverse to the land so that an intending purchaser (including a mortgagee) will be aware of what they are about to buy (minor interests).

The three principles of registered land

(1) The mirror principle, encapsulating the idea that the register should reflect the totality of rights in and over the land. The mirror is not perfect under the LRA 1925 due to the existence of overriding interests but it will become considerably more accurate under the LRA 2002.

(2) The curtain principle, encompassing the idea that equitable interests existing behind trusts of land should be kept off the register and dealt with through the mechanism of overreaching. This has been largely achieved, although the cases where overreaching is not possible has meant that sometimes the purchaser must lift the curtain.

(3) The insurance principle, encapsulating the idea that the State will guarantee the efficacy of the system by providing statutory compensation (indemnity) to persons suffering loss by reason of the operation of the system.

An overview of registered land and the various classes of estates and interests

Under the LRA 1925, proprietary rights fall into four classes, not necessarily coterminous with their quality as legal or equitable interests:

(a) registrable interests, being the registrable titles to land. These are the legal freehold absolute in possession and currently the legal leasehold of over 21 years' duration. The grade of title with which the registered proprietor is registered may be absolute, good leasehold, possessory or qualified. The grade of title helps to determine the extent to which the proprietor is bound by pre-existing adverse rights. Registration as registered proprietor confers the relevant estate at law, subject to the rights specified in s 20 of the LRA 1925. The position is similar under the LRA 2002 save that legal leases over seven years will become registrable in their own right. Note also that dealings with the title will be undertaken electronically;

(b) registered charges, being legal mortgages;

(c) overriding interests, being interests which bind a purchaser automatically, without registration. The most important rights are legal easements and certain equitable easements (s 70(1)(a) of the LRA 1925), the rights of an adverse possessor under the Limitation Acts (s 70(1)(f)), the rights of persons in actual occupation of the land or in receipt of rents and profits thereof (s 70(1)(g)) (these are not 'rights of occupation', but the proprietary rights of people who are *in actual occupation*); and legal leases of 21 years or less duration (s 70(1)(k)). The concept of such rights is retained by the LRA 2002, but is renamed as 'interests that override' under Scheds 1 or 3 and has been reduced significantly in scope;

(d) minor interests, being a residual category of rights, comprising those rights which do not fall within the other categories. Except where overreaching occurs, minor interests are protected if entered on the register by either a *restriction*, an *inhibition*, a *notice* or (with limited effect) a *caution*. Unregistered minor interests are generally void against a purchaser for value who is registered as the proprietor. The one considerable exception to this is if the potential minor interest qualifies in some way as an overriding interest. The concept is retained by the LRA 2002, but with some modifications. The method of protecting these interests will change and fewer that are not registered will be saved as interests that override.

Overreaching

This is a process whereby certain equitable interests are removed from the land and transferred to the cash proceeds of a sale of that land. Overreaching will occur when the equitable right is overreachable *and* a proper overreaching transaction occurs. If these conditions are satisfied, the equitable interest cannot be protected as either a minor interest or as an overriding interest.

Indemnity and rectification

The Register may be rectified and/or a person may claim an indemnity under ss 82 and 83 of the LRA 1925. The latter has been amended by the LRA 1997 in order to increase the circumstances in which a person can claim compensation because of loss caused by the operation of the system of registered land. The power of rectification is circumscribed by statute and should not be regarded as giving the court unfettered discretion to disrupt the sanctity of the register. It will be restated by the LRA 2002.

Reform

- The reclassification of overriding interests in to rights that override a first registration (Sched 1) and rights that override a subsequent registered disposition (Sched 3). The former is more extensive than the latter. The role of rights binding by actual occupation and easements is severely restricted for Sched 3 rights. Undiscoverable overriding interests will be eliminated in respect of Sched 3 rights.

- The new system of adverse possession as it applies to registered land. In essence, rarely will a registered proprietor lose title through adverse possession if he is prepared to take action to evict the adverse possessor. There will be no 'limitation period' *per se* for registered land.

- The provisions relating to the introduction of electronic conveyancing. Thus at first, it will be possible to create and transfer property rights by electronic 'written contracts' and 'deeds' (the intended s 2A of the LP (Misc Prov) A 1989 and s 91 of the LRA 2002 respectively). More importantly, in due course, the creation or transfer of most rights in or over registered land will be ineffective unless completed by registration. Rights not so electronically registered will not exist. Registration and creation will be simultaneous, the registration gap will disappear and the register will be a truer mirror. In time, and subject only to the limited rights in Scheds 1 and 3, rights not entered on the register will not exist at all.

- Rights arising by proprietary estoppel and 'mere equities' will be treated as proprietary (s 116 of the LRA 2002).

- Legal leases of over seven years' duration will be substantively registered with their own title number.

- The way in which so called 'minor interests' are protected will be rationalised.

- Mortgages of registered land may be created only by the 'charge' and the charge certificate will be abolished.

- The circumstances in which the register may be altered are clarified and the indemnity provisions are recast.

- The Crown will be able to register its land for the first time.

CHAPTER 3

UNREGISTERED LAND

3.1 Introduction to the system of unregistered conveyancing: unregistered land

As we have seen in Chapters 1 and 2, land law in England and Wales underwent radical reform with effect from 1 January 1926. However, it was as obvious then as it is now that the task of transforming a basically feudal system of law into one which could adequately serve the 20th century and beyond would not be accomplished overnight. Thus, at the outset, it was intended that registration of title and the accompanying provisions of the Land Registration Act (LRA) 1925 would be phased in: at first, in discrete geographical areas, and only later, to embrace the whole country. This meant that much land would remain within the old system of conveyancing, sometimes known as the system of 'private unregistered conveyancing', in order to distinguish it from the State guaranteed system of the Land Registration Acts. Yet, it is also apparent from Chapter 1 that the old system was complicated and unwieldy, and offered neither certainty to a purchaser of land, nor adequate protection to a person who enjoyed rights over that land. For example, the doctrine of notice, and especially the development of constructive notice, could make a purchaser bound by a third party right even if it did seriously devalue the use and enjoyment of their land, and in circumstances where the purchaser 'knew' of the right only in the most vague way. Conversely, a person seeking to enforce an equitable right over land owned by somebody else could find their right destroyed through no fault of their own, and in circumstances where they could have done nothing to protect it. Furthermore, the lengths to which a purchaser had to go to investigate title, and the potential number of persons with whom he had to agree a sale, made conveyancing time consuming and expensive.

To meet these problems, and bearing in mind that an immediate move to wholesale adoption of registered title was not possible, a great part of the 1925 legislative reforms were directed at establishing an intermediate, but temporary, system of conveyancing. This temporary system was meant to last only 30 years as it was hoped that registration of title would cover England and Wales by 1955. As we now know, this was a forlorn hope and first registration of title only became compulsory across the country in December 1990. Of course, the fact that compulsory first registration is now geographically universal and that registered titles now comprise the great majority of all titles does mean that the system of unregistered conveyancing will diminish in practical importance, but the time has not yet come when it can be abandoned completely. That happy day will not be with us even when the reform of registered land begins to take effect in 2003.

3.1.1 What is unregistered land?

To describe a piece of land as 'unregistered' means one thing only: viz, that title to the land is not to be found in the Land Register established by the Land Registration Acts, but rather that it is located in the old fashioned title deeds. Unregistered land is land to which the *title* is not registered. It does not mean that there is no provision or opportunity for the registration of other rights and interests affecting the land, for, as we shall see, 'unregistered land' has its own system of partial registration. It is important that this is appreciated fully. Indeed, it is essential from the outset to remember that the system of unregistered land (with its partial system of registration) operates *completely separately* from the system of registered land. Of course, they both deal with the same substantive property rights (freeholds, leaseholds, easements, covenants, etc), and they share the concept of overreaching, but they do so in different and mutually exclusive ways. So, if title to land is not registered, it is unregistered land and is to be dealt with according to the principles considered below. It does not borrow from the system of registered land, or vice versa.

3.2 An overview of unregistered land

Given that it was intended to be a temporary modification of pre-1925 practice, it should come as no surprise that the system of unregistered land relies heavily on many of the old doctrines that characterised dealings with land before the great reforms. Thus, unlike registered land, the distinction between legal and equitable rights is still of crucial importance when considering dealings with unregistered land, although the doctrine of notice has been replaced in all but a few instances by the partial system of registration referred to above. In essence, unregistered land can be viewed in the following way.

3.2.1 Estates in unregistered land

Title to land is not recorded in a register, nor is it guaranteed by the State through any indemnity legislation. However, the same type of estates may exist at law and in equity in unregistered land as exist in registered land on or after 1 January 1926. The substantive law of estates is governed by the Law of Property Act (LPA) 1925 and the 'freehold' or 'leasehold' are the same creatures in either system, albeit that the machinery governing their conveyance (transfer) is different. Thus, in the absence of title registration, any purchaser of unregistered land must seek out the 'root of title' in order to ensure that the seller has a good and safe title to pass on. Title is proven by an examination of the title deeds and documents relating to previous dealings with the land. In addition, a prudent purchaser will make a thorough physical inspection of the land in order to ascertain whether there are any obvious defects of title *and* whether there are any obvious third party rights (for example, frequently used easements) which might prejudice his use of the land.

As title is not registered, the quality of an estate owner's interest is determined according to the old common law as modified by the LPA 1925. A legal title, whether fee simple absolute (freehold) or leasehold, encapsulates the essence of ownership for the duration of the estate granted. A legal estate owner has no fear that his title will be compromised by any extraneous issues affecting the land, other than those interests binding as proprietary rights according to the rules of unregistered conveyancing. With an equitable estate (as where, for example, the proper formalities for the creation of a legal estate were not observed), the estate owner also enjoys full rights over the land, subject to the difficulties affecting all equitable interests, viz, that they rank second to any previously created equitable right and are vulnerable in the face of a sale of the land to a purchaser of a legal estate for valuable consideration.

3.2.2 Interests in unregistered land: rights over another person's estate

'Interests' in unregistered land are of the same type as interests in registered land. There are easements, covenants, profits, etc, as these are creatures of the substantive law. Once again, however, it is the machinery of unregistered land – the way in which these interests affect land – that is different. As before, 'interests' can be described conveniently as proprietary rights over someone else's land (in reality, over their estate in it) and interests in unregistered land may be split into the following four categories: legal rights; equitable rights which are registrable under the Land Charges Act (LCA) 1972; equitable rights which are not registrable under the LCA 1972 because they are subject to overreaching; and equitable rights which are neither overreachable nor registrable under the LCA 1972.

3.2.3 Legal rights

Legal rights, such as legal easements, legal mortgages and legal leaseholds are, in the main, automatically binding on the land over which they exist. They will bind automatically any person coming into ownership or occupation of the land, be they a purchaser, donee of a gift, devisee under a will or an adverse possessor. This is the old pre-1926 rule that 'legal rights bind the whole world'. This is a principle of utmost importance in unregistered land and necessarily requires that a clear distinction can be made between legal and equitable estates and interests. As we have seen (Chapter 1), this distinction turns primarily on the definition in s 1 of the LPA 1925, the way in which the interest has been created and the possible existence of a trust. However, once a legal right has been established, there is no need to make further enquiries as to the 'state of mind' of the potential new owner, the nature of his title or indeed any other matter: legal rights bind the whole world. In reality, however, this unbending rule rarely causes hardship because the manner of creation of legal rights means that generally they are obvious either from inspection of the title documents or inspection of the land itself.

The singular exception to the rule that legal rights bind the whole world is provided by the *'puisne* mortgage'. A *puisne* mortgage is a legal mortgage over land where the documents of title have not been deposited with the mortgagee (lender), usually because a prior legal mortgage has already been created and that first mortgagee has the documents. As the *puisne* mortgagee does not have the documents of title, he does not have the ability to prevent dealings with the land, and so the *puisne* mortgagee may not be protected adequately against further dealings. Consequently, a *puisne* mortgage is registrable, in unregistered land as a Class C(i) land charge (on which, see below, 3.6) and such registration ensures that any subsequent dealings with the land are subject to the mortgage. (For a recent discussion, see *Barclays Bank v Buhr* (2001).)

3.2.4 Equitable rights which are registrable under the Land Charges Act 1972

The second category of interests in unregistered land are those equitable rights requiring registration as land charges under the LCA 1972 (replacing the LCA 1925). The majority of third party equitable rights in unregistered land fall into this category, including equitable easements, restrictive covenants, equitable mortgages and estate contracts. In order to bind a purchaser of unregistered land, a land charge must be registered in the appropriate way. Failure to register when required renders the interest void against a purchaser, and the old doctrine of notice is irrelevant. Note also, that the registration of land charges has *absolutely nothing* to do with registered land. It is an independent register, which operates purely in the field of unregistered conveyancing.

3.2.5 Equitable rights which are not registrable under the Land Charges Act 1972 because they are subject to overreaching

Certain equitable rights may not be registrable under the LCA 1972 because they are subject to overreaching. These equitable interests are overreachable in the same way as their counterparts in registered land. Again, they comprise equitable co-ownership interests existing behind a trust of land and equitable interests operating behind a settlement established under the Settled Land Act 1925. These rights are capable of expression in monetary terms and are kept off the Land Charges Register in order to prevent the title becoming clogged.

3.2.6 Equitable rights which are neither overreachable nor registrable under the Land Charges Act 1972

Equitable rights which are neither overreachable nor registrable under the LCA 1972 form a miscellaneous category of equitable rights that were either deliberately or accidentally left out of the land charges system, or have developed since that system came into operation. As they are neither overreachable nor registrable, the only way in which it is possible to determine whether these rights affect the unregistered title (that is, a person purchasing the land) is to utilise the old doctrine of notice. This is virtually the only time that the doctrine of notice remains applicable in land law after 31 December 1925. As we shall see, the number of equitable rights that fall into this category is small, and all but one or two arise in very untypical situations. Nevertheless, this category represents a 'hole' in the system of unregistered conveyancing and is one of the main reasons why an understanding of pre-1926 law is still important.

3.3 Titles in unregistered land

As with registered land, the reforms of the LPA 1925 apply in equal measure to unregistered land. After all, the substance of the law is the same, it is the machinery for dealing with the two types of land that is different. Thus, the number of possible legal estates (titles) is limited to two, being the freehold (fee simple absolute in possession) and the term of years absolute (leasehold) (s 1 of the LPA 1925). As noted above, the title in unregistered land is not registered, but remains provable from the title deeds. In effect, when a purchaser wishes to buy unregistered land, there has to be an investigation of the 'root of title' in order to determine whether the seller owns the land and in order to determine the quality of their ownership. This will still be relevant on the occasion of a sale of unregistered land today, save that, after this last sale, the new owner must apply for first registration of title under s 123 of the LRA 1925 (as amended by s 1 of the LRA 1997). This is what is meant by the spread of compulsory registration to all England and Wales and an outright sale of unregistered land is only one of the 'triggers' for compulsory registration (see Chapter 2). Obviously, then, the search for root of title will become less frequent as more land becomes subject to registration of title.

The search for root of title in order to prove ownership by a potential purchaser was once a mammoth task. Prior to 1926, the number of potential legal owners of the land was unlimited and, in co-ownership situations, this meant that the title of every individual co-owner/seller might have to be investigated (for example, if they were tenants in common – see Chapter 4). After 31 December 1925, as we will see in Chapter 4, the maximum number of legal owners of an estate is restricted to four and any other co-ownership interests will exist in equity and will be overreachable. Likewise, in the 'modern' era if two or more persons own the legal estate in co-ownership, this must be under a joint tenancy. In essence, this means that there is but one title to investigate, irrespective of whether there are the maximum of four legal owners. Undoubtedly, this has made the search for root of title considerably easier. Moreover, since 1970 (s 23 of the LPA 1969), the search for 'root of title' through the title deeds and documents has been reduced to an examination of only the last 15 years of dealings with the land, not the 30 years prior to 1970. What this means is that, when the purchaser is searching the title deeds for an unbroken chain of ownership to the present seller, the purchaser need only find proper conveyances stretching back a minimum of 15 years. So, if a purchaser wishes to buy unregistered land in 2002, he must seek out a sound root of title going back to the first proper conveyance that was executed before 1987. A purchaser is entitled to rely on this proof of ownership, even if there is some defect in the title beyond the 15 year period which was not disclosed by the abstract of title sent by the seller to the purchaser. In practice, this search for a good root of title now causes little hardship to prospective purchasers, especially since most title deeds to property are kept together or even deposited with a bank which has advanced money by way of mortgage. As we shall see, however, the shortened period for establishing root of title has caused unfortunate difficulties in other areas of the system of unregistered land, especially in relation to the operation of the Land Charges Register.

The mechanism for the transfer of estates in unregistered land is essentially a matter of conveyancing procedures and falls largely outside the scope of the present work. Briefly, the vendor and purchaser will enter into a contract for the sale/purchase of the property ('exchange of contracts'), after settling a number of pre-contractual matters, such as price, general area of land to be sold, existence of planning law obligations, and (usually) the existence of any local authority charges over the land (known as local land charge, and not to be confused with land charges under the LCA 1972). This contract commits each party to the bargain, and may be specifically enforced if one party later tries to withdraw. The actual transfer is perfected by 'completion', this being the effective conveyance of the property by deed to the purchaser. In the interval between exchange of contracts and completion, the vendor must have produced an 'abstract of title', from which the purchaser can deduce a good root of title beyond the 15 year period. The failure of the vendor to produce a good title permits the purchaser to rescind the contract. Also in the period between exchange and completion, the purchaser will search the Land Charges Register to discover whether any LCA 1972 land charges are binding on the land. The problem of searching for, and discovering, binding land charges when the purchaser is already committed by contract to purchasing the property is discussed below.

3.4   Third party rights in unregistered land

It is inherent in what has been said already about land law and the 1925 reforms that a major purpose of the LPA and the specific regime of unregistered conveyancing is to bring certainty and stability to the status of third party rights in land. There are two reasons for this, whose fundamental importance bears repetition:

(a) a purchaser of land needs to know with as much certainty as possible whether any other person has enforceable rights over the land and the extent and nature of those rights; and

(b) the owner of those rights needs to be sure that his rights are protected when the land over which they operate is sold or otherwise disposed of.

It is, then, in everybody's interest to have a workable conveyancing system, wherein there is a balance between potential purchaser and third party, and which is so uniform in its operation as to allow accurate predictions of what will happen to third party rights in the majority of real life situations. Unfortunately, the system of unregistered conveyancing does not achieve these goals to the extent necessary to pronounce it a success. Of course, it does work – or, rather, it is made to work – but there is no doubt that the temporary measures adopted with effect from 1 January 1926 have not stood the test of time. There are few who are sorry to see the near death of unregistered conveyancing.

Before examining in detail the operation of third party rights in unregistered land, three preliminary points of crucial importance should be noted:

(a) first, that we are about to consider whether a person who obtains title to unregistered land, over which an adverse third party interest *already* exists, is bound by that interest (for example, a right of way or easement). In other words, does the third party interest survive a transfer of the land? This may depend on both the nature of the third party interest and/or the status of the new owner;

(b) secondly, in *all* cases, it is vital to know whether the third party right is legal or equitable. This will, in turn, depend both on the definition of legal interests contained in s 1 of the LPA 1925 and the way in which the interest was originally created. Hence, an easement may be legal or equitable (s 1 of the LPA 1925) and everything will depend on how it was created. Conversely, the burden of a restrictive covenant can only ever be equitable, irrespective of how it is created (s 1 of the LPA 1925). A knowledge of the distinction between legal and equitable rights is vital if the system of unregistered conveyancing is to be properly understood;

(c) thirdly, if it should prove that a third party right is not binding on a new owner of the land, the right may still be enforceable between the parties that created the right. For example, in *Barclays Bank v Buhr* (2001), the Buhrs had granted a mortgage (actually a *'puisne* mortgage' – see below

3.6.1 (c)) over their land. As we shall see, this proprietary right should have been registered as a Class C(i) land charge in order to remain enforceable against the land should that land come into the hands of another person. It was not so registered and hence was not enforceable ('void') by the Bank against the new owner of the property. Nevertheless, as between the Bank and the Buhrs, the mortgage remained enforceable as these were the parties that had created the right in contract and so the Bank were able to recover some of their money from the proceeds of the sale of the house.

3.5 The purchaser of unregistered land and the protection of legal rights

With the one exception noted above (the *puisne* mortgage), a fundamental principle of unregistered conveyancing is that 'legal rights bind the whole world'. So, if a person buys, or is given, or comes to possess, a piece of unregistered land, he will take that land subject to virtually every legal interest over it. Such legal interests may be, for example, a legal lease granted by the previous owner or a legal easement conferring a right of way over the land. Short of obtaining a waiver or release of the right from the person entitled to the benefit of it, there is little a transferee can do to avoid being bound. However, lest this be thought to be a harsh and unfair rule, we must always remember that only specified estates and interests may be 'legal', and even then they must be created in the proper fashion. Indeed, the most important reason why it is not unfair that legal rights should bind the land automatically is that they are usually perfectly apparent to a purchaser who investigates title properly and makes a physical inspection of the land. In other words, a potential purchaser will nearly always know of the existence of these rights and can act accordingly, either by offering a lower price or walking away. For the sake of clarity, however, the correct view is *not* that these rights are obvious and that this is why it is acceptable that they bind the land; rather, it is that it is necessary to have some rights that are capable of automatically surviving changes of ownership in land, and one way of avoiding any undue hardship is to ensure that only those rights that are apparent or obvious have this effect. The two reasons why legal rights are so apparent to a potential purchaser are:

(a) that most are created formally, by use of a deed. This is then kept with the title documents for all future purchasers of the land to see; or

(b) the rights are obvious to any prudent purchaser making a physical inspection of the land, as is the case where a tenant occupies the land or the existence of an easement is indicated by a driveway.

Of course, the rule now is that legal rights bind a transferee *whether or not* he knew about them, and *whether or not* they were, in fact, obvious from an inspection of the title deeds or land. However, the origin of the rule is plain to see.

3.6 The purchaser of unregistered land and the protection of equitable rights: the Land Charges Act 1972

A major part of the unregistered land system is devoted to the protection of equitable third party interests in land. The most important method by which this is attempted is through a system of registration introduced by the LCA 1925 and now codified in the LCA 1972. To reiterate, this has nothing to do with any of the registration facilities available in registered land.

In order to understand the system of registration of land charges, it is important to appreciate that there are three stages in assessing whether an equitable right binds the land when the land passes to a new estate owner:

(a) the first issue is whether the equitable interest is *registrable* under the LCA 1972. In other words, does the equitable interest fall within the classes of right that are required to be registered as a land charge in order to bind a purchaser of the land? If it does *not*, and so is *not* registrable (and this depends on the statutory definition contained in the LCA 1972), then the equitable interest is either overreachable, or within the exceptional class discussed below, 3.7 and 3.8;

(b) the second question is, assuming that the equitable interest is registrable, has it in fact been registered, and what is the effect of the registration?;

(c) thirdly, if the right is registrable, but has not been registered, what is the effect (if any) on a transferee of the unregistered land?

These three issues will be addressed below, but first the *machinery* of land charge registration needs to be examined. This is of a unique character. Unlike registered land, land charges are not entered against the title to the land – after all, this title is not entered on any register but is provable from the title documents. Consequently, land charges are registered against 'the name of the estate owner whose estate is intended to be affected', s 3(1) of the LCA 1972. For example, if a registrable equitable interest is alleged to bind the land owned by Mr X, having been created during Mr X's ownership, it must be entered against the name of Mr X. Indeed, even if the land is then sold to Mrs Y and then to Miss Z, the land charge will remain entered against the name of Mr X. This is the 'named-based' system of registration, and it has given rise to a number of practical difficulties for purchasers, as we shall see below in 3.9.

As briefly discussed above, when a person wishes to purchase unregistered land, he will make a search of the Land Charges Register to determine the existence of any registered land charges. The name-based system means that the purchaser must make an official search *against the names* of all previous estate owners revealed in the root of title in order to discover whether any charges are registered. These names are usually readily discoverable from the documents of title provided by the vendor, although the search is usually undertaken *after* the vendor and purchaser have entered into an enforceable contract to sell the property, because it is only then that the purchaser has access to the title deeds and so may discover the relevant names. Of course, this means that a purchaser might discover a registered land charge that would seriously diminish the value of the land they propose to buy, yet he is bound by contract to go through with the sale. To meet the obvious injustice that this situation can create (because, by virtue of s 198(1) of the LPA 1925, the registration of the charge constitutes notice of its existence, and is, therefore, binding on the intending purchaser, even though it could not have been discovered until after contracts were made), s 24(1) of the LPA 1969 provides that a purchaser shall be entitled to escape from the contract if he did not have real notice of the registered land charge at the time he entered the contract. This is a necessary modification to the normal rule that contracts for the sale of land can be specifically enforced as the difficulties are generated entirely by the name-based system of registration of land charges and not because of some act of the parties.

Bearing this in mind, two important consequences flow from the making of an official search of the Land Charges Register:

(a) first, if a search is made in the proper manner, an official search certificate is issued to the purchaser and this (not the register itself) is conclusive according to its terms (s 10(4) of the LCA 1972). This is so even if there has been a mistake by the Registry in issuing a certificate, as in *Horrill v Cooper* (1998). Thus, if a registered charge is not revealed through error, the purchaser still takes the land free of that charge (the certificate is conclusive), and the right as a right enforceable against the land is lost. However, the owner of the registered charge may seek compensation from the Registrar via the tort of negligence (*Ministry of Housing and Local Government v Sharp* (1970));

(b) secondly, the purchaser has a 15 day 'priority period' from the date of the official search in which to complete his purchase, safe in the knowledge that only those charges revealed by the official search will be binding against him. Charges registered in the interim (that is, *within the purchaser's priority period*) will not be binding if completion of the purchase occurs within that period (s 11(5)). However, this presupposes that the purchaser has searched the names correctly, and that all the relevant names have been searched. In this connection, it must always be remembered that the certificate is conclusive as to the search *requested*, and not as to the search that the purchaser should have made. This has caused some difficulties where defective searches or defective registrations take place: see below, 3.9.

3.6.1 The classes of registrable charge under the Land Charges Act 1972

Broadly speaking, the interests that are capable of registration as land charges are those rights which have an adverse affect on the value of the land or the enjoyment of it, *and* which are not suitable for overreaching, being interests which are not easily translated into a monetary equivalent. With the exception of the *puisne* (legal) mortgage, they can be referred to as 'commercial' equitable interests in order to distinguish them from the overreachable 'family' equitable interests. Although there are some other matters which can be registered under the LCA 1972 so as to bind transferees (for example, pending land actions, writs: see below, 3.6.5), we are concerned primarily with the six classes of land charge defined in s 2 of the Act:

(a) Class A: certain statutory charges which are created on the application of an interested person under an Act of Parliament (s 2(2) of the LCA 1972). These statutory charges usually relate to some work undertaken by a public body in relation to the land (not being a local land charge), the cost of which is chargeable to the owner, or where an Act of Parliament charges land with the payment of money for very specific purposes. In either case, the 'cost' is secured by means of the Class A land charge. Although not rare, rarely do they generate problems, being extinguished by payment of the sum charged;

(b) Class B: certain statutory charges that arise automatically (s 2(3) of the LCA 1972). These are very similar to Class A land charges, save only that the charge is not created by some person petitioning the Registrar but arises automatically by effect of the relevant legislation. A charge for the costs (or part thereof) of recovering property with the assistance of legal aid falls within Class B;

(c) Class C is one of the most important classes of land charge. Herein lie many interests that can have a profound effect on the land against which they exist. Many are genuinely 'adverse' to the estate owner, being rights which control his use and enjoyment of the land, or detract from its capitalised value on sale. Class C is divided into four sub-classes:

- C(i): a legal mortgage which is not protected by the deposit of the title deeds of the property with the lender. This is the *puisne* mortgage, and is an exceptional example of a *legal* interest being registrable as a land charge (s 2(4)(i) of the LCA 1972). As with all land charges, failure to register a *puisne* mortgage means that it will be void against a purchaser – see *Barclays Bank v Buhr* (2001) and below. This exceptional need to register a legal right is motivated by a desire to offer protection to the *puisne* mortgagee, given that it will not have control of the documents of title. It is interesting, then, that if the mortgagee fails to make use of the registration machinery that exists for *the mortgagee's* protection, that mortgagee will suffer the voidness of its charge if the land is transferred to a purchaser. Another solution could have been to allow the *puisne* mortgage to be binding automatically as with other legal interests, but to ensure that, if the mortgagee wished to prevent the estate owner from granting further mortgages without the mortgagee's consent, registration as a land charge was also available. The opposing argument is that if this were the scheme then the purchaser could not rely on an inspection of the relevant Land Charges Register to determine the existence of a *puisne* mortgage (although, of course, this is true already of all other legal interests);

- C(ii): 'a limited owner's charge', being a charge or mortgage which a person such as a life tenant under the Settled Land Act (a limited owner) may be entitled to levy against the land because of obligations discharged by him, for example, because of the payment of inheritance tax (s 2(4)(ii) of the LCA 1972). Note, it is the charge or mortgage which is registrable, *not* the life interest itself (see below);

- C(iii): 'a general equitable charge', being a residual category that catches specific charges not mentioned elsewhere. However, this is not a completely open-ended category, for by statute it does not include an equitable co-ownership interest behind a trust of land or a successive equitable interest under a strict settlement (because they may be overreached) and it does not include any charge which is, in reality, a charge over the proceeds of sale of land rather than the land itself (as in *Re Rayleigh Weir Stadium* (1954)). Neither, so it would seem, does it include equitable interests arising by virtue of proprietary estoppel (*Ives v High* (1967); s 2(4)(iii) of the LCA 1972);

- C(iv): 'estate contracts', being enforceable agreements to convey a legal estate (s 2(4)(iv) of the LCA 1972). This class is important as it effectively includes all manner of equitable interests, providing that they are 'equitable' because of a failure to observe the proper formalities that would have constituted them as legal interests. Thus, equitable leases are registrable as Class C(iv) land charges, as they result from an enforceable contract to grant a legal lease (*Walsh v Lonsdale* (1882) and Chapter 6), as are equitable mortgages of a legal estate. Also included are options to purchase land (*Armstrong v Holmes* (1993)) and certain rights of first refusal to buy land (rights of pre-emption). However, it is clear that only those contracts which are for the grant of a proprietary interest in land fall within this head. Class C(iv) cannot confer any protection for contracts for personal interests in land (*Thomas v Rose* (1968)). The 'estate contract' is one of the most frequently registered classes of land charge, both because it can arise in a wide variety of situations and because of the effect an estate contract can have on the value of the land when the time comes to sell it. For example, if A, the freehold owner, has granted B an option to purchase the land, this is an estate contract. If B then registers against A's name, A's ability to deal subsequently with the land is much reduced: any other purchaser from A takes the land subject to B's prior right to buy it. Note, however, that in order to be registrable as an estate contract under Class C(iv), the 'contract' must be validly created. As discussed in Chapter 1, the majority of contracts for the disposition of an interest in land currently must be made in writing, incorporating all the terms and signed by both parties (s 2 of the Law of Property (Miscellaneous Provisions) Act (LP (Misc Prov) A) 1989). A contract which does not fulfil these conditions is not registrable as a Class C(iv) land charge because it is no contract at all. (The same will be true for attempted electronic contracts that do not meet the required format.) Likewise, those proprietary rights that may be created informally (for example, by proprietary estoppel) are not registrable under this Class, as they do not spring from a contract;

(d) Class D, which is divided into three sub-classes:

- D(i): an Inland Revenue charge, being in respect of taxes payable on death under the Inheritance Tax Act 1984 (s 2(5)(i) of the LCA 1972);

- D(ii): restrictive covenants created after 1925, not being covenants between a lessor and lessee (s 2(5)(ii) of the LCA 1972; *Dartstone v Cleveland Petroleum* (1969)). For example, where one landowner (A) promises his neighbour (B) that he will not carry on any trade or business on his own land, the neighbour may register the 'restrictive covenant' against A's name. If the covenant *is* made between lessor and lessee, and affects the leasehold land (as where a tenant promises not to keep pets on the leasehold premises), special rules apply and these are discussed in the chapter on leases (Chapter 6). These special rules – themselves a mix of common law and statute – provide an adequate system for the enforcement of leasehold covenants outside the registration scheme of the LCA 1972 (and indeed that of the LRA 1925);

- D(iii): equitable easements, rights or privileges over land created after 1925, being easements/rights which are equitable because they are created informally or for an estate that is not itself legal (for example, an easement attached to an equitable lease) (s 2(5)(iii) of the LCA 1972). However, this category does not include equitable easements which arise by proprietary estoppel (*Ives v High* (1967)), because the category relates only to those rights which could have been 'legal' if properly created, not to those rights which are creations of equity alone, see also *Shiloh Spinners v Harding* (1973);

(e) Class E: annuities created before 1926 (s 2(6) of the LCA 1972), being yearly sums payable to a specific person. Annuities created after 1925, provided they comply with certain conditions, are registrable as Class C(iii) land charges;

(f) Class F: a spouse's 'matrimonial home right' arising under s 30 of the Family Law Act (FLA) 1996 and registrable as a land charge by virtue of s 31 of that Act. This replaces the former regime of the Matrimonial Homes Act 1983, and is, in most respects, identical. These rights are essentially personal rights, which spouses enjoy against their partners, to occupy the matrimonial home. However, these rights are treated as being equivalent to proprietary rights by the registration machinery. If registered against a spouse, the spouse owning a legal estate in the land (s 31(13) of the FLA 1996), and any subsequent purchaser, may be bound by the registered right of occupation. Such registration is relatively uncommon, and arises, usually, when the husband and wife are in some domestic dispute. In fact, however, given that the spouse against whom the charge is registered is taken to promise any purchaser that he will give vacant possession (Sched 4, s 3(1) of the FLA 1996), the effect of registering a Class F land charge is likely to be that the husband and wife are forced to settle their differences before the house is sold. Should they fail to do so, the consequences can be serious, as in *Wroth v Tyler*, where the husband's inability to complete the contract with the innocent purchaser due to the registered Class F land charge led to legal action and bankruptcy.

3.6.2 The effect of registering a land charge

It has been noted already that the machinery of the LCA 1972 requires a registrable charge to be entered on the register against the name of the estate owner whose land is to be affected. This has three important consequences.

First, in order to be sure that a registrable interest will be enforceable against a subsequent purchaser of the land, the land charge must be entered against the correct name of the estate owner that first created the right. Normally, it would be registered by the person (that is, his solicitor) who was first given the benefit of the right. For these purposes, the correct name is the full name of the current estate owner as it appears on the title deeds of the land to be affected (*Standard Property Investment plc v British Plastics Federation* (1987)). If an entry is made against the wrong name (or more likely an incorrect version of the right name, for example, as in *Diligent Finance v Alleyne* (1972)), then an official search against the correct name will confer protection on the purchaser within the priority period, because the charge will not be revealed by the certificate, and the certificate is conclusive. The purchaser will take the land free of the incorrectly registered charge. For example, if the estate owner's name is William Smith, but the land charge is registered against Bill Smith, a purchaser who searches against 'William Smith' will take the land free of the charge. However, as is illustrated by *Oak Co-operative Society v Blackburn* (1968), if the purchaser also searches against the wrong name, then the registration of the land charge against a version of the correct name (albeit actually incorrect) will protect the land charge. In other words, if both registration and search are defective as to the correct name, the registration of the charge will be effective to protect the interest, providing the name against which it was actually registered is a reasonable version of the correct name. For example, assuming that the estate owner's name is William Smith, and the land charge is registered against Bill Smith, if the purchaser searches against Walter Smith, the land charge binds the purchaser. Of course, a defective search will always lose priority to a correctly registered charge. Thus, if the estate owner's name is William Smith and the land charge is registered against William Smith, a purchaser will be bound by the land charge if he searches against the wrong name (for example, Bill Smith) and the charge is (obviously) not revealed.

Secondly, the charge must be entered against the name of the person who is the estate owner of the land intended to be bound at the time the charge is created. So, for example, if A contracts to sell land to B, B must register this estate contract (Class C(iv) land charge) against the name of A. This is perfectly straightforward. If then B enters into a subcontract to sell the land to C before B actually acquires title, C must also register their estate contract against A, because A is the estate owner of the land which is to be bound at the time the charge is created. C can only safely register against B if B has acquired title before making the contract with C (*Barret v Hilton Developments* (1975)). There are then some pitfalls for purchasers involved in a series of sub-sales if they do not know the name of the estate owner (or, more likely, that it is a sub-sale at all!)

Thirdly, having taken account of the two points above, a correct registration of a land charge has a powerful affect on the land over which it operates. According to s 198(1) of the LPA 1925, registration of a land charge is 'deemed to constitute actual notice of the fact of such registration, to all persons and for all purposes connected with the land'. This means (although it is expressed rather elliptically) that, if the charge is registered, it will bind all future purchasers (and other transferees of the land, for example, by gift or under a will) of the land (unless they are given a mistakenly clear search certificate: *Horrill v Cooper* (1998)). This 'bindingness' is expressed in terms of notice, because from 1 January 1926, this system of registration was to replace the doctrine of notice. However, it is vital to remember that, for a registrable land charge, registration alone means that it is binding. It does not matter that the purchaser either actually knew or did not actually know of the existence of the charge. Registration is not just one form of alerting the purchaser to the existence of the charge; it is the only method of alerting the purchaser, and therefore making them bound. As discussed below, a person who has knowledge of such an adverse right by another route, but where there is no registration of it, will not be bound – *Midland Bank v Green* (1981).

The powerful effect of properly registering a land charge against the name of the current estate owner – in that it becomes binding on all future purchasers and other transferees – is further illustrated by the fact that a registered land charge remains binding on a purchaser even if he could not possibly have discovered the names of the estate owners against whom to make a search. So, a purchaser of a leasehold estate will be bound by charges registered against the name of the former owner of the leasehold estate *and* by charges registered against the names of the owners of the freehold estate out of which the lease is carved. This is so even though a leaseholder has no right to investigate their landlord's title (*Patman v Harland* (1881)), and hence has no way of discovering the names of the freeholders against which to search. According to *White v Bijou Mansions* (1938), this is the effect of s 198(1) of the LPA 1925, even though s 44(5) of the LPA 1925 would seem to say that a tenant in such circumstances is not fixed with notice of the relevant charge. Likewise, a purchaser has no right to view title documents that exist behind the root of title. Yet, root of title is only 15 years, so a purchaser may well be bound by charges registered against a name which appears in a conveyance made more than 15 years ago. This name is potentially undiscoverable, but the registered charge is binding (s 198 of the LPA 1925). To meet this unjust situation (which was exacerbated when root of title was reduced to 15 years, instead of 30, in 1970), s 25(1) of the LPA 1969 provides that a purchaser may obtain compensation for being bound by a registered charge hidden behind the root of title if:

(a) the transaction causing loss takes place after 1 January 1970; and

(b) the purchaser had no actual (that is, real) knowledge of the hidden charge; and

(c) the charge is registered against the name of an estate owner which is not revealed in any of the documents of title.

3.6.3 The consequences of failing to register a registrable land charge in general

As the paramount policy of the LCA 1972 is to protect both the purchaser of land and the owner of any third party rights in that land (by bringing a measure of certainty to dealings with unregistered land), it is not surprising that there is a heavy penalty for failure to register a registrable interest. The fundamental point is that, while failure to register the land charge does not affect its validity as between the parties that created it (*Barclays Bank v Buhr* (2001)), it does destroy its validity against any future purchasers of the land. In simple terms, if a person purchases land over which there exists a registrable, but unregistered, land charge, that purchaser and all subsequent transferees are not bound by the charge. Lack of registration equals voidness *even if the purchaser actually knew of the charge* (s 199 of the LPA 1925) (*Hollington Bros v Rhodes* (1951); *Midland Bank v Green* (1981); *Horrill v Cooper* (1998)).

In practice, the precise circumstances in which an unregistered land charge is void depends on the particular class of land charge and, although we have been talking about purchasers of the land, it is clear that some persons who come into possession of the land may still be bound by an unregistered charge if they are not purchasers. Finally, there are some circumstances where an unregistered charge may be upheld against a purchaser for other reasons not connected to the principles of charge registration. The rules are not really complicated, and can be expressed as follows.

3.6.4 The voidness rule

The voidness rule is as follows:

(a) a purchaser or transferee's knowledge of the existence of a registrable, but unregistered, land charge is generally irrelevant in determining whether it binds them (s 199 of the LPA 1925) (*Hollington Bros v Rhodes* (1951); *Midland Bank v Green* (1981); *Horrill v Cooper* (1998));

(b) Class A, B, C(i), C(ii), C(iii) and F land charges, if not registered, *are void against a purchaser of any interest in the land* (that is, a legal or equitable estate) *who gives valuable consideration* (ss 4 and 17 of the LCA 1972). In other words, a person who buys an equitable or legal freehold or leasehold, or who takes an equitable or legal mortgage, will obtain the land free of the relevant unregistered charge if they gave 'valuable consideration'. Actual knowledge of the charge is irrelevant. Moreover, the consideration need only be valuable; it need not be adequate (*Midland Bank v Green* (1981));

(c) Class C(iv) and D land charges, if not registered, *are void against a purchaser of a legal estate in the land who gives 'money or money's worth'* (s 4 of the LCA 1972) as in *Lloyds Bank v Carrick* (1996), where the defendant's estate contract (being a contract to purchase the remainder of a long lease) was held void against the bank (a subsequent mortgagee) due to lack of registration. That the voidness rule for Class C(iv) and D land charges operates only in favour of a purchaser of a *legal* estate means that its effect is more limited than that applying to the other classes. So, a purchaser of an equitable lease, or a bank lending money by means of an equitable mortgage, remain bound by unregistered Class C(iv) and D land charges. There is also a difference between 'valuable consideration' and 'money or money's worth', the latter being what the purchaser of a legal interest must give to take free from Class C(iv) and D. So, for example, a transfer of a legal estate in land to a newly married couple 'in consideration of marriage' is valuable consideration, but it is not 'money or money's worth'. Again, however, the purchaser need not pay adequate 'money or money's worth' (*Midland Bank v Green* (1981)). Finally, although it is quite possible to come across persons who only purchase an equitable interest in property, it should be noted that, in practice, the majority of cases concerning the enforceability of Class C(iv) and D land charges do concern purchasers of a legal interest for money or money's worth;

(d) all land charges, *even if unregistered, are valid against a transferee of the land who is not a purchaser*. This includes:

- a donee of the land by way of gift;

- a devisee (that is, beneficiary) under a will;

- an adverse possessor (squatter) whether in the process of completing, or having completed, the requisite period of possession;

(e) all land charges, *even if unregistered, will be valid against a purchaser who has indulged in fraud*. This is another example of the maxim that 'equity will not permit a statute (that is, the voidness rule of the LCA 1972) to be an instrument of fraud'. The really difficult problem is to identify what constitutes fraud. Certainly, mere notice of the unregistered charge does not constitute fraud (*Hollington Bros v Rhodes* (1951)), but neither does notice coupled with a deliberate sale to a purchaser at an absurdly low price for the express purpose of defeating the unregistered interest (*Midland Bank v Green* (1981)). In *Green*, a father granted his son an option to purchase a farm. This was an estate contract and should have been registered as a Class C(iv) land charge. It was not registered. Subsequently, the father sold the farm to the mother for £500 (it being worth nearer £40,000) deliberately to defeat the unregistered option. Nevertheless, as was made clear by the House of Lords, it is not a fraud to take advantage of one's legitimate rights, even if it seems that there has been some element of 'bad faith'. Consequently, as the mother was a purchaser of a legal estate for money or money's worth, the unregistered option was unenforceable against the land, even though it also amounted to a clear breach of contract by the father with his son. Clearly, the courts have taken a strict line with the enforceability of land charges, and have not been prepared to permit the fraud exception to make large inroads into the voidness rule. Undoubtedly, this has much to do with the powerful decision of the House of Lords in *Midland Bank v Green* (1981), where there is a clear preference for the certainty of the register (by limiting the fraud exception), over the apparent 'justice' of individual cases. Indeed, although in *Green* the owner of the option had recourse to other remedies (for example, suing the solicitor successfully for negligently failing to register the option), the case illustrates that there is more to the fraud exception than simply that the person who granted the land charge has attempted to defeat it. Perhaps the result would have been different if, say, the father had assured his son that the option needed no registration and then had sold the land to his wife. This might have generated an 'estoppel' (see Chapter 9) capable of affecting the mother;

(f) all land charges, *even if unregistered, will be valid against a purchaser who is estopped from denying their validity through proprietary estoppel or the doctrine of constructive trusts.* This is very similar to the position above, and many would argue that they are analytically indistinguishable. The point is that, if a purchaser has either promised or agreed to give effect to an unregistered land charge, and that promise or agreement is relied upon by the person entitled to the benefit of the land charge to their detriment, the purchaser will not then be able to plead statutory voidness against that person. He will be held to the promise or agreement, although subsequent purchasers may not. As with a similar scenario in registered land (minor interests), this appears to be a personal remedy against a particular purchaser because of their conduct (*Taylor Fashions Ltd v Liverpool Victoria Trustees* (1982); cf *Lyus v Prowsa Developments* (1982) for registered land). For example, in the *Green* case, if the mother (the purchaser) had promised that she would give effect to the unregistered option, she may have been bound by an estoppel or constructive trust to give effect to it even though it was unregistered. Once again, however, this must be a very narrow exception to the voidness rule and one that will be rare in practice.

3.6.5   Other registers

In addition to the Land Charges Register, there are four other registers of matters affecting land regulated by the LCA 1972. These are the register of annuities, the register of deeds of arrangement, the register of writs and orders affecting land and the register of pending actions. These four registers contain information relating to rights, remedies and related interests affecting land that are not the typical third party interest registrable under the LCA 1972. The register of pending actions is used for the registration of disputes pending in court relating to title to land or to the existence of a proprietary interest. For example, a dispute concerning the existence of easement or whether an estate contract was made validly, may be registered here. Registration ensures that any subsequent purchaser of the land is given notice of the dispute affecting his land. Similarly, the register of writs and orders affecting land contains details of any order or writ issued by a court affecting land, such as a charging order securing a debt on the debtor's land, and if registered, are binding on all persons. The register of annuities contains details of certain pre-1926 annuities that do not fall within Class E land charges, and the register of deeds of arrangements records deeds executed by a bankrupt in settlement with creditors. Again, registration ensures their validity against future purchasers of the land.

The Land Charges Register and the four other registers operating under the LCA 1972 are administered centrally by the land charges department of the Land Registry. In addition, there are registers of land held locally by district councils and other local authorities which record 'local land charges'. These have nothing to do with land charges under the LCA. In fact, 'local land charges' are registered against the land itself and concern charges on land or matters affecting land that may have been recorded by a local authority in pursuit of its statutory responsibilities, such as planning matters. They are discussed here, because some categories of land charge proper exclude 'local land charges'. In fact, local land charges operate in unregistered and registered land in exactly the same way: a prospective purchaser of land will make a search of the local land charges register held by the relevant local authority prior to concluding the contract of sale. This will inform him of any matters which may affect adversely the use to which he proposes to put the land.

3.7 Overreachable rights

The second category of equitable rights operating in unregistered land are those which are subject to the process of overreaching. These are those equitable rights that are excluded from the category of land charges (that is, they cannot be registered), because a properly conducted overreaching transaction will sweep the interests off the land and cause them to take effect in the monies paid by the purchaser. Overreaching occurs in unregistered land in precisely the same circumstances as registered land. To recap briefly, overreaching will occur when:

(a) first, the equitable right is capable of being overreached: these are mainly equitable co-ownership rights existing behind a trust of land (for example, *City of London Building Society v Flegg* (1988)) or behind a strict settlement (s 2 of the LPA 1925); *and*

(b) secondly, the sale is made by those persons and in those circumstances that are capable of effecting an overreaching transaction (s 2(1) of the LPA 1925). These circumstances are four in number, although the first is the one most frequently encountered, viz:

(i) the transaction is made by at least two trustees of land (or a trust corporation) under a trust of land; or

(ii) the transaction is made under the provisions of the Settled Land Act 1925 relating to the operation of strict settlements; or

(iii) the transaction is made by a mortgagee or personal representative in exercise of their paramount powers; or

(iv) the transaction is made under order of the court, for example, s 14 of the Trusts of Land and Appointment of Trustees Act (TOLATA) 1996.

As with registered land, it is only if both of these requirements are met that overreaching can occur and the equitable right can then be given effect to in the purchase money paid for the land. However, what is important for present purposes is that these overreachable equitable rights are *not* capable of registration under the LCA 1972 (s 2(4)(iii) of the LCA 1972). The owner of such an interest cannot obtain protection through the system of registration just described. The reason for this is clear enough, viz, that the protection of these rights is found in the fact that, on overreaching, the equitable rights will take effect in the purchase money paid by the purchaser. In theory, they are not lost, but transformed into a share of the purchase money equivalent to the share the equitable owner held in the property. Unfortunately, as we have seen in relation to registered land, *State Bank of India v Sood* (1997) decides that no purchase money need be paid to the trustees to overreach the equitable interests if no such money was contemplated by the transaction: for example, as in *Sood*, where the legal owners mortgaged the property to secure future borrowings not an immediate lump sum payment. In such cases, there is no real protection for the equitable owners through overreaching, because there is no money in which their interests can take effect.

It might be wondered why these equitable rights are not capable of registration as land charges. The reason is, quite simply, that the 1925 legislation presupposes that the overreaching machinery itself will always be effective to guarantee the equitable owners' rights. Yet, as we have seen, before overreaching can occur, certain formalities (for example, *two* trustees) must be observed. If these formalities are not observed – because there may, in fact, be only one trustee (see Chapter 4) – the equitable rights are not overreached and the purchaser does not take the land automatically free of them. Yet, if these rights are not registrable as land charges, how can the person who owns the equitable right gain protection? The answer is that a purchaser who fails to overreach (for example, because there is only one trustee) will be bound by these equitable interests if he has notice of them (*Kingsnorth v Tizard* (1986)). This is one example when the old doctrine of notice is still relevant after 1925, and it arises because of the non-registrable nature of these equitable rights coupled with the rise of 'one trustee' cases of co-ownership. This is discussed more fully in Chapter 4, but, for now, the two important points are:

(a) certain equitable rights (those existing behind trusts of land) cannot be registered as land charges, because they are susceptible to overreaching. Overreaching will occur whenever the statutory formalities are complied with, even if no purchase money is actually paid (because it is not payable); and

(b) if these rights are not overreached, their effect on a purchaser is determined by the old equitable doctrine of notice.

3.8 A residual class of equitable interests

So far we have considered three different types of third party rights over land: legal rights, rights capable of registration under the LCA 1972, and rights capable of being overreached. In essence, this tripartite scheme was intended to encapsulate the totality of third party rights over land, with only minor exceptions. However, in the same way that land law in this country had developed up to 1926, it has continued to develop since the 1925 legislation and it is now clear that there is a fourth category of third party equitable rights that do not fit into this schema. Some of these were deliberately excluded from the tripartite pattern, being minor exceptions made for policy reasons. Others are new rights, developed since 1 January 1926. However, whatever the reason for their exclusion from the tripartite system, the fundamental rule governing their effect on land is clear.

When a purchaser buys land over which there is alleged to be an equitable right that is neither registrable as a land charge, nor overreachable, that equitable right is binding on the purchaser if he has actual, constructive or imputed notice of it. In other words, the ability of these rights to bind a purchaser depends on the historical doctrine of notice, and this is the one significant situation where the doctrine is still relevant in the land law of this country. The equitable rights which fall into this residual category are:

(a) equitable co-ownership interests behind a trust of land and equitable successive interests under a Settled Land Act settlement (s 2(4)(iii) of the LCA 1972), but *only* when there is no overreaching (*Kingsnorth v Tizard* (1986)). As noted above, 3.7, these equitable rights were deliberately omitted from the land charges system because it was believed most would actually be overreached. The relevance of notice in this context is a result of other, unforeseen changes in the law, such as the development of 'one trustee' co-ownership;

(b) pre-1926 restrictive covenants and easements (s 2(5)(ii) and (iii) of the LCA 1972) are also deliberately excluded;

(c) equitable mortgages protected by deposit of title deeds, because absence of the title deeds will always be notice to an intending purchaser of the land of the existence of such a powerful adverse right. Note, however, it is now clear that deposit of title deeds alone cannot actually create an equitable mortgage because such a mortgage does not spring from a *written* contract as required by s 2 of the LP (Misc Prov) A 1989 (*United Bank of Kuwait v Sahib* (1995)). Consequently, this is a category diminishing in significance;

(d) pre-1926 Class B and C land charges, until they are conveyed into different ownership, when they must be registered (s 4(7) of the LCA 1972);

(e) restrictive covenants between a lessor and lessee relating to the land held under the lease (s 2(5)(ii) of the LCA 1972), because such covenants will bind subsequent purchasers of the freehold reversion of the lease by virtue of the self-contained rules relating to the operation of leasehold covenants (see Chapter 6);

(f) restrictive covenants between a lessor and lessee relating to other land, that is, to land which is not part of the lease. These are also outside the registration system (because they are between lessor and lessee (s 2(5)(ii) of the LCA 1972), as above) but, because they do not relate to the land which is the subject matter of the lease, they cannot be enforced under the leasehold covenant rules. Thus, they bind purchasers of the relevant land through the doctrine of notice (*Dartstone v Cleveland* (1969)). The position is unlikely to be affected by the Landlord and Tenant (Covenants) Act 1995, because that Act annexes covenants to 'the premises demised by the tenancy and of the reversion in them', not to land outside the lease (s 3(1)(a) of the Landlord and Tenant (Covenants) Act 1995), a view confirmed by *Oceanic Village v United Attractions* (1999);

(g) a landlord's 'right of re-entry' which is implied in equitable leases (*Shiloh Spinners v Harding* (1973)). Being implied into an equitable lease, this right of re-entry is itself equitable, but non-registrable. It is used when a landlord wishes to forfeit a lease because the tenant has broken a promise (covenant) in the lease (see Chapter 6). It is enforceable against subsequent purchasers of the equitable lease, or an interest in it (for example, a subtenancy), through the doctrine of notice;

(h) a tenant's equitable right to enter the property and remove 'tenant's fixtures' at the end of an equitable lease (*Poster v Slough Lane Estates* (1969));

(i) interests acquired through proprietary estoppel (*Ives v High* (1967)). These are equitable interests which appear to be non-registrable even if (as in *Ives*) the interest created is similar to a class of land charge, such as an equitable easement. The point is, however, that these rights derive from pure equity and their mode of creation is such that their owner may not be aware that they actually have an interest until the land over which they exist is sold to a purchaser. In other words, there may be no dispute about the right until a new owner comes along. It would be unfair in such circumstances to require the owner of an estoppel interest to register something they did not know they had! It is likely that all interests generated by proprietary estoppel will be regarded as non-registrable, at least on the occasion of a sale of the land over which they exist to the first purchaser after they have been created. Subsequent to that, the existence of the interest will be known, and the owner might be required to register it. This issue has not been settled, and cases where the matter was relevant (for example, *Bibby v Stirling* (1998)) have sidestepped this problem;

(j) note, also, that a 'charging order' (that is, an order over a debtor's property enforcing a judgment debt), made under the Charging Orders Act 1979, against the interest of an equitable owner of property that exists behind what was then called a trust for sale, is apparently not registrable in the register of writs and orders affecting land, because such an interest is theoretically not an interest in land, but merely an interest in the proceeds of sale of land (*Perry v Phoenix Assurance* (1988)). It would, it seems, bind only by notice. This is a consequence of an application (some would say misapplication) of the doctrine of conversion, rather than an inherent problem with the system of land charges. The abolition of the relevant aspect of the doctrine of conversion by the TOLATA 1996 appears not to reverse *Perry* because the LCA 1972 is amended to provide that no writ or order 'affecting an interest under a trust of land' may be registered: see Sched 3, s 12(3) of the TOLATA 1996.

3.9 Inherent problems in the system of unregistered land

Throughout the analysis presented above, reference has been made to both the nature of the system of unregistered land and the machinery for the registration of land charges. Some of the problems and difficulties that surround the operation of unregistered land are inherent in the system itself, and some have emerged because of legal, social and economic developments in the years after 1925. Some of the more important points are reiterated below.

First, the system of the registration of land charges is incomplete, in that some equitable rights are non-registrable. This means that the old doctrine of notice still has a part to play, albeit of rapidly diminishing importance since the introduction of compulsory first registration of title. Nevertheless, it is a serious criticism that a system that was intended to bring certainty to dealings with land was unable to do away with the vagaries of the doctrine of notice.

Secondly, the Land Charges Register is a name-based register, and this brings several problems of varying importance:

(a) the use of wrong names or incorrect versions of names, both in the registration of a land charge and in a search of the register. This causes obvious problems, as charges are not properly protected and a purchaser may obtain a search certificate on which he cannot rely safely;

(b) long-lived land charges may be registered against names which the purchaser cannot discover and cannot, therefore, search against, as where a purchaser of a lease cannot discover the names of previous freeholders and, more importantly, where names are hidden behind the root of title;

(c) land charges must be registered against the estate owner of the land which is intended to be bound; thus, sub-purchasers in a chain of uncompleted transactions may register against the wrong person.

Thirdly, the official search certificate is conclusive. Consequently, in the event that the Registry fails to carry out an accurate search, a properly registered charge may be lost, as in *Horrill v Cooper* (1998). The remedy for the person prejudiced by this error lies in the law of tort.

Fourthly, some would question whether the absolute voidness of an unregistered charge is justifiable, especially where the purchaser has full knowledge of the unregistered charge and acts deliberately to defeat it (*Green*). The LCA 1972 is morally neutral and is premised on the paramount need for certainty. Although the steady demise of unregistered conveyancing makes the matter less pressing, there has been much debate about whether the LCA 1972 should be applied as vigorously as it was in *Green*, or whether the purchaser's 'actual' state of mind should be as important as the registration requirement.

Fifthly, the LCA 1972 does not protect the rights of persons in actual occupation of the land. Rather, the position is that, if a person has a proprietary right over another person's land, that right will be binding if it is either legal or registered as a land charge, or occasionally protected through the doctrine of notice. If, however, a right is registrable, but not registered, then the right is lost and the owner cannot rely on the fact that they are occupying the property. For example, in *Hollington Bros v Rhodes* (1951), equitable tenants had not registered their equitable lease as a Class C(iv) land charge and so it was void against a purchaser. Again, in *Lloyds Bank v Carrick* (1996), the occupier was held also to have rights under a Class C(iv) land charge, which were void through lack of registration. Yet, in both cases, if this had been registered land, the interests would have been protected as overriding interests under s 70(1)(g) of the LRA 1925 through 'actual occupation'. This is a serious defect in the system of unregistered conveyancing and means that the continuing validity of a person's rights might actually turn on the chance of whether the land is registered or not. Such a disparity in the systems is not justifiable, and there is evidence to suggest that it was not intentional, caused possibly by accidental omission of a provision protecting occupiers of unregistered land when the land charges legislation was consolidated in the LCA 1925.

3.10 A comparison with registered land

The regimes instituted by the LCA 1972 and the LRA 1925 were intended to achieve the same objective, albeit that the latter was far more wide ranging than the former. In essence, both of these systems were intended to bring stability to the system of conveyancing in England and Wales by protecting purchasers of land and owners of rights over that land. The following points highlight the different methods used to achieve these goals:

(a) in registered land, title to land is recorded on a register with a searchable, unique title number. In unregistered land, a purchaser must rely on the title deeds, and has to investigate the title in order to secure a proper root of title;

(b) in registered land, third party rights are protected through registration as minor interests, or under the provisions relating to overriding interests (s 70(1) of the LRA 1925). Of especial importance is the protection given to the rights of persons in actual occupation (s 70(1)(g)). In unregistered land, 'legal rights bind the whole world' and equitable third party rights are protected through a flawed 'name-based' system of land charge registration, or, even worse, by reliance on the old doctrine of notice. In both systems, overreaching is available, but not always possible;

(c) in registered land, an owner of an equitable right need not always register his right as a minor interest, but in many circumstances can fall back on the protection provided by overriding interests, especially through 'actual occupation' under s 70(1)(g) of the LRA 1925. Although this compromises the integrity of the register, and poses problems for purchasers, it serves an important social purpose. In unregistered land, there is no protection for the rights of people in actual occupation;

(d) in registered land, the methods of protecting a minor interest currently are complicated, although effective (they will change under the LRA 2002). In unregistered land, the name-based system can cause considerable problems with defective searches and registrations;

(e) in registered land, there have been some attempts to attack the automatic voidness of an unregistered minor interest when the land is sold to a purchaser for value. Similar moves have been made in unregistered land as regards the voidness of unregistered land charges. In both systems, the penalty of voidness for lack of registration has been largely upheld;

(f) in registered land, it is the register that is conclusive, not any search thereof. In unregistered land, it is the other way around.

UNREGISTERED LAND

Unregistered land and unregistered conveyancing

'Unregistered land' is land to which title is not recorded in an official register. 'Title' is found in the title deeds and related documents held by the estate owner (or his mortgagee). The purchaser will identify a good 'root of title' by examining the deeds and the land before completing the purchase.

The basic rules of unregistered conveyancing

A purchaser of unregistered land can become subject to another person's proprietary rights over the land, such as another's lease or easement. In order to determine the precise effect of another person's proprietary rights on a purchaser's land, the following principles apply:

- legal rights bind the whole world, so ensuring that any legal estates or interests affecting the purchaser's land are binding on him. These legal rights may well have been obvious from inspection of the title deeds or the land itself. The exception is the *puisne* mortgage, a legal interest that is a land charge (see below);

- equitable rights fall into three categories:
  - (a) land charges (being defined in six classes in the LCA 1972) must be registered against the name of the estate owner of the land that is to be bound. If registered, they are binding on a prospective purchaser of the land, even if 'hidden' from that purchaser. If they are not registered, they are void against a purchaser of either a legal estate, or a purchaser of any interest, depending on the category of land charge. This rule of voidness is strictly applied. The land charges system suffers from many defects, not least that it is name-based. It also fails to protect the rights of those in occupation of the land, even though this protection is automatic in registered land;
  - (b) overreachable rights, being 'family' equitable interests (such as co-ownership rights) that are capable of being accurately quantified in money. They are not registrable as land charges because it was believed they would be swept off the title by overreaching. The same conditions for overreaching apply in unregistered land as in registered land and the same difficulties exist resulting from the *Pettitt v Pettitt* rules on implied co-ownership (that is, only one trustee);
  - (c) equitable interests protected by the doctrine of notice, being a residual category of rights that were either deliberately or accidentally excluded

111

from the land charges system. The most important are the equitable right of co-ownership where there is no overreaching and rights generated by proprietary estoppel. Whether a purchaser is bound by any of these rights depends on the doctrine of notice with all its vagaries.

Inherent problems in the system of unregistered land

Some of the problems and difficulties that surround the operation of unregistered land are inherent in the system itself and some have emerged because of legal, social and economic developments in the years since 1925:

- the system of the registration of land charges is incomplete, in that some equitable rights are non-registrable. This means that the old doctrine of notice still has a part to play;

- the Land Charges Register is a name-based register and this brings several problems of varying importance. For example, the use of wrong names or incorrect versions of names both in the registration of a land charge and in a search of the register; that land charges may be registered against names which the purchaser cannot discover and cannot search against; that subpurchasers in a chain of uncompleted transactions may register against the wrong person;

- the official search certificate is conclusive, thus, in the event that the Registry fails to carry out an accurate search, a properly registered charge may be lost;

- some would question whether the absolute voidness of an unregistered charge is justifiable, especially where the purchaser has full knowledge of the charge and acts deliberately to defeat it (*Green*);

- the LCA 1972 does not protect the rights of persons in actual occupation of the land.

A comparison with registered land

- In registered land, title to land is officially recorded whereas, in unregistered land, a purchaser must make his own investigation based on the title deeds.

- In registered land, third party rights are protected through registration as minor interests or under the provisions relating to overriding interests. In unregistered land, legal rights are safe, but equitable third party rights are protected through a flawed 'name-based' system of land charge registration or, even worse, by reliance on the old doctrine of notice. In both systems, overreaching is available.

- In registered land, an owner of an equitable right may be able to fall back on the protection provided by overriding interests, especially through 'actual occupation' of the relevant land. In unregistered land, there is no protection for the rights of people in actual occupation.

- In registered land, there have been some attempts to attack the automatic voidness of an unregistered minor interest. Similar moves have been made in unregistered land as regards unregistered land charges. In both systems, the penalty of voidness for lack of registration has been largely upheld.

- In registered land it is the Register that is conclusive, not the search certificate. In unregistered land, it is the other way around.

CHAPTER 4

CO-OWNERSHIP

The law relating to co-ownership (or concurrent interests in land) forms a major part of most land law syllabuses. More important than that, however, is the fact that this is one area of land law that can have a powerful impact on the lives of ordinary men and women in England and Wales. In simple terms, the law of co-ownership operates whenever two or more people enjoy the rights of ownership of property at the same time, either freehold or leasehold. The co-owners may be husband and wife, romantic partners, friends, neighbours, business partners (see, for example, *Rodway v Landy* (2001): a doctors' surgery), or stand in any other relationship to each other that we can think of. In other words, 'the law of co-ownership' is a set of rules that governs dealings with property that is owned simultaneously by more than one person. It is not specifically concerned with the property law problems of married, or even unmarried, couples. It is not a species of family law. Of course, many of the problems that exist with co-owned property arise precisely because an emotional relationship has broken down, or friends have fallen out, or a mortgage cannot be paid. But, these are the causes of the problem and the rules of co-ownership are not designed specifically for these domestic eventualities. It is important to remember the fundamental 'property law' nature of co-ownership when considering the issues discussed below.

The law of co-ownership is to be found in the 1925 property legislation (particularly the Law of Property Act (LPA) 1925), common law, and the Trusts of Land and Appointment of Trustees Act (TOLATA) 1996. The last of these has amended significantly the original 1925 scheme. Moreover, social and economic changes have also had a great impact on the frequency with which co-ownership can arise and the consequences it brings. It is no longer true that co-ownership is limited to large, country estates or to land held for investment purposes. Neither is it true that co-ownership can arise only on a deliberate conveyance of land to two or more people. As we shall see, much of the law of co-ownership today concerns the rights and responsibilities of the co-owners of the family home and the way they interact with banks, building societies and other purchasers. This change in the role of co-ownership – or, rather, this broadening of the reach of the law on co-ownership – has generated fundamental changes to the scheme of co-ownership as it was intended to operate originally.

The law of co-ownership can be broken down into its various component parts, at least for the purposes of exposition. There is, first, the nature of co-ownership, and the types of co-ownership that can exist since 1 January 1926. Secondly, there is the statutory machinery that regulates the use and enjoyment of co-owned land, and the all important question of why the 1925 legislation made the radical changes that it did, and why it was felt necessary to amend these in 1996. Thirdly, there are those statutory and common law rules governing the creation of co-ownership, both when this is deliberate, and where it arises informally from the potential co-owners' dealings with the property and each other. Fourthly, there is the impact of co-ownership on third parties, such as banks and building societies (who may have lent money to finance the purchase of the property), and on purchasers and other occupiers. Fifthly, there are matters relating to the termination of co-ownership, and the methods by which one form of co-ownership may replace another.

4.1 The nature and types of concurrent co-ownership

Concurrent co-ownership of property describes the simultaneous enjoyment of land by two or more persons. It is important to remember that we are concerned here with the *simultaneous* enjoyment of property, that is, enjoyment of the rights of ownership by two or more persons at the same time. Successive interests in land, whereby two or more people are entitled to the enjoyment of land in succession to each other, are dealt with in Chapter 5. Prior to 1 January 1926, concurrent ownership of property could take a variety of forms, but, for all practical purposes, co-ownership since 1 January 1926 will either be by way of a *joint tenancy* or a *tenancy in common*. At the outset, it is best to note that 'tenancy' here does not mean a lease òr leasehold interest: it is the description given to the type of co-ownership enjoyed by the co-owners, whether they own freehold or leasehold land.

4.2 Joint tenancy

When land owned by two or more people is owned by them on the basis of a joint tenancy, each co-owner is treated as being entitled to the whole of that land. There are no distinct 'shares', and no single co-owner can claim any greater right over any part of the land than another. As far as the rest of the world is concerned, the land is treated as if it is owned by one person only and all the joint tenants share in that one ownership. In practical terms, this means that, when land is subject to a joint tenancy, there is only one formal title to it, and that title is owned jointly by all the joint tenants. So, if four student lawyers co-own legal title to a house under a joint tenancy, it is *not* possible to say that they own one quarter each: they each own the whole. Moreover, if the land is registered, there will be but one title registered at the Land Registry, with each co-owner registered as proprietor of that title in the proprietorship section of the register. If the land is unregistered, there will be but one set of title deeds, specifying the four owners. In essence, each joint tenant owns the total interest in the land. This really is 'co-ownership', because there are no shares, no partition of the land, but a right of ownership of the whole of the land enjoyed simultaneously with all the other owners. The nature of the joint tenancy as a single title owned by more than one person is reflected in the legal attributes of a joint tenancy. These attributes – discussed immediately below – are regarded as the touchstone of a joint tenancy and the absence of any one is fatal to the existence of this form of co-ownership.

4.2.1 The right of survivorship (the *ius accrescendi*)

By virtue of this principle, if one joint tenant dies during the existence of the joint tenancy (that is, before it has been 'severed', see below, 4.11), his interest in the joint tenancy (being his right to enjoy the whole of the land and its cash value on sale) automatically passes to the remaining joint tenants. In fact, it is a mistake to talk of anything 'passing' at all, because all that is happening is that the dead joint tenant drops out of the joint tenancy and the remainder continue to enjoy their rights over the whole land. The important practical point is, however, that when a joint tenant dies, no formal conveyance or written document is needed to reflect the new *status quo*. There is nothing to convey or pass, so no conveyance or transfer is needed. Indeed, the right of survivorship takes precedence over any attempted transfer by will of the interest of the dead joint tenant because unless that joint tenancy had been severed before death, there is no share to transfer (*Gould v Kemp* (1834)). This means that a joint tenancy can either be very useful (as where it avoids the need for formal documentation when a co-owner dies) or very unfair (as where a co-owner dies and is unable to leave an interest in the property to his family).

4.2.2 The four unities

Before a joint tenancy can exist, the four unities must be present (*AG Securities v Vaughan* (1988)), and it is the presence (or absence) of these factors that enables us to distinguish a joint tenancy from a tenancy in common:

(a) the *unity of possession* means that each joint tenant is entitled to physical possession of the whole of the land. Unity of possession means that there can be no physical division of the land and no restriction on any joint tenant's use of each and every part of it. This includes the right to participate fully in the fruits of possession, such as receipt of rents and profits derived from the land. As we shall see, although unity of possession must exist before a joint tenancy can exist, the practical effects of it have been modified by statute, so that, in some circumstances, a joint tenant may be excluded in practice from the land (ss 12 and 13 of the TOLATA 1996; and see *Chun v Ho* (2001)). This does not destroy the unity of possession *per se*; rather, the court's power under ss 12 and 13 of the TOLATA modifies the co-owner's entitlements. An additional power exists in relation to certain family oriented disputes: Pt IV of the Family Law Act 1996;

(b) the *unity of interest* means that each joint tenant's interest in the property must be of the same extent, nature and duration. Thus, all must be joint tenants of the freehold, or of the leasehold, and in remainder or possession (as the case may be). Different qualities of right are inconsistent with the nature of a joint tenancy as a single title, jointly owned;

(c) the *unity of title* means that each joint tenant must derive their title (that is, ownership) from the same document. Note, however, that in certain circumstances, occupiers may still have a joint tenancy, even though as a matter of formality they have each signed different documents, as where leaseholders may be treated as joint tenants despite signing separate agreements because this reflects the true nature of the agreement between all the parties (see Chapter 6; *Antoniades v Villiers* (1990)). The point is that *as a matter of law*, all joint tenants must have derived their title from the same document, even if there is more than one piece of paper. In the normal course of events, the title will, indeed, have been conveyed to the joint tenants by the same document, as where man and woman buy a new house as the family home;

(d) the *unity of time* means that the interest of each joint tenant must arise at the same time, as befitting their ownership of a single title. For example, if a woman purchases a house in 1997 and, in 1999, on the occasion of her marriage, grants an equal share in the house to her husband, this cannot be a joint tenancy: the interests of the co-owners arose at different times. The same is true if, say, the interest of the husband arises informally through some act of the parties (on which see below, 4.10). It would be otherwise if the entire house was reconveyed into the joint names.

4.3   Tenancy in common

When two or more people own land under a tenancy in common, it is often said that they have an 'undivided share in land'. In other words, a tenant in common can point to a precise share of ownership of the land (for example, one half, one fifth, one quarter, etc), even though the land at present is undivided and treated as a single unit. The distinguishing feature of a tenancy in common is, then, that each co-owner has a distinct and quantifiable share in the land. That does not mean, however, that a particular tenant can physically demarcate a portion of the land and claim it as their own. The land is still 'undivided', and the tenant in common owns a quantifiable share in it, which can be realised if and when the property is sold. To put it another way, there is 'unity of possession' with a tenancy in common despite the fact that such a tenant can legitimately say that they own, say, one fifth of the land. So, following through the example, if four student lawyers co-own the house in which they live under a tenancy in common, it will be possible to say that they each own a defined share. This may be one quarter each, but it is equally possible that A owns one third, B owns one third and C and D own one sixth each. In fact, any combination of shared ownership is possible with a tenancy in common. Nevertheless, as a tenancy in common also requires unity of possession, each co-owning tenant in common is entitled to possess the whole of the land, irrespective of their actual share. The land is undivided. Were the house to be sold then the actual shares would take effect in the purchase money. Importantly, none of the other unities need be present for a tenancy in common (although one or other may be, especially 'time'). Likewise, the right of survivorship does not apply to a tenancy in common, so that a co-owner, under a tenancy in common, may leave his share to a relative on death. It is for this reason that a tenancy in common is often preferred where the co-owners are not closely related by family or business ties. Thus, to summarise the tenancy in common:

(a) there is an undivided share in land;

(b) there is unity of possession;

(c) no other unities need be present;

(d) there is no right of survivorship: a tenant's share may be passed on in the normal way by will on death or in writing during their life.

Finally, we should note that a tenancy in common may come about through the 'severance' of a joint tenancy. This is discussed more fully below, 4.11, but means, in essence, that the parties to a joint tenancy may choose to terminate this form of co-ownership and be governed instead by a tenancy in common, often because of a desire to avoid the right of survivorship.

4.4 The effect of the Law of Property Act 1925 and the Trusts of Land and Appointment of Trustees Act 1996

It goes without saying that it is vital to distinguish between the existence of a joint tenancy and a tenancy in common, not least because of the right of survivorship. However, before we can examine that in detail, it is necessary to consider the changes made by the LPA 1925 to the manner in which co-ownership operates today, and the further changes made by the TOLATA 1996. This last statute does not change the basic principles of the LPA 1925 regarding co-owned land (and so the LPA 1925 must still be regarded as the source statute), but it does make significant changes to the detail. Reference will be made to the 1996 Act where appropriate as this came into force on 1 January 1997. To recap then, the changes made by the LPA 1925 were both changes in substance and procedure and were part of the wider plan to simplify all dealings with land to meet the economic and social challenges of the 20th century. The reasons for these changes are considered below, but, essentially, they stem from the advantages of the joint tenancy as a form of co-ownership, involving as it does a single title to land in which many may share. This contrasts with the tenancy in common, which presupposes several individual titles.

4.4.1   Before 1 January 1926

Before 1 January 1926, it was possible for a joint tenancy and a tenancy in common to exist in both the legal and equitable estate in the land. So, if land was conveyed 'to A and B as tenants in common', they would be tenants in common of the legal title. Likewise for a joint tenancy. Again, if land was conveyed 'to X and Y on trust for A and B as tenants in common', A and B would be tenants in common of the equitable title (in equity), with the legal title held by X and Y. So, if a purchaser wished to buy the legal title of land which was co-owned, he would either have to investigate one title (joint tenancy) or all the individual titles of the various co-owners (tenancy in common). While this caused no great hardship for a purchaser investigating the one title held by the joint tenant legal owners, if the land was co-owned under a tenancy in common, the complexity of the transaction increased as the number of tenants in common increased. To purchase from A and B as tenants in common is only two titles to investigate, but to purchase from A, B, C and D is four, and so on.

4.4.2   On or after 1 January 1926

We have noted above that one change made by the LPA 1925 was to limit the types of co-ownership to two: the joint tenancy and tenancy in common. However, the Act also placed restrictions on the manner in which these forms of co-ownership could come into existence (see ss 34 and 36 of the LPA 1925, as amended by the TOLATA 1996; see also ss 4 and 5 of the TOLATA 1996).

The first point is that it has been impossible, since 1 January 1926, to create a tenancy in common at law: a tenancy in common of the legal title to land cannot exist (s 1(6) of the LPA 1925). Only joint tenancies of the legal title are possible and this is true irrespective of the words used when the land is transferred to the co-owners or their own intentions. No longer is it possible to convey the legal title to land to A, B, C and D as tenants in common. This must, on or after 1 January 1926, operate as a conveyance of the legal title to A, B, C and D as joint tenants, even though the words are plain and the intentions clear. Note also, that this must mean that a joint tenancy of a legal title is 'unseverable' (s 36(2) of the LPA 1925), because it is impossible to turn it into a legal tenancy in common.

Secondly, however, this joint tenancy of the legal title is of a special kind, because the persons to whom the legal title to the land is conveyed (that is, the intended co-owners) are trustees of the legal title for the persons interested in the land under a statutorily imposed trust of land (ss 34 and 36 of the LPA 1925, as amended). Thus, in every case of co-ownership, legal title to the land is held by joint tenant trustees on trusts of land (ss 4 and 5 of the TOLATA 1996). These statutory trusts are defined in the LPA 1925 and the TOLATA 1996, but essentially impose on the trustees (the legal owners, the co-owners) a duty to hold the land for the benefit of the persons interested in the land (that is, the equitable owners) and for the purpose for which it was purchased, to which end they are given various powers of management, including the power of sale. So, given that, in the example above, the conveyance to A, B, C, and D operated as a conveyance to them as joint tenants (irrespective of the words used), they will hold this land as trustees on the statutorily imposed trust of land for the 'real' owners. In this case, the 'real owners' are, in fact, A, B, C and D themselves, also known as the equitable owners. The reasons for this apparently complicated machinery are discussed below, 4.8.

Thirdly, although the legal title to co-owned land must be held under a joint tenancy, the equitable title (the real and valuable interest) may be either a joint tenancy or a tenancy in common. Which form of co-ownership is most appropriate will depend on the words used to create the co-ownership, the intentions of the parties and the surrounding circumstances. Again, in our case, although A, B, C and D are in law joint tenant trustees of the land, in equity, they are equitable tenants in common because a tenancy in common was the intended form of co-ownership of the land. They could have been joint tenants in equity instead (that is, as well as legal joint tenants), *if* this had been established on the facts.

To sum up, all co-ownership operates behind a mechanism whereby the formal, legal title is held by joint tenant trustees on the statutorily imposed trust of land. The real, equitable interest takes effect behind this trust and may be either a joint tenancy or a tenancy in common. Furthermore, in many cases, the 'trustees' will be the same people as those who share in the equitable co-ownership. So, if land is conveyed to husband (H) and wife (W), this will operate as a conveyance to them as joint tenant trustees of the legal title as trustees of land, holding on trust *for themselves* as either joint tenants or tenants in common in equity, depending on the circumstances in which the property was purchased. This is so even if the conveyance says 'to H and W as tenants in common': they will still be joint tenants of the legal title (s 1(6) of the LPA 1925), albeit tenants in common of the equitable interest. The same mechanism operates irrespective of the number of intended co-owners, save that, by statute, the number of legal joint tenant trustees is limited to four (ss 34 and 36 of the LPA 1925). The number of co-owners in equity is not limited, be they joint tenants or tenants in common. If the land is, in fact, conveyed to more than four people, it is the first four named in the conveyance who become the joint tenant trustees of the land, with all five, six, etc, owning in equity as either joint tenants or tenants in common.

The use of the trust is, therefore, a device to ensure that all legal title to co-owned land is held under a joint tenancy, while also ensuring that, in equity (where the real interest lies), the co-owners can be either joint tenants or tenants in common as before. Indeed, given that, in many cases – particularly of residential property – the trustees will be the same people as the beneficiaries (equitable owners), there is no real change to the rights of the co-owners to use and enjoy the land.

4.5 The distinction between joint tenancy and tenancy in common in practice: the equitable interest

It follows from the fact that legal title to co-owned land must be held under the special joint tenancy trusteeship, that the important issue is to determine the nature of the co-ownership in equity for herein lies the substantive interest. Generally, the principles here are much the same as they were before 1926, although, as ever, there are no immutable rules and each case must be decided on its own facts. The following are offered as guidelines only and their influence will vary from case to case. Remember at all times that we are now talking of the equitable interest: legal title must be held on a non-severable joint tenancy:

(a) if the unities of interest, title or time are absent, a joint tenancy in equity cannot exist. It must be a tenancy in common. If the interest of one co-owner arises later than the other – as where a husband makes a successful claim to a share in his wife's property by way of constructive or resulting trust (see below, 4.10) – the equitable interest will be a tenancy in common;

(b) if the original conveyance to the co-owners stipulates that they are 'joint tenants' or 'tenants in common' *of the beneficial or equitable interest*, this is normally conclusive as to the nature of their co-ownership in equity. So, if land is conveyed to 'Minnie and Mickey as tenants in common beneficially', they will be tenants in common as (in the absence of fraud, misrepresentation or some other vitiating factor) the conveyance is conclusive as to the nature of the equitable ownership, irrespective of later events (as in *Goodman v Gallant* (1986); *Hembury v Peachey* (1996)). In *Roy v Roy* (1996), a conveyance to P and D jointly was held conclusive between them as to the existence of a joint tenancy, despite the fact that D had contributed significantly more to the purchase and upkeep of the property over the years, and that P had lived in the property for only a few months just after it was purchased. Note, however, that a conveyance is conclusive only for the parties to it. So, in the *Roy* case, if an imaginary third party (W) had made a claim to an interest in the property, she would not have been bound by the conveyance to accept a joint tenancy;

(c) if words of severance are used, then a tenancy in common will exist in equity. Thus, a description of the share of each owner, or the creation of unequal interests in different co-owners will mean that a tenancy in common exists. A conveyance to 'A and B, two thirds to A', will necessarily create a tenancy in common in equity. The same is true of a conveyance to 'A and B, half each', as this specifies a share. If land is given 'equally' (as in 'to A and B equally') this can mean either a joint tenancy or a tenancy in common, depending on whether this means 'half each' or 'jointly', although in such cases the next presumption will usually operate;

(d) in the absence of an express declaration of the type of ownership or words of severance, and if all the four unities are present, there is a presumption that 'equity follows the law'. Consequently, because the legal title must be a joint tenancy, in the absence of all other evidence, the equitable title 'follows the law' and is deemed to be a joint tenancy also. So, a conveyance 'to A and B' will be taken to be a conveyance to A and B in law as joint tenants (as it must be), and in equity also. There are, possibly, some exceptions to this, such as situations where the presumption that 'equity follows the law' can be displaced by a counter-presumption, arising from special facts, that a tenancy in common must have been intended. These are cases where it is recognised that the existence of a joint tenancy may cause hardship to the co-owners, being cases where the right of survivorship is inappropriate. In such cases, there will be a tenancy in common in equity behind the trust of land: viz, business partners and in related business arrangements (*Malayan Credit Ltd v Jack Chia-MPH* (1986)); for the interests of co-mortgagees, so that the death of one mortgagee will not deprive their estate of the security for the loan made (*Re Jackson* (1887)); where the purchasers have provided the purchase money in unequal shares, which, in the absence of other evidence (for example, that one co-owner was making a gift to another) establishes lack of a unity of interest (*Lake v Craddock* (1732)).

4.6 The statutory machinery and the operation of co-ownership

At first glance, the changes made by the LPA 1925, and then by the TOLATA 1996, seem complicated and unwieldy. In fact, as we shall see, the statutory framework for co-ownership established by these statutes is designed to ensure that dealings with co-owned land (particularly sale and mortgage) can be accomplished with more ease than was the case previously. Although complicated as a legal mechanism, the law of co-ownership is now much simpler in practice. To summarise the situation:

(a) it is impossible for a tenancy in common of a legal estate to exist. All legal co-ownership must be by way of joint tenancy;

(b) however, the joint tenants are trustees of the legal estate for the equitable owners, holding the property as trustees of land within the LPA 1925 and the TOLATA 1996. They hold the property on trust for the equitable owners;

(c) the equitable owners are often the same people as the legal owners (the trustees), but there is no necessary reason why this should be so. In equity, the co-owners may be either joint tenants or tenants in common;

(d) the number of equitable owners is not limited, although the number of legal joint tenant trustees is limited to four, usually the first four co-owners named in the transfer to them. The non-legal co-owners remain entitled in equity.

4.7 The nature of the unseverable legal joint tenancy: the trust of land

It has already been indicated that the owners of the legal title hold the property as joint tenant trustees of land, with powers specified in the LPA 1925 and the TOLATA 1996. This trust is effectively defined in ss 34 and 36 of the LPA 1925 and Pt I of the TOLATA 1996 (s 35 of the LPA 1925 is repealed). The trustees will hold the land for the persons interested in it and, subject to any express terms of the trust and statute, with the powers of an absolute owner. They may delegate any of their functions to the beneficiaries, save that only the trustees may give a valid receipt to a purchaser if the land is sold. In fact, it is unlikely that the provisions of the Acts relating to trustees' powers and the ability to delegate will be useful in most cases of domestic co-ownership, certainly if the trustees and equitable owners are the same people. They will be more relevant in cases concerning successive interests in land (Chapter 5) or where the trust of land is used as an investment vehicle rather than as a statutorily imposed device for jointly owning a home.

Perhaps the most important point to grasp when considering the nature of the trust of land is that the trustees are under no duty to sell the land, as was the case prior to the TOLATA 1996 when the LPA 1925 imposed a trust on the land known as a 'trust for sale'. This important change means that the legal mechanism of co-ownership (the trust of land) now more accurately mirrors how most co-owned land is used in practice – not as land to be sold, but as land to be occupied. As we shall see, if the trustees (or equitable owners, if such power has been delegated to them) cannot agree whether to sell the land at an appropriate time (for example, on divorce or separation of the co-owners or on bankruptcy), any interested person may apply to the court under s 14 of the TOLATA 1996 (replacing s 30 of the LPA 1925) for an order for sale or other order concerning the land. However, there is now no duty to sell the land and the trustees have every right to hold the land for the purpose for which it was acquired, or indeed any other lawful purpose which benefits the equitable owners.

As noted above, the TOLATA 1996, with its amendments to the 1925 scheme of co-ownership, came into force on 1 January 1997. Many of its provisions are retrospective – in that they apply to co-ownership trusts already in existence – but it will be some time before the full import of the changes are worked out in practice through judicial interpretation. Some commentators believe that the TOLATA 1996 leaves much of the pre-1997 law intact and doubt whether much of the legislation was really necessary. Although perhaps an over-simplification, there is merit in this argument, not least because many of the 1996 Act's changes simply brought the legal structure of co-ownership into line with the way in which the courts had interpreted the 1925 legislation. For example, prior to 1 January 1997, the equitable owner, in theory, did not have an interest in the land itself, but an interest in the proceeds of sale of that land – because of the trustees' duty to sell under the old 'trust for sale'. In fact, for nearly all practical purposes, such equitable owners were treated as having interests in land (for example, *Williams and Glyn's Bank v Boland* (1981)), and now this has been recognised by s 3 of the TOLATA 1996. With these considerations in mind, the following are the specific attributes of the unseverable legal joint tenancy under the new trust of land established by the TOLATA 1996:

(a) the trustees (legal owners) are under a duty to hold the land for the persons interested in it (often themselves). The TOLATA 1996 gives these trustees the powers of an absolute owner in relation to the land (s 6) subject to any listing on the register of title, although they must have regard to the wishes of the equitable owner. However, the trustees may delegate 'any of their functions' to a beneficiary of full age (s 9) and the court may intervene by way of an order under s 14. The trustees' powers may be restricted by the instrument (document) creating the trust, except in the case of charitable trusts (s 8). Note here, however, that not everything done by a trustee will be a 'function relating to' the trust. So in *Brackley v Notting Hill Housing Trust* (2001), the giving of notice by one joint tenant trustee of a lease (thereby terminating the lease) was not such a function, at least in the case of a periodic tenancy;

(b) if the trustees do sell the land (voluntarily or otherwise), the trustees hold the proceeds of sale on trust for the equitable owners in the same way that they held the land itself. As discussed in Chapters 2 and 3, the equitable owners' interests are overreached and take effect in the purchase money, if any. Often, the money is distributed;

(c) as mentioned above, prior to the 1996 Act, the trust of land was actually a trust for sale and this had the unfortunate consequence that, for some purposes, the interests of the equitable owners were treated as interests in the proceeds of the sale, not as interests in the land itself, even if the land had not actually been sold (see, for example, *Perry v Phoenix Assurance* (1988) and the 'doctrine of conversion'). As a statutory creation, there is no reason why the new trust of land should be subject to this rule, but, in any event, s 3 of the TOLATA 1996 abolishes the doctrine of conversion for all new trusts of land and most old ones. Now, it is certain that the interests of the equitable owners behind the statutorily imposed trust of land are interests in that land (that is, proprietary rights) for all purposes;

(d) although the trustees of land now have no duty to sell, they do have a power to do so (which may be delegated to the equitable owners). Trustees are the legal owners of the property: it is their names on the title deeds or entered on the title register at the Land Registry. All legal owners (trustees) must formally join in a conveyance if the land is sold and, therefore, there must be a mechanism for dealing with disputes between trustees, particularly where some wish to sell and others do not. This mechanism is found in s 14 of the TOLATA 1996 (replacing s 30 of the LPA 1925) and involves an application to the court. It is considered more fully below;

(e) a catalogue of the trustees' functions and powers are found in the TOLATA 1996 itself. As stated above, most will not be relevant in a 'normal' co-ownership situation where the co-owners (often a romantically linked couple) are trustees of land holding for themselves in equity. Similarly, many of these powers will be redundant when there is but one trustee of land (no overreaching, see below, 4.9.7) holding for himself and for others in equity. However, in those relatively rare cases of residential co-ownership where there is *not* complete identity between the two or more trustees of land and the beneficiaries (as in *City of London Building Society v Flegg* (1988), where man and wife held on trust for themselves and one set of parents), the powers and functions of the trustees under the TOLATA 1996 may become important if the trustees and equitable owners cannot agree on the future use of the land. The powers and functions of the trustees remain central when the land is non-residential, as where it is held by trustees as an investment for the equitable co-owners;

(f) it is intrinsic in everything we have said so far that the ability to deal with the land lies with the legal owners – the trustees. If, as is often the case in a domestic context, these are the same people as the legal owners, few practical problems arise. However, if the trustees are completely unconnected with the equitable interest (as in an investment situation) or if there are more than four co-owners, or if the legal title was conveyed only to certain of the co-owners, or if some of the co-owners acquired their interests at a later date, there will not be this identity between legal and equitable owners, and problems can occur. We will examine these more closely below, but, for now, three factors need be noted:

- a sale by all the trustees, providing they are two or more in number, will overreach the interests of the equitable owners (ss 2(1)(ii) and 27 of the LPA 1925). The equitable owners' interests will take effect in the proceeds of sale, and only a very astute equitable owner may be able to stop this happening (see below, 4.9);

- if there is only one trustee of the land (as where the co-ownership has not been created expressly, see below, 4.10.2), the interests of the equitable owners cannot be overreached. Consequently, whether the equitable interests can bind a purchaser will depend on the law of registered or unregistered conveyancing (as the case may be);

• if the trust is created by 'a disposition' (which probably means a trust created expressly in writing, and not one arising informally), the exercise of the trustee's power of sale (among others) can be made subject to an express requirement that the consent of the beneficiaries be obtained. This is an attempt to ensure that a sale does not take place contrary to their wishes (s 10 of the TOLATA 1996), or at least forcing a reference to the court under s 14 of the TOLATA 1996. Although it is unclear, it may have been possible to restrict the powers of the trustees in a similar way prior to the entry into force of the TOLATA 1996 (see, for example, *Re Herkelot's Will Trusts* (1964)).

4.8 The advantages of the 1925 and 1996 legislative reforms

In discussing the property legislation of 1925–96 in general, and the law of co-ownership in particular, it is always important to remember that the wholesale reshaping of English property law was prompted by two fundamental objectives:

(a) to ensure that the value of land as an economic asset was utilised to the full and, to that end, to promote the free alienability of land. This would entail both simplifying the conveyancing procedure and providing for the protection of purchasers of land from the myriad rights and interests which might encumber their use of the land;

(b) to ensure, as far as was compatible with this first objective, that no owner or occupier of land and no person with any interest in land was unreasonably prejudiced by the procedural and substantive changes that were to be made. It was recognised, however, that some people would find that their rights over the land itself had diminished, albeit that such rights could now take effect in its exchange product, that is, money.

These two goals remain, but changes in the way land was used, and the explosion of 'private' ownership meant that the 1925 machinery was out of date. For example, land is no longer owned by the few, nor is it used only for investment purposes. The 'property owning democracy' is a clichéd but accurate description for the much more widespread land ownership of our time and the more diffuse purposes property ownership serves. It was almost ludicrous that normal domestic co-ownership should have been forced to operate under a statutory mechanism (the old trust for sale) that was designed to promote the sale of land rather than its retention for use by the owners. Hence, the reforms of 1925 were rightly amended by the 1996 Act in order to reflect the reality of property use and ownership in 1997 and beyond. This should be remembered in the following discussion about the advantages of the 1925 and 1996 legislative reforms.

Prior to 1 January 1926, any person wishing to purchase co-owned land would have to investigate the title of every single tenant in common (if that was the mode by which the land was held). Obviously, not only was this time consuming, but the objection of just one tenant in common might prevent the land from being sold, even if this would have been for the benefit of every other tenant. By abolishing tenancies in common at law, the LPA 1925 has ensured that there is but one title to investigate: the legal joint tenancy. Moreover, the number of legal joint tenants is limited to a maximum of four (irrespective of the number of equitable owners), so that a purchaser need only concern himself with obtaining the consent of these people.

If there are two or more trustees of land (that is, two or more legal owners), and the purchaser obtains the consent of all to a sale, the purchaser may safely ignore all the equitable owners, subject only to any entries on the register of title restricting the trustees' powers such as a requirement to obtain the equitable owners' consent (see below, 4.9.5). This is the magic of statutory overreaching whereby the interests of the equitable owners behind a trust of land (be they joint tenants or tenants in common) are transferred from the land to the money paid by the purchaser on a sale or mortgage. Indeed, such is the power of overreaching that it will operate even if no money is actually paid over in one large sum (*State Bank of India v Sood* (1997): legal owners could draw money from a bank by way of overdraft facility).

Although a tenancy in common cannot exist at law, the co-ownership in equity may take this form (or a joint tenancy). Indeed, in the normal case, the equitable owners are theoretically secure in the knowledge that their interests, however held, will take effect in any money received for the property should it be sold or mortgaged. Moreover, the existence of a trust means that the equitable owners have powerful proprietary remedies in the event of default by the trustees. For example, the beneficiaries may secure ownership of any assets purchased by the trustees with the proceeds of sale or, failing that, may sue the trustees personally if they have spent the money on untraceable assets.

The existence of a power to sell under the trust of land prevents co-owned land becoming inalienable should there be a dispute between the co-owners (or other interested persons: for example, a mortgagee). Although all trustees must agree if the power of sale is to be exercised voluntarily, if the trustees do disagree about how the land should be used, application can be made to the court under s 14 of the TOLATA 1996 for an order for sale (or other order) and, if granted, the equitable interests will take effect in the purchase money. Consequently, co-owned land will not stagnate through inability to secure the agreement of all interested parties. This is entirely consistent with the general aim of the 1925 reforms which was to ensure the free alienability of co-owned land through simplifying the conveyancing process and offering protection for the purchaser against any adverse equitable interests (the overreaching machinery). The 1996 statute, which has now modified co-ownership trusts, reflects the fact that much co-owned land is not held in order to sell, but in order to be occupied. Its replacement of the old trust for sale with the trust for land as the statutory machinery for regulating co-owned land, comprising a power (but not a duty) to sell the land, puts this into practice. The 1996 statute holds more evenly the balance between the needs of the purchaser and the needs of the equitable owners. Although the *express* and deliberate creation of a trust for sale is still possible, such trusts will be subject to the strictures of the TOLATA 1996 and now carry very few advantages. A synopsis of the effect of the 1996 Act is given below, 4.9.12.

4.9 The disadvantages of the trust of land as a device for regulating co-ownership

Given what we have just learnt about purchaser protection through the overreaching machinery, it is not surprising that many of the disadvantages of the current mechanism, even after the 1996 amendments, focus on the other half of the equation: the equitable co-owner, particularly that equitable owner who is not also a trustee of the legal estate. However, as we shall see, not even the legal owners of the co-owned land always benefit from the imposition of a trust of land.

4.9.1 Disputes as to sale

An immediate difficulty of utilising the trust as a mechanism for co-ownership is that there may well be disputes between the trustees as to whether the property should be sold or retained for occupation by the equitable owners. This problem becomes more acute if the consent of the equitable owners is also required before a sale can take place. Admittedly, the difficulty is not as pressing as it was prior to the 1996 Act – there is now no *duty* to sell, only a power – but the potential remains for dispute and litigation. In the normal course of events for residential property, the legal owners and the equitable owners will be the same people and the property will have been acquired for a purpose (domestic occupation) and both will be happy to retain the property. Yet, should the co-owners' relationship break down, or one of the co-owners go bankrupt, the other co-owner or co-owners (of a legal or equitable interest) may wish to sell the property to realise its capital value or may be forced to do so to satisfy creditors.

To deal with such disputes, s 14 of the TOLATA 1996 (replacing s 30 of the LPA 1925) provides that any trustee of land, or any person having an interest in land subject to such a trust (for example, equitable owner, mortgagee, trustee in bankruptcy) may apply for an order concerning the property. Among other things, such an order may be for sale of the property. Unless the application is made by a trustee in bankruptcy in respect of property in which a bankrupt has an interest (see below, 4.9.3), when considering the application, the court is to have regard to the intentions of the persons who established the trust, the purposes for which the property is held, the welfare of any minor who occupies the land as his home (whether or not as a child of the owner), the interests of any secured creditor, and, in most circumstances, the wishes of any equitable owner (s 15 of the TOLATA 1996; as considered in *Chun v Ho* (2001)). This list of factors is generally thought to be all-inclusive and is likely to cover most situations. Importantly, these factors mirror many of the factors developed by the courts when interpreting the old s 30 of the LPA 1925 (which had no statutory list). Thus, it is the Law Commission's view that much of the pre-1996 case law will be relevant in interpreting ss 14 and 15 of the TOLATA 1996. The following are examples of factors considered by the court in deciding whether to exercise its discretion under the old s 30. They now fall within s 15 of the TOLATA 1996:

(a) whether the property is needed for the maintenance of a matrimonial home (*Jones v Challenger* (1961)). *A fortiori*, maintenance of a home for a stable unmarried couple;

(b) whether the property is required in order to provide accommodation for the lives of the co-owners, or that of the survivor (*Harris v Harris* (1996)) or until the occurrence of any event (*Chun v Ho* (2001), completion of education of one co-owner);

(c) whether the property is needed for the provision of a family home for the children of a relationship that has broken down (*Williams v Williams* (1976)). Under s 15 of the TOLATA 1996, the welfare of any minor occupying the land as his home is made relevant expressly, resolving the doubts expressed in *Re Holliday* (1981) and *Re Evers' Trust* (1980);

(d) whether the property is required to continue a business for which the land was purchased (*Bedson v Bedson* (1965));

(e) where the person seeking a sale may be estopped from obtaining an order for sale by their conduct, this having been relied upon to detriment by other co-owners. This is a manifestation of the principle of proprietary estoppel (*Re Buchanan-Wollaston's Conveyance* (1939); and see *Chun v Ho* (2001));

(f) whether there has been any misconduct by the person applying for sale, or his legal advisers, as in *Halifax Mortgage Services v Muirhead* (1998),where sale was refused because the claimant's solicitors had wrongly altered relevant documents;

(g) the general desire not to keep a creditor out of its money: *Bank of Ireland v Bell* (2001), although this is not always paramount (*Mortgage Corp v Shaire* (2001)).

4.9.2 When is it likely that a court will order sale?

Apart from the special case of bankruptcy, the old law, of s 30 of the LPA 1925, indicates when a court would be minded to order a sale. There is no doubt that these precedents will remain useful, subject to one very important proviso. Before the 1996 Act, as we have seen, co-owned land was subject to a trust for sale, with a duty to sell. Thus, in any dispute as to sale, the default position was that a sale *must* take place, and this is reflected in applications made under the old s 30. Consequently, pre-1996 statements unequivocally favouring a sale of co-owned property in cases of dispute must be read with some care and cannot apply to applications under the new s 14, where there is *no* presumption of sale in default. So, in *Banker's Trust v Namdar* (1997), a sale was ordered under s 30 of the LPA 1925, but Peter Gibson LJ thought that it was 'unfortunate' that the TOLATA 1996 was not applicable (the case arose before the TOLATA 1996 came into force) 'as the result might have been different'. In *TSB v Marshall* (1998), the county court judge used pre-TOLATA 1996 principles to assess an application under ss 14 and 15. For example, a court is still likely to order a sale when only the co-owners are in dispute and there are no extrinsic factors (for example, no children), as this supports the alienability of the co-owned land. Conversely, no sale is likely if there are children living in the property and the co-owner wanting a sale is not in desperate financial straits and in *Chun v Ho* (2001) sale was postponed until the co-owner completed her studies, not least because the other co-owner had behaved inequitably, there was no real evidence that the money was needed to pay debts and the co-owner resisting sale had provided most of the original purchase price. A sale is likely if the land was purchased as an investment, rather than a home, or if it would be inequitable to deny a co-owner their share of the capital value of land (cf *Barclay v Barclay* (1970)). Again, a sale might be favoured if the rights of creditors are in issue (for a non-bankrupt), but only if there are no countervailing circumstances (*Bank of Ireland v Bell* (2001), but contrast *Mortgage Corp v Shaire* (2001)) and only if the rights of the creditors would be prejudiced by not ordering sale (*Chun v Ho* (2001)). Clearly, if the non-trustee equitable owners' consent is required before a sale takes place (for example, where such requirement is required by the conveyance to the trustees), a court will be careful before it dispenses with such consent and actually orders a sale against their wishes. Likewise in *Dear v Robinson* (2001) where the wishes of the beneficiaries were critical (even though they had no consent powers), especially as a postponement of sale was also in accordance with the original intention of the creator of the trust. Moreover, even if the equitable owners' consent is not a *requirement* of a sale or mortgage by the trustees, their wishes are relevant (see s 11 of the TOLATA 1996), although it is unlikely that they will be pivotal. As is obvious, the court's approach to a s 14 application will vary according to the circumstances. It may have altered the emphasis against a sale (*Shaire*) or it may not (*Bell*) although the decision in *Chun Ho* (2001) indicates a more sympathetic attitude to the position of occupying co-owners. What we can be sure of, however, is that, in registered land, an equitable owner will be able to place a restriction on the title of the co-owned land in order to influence any proposed dealings. If then alerted by the restriction of an attempt to deal with the land, the non-trustee equitable owner can then utilise s 14 of the TOLATA 1996 to try to prevent sale, or to ensure that it proceeds only on certain conditions. If a restriction has been entered, this will ensure that no dealings take place unless the conditions specified in the restriction are fulfilled, for example, that there are indeed two trustees of the land (that is, overreaching) or that the consents of the equitable owners (if required) are, in fact, obtained. Note finally, that a court is empowered under s 14 of the TOLATA 1996 to revisit a previous application if circumstances change prior to a sale actually taking place. So, in *Dear v Robinson* (2001) a previous order for sale was rescinded because circumstances had changed and a majority of the beneficiaries did not want an immediate sale.

4.9.3   The special case of bankruptcy

The list of factors in s 15 of the TOLATA 1996 do not apply to disputes concerning sale of co-owned property when an application is made by the trustee in bankruptcy of a person interested in co-owned land. In that case, an application is made under s 14 of the TOLATA 1996, but s 335A of the Insolvency Act 1996 provides the list of relevant factors (see s 15(4) of the TOLATA 1996). Section 335A of the Insolvency Act 1986 is inserted by the TOLATA 1996 (see Sched 3), and replaces the similar (but not identical) s 336(3) of the Insolvency Act 1986.

If one of the persons interested in the co-owned land is made bankrupt (whether they are a legal or equitable owner), his assets vest in a 'trustee in bankruptcy'. A trustee in bankruptcy is simply the name given to the person who administers the bankrupt's assets with a view to paying off his creditors, and, to that end, becomes vested with his property. In a co-ownership situation, therefore, a trustee in bankruptcy will step into the shoes of a legal or equitable owner. Naturally, the trustee in bankruptcy will want to sell the co-owned property to realise some of the bankrupt's assets, and, equally naturally, this will be resisted by the other legal or equitable owners, often the bankrupt's domestic partner wishing to stay in the house. If a sale is opposed, the trustee in bankruptcy will apply to the court for an order for sale under s 14 of the TOLATA 1996, and the court will have to balance the needs of the innocent creditors and the needs of the innocent co-owner within the framework of s 335A of the Insolvency Act 1986.

On hearing an application for sale by a trustee in bankruptcy, the court must consider a number of factors, such as the interests of the bankrupt's creditors, the conduct of the bankrupt's spouse as a contributing factor to the bankruptcy, the needs of the spouse and the needs of any children and all other circumstances, and may make such order as it thinks just and reasonable. However, if the application under s 14 of the TOLATA 1996 is made more than one year after the bankruptcy, the interests of the creditors are deemed to outweigh the interests of the resisting co-owners unless the circumstances are 'exceptional'. What this means is that, after one year, the court is extremely likely to order a sale of the property in order to satisfy the creditors, but, up to then, the matter could go either way. So, in *Harrington v Bennett* (2000) an application for sale by the trustee in bankruptcy more than one year after the bankruptcy was granted. It was not an exceptional circumstance that the bankrupt appeared to have a purchaser in view who might pay a higher price than that achievable by the bankruptcy trustee. On its face, the s 14/s 335A procedure applies whether or not the co-owners were married, or, indeed, in any emotional relationship. This is different from the repealed s 336(3) of the Insolvency Act 1986, which applied only to spouses and only to bankruptcies of the legal owners. However, it is only in the case of spouses (not unmarried couples) that spousal conduct and the needs of children are expressly mentioned as relevant factors for the court's scales. It is not clear whether this means that the needs of children of non-married couples are irrelevant under the statute (surely not: see s 335A(c)), but, in any event, the law relating to unmarried couples was assimilated to the old s 336(3) by *Re Citro* (1991), and this should remain the case for the new s 335A.

Summary

It is convenient at this stage to summarise the position in respect of the court's approach when an application is made under s 14 of the TOLATA 1996. In most cases, the court must consider the factors listed in s 15 of the TOLATA 1996 (the intentions of the creator of the trust, the purposes for which the property is held, the welfare of any child who occupies or might occupy the property as his home, the interests of a secured creditor, the wishes of any beneficiaries), but in cases of bankruptcy must consider instead those factors listed in s 355A of the Insolvency Act 1986 (the interests of the creditors, for dwelling houses the interests and conduct of the bankrupt's spouse, the needs and resources of the spouse, the needs of any children, the requirement to sell after one year barring exceptional circumstances). Importantly, much may turn on who is making the application:

(a) In disputes purely between co-owners, without the intervention of any third party, the court may well be happy to postpone sale and make some other order: for example, that one co-owner pays rent to another (or does not have to: *Chun v Ho* (2001)), that the land is partitioned etc. It is likely that that there will be much less emphasis on a sale in these circumstances. Under the TOLATA 1996, the *trust of land* is no longer a *trust for sale* of land.

(b) In disputes between a co-owners and a third party secured creditor (for example, a mortgagee), it is important to assess why the creditor wishes a sale. It is worth noting here that a mortgage does not have to resort to s 14 for a sale if the mortgagee has overreached the beneficial interests by paying capital money to two or more trustees or otherwise takes free of the mortgage (for example, having obtain relevant consents). In such cases, like *City of London Building Society v Flegg* (1988) (overreaching) and *LF v LF* (2001) (consent), the mortgagee may sell in virtue of its paramount mortgage powers. Consequently, a mortgagee using s 14 of the TOLATA 1996 is by definition a mortgagee bound as a matter of property law by the prior right of one of the co-owners. This may be important as the court legitimately may ask why it should deprive a co-owner of possession of the land when the co-owner's right is paramount to that of the creditor. Consequently, a creditor may not get an order for sale under s 14 where they simply have failed to protect themselves adequately (as in *Boland*). Nevertheless, a sale has been ordered in favour of a 'bound' creditor where it seems unjust to keep the creditor out of its funds, especially where the 'unjustness' is that the bank believed that all the co-owners had consented to the mortgage but where this was untrue because of a fraud by one co-owner in forging the consent of the others (*Bank of Ireland v Bell* (2001); *Bankers Trust v Namdar* (1997)). Of course, the court may well conclude that even this is not sufficient to justify a sale, at least not without terms and conditions to protect the innocent co-owners (*Mortgage Corp v Shaire* (2001)).

(c) Where one of the co-owners goes bankrupt and his trustee in bankruptcy applies for an order for sale, it will take very exceptional circumstances for a sale to be postponed for more than a year. Such a postponement will be rare indeed, see *Harrington v Bennett* (2000).

(d) It is open to a mortgagee (a secured creditor) who cannot get a sale themselves under s 14 to make a co-owner bankrupt. This will mean the mortgagee giving up its secured status – and becoming an 'ordinary' creditor losing its priority right over the property – but it is likely to generate a sale under the more powerful bankruptcy rules. Although this appears to be getting in by the back door – after all, the mortgagee could not themselves get a sale under s 14 – it is not an abuse of the process and will not be prevented by the court, as made clear *in Alliance & Leicester v Slayford* (2001).

4.9.4 The position of a purchaser who buys co-owned land: when overreaching occurs

If a purchaser buys co-owned land from *two* or more legal owners (that is, there are two or more trustees of land), then the interests of the equitable owners are overreached. The effect is that their co-ownership interest is transferred from the land and takes effect in the purchase money. The purchaser obtains the land free from their rights (*City of London Building Society v Flegg* (1988); *Birmingham Midshires Building Society v Saberhawal* (2000)). This is the same in registered and unregistered land. Usually, of course, the two trustees will be the man and woman who together own the home in its entirety, both also being the only equitable owners. In such cases, there is no difficulty, as the equitable owner could have objected to the sale in their capacity as a legal owner. However, in some cases, the equitable owners will be different from the legal owners, and *if there are two legal owners* (trustees), overreaching can still occur. In that situation, the purchaser still obtains the land free from the equitable rights, and those equitable rights still take effect in the purchase money, even if the equitable owners objected to the sale (*City of London Building Society v Flegg* (1988)). In other words, overreaching can occur against the wishes of the equitable owners: they lose their rights to occupy the land, although they do receive their share of the purchase money (assuming, of course, that purchase money is payable on the overreaching transaction: see *State Bank of India v Sood* (1997); Chapter 2). This is the position even though, under s 11 of the TOLATA 1996, the trustees under the trust of land must consult the equitable owners and 'in so far as is consistent with the general interest of the trust' give effect to such wishes. Section 11 imposes a duty to consult and pay attention to such wishes, not to follow them slavishly, and the duty does not affect the overreaching effect of conveyances. Not surprisingly, the powerful effect of overreaching has caused some concern, and the Law Commission once proposed alternative ways of protecting the equitable owner. These proposals are considered below but, for now, it is important to consider the impact of the TOLATA 1996 on the effectiveness of overreaching. As we have seen, it is now possible for a settlor (that is, the person who sets up the trust of co-owned land) to provide that the exercise of the trustees' powers should be subject to the consent of the beneficiaries (s 10 of the TOLATA 1996) and, further, that any interested person (for example, non-legal equitable owner) may make an application for an order 'relating to the exercise by the trustees of any of their functions' (s 14). How does this effect the 'trump card' of overreaching when there are two or more trustees of the land?

4.9.5 If consents are required

If the disposition originally conveying the land to the co-owners makes the trustees' powers (for example, of sale or mortgage) dependent on obtaining the prior consent of the equitable owners (as envisaged by s 10 of the TOLATA 1996), there is a potential conflict with the ability of the trustees to sell the land and overreach the equitable interests. For example, what is the position if the land is sold by the two trustees, but the required consents are not obtained? Is the purchaser bound by the equitable interests, or are they overreached? This is not such an easy question to answer, as the new Act is not entirely clear on this point. Although it will be rare for consent requirements to be built into a trust of residential property that is co-owned (because the trustees/equitable owners will usually be the same people), the matter will not be settled conclusively until there has been some case law. Moreover, it should also be remembered that trustees can apply under s 14 of the TOLATA 1996 for removal of a consent requirement just as equitable owners can apply for one to be imposed.

With these qualifications in mind, the TOLATA 1996 appears to envisage the following results if land is sold by two or more trustees of land by a proper overreaching transaction, yet in violation of a consent requirement. In registered land, because the consent requirement must, first, be expressed in the 'disposition' establishing the trust (that is, it will be written into the conveyance to the two trustees: s 10 of the TOLATA 1996), there is every chance that the consent requirement will be entered on the register in the form of a restriction against dealings. This means that no dealings with the land can occur until the conditions of the restriction (that is, obtaining consent) have been complied with. If, by some chance, no restriction is entered (most unlikely), the marginally better view is that the purchaser obtains a good title to land, the equitable interests are overreached, and the equitable owners are left to sue the trustees for breach of trust. This is despite s 8 of the TOLATA 1996, which says that the power of sale 'may not be exercised without that consent'. Although there has been some academic criticism of this view, there is no doubt that TOLATA 1996 was not intended to restrict the power of overreaching and such case law as there is supports the primacy of overreaching in these circumstances (*Birmingham Midshires Building Society v Saberhawal* (2000)). This is also the Law Commission's view and any lingering doubts have been dealt with by s 26 of the Land Registration Act (LRA) 2002. Overreaching is effective save where some restriction is entered on the title, even if a sale by the trustees violates some term of the trust. Note finally that a consent requirement granted by reason of an order of the court under s 14 of the TOLATA 1996 of necessity will be registered as a restriction consequent on the court order.

In unregistered land, although any deliberate consent requirement will again be expressly declared in the disposition establishing the trust, there is no mechanism to register it under the Land Charges Act (LCA) 1972: these are not land charges falling within Classes A–F, nor does a consent requirement appear to fall within any of the other registers of the LCA 1972. However, s 16 of the TOLATA 1996 (which applies *only* to unregistered land) says that a purchaser is not affected by the trustees' failure to observe a consent requirement included in a disposition provided that the purchaser had no actual knowledge of the consent requirement. In other words, if the purchaser (or his legal adviser) did not actually know that the land was being conveyed in breach of a consent requirement, then overreaching remains effective. By analogy, the same rule should apply if a consent requirement is imposed as a result of an application under s 14 of the TOLATA 1996 (although the Act does not address this possibility). This means that the position in registered and unregistered land is broadly similar in effect. Note, however, that the chances of consents being required in unregistered land is minimal – new trusts will usually take effect in registered land, and rare will be the circumstances when a consent requirement is imposed on an existing trust in unregistered land (see below, 4.9.8).

4.9.6 If consents are not initially required

If no consents are required, then, clearly, the matter is straightforward – overreaching takes its usual course. However, we need to be aware of two possibilities which arise, even when a consent requirement is not required by the original disposition. First, an equitable owner may apply under s 14 of the TOLATA 1996 for a court order that the trustees seek his consent before a sale. This is not precluded by s 14, which says that the court may make any order 'relating to the exercise by the trustees of any of their functions'. The court may have to develop criteria to determine whether a consent requirement should be imposed. If that happens, the position should be as above, 4.9.5. Note, however, that s 8 of the TOLATA 1996 talks only of a consent requirement imposed by the disposition creating the trust, that is, for original and express consent requirements. It could be that consent requirements imposed under s 14 will be treated differently. Secondly, if the co-owned land is registered land, an equitable owner who does not enjoy the protection of a consent requirement may place a caution (or a unilateral notice under the LRA 2002) against dealings on the title, thus ensuring that the Registrar will alert her to any proposed dealing with the land by the two trustees. If that happens and the caution is activated the equitable owner may apply to the court under s 14 for an order postponing sale or requiring other conditions to be met.

4.9.7 When overreaching does not occur

The usual reason why overreaching does not occur is that there is only *one trustee* (legal owner) of the property (*Williams and Glyn's Bank v Boland* (1981)). This, in turn, is usually caused by someone else gaining an equitable interest in the property under the *Pettitt v Pettitt* (1970)/*Lloyds Bank v Rosset* (1991) rules after it has been conveyed into one person's name alone. For example, where a single woman buys a house (which is conveyed to her name alone) and then she invites her lover to live with her, the lover may acquire an equitable interest under the principles (discussed below, 4.10). If that happens, a trust of land arises (*Bull v Bull* (1955)), but there is only one legal owner. If the purchaser buys the property (or a bank lends money on it), but pays the purchase money to the single trustee only, then the purchaser cannot rely on overreaching to protect him from the rights of the equitable owners: the purchaser may be bound by the rights of the equitable owners and his use of the land severely restricted or completely disrupted. In fact, in the absence of overreaching, the normal rules of registered or unregistered land (as the case may be) take over. Thus, in registered land, if the equitable owner is a person in actual occupation of the property at the time of the purchase or mortgage (*Abbey National Building Society v Cann* (1991)), he will have an overriding interest against that purchaser or mortgagee (currently s 70(1)(g) of the LRA 1925). Alternatively, he may have registered his interest as a minor interest, and so secured its priority. However, if neither of these has occurred, the purchaser takes the land free of the equitable interests, in the same way that he would for any other unprotected equitable interest.

In unregistered land, these equitable interests *cannot* be registered as land charges under the LCA: see s 2(4) of the LCA 1972. Consequently, whether they bind a purchaser or mortgagee who has not overreached depends on the old doctrine of notice (this being one of the very few cases where it is relevant). Usually, if the equitable owner is residing in the property, the purchaser or mortgagee will be deemed to have constructive notice of their interest, and be bound by it (*Kingsnorth Trust v Tizard* (1986)).

However, in both registered and unregistered land, a purchaser who has failed to overreach, and is presumptively bound by the equitable interest according to the above rules, may be able to plead that the equitable owner has expressly or impliedly consented to the sale/mortgage taking place. In such cases, although it appears that the purchaser should have been bound, a court of equity will respect the express or implied consent of the equitable owner with the consequence that the purchaser gains priority over their interest (*Paddington Building Society v Mendelson* (1985) (registered land); *Bristol and West Building Society v Henning* (1985) (unregistered land)). In order to give the purchaser this relief, the court must be satisfied that the expressed or implied consent is real: it does not exist simply through knowledge of the proposed sale or mortgage (*Skipton Building Society v Clayton* (1993)). So, for example, if the legal owner attempts to mortgage the land to a bank and his lover (the equitable owner) signs a consent form postponing her interest to that of the bank, we need to be sure that (in the absence of undue influence) the consent was real. Likewise, even in the absence of a signature on a consent form, the lover may have so acted in relation to the mortgage (for example, attending the bank, explaining the need for a mortgage to the bank's employee) that her consent can be implied and is beyond doubt. Likewise, clear consent to one mortgage will be taken to be effective in favour of a different mortgagee that provides funds to pay off the first mortgage (at least up to the value of the first mortgage) on the basis that the equitable owner should not benefit merely because of a change in identity of the lender (*Equity and Home Loans v Prestige* (1992); *LF v LF* (2001)). On the other hand, an equitable owner who knows that the legal owner is about to mortgage, but who does not consent expressly or impliedly, does not, thereby, lose her interest. It is up to the bank to seek consent, not for the equitable owner to offer it. In practice, most mortgagees will ensure that all possible equitable owners sign a consent form, thus securing the priority that is not available through overreaching.

However, in *Woolwich Building Society v Dickman* (1996), the Court of Appeal reconsidered the principle that a purchaser may plead the consent of an equitable owner as a means of taking the land free of the interest. In a surprising decision, the court seems to suggest that such consents can have no effect (that is, will not aid a purchaser) unless they are 'expressed on the register', at least when the person alleged to have consented is in actual occupation of the property, and could otherwise claim an overriding interest under s 70(1)(g) of the LRA 1925. Previous cases have not suggested that such consents have to be entered against the title in order to be effective and it is submitted that this decision misreads s 70(1) of the LRA 1925. Under that section, the purchaser's land is subject to certain rights unless such is 'expressed on the register', but only for rights 'for the time being subsisting in reference' to the land. The giving of consent by the equitable owner means that the right no longer 'subsists in reference' to the land in respect of the purchaser to whom the consent is given. Hence, s 70(1)(g) is not relevant, because there is no right that could bind *that* purchaser. *Dickman* itself can be justified on other grounds – the relevant right being protected under the Rent Act 1977. In *Gracegrove Estates v Boeteng* (1997), the Court of Appeal upheld the validity of an express consent in registered land where it had not been registered against the title. In fact, the *Dickman* view was not even considered, and it is now very doubtful whether *Dickman* is correct on this point (see also *Saberhawal* (2000)). The Law Commission has expressed the view (Report No 254) that these consents are effective to postpone the rights of the equitable owner without the need to enter them on the register of title.

4.9.8 The position of the equitable owners: problems and proposals

We have noted above that if a purchaser pays the purchase price to two trustees (legal owners) of the property, the equitable owners' rights are overreached. This means that the equitable rights are automatically transferred to the purchase money and the trustees hold that money on trust for the equitable owners in the same way as they held the land, that is, as tenants in common or joint tenants. Often, the sale would have been caused by one or all of the co-owners wishing to realise their investment and it is quite likely that the money will be distributed and the trust brought to an end. Alternatively, where the legal and equitable owners are the same people (for example, husband and wife), the money may be used to finance the purchase of a new property, which will then become co-owned.

Of course, these are the 'normal' cases and the great majority of dealings with residential co-owned land follow this smooth path. However, there will always be some legal owners who decide to sell without telling the equitable owners, perhaps in order to abscond with the proceeds, or raise a loan (mortgage) on the property for their own purposes. What happens then?

The first question is always whether overreaching has occurred and, if not, is the purchaser or mortgagee bound by the equitable interests (see above, 4.9.7). If overreaching has not occurred and the purchaser is bound, the problem has gone away. The equitable owners remain entitled to use the land, save only that a purchaser could apply to have the land sold under s 14 of the TOLATA 1996. The court is unlikely to order such a sale, given that the equitable owners have priority, although it is clear that they may do so in an exceptional case, as in *Bank of Baroda v Dhillon* (1997) and *Bank of Ireland v Bell* (2001) and see above, 4.9.3.

If overreaching has occurred, the fundamental rule is that the equitable owners have no claim against the purchaser or mortgagee to remain in possession of the land (*City of London Building Society v Flegg* (1988)). They are overreached and their interest now takes effect in the purchase money. If, therefore, the legal owners have absconded or are unable to pay, the equitable owners will have only the normal remedies for breach of trust, for example, a personal action, a tracing claim. Unfortunately, all this may be of little comfort to an equitable owner who did not want to have the land sold, especially as their share of the proceeds (for example, one half) may not be sufficient to pay for alternative accommodation. This is particularly acute in cases where the property has been used as a family home, and the rationale for overreaching disappears completely if no purchase money was actually payable on the transaction (*Sood*). Thus, in response to the decision in *Flegg*, and as a way of limiting the effect of overreaching on an 'unwilling equitable owner', the Law Commission once suggested three alternative reforms (Report No 188):

(a) that overreaching should not be possible unless one of the trustees (legal owners) is a solicitor or licensed conveyancer. The idea is simply that such a person might offer protection to an equitable owner by looking after their interests and possibly objecting to a sale.

This is a poor solution, as it would make conveyancing more expensive, as well as requiring an 'outsider' to become involved in personal affairs. Moreover, would it work? Does a solicitor have the time or inclination to be the guardian of the equitable owner?;

(b) that overreaching should not be possible if the equitable owner had registered their equitable interest.

This is superficially attractive, as the register could be relied on by the purchaser to indicate whether it was safe to proceed and the equitable owner would be protected. Unfortunately, however, this 'solution' presupposes that equitable owners are *prepared* to register, even if they *know* they must register. For example, given that many of these equitable interests arise informally, without writing or solicitors, will a housewife know that she should register her interest 'against' her husband's land?

Will she be prepared to register, especially as this might be regarded as a hostile act? It is no accident that, where there is no overreaching, these equitable rights are, at present, capable of being overriding interests which bind *without* the need for registration. In fact, this result might be achieved by an equitable owner obtaining a consent requirement under s 14 of the TOLATA 1996;

(c) that overreaching should not be possible without the consent of all the equitable owners who are of full age and in possession of the property.

The first point is that this would certainly work. An equitable owner's right to the land would be safe from overreaching under this proposal. However, what this also does is to destroy the entire overreaching mechanism of the LPA 1925. The whole point behind the abolition of legal tenancies in common, the institution of the joint tenant trusteeship and the concept of overreaching is precisely that a purchaser should be able to buy co-owned land *without* having to search for every legal and equitable owner and obtain their consent. This proposal very nearly returns to the pre-1926 law, and it would be much easier to reinstate legal tenancies in common if that is what is wanted. That said, it will be obvious from the above discussion of the effect of the TOLATA 1996 that some form of 'consent requirement' may now exist. This may not actually prevent a sale by two trustees (see above, 4.9.5), but it could trigger an application under s 14 of the Act. In essence, then, a partial 'consent bar' may have been created by the 1996 Act, not entirely deliberately, and whose effect is not necessarily to prevent a sale by two trustees, but to trigger the intervention of the court under s 14.

4.9.9 The position of the equitable owners faced with overreaching: the problem in perspective

If none of the solutions once proposed by the Law Commission (but now abandoned) deal satisfactorily with the problem of overreaching (even allowing for the effect of the 1996 Act), what is to be done?

If there is one trustee for sale, overreaching cannot occur. In the very great majority of cases, this will mean that the purchaser is bound by the rights of the equitable owners, both in registered land (overriding interest or registered interest) and unregistered land (the doctrine of notice). *There is no problem for the equitable owner,* save the relatively remote possibility of a sale against their wishes after a purchaser's or mortgagee's application under s 14 of the TOLATA 1996. Even then, the equitable owner would be paid the full value of their share before any claim of the mortgagee.

If there are two trustees for sale, overreaching can occur, but, in most residential property cases (that is, where the Law Commission once believed the problem to exist), the two trustees will also be the *only* two equitable owners; for example, where man and woman hold the house on trust for themselves. Again, there is no problem, because either party can object to a sale in their capacity as legal owner. In any event, an application to prevent sale may be made under s 14 of the TOLATA 1996.

So, then, it is only where there are two trustees for sale and *different* equitable owners that the problem really occurs. Such was the case in *Flegg*, where the property was held by the married couple on trust for themselves and one set of parents, that is, two trustees and four equitable owners. Yet, the question the Law Commission did not ask themselves is, how often does this factual situation occur in the context of residential property? How often, in a domestic context, will there be two legal owners and different or additional equitable owners? Perhaps *Flegg* raises an *exceptional* factual scenario, not a normal one. Should the law be changed to meet the 'hard case'? One view is that all that needs to be done is to prevent *single* trustees from appointing a second trustee (in order to overreach) without the leave of the court or the consent of the equitable owners. Such a move would prevent the artificial creation of a 'two trustee' situation by a knowledgeable legal owner preparing to sell or mortgage the property. Moreover, with the arrival of the TOLATA 1996, equitable owners in the *Flegg* position may apply, under s 14, for an order preventing sale, and the court will exercise its discretion to see which interest shall prevail – those of the two legal owners, or those of the non-legal equitable owners.

4.9.10 The question of possession

Prior to the TOLATA 1996, the question of who had a *right* to occupy the co-owned land caused unnecessary difficulty. There was no doubt that the legal owners (the trustees) had a right to occupy the land (subject to the trust instrument) – they had a legal estate in the land, with all the rights this entailed. If the land was held for investment purposes, the trustees may have chosen to relinquish possession to another (or it may have have been impliedly or expressly excluded), but theirs was the right by virtue of their legal estate. However, in reality, most co-ownership situations concern property purchased for residential purposes, and if all the co-owners were also legal owners (for example, man and woman), each could occupy by virtue of their legal estate. Unfortunately, problems did arise for non-legal equitable owners. In theory, such persons had only an interest in the proceeds of sale of the land, not the land itself, and consequently could be denied possession. Obviously, this misrepresented the reality of the situation and cases such as *Bull v Bull* (1955) and then *Williams and Glyn's Bank v Boland* (1981) ignored the theory and recognised an effective right to possess, enforceable against the legal owners and (in the absence of overreaching) against a purchaser. This situation has now been regularised by the TOLATA 1996. The Act has not altered the trustees' position as legal owners of the land, as they have all the powers of an absolute owner unless restricted. However, not only does the Act abolish the doctrine of conversion, and effectively declare that the equitable owners shall be regarded as having rights in the land (s 3 of the TOLATA 1996), it also provides in s 12 that an equitable owner has a right to occupy the land if this was the purpose for which the trust came into existence (as demonstrated by *Chun v Ho* (2001)). Such a right can be excluded by the trustees in exceptional circumstances, under s 13, if there are two persons entitled to occupy, but this will be rare in domestic cases and cannot, in any event, result in the removal of a person already occupying land unless they consent (s 13(7)). The TOLATA 1996 has effectively solved any problem that might remain in this regard – as it was intended to do.

4.9.11 The payment of rent

Once again, before the TOLATA 1996, there were difficulties in requiring one co-owner to pay rent to the other if only one enjoyed occupation of the property. This was because the nature of co-ownership meant that each co-owner was, in theory, entitled to occupy the whole property (not any defined share) and could not be made to 'pay' for enjoying that to which they were already entitled. So, if one co-owner did not occupy, the other could not be forced to pay them 'rent' or 'compensation' by way of recompense for the sole use. This could have meant hardship for the 'ousted' co-owner, especially if the reason why only one was in possession of the property was because of a breakdown in their domestic relationship. Fortunately, even prior to the TOLATA 1996, the courts took a pragmatic view, and would order the payment of a monetary sum where it was equitable to do so, irrespective of the theoretical niceties (*Re Pavlou (A Bankrupt)* (1993)). Now, s 13 of the TOLATA 1996 provides that compensation may be paid by one co-owner occupying the land to the exclusion of the other if certain conditions, specified in s 13, are met. Note, however, that this will not be automatic. In *Chun v Ho* (2001) the co-owner was not required to pay rent to the non-occupying co-owner because the latter had had the benefit of the large amount of money that the occupying co-owner had contributed to the purchase price.

4.9.12 A summary of the Trusts of Land and Appointment of Trustees Act 1996

The effect of the TOLATA 1996 has been woven into the preceding text and the picture presented there is of how trusts of land will work since 1 January 1997. The following is a short summary of how the Act changed the original 1925 co-ownership scheme:

(a) it will not be possible to create new strict settlements of land (see Chapter 5) and the entailed interest is abolished (see s 2 and Sched 1). Existing settlements will remain valid;

(b) the doctrine of conversion is abolished, effective for all new and nearly all existing trusts of land (s 3);

(c) unless a trust for sale has been created expressly, existing trusts for sale of land become trusts of land (ss 4 and 5) and trusts of land will become the model for all future trusts. There is no duty to sell the land. It remains possible deliberately and unequivocally to create a 'trust for sale' of land, but, given that even these deliberate creations are subject to the TOLATA 1996, there is very little to be gained practically;

(d) the trustees have all the powers of an absolute owner, but may delegate these to an equitable owner (ss 6–9). Only the trustee can give a valid receipt for purchase money, hence preserving their role in overreaching;

(e) the trustees must consult with the equitable owners, and give effect to their wishes in so far as is consistent with the purposes of the trust of land (s 11);

(f) the trustees' powers may be made subject to the consent of the beneficiaries, but only if stated in the instrument creating the trusts (s 10), or if imposed by the court under a s 14 application. This may have consequences when a sale is proposed;

(g) the equitable owners have a right to occupy the property (s 12), which can be modified subject to safeguards (s 13). Compensation may be ordered for exclusive use of the land by one co-owner;

(h) any person with an interest in the land can make an application to the court under s 14 for a variety of orders, for example, sale, no sale, override consent requirement, impose consent requirements. The criteria specified in s 15 do not apply in cases of bankruptcy (see s 335A of the Insolvency Act 1986).

4.10 The express and implied creation of co-ownership in practice: express, resulting and constructive trusts

So far, we have considered the nature of co-ownership in general, and the statutory machinery that governs it. Much has been said about the existence of two trustees or one trustee and the rights of the equitable owners. Now it is time to examine the way in which this co-ownership can come about. Put simply, how is it that land becomes 'co-owned' so that the panoply of legal rules just discussed come into play?

4.10.1 Express creation

Any land may be deliberately conveyed to two or more people, a typical example being the purchase of a new house by a couple. In such circumstances, the persons to whom legal title is transferred (that is, in the formal conveyance) will be the legal owners. In the absence of any statement to the contrary, these legal owners will also be taken to be the equitable owners. The result is that land conveyed to A and B as legal owners will be held on trust by them for themselves as either joint tenants or tenants in common. This was effectively the case in *Roy v Roy* (1996), where two brothers were held bound by the joint ownership of a house that had been transferred to them both. As we shall see, this presumption that the legal owners are also the only equitable owners may be challenged by proof of a 'resulting' or 'constructive' trust. Before we come to that, however, it is important to note that it is quite possible for a conveyance of land expressly to declare who are the equitable owners, and also the nature of their ownership. Thus, land might be conveyed 'to A and B as legal owners on trust for A and B beneficially as tenants in common' or 'to A and B as legal owners on trust for A, B, C and D as tenants in common'. In these cases, both where the legal and equitable owners are the same people, and when they are not, the trust of land and the equitable ownership is 'expressly declared'. Two points are of importance here:

(a) in order for a trust of land to be valid, it must satisfy s 53(1) of the LPA 1925. This means that an express declaration of the beneficial (equitable) interests of the co-owners can only be relied upon to establish ownership if it is 'manifested and proved by some writing'. Usually, the 'writing' is the deed of conveyance to the co-owners. However, there is one vital exception to the requirement of writing, namely, that a person who is *not* a party to any *valid* express declaration of trust may establish a beneficial interest in the property by proving a resulting or constructive trust, s 53(2) of the LPA 1925 (see below, 4.10.2). Note, also, that even in the absence of an express declaration of the beneficial interests in the land (that is, that no trust is declared), the very conveyance of the land to two or more people will be strong evidence of joint ownership in law and in equity (*Roy*) unless it is clear that the conveyance to two persons was merely administrative in order to enable the single 'true' owner to purchase the land in the first place (*Goodman v Carlton* (2001));

(b) if the beneficial interests are expressly declared in writing, this is conclusive as to the beneficial ownership *for the parties to that express declaration* (*Goodman v Gallant* (1986)). In other words, persons who are parties to the writing that establishes the trust cannot, thereafter, plead a resulting or constructive trust to establish different interests. The only exception to this is if the express declaration has been procured by fraud or some other vitiating factor such as undue influence. Of course, persons not party to the express written declaration of the trust may rely on resulting or constructive trusts. Moreover, *Roy* also suggests that any of the parties to a conveyance which does not actually declare the trusts – but merely records the transfer of the land to them – may also rely on resulting or constructive trusts to prove an enlarged share.

4.10.2 Creation of co-ownership even though the legal title is in one name only

It often happens that property is bought by one person and conveyed into their sole name. Of course, this has nothing to do with co-ownership, for the land is owned by that person. However, what happens if someone else (for example, a spouse or a lover) comes to live in that property, or makes some contribution to its purchase price? Is it possible that this new person may acquire an equitable interest in the house which is legally owned by the other? To put the question another way, even though legal title to the land is held by its original owner, in what circumstances may some other person gain a share in that ownership, which interest must necessarily be an equitable interest, given that the original owner is already holding the legal title on their own? The answer is provided by the law of resulting and constructive trusts. Before considering the matter in detail, it is vital to understand why it is so important to determine whether such an equitable interest is created.

Although there is only one legal owner (A) (the person who originally purchased the property), the fact that another person (B) has established an equitable interest means that *in equity* the property is co-owned. According to *Bull v Bull* (1955), this means that a trust of the land comes into existence whereby the original legal owner (A) holds the property on trust for himself and B in equity. In other words, there is *one* trustee of the land, but at least two co-owners in equity. Because there is only one trustee, a person who wishes to buy the property from the sole legal owner (or a bank that lends money to that owner on the security of it) cannot rely on overreaching to give them priority over any equitable owners. Thus, the purchaser may be bound by B's equitable interest according to the rules of registered and unregistered land. Moreover, because B's equitable interest has arisen informally under the rules of resulting and constructive trusts, without writing, the purchaser may be unable to discover its existence, and may fail to take avoiding action before completing the purchase.

4.10.3 Establishing the equitable interest

The rules considered below are applicable whenever a person seeks to establish a share of ownership in land, legal title to which is held by someone else. Usually, legal title will be held by one person, and the claimant will be their partner or former partner in a domestic relationship. Often, the man will have legal title and the woman will be a claimant, but the law is the same whatever the factual matrix (for example, *Tinsley v Milligan* (1993), two women; *Babic v Thompson* (1999), two businessmen). These rules are also equally applicable when legal title is held by two, three or four people, the only difference being that the legal owners would then be able to overreach the new equitable interest on a sale or mortgage. Bearing this in mind, it is possible to categorise the methods by which an equitable interest may be claimed. However, it is to be remembered that, while these categories are convenient for the purposes of exposition, in reality, the claimant's and defendant's lives tend to be much more complicated, and much less susceptible to objective, forensic analysis.

4.10.4 The express trust

Although it rarely occurs, it is perfectly possible for the legal owner (or owners) deliberately to generate an interest in the land for another by means of an express trust. In short, the legal owner (A) may declare expressly and in writing (as required by s 53(1) of the LPA 1925) that he holds the land on trust for the claimant (B), usually in co-ownership with himself. As an express trust, the equitable co-ownership thereby created is conclusive according to its terms. It is also possible for the legal owner actually to convey the legal title to himself and another, in which case there will be co-ownership of the legal and equitable title. This is even rarer.

4.10.5 The immediate, the deferred and the indirect 'purchase money' resulting trust

A second means by which a person may claim an equitable interest in another's property – thereby triggering co-ownership – is by contributing to the purchase price of the property, despite the fact that their name is not on the legal title. Unless it can be established that the money was given to the legal owner by way of gift or loan (as in *Bradbury v Hoolin* (1998)), the claimant will have an equitable interest in the land in direct proportion to their contribution to the purchase price. This is the resulting trust. It is said to arise from the 'common intention' of the legal owner and the claimant that the latter should have an interest in the property, as manifested by their contribution to the acquisition of the property through part provision of the purchase price (*Tinsley v Milligan* (1993)). A typical example is where the intended legal owner provides some of the purchase price and the balance is provided by a husband, wife or other partner. In such cases, legal ownership is in one person and equitable ownership is shared among the contributors, usually on the basis of a tenancy in common in proportion to the contribution provided. The principles are the same if all that is provided is the deposit (*Halifax Building Society v Brown* (1995)) and in certain circumstances may include a notional payment because of a 'right to buy' discount off the purchase price – *Mumford v Ashe* (2000). Note, however, that the contribution must be made to the acquisition of property, not merely to its repair (*Bank of India v Mody* (1998)), and it seems that an interest will not arise if there is evidence that no common intention as to joint ownership in fact existed (*First National Bank v Wadhwani* (1998)).

As a variation on this, an equitable interest may arise in much the same way when a financial contribution is made to the purchase price over a period of time. Thus, where a person contributes to a mortgage which has been used to purchase the property, this can be regarded as a deferred contribution to the purchase price, thereby generating an interest under a resulting trust. Subject to what will be said below concerning constructive trusts, the interest thus acquired, as a matter of principle, is directly related to the amount of deferred contributions. Of course, there may be problems of quantification (for example, who paid what and when), but as the basis of the claim is a payment towards the purchase price, the interest should be related to this.

Finally under the rubric of resulting trusts, we must consider those cases where the claimant makes a financial contribution to the cost of running the household, the value of which may have enabled the legal owner to pay the purchase price of the property. Although it is more doubtful, perhaps even these may be regarded as an indirect means of helping to purchase the property. An example is where the woman pays all the regular domestic outgoings and the man pays the mortgage. Providing that such indirect financial contributions are evidence of a common intention as to ownership (*Wadhwani*), the claimant has a chance to establish an interest in the property under a resulting trust as with the right to buy discount cases: *Springette v Defoe* (1992). However, it is not enough that financial contributions to the running of the household simply have been made (*Lloyds Bank v Rosset* (1991)). It seems that they may give rise to an interest only if made in circumstances that enabled the legal owner to purchase the property. This is very difficult to prove and the claimant is unlikely to succeed in all but the most obvious cases. Such a claim failed in *Burns v Burns* (1984), and appears to be rejected as a matter of principle in the all-important judgment of Lord Bridge in *Rosset*.

It has been assumed above that if a claimant establishes a resulting trust – by payments to the purchase price – their interest in the property is to be quantified in direct proportion. So, a contribution of 25% entitles the claimant to a 25% interest, and so on. However, it now seems possible that if a claimant has established an interest by means of a payment to the purchase price, the court may be free to quantify that interest by taking into account the whole course of dealings between the parties. It is as if the payment to the purchase price opens the door to an interest, but once through the door, the interest can be out of proportion to the payment. In *Midland Bank v Cooke* (1995), the claimant paid just under 6.5% of the purchase price, but the Court of Appeal felt able to expand this into a 50% share because the subsequent conduct of the parties revealed that this was their true intention. To a purist, this seems rather awkward, as it confuses principles of resulting and constructive trusts (see below. Note also *Drake v Whipp* (1995), arguing for a distinction between the concepts). However, it does seem to be the way forward and it has been expressly followed in *LF v LF* (2001) where the whole conduct of the parties was relevant in quantifying the interest. It would be supportable if the expanded interest is based on a real intention of the parties as manifested by their words or conduct (of which the small payment to the purchase price is merely evidence) and not some 'intention' manufactured by the court in its infinite wisdom. So, if the claimant pays 10% of the purchase price (by whatever method), but there is evidence of a real intention that the property should be held (say) 50:50, then the court might be justified in quantifying the interest on the basis of the intention, not the contribution. While this may be acceptable, it would be unfortunate, and the cause of great uncertainty, if the courts were to follow *Cooke* in all respects and permit the expansion of a 'payment interest' on the basis of what the parties would have intended had they actually thought about it. In *Cooke*, for example, the parties were honest about the fact that they had no real intention as to ownership. In other words, to expand a proportional interest on the basis of a real intention is defensible, to expand it on the basis of an intention supplied by the court is not. Adoption of this broadest of approaches has now been rejected in constructive trust cases, and the same should follow here (see below, 4.10.6).

4.10.6 The constructive trust

A second method of establishing an interest is through the 'constructive trust'. In these cases, the legal owner may have made an oral promise or assurance to the claimant that they 'owned' the property or had a share in it. If the claimant then relies on this to their detriment, the legal owner will not be able to deny the interest promised (*Lloyds Bank v Rosset* (1991); *Grant v Edwards* (1986)). Again, this is a form of 'common intention', and proof of an absence of such intention may be fatal (*Wadhwani*). There are three elements to a successful claim:

(a) a promise or assurance made. In many cases, the promise will be truly express, as where A says to B: 'Of course half this house is yours' or 'This house is as much yours as mine'. However, promises are also expressly made for the purpose of establishing a constructive trust when the legal owner makes a statement reassuring the claimant that they have a stake in the property. This can take many forms and is, ultimately, a matter for construction in each case. For example, does 'this will always be your home' or 'I would never sell without your agreement' imply a promise as to ownership? If it does, a constructive trust is a possibility. Moreover, it appears that such a promise can be enough to trigger a constructive trust case, even if it is not meant. So, in *Eves v Eves* (1975), a promise was held to have been made where the legal owner said, by way of excuse, that the only reason that the property was not conveyed originally to the woman was because she was too young. Likewise, telling the claimant that the property will be conveyed to them in due course can be a promise, even if it is a lie. The only rule is that an express assurance must be made, in whatever form, and it matters not that this occurs after the legal owner has acquired the property (*Clough v Kelly* (1996));

(b) reliance by the claimant on that assurance. It is not enough that an assurance is made. It must also be established that the claimant relied on the assurance. So, if it is clear that the claimant would have behaved the same way irrespective of the legal owner's words, no constructive trust arises. A constructive trust arises because of the need to remedy an inequity: there is no inequity if a promise has made no impact on the conduct of the claimant. Of course, such reliance may also take many forms, and can be notoriously difficult to prove. Does the woman who has been promised that 'this house is yours as well as mine' actually rely on that promise when selling her own house and moving in, or would she have done that anyway? In view of these difficulties, Lord Denning, in *Greasley v Cooke* (1980), suggests that, if there is evidence of 'detriment' (see below), there is a presumption of reliance: that is, in the absence of evidence to the contrary adduced by the legal owners, the court is entitled to assume that the claimant did, indeed, rely on the assurance made (as in *Chun v Ho* (2001)). This is, of course, a generous presumption and it reverses the burden of proof. Nevertheless, it is wholly necessary if the legal owners were not to avoid all claims of constructive trust merely by pleading that the claimant could not actually prove that he relied on the promise made;

(c) detriment. Following the established equitable principle that 'equity will not assist a volunteer', no constructive trust can arise unless the claimant can show that they acted to their detriment when relying on the promise. Once again, detriment may take many forms: it can be in the conduct of the claimant, as in doing extraordinary work about the house (*Eves v Eves* (1975); *Ungurian v Lesnoff* (1990)); or it may be financial in substance: perhaps paying bills, or settling other household expenses. Whatever form it takes, however, the key is that the claimant does something concrete in relation to the promise. In this connection, it seems that the 'detriment' does not need to have been detrimental in the sense of harmful. So, giving up existing accommodation in order to move into the legal owner's luxurious property is a 'detriment' (no house to fall back on), as is spending one's life savings on a Porsche in reliance on the legal owner's property that 'you will never have to find another house' (no money to purchase another property). As both these examples illustrate, it is also true that the detriment need not be related to the property in which the claimant acquires an interest.

If the claimant establishes these three elements, he will be the beneficiary of a constructive trust, and be entitled to an equitable interest in the property. As ever, legal title will be held by the legal owner, as trustee for himself and the successful claimant. Difficulties do arise, however, when trying to quantify this interest. As a matter of principle, the interest of the 'promisee' should be equivalent to that which they have been promised: this is what they have been unfairly denied. So, if the claimant has been promised 'a home for life', a life interest is suitable, and 'this is as much yours as mine' should generate a 50% share. However, the temptation to adopt a broad brush approach is almost overwhelming – not least because it is simpler. Consequently, many of these cases do, in fact, result in an equal division between the legal owner and claimant, even if the terms of the promise are otherwise, or unclear. Recently, however, in *Clough v Kelly* (1996), the Court of Appeal has confirmed that, if that the terms of the express promise (that is, the common intention) are clear, the court should not depart from this as the basis for quantification. So, in that case, the promise was that the wife should have a joint interest, and this is what she received, even though there was evidence that the share of interest 'earned' by her detriment should have been only 25%. To put it another way, in quantifying interests under a constructive trust, the court usually will satisfy expectations rather than compensate for loss (detriment).

To sum up then, a person may claim an interest in property belonging to another in these three circumstances: the express trust; the resulting trust; and the constructive trust. All are examples of how an interest arises because of a common intention between the legal owner and the claimant. They are, however, different in principle, even though the resulting trust and constructive trust appear very similar and are often treated as synonymous (see, for example, *Rosset* (1991) and *Midland Bank v Cooke* (1995); *contra* is *Drake* (1995)). For example, if the detriment which supports a constructive trust consists of financial contributions, this is not the same as the financial contributions which support a resulting trust. In a resulting trust, the interest arises *because* payments are made; in a constructive trust, the interest arises *because* promises were made which have been relied on: the financial detriment is not the reason for the interest. So, in a resulting trust, the equitable interest given to the claimant might be thought to be equivalent to the money he contributed to the purchase price, whereas, in a constructive trust, it is equivalent to the promise made or that which is necessary to do justice between the parties, even if the financial contribution (or detrimental conduct) is relatively small. *Cooke* blurs this distinction in an effort to do justice to the claimant.

4.10.7 Where there is no interest

For the sake of completeness, and because of uncertainties in the earlier case law, we should note the circumstances which will not give rise to an interest under either a resulting or constructive trust. As the law stands at the moment, unless the claimant has 'paid' (in some way) towards the purchase price, or has relied on a 'promise' as to ownership, they have no interest in the property. So, a woman who has looked after her lover for 30 years, but has never paid part of the purchase price and to whom no promises have been made, has no interest. Lord Bridge makes this very clear in *Rosset*; 'pure' conduct (not being a financial contribution to the purchase price), which is not referable to a promise, will not raise an interest. Likewise, if the payments were for repairs, not acquisition (*Mody*), or were a gift (*Bradbury*), or there was clear evidence of an absence of a common intention (*Wadhwani*). Of course, if the couple are married, and then divorce or separate, a 'property adjustment order' can be made in the family court under the Matrimonial Causes Act 1973, but there is no equivalent power if the couple are unmarried or are just friends. Finally, we should also note that the court has a power under s 37 of the Matrimonial Proceedings and Property Act 1970 to award a beneficial interest consequent upon spousal improvements to property. This is a fairly limited power, restricted by definition to married couples. It appears that the value of the interest awarded must be commensurate with (that is, restricted to) the value added to the property by way of the improvement.

The apparently limited circumstances in which a non-owner can claim a proprietary (ownership) interest in another's property has given rise to much criticism. It seems unfair that, say, a long term emotional partner should be unable to claim a share in the family home simply because she cannot prove the existence of an express promise or a payment towards the purchase price. However, in reality, things can be different. First, as mentioned above, if the couple are married, the court has a discretion to readjust property rights on divorce or judicial separation. Of course, this does not help a happily married couple in a fight with a mortgage lender (or an unmarried couple at all: see *Burns v Burns* (1984)), but it does mean that the non-owning half of a married couple at least has some hope of securing a 'fair share' of the main family asset. Secondly, there are relatively few reported cases where a claimant in a normal domestic context has actually failed to secure an interest under the *Rosset* rules (*Rosset* was one!) and this is irrespective of whether the couple are married or unmarried, hetero or homosexual. The courts are adept at finding some kind of payment to the purchase price (which they might then enlarge under the *Cooke* approach) and even keener to identify some kind of promise about ownership. It seems sometimes that even casual remarks can trigger an interest. Thirdly, the Law Commission has just completed a thorough analysis of the rights of 'homesharers' and a consultation document is expected in June 2002. It is certain that this will contain proposals relating to the ownership and use of family property. Fourthly, while it is true that the courts take a tougher line with property acquired for business purposes, we might argue that this is as it should be. After all, the business partners could have deliberately conveyed the land into joint names. Only rarely might there be the kind of emotional pressures and concerns that require a more generous intervention in the context of family property. Finally, we should always remember that ownership of family property might actually be of great concern to third parties –banks, lending institutions, creditors etc. As we have seen in cases like *William and Glyn's Bank v Boland* (1981) and cases following it, a simple way to keep a mortgagee out of possession of the family home after non-payment of the mortgage is to prove that the non-legal owner has acquired an equitable interest before the mortgage which then overrides the bank's interest. Sometimes, some cases feel as if the alleged co-owners have manufactured an interest in favour of the non-legal owner precisely (as it turned out) to defeat the claims of a creditor. As Fox LJ said in *Midland Bank v Dobson* (1985), 'assertions made by a husband and wife as to a common intention formed 30 years ago regarding joint ownership, of which there is no contemporary evidence and which happens to accommodate their current need to defeat the claims of a creditor, must be received by the courts with caution'.

4.10.8 The nature of the interest established: joint tenancy or tenancy in common

In the usual case of an equitable interest established by means of a resulting or constructive trust, there will be little doubt that the co-ownership in equity takes the form of a tenancy in common. This is simply because one of the four unities is almost certainly lacking. For example, the claimant's equitable interest may have arisen later in time than the legal owner's (no unity of time), or it may be of a lesser or greater extent depending on any promises made or the amount of money paid (no unity of interest). However, if co-ownership of the equitable interest is established at the time the property was originally purchased, either because it was expressly declared in the conveyance of the legal title to a sole owner, or because all co-owners pay an equal proportion of the purchase price, then there may be a joint tenancy.

4.11 Severance

As we have seen above, co-ownership of the equitable interest in property may be either as a joint tenancy or a tenancy in common. A tenancy in common is clearly an 'undivided share' in land, with each co-owner being able to identify their portion of ownership (for example, one quarter, one fifth, etc), even though there is unity of possession of the whole. Conversely, with a joint tenancy, no co-owner has a defined share, but each is the owner of the whole and subject to the right of survivorship. In practical terms, this means that a joint tenant has no individual share in the equitable interest in the land which he can sell, give away or leave by will. For some, this may be perfectly acceptable, but for others it means that they or their families are denied the opportunity to liquidate the capital value of the land. In order to meet these difficulties, any joint tenant may 'sever' their joint tenancy, and, thereby, turn it into a tenancy in common. Of course, because of the 1925 reforms, it is only possible to sever an equitable joint tenancy (not that of the legal title), because tenancies in common may exist only in equity. That said, there are several methods by which a joint tenant may sever their interest, and thereby constitute themselves a tenant in common in equity. One is statutory, and three arise under common law, as codified in *Williams v Hensman* (1861). After severance has occurred, if there were only two joint tenants, necessarily, both are now tenants in common, but if there were three or more joint tenants, the others can remain as joint tenants between themselves. So, if land is held by A, B, C and D as legal and equitable joint tenants, and then C and D carry out an act of severance, legal title remains held by A, B, C and D as joint tenants (it is not severable), but the equitable title now exists as a joint tenancy between A and B, with C and D as tenants in common.

4.11.1 By statutory notice: s 36(2) of the Law of Property Act 1925

Under s 36(2) of the LPA 1925, any equitable joint tenant may give notice in writing to the other joint tenants of his intention to sever the joint tenancy. The giving of such notice results in a severance of that co-owner's interest, and they become a tenant in common (*Burgess v Rawnsley* (1975)). Indeed, so long as there is evidence that the written notice was sent (for example, by registered post), it seems that it does not have to be received by the other joint tenants to be effective to sever (*Re 88 Berkeley Road* (1971)). So, in *Kinch v Bullard* (1998), a notice was sent by one joint tenant to the other and arrived at the receiver's address. He never saw it, having suffered a heart attack, and the notice was destroyed by the sender (hoping to benefit from the survivorship she had sought to end!). Not surprisingly, the court held that the notice was served by delivery – even if not seen – and that it could not be withdrawn after service. Severance had occurred. Moreover, it is also clear that the notice may take many forms. For example, in *Re Draper's Conveyance* (1969), a summons claiming sale of the co-owned property was held to constitute written notice of severance under s 36(2). Unusually, however, it also seems true that a mere oral agreement *not* to sever can prevent any later act of severance by written notice taking effect (*quare* whether this applies to *William v Hensman* methods also). In *White v White* (2001), the property had been conveyed expressly to three people as equitable joint-tenants and there had been an oral agreement not to sever. In such circumstances, a clear attempted severance by written notice under s 36(2) was held ineffective on the ground that the oral agreement supported the original declaration of the owners as joint-tenants. Of course, the whole point of severance is that it can destroy an expressly declared equitable joint-tenancy, so perhaps the case is best explained on the basis that the person wishing to sever was estopped from so doing by their conduct (the oral agreement) because it would have been unconscionable in the circumstances to permit that severance. There is one possible limitation to statutory severance, and this emerges from the words of s 36(2) itself. The section talks of severance by written notice where land 'is vested in joint tenants beneficially'. This seems to encompass only those situations where the legal and equitable joint tenants are the same people, and not where, for example, A and B hold on trust for A, B, C and D as joint tenants. Fortunately, this limited interpretation of s 36(2) has not been adopted, and statutory severance is presumed to be available for all joint tenants, whether they are also legal owners or not (*Burgess v Rawnsley* (1975)).

4.11.2 By an act operating on his own share

In addition to statutory severance, the common law recognises three other ways in which it is possible to sever the joint tenancy. These were explained in the case of *Williams v Hensman* (1861), and this case is now regarded as authority for the 'methods' outlined here and below, 4.11.3 and 4.11.4. These three methods may still be used, although it will be appreciated that statutory severance is by far the most reliable and easily proved.

The first *Williams v Hensman* (1861) method of severance is 'by an act operating on one's own share'. This occurs when one equitable co-owner seeks to deal with 'their share' of the land, so manifesting an intention no longer to be part of the joint tenancy. The very action of dealing with one's own share thereby severs that share. Typical examples are where the equitable owner sells their share to a third party, mortgages it in favour of a bank, or becomes bankrupt, so that their property becomes vested in the 'trustee in bankruptcy' (for example, *Re Dennis* (1992)). Likewise, attempting to deal with the legal title by forging the consent of the other legal owners in fact operates to transfer that person's equitable interest, so also effecting a severance (*Banker's Trust v Namdar* (1997) and s 63 of the LPA 1925). Note, however, that leaving one's 'share' in a subsisting joint tenancy by will can *never* constitute severance, as the right of survivorship takes precedence over testamentary dispositions (*Gould v Kemp* (1834)). Finally, for this method of severance to be effective, the 'act' operating on the joint tenant's share must be valid and enforceable, unlike 'mutual agreement' (below, 4.11.3). This means that the 'act' which effects the severance must be one which is valid according to the formality rules for that type of disposition. So, given that nearly all dispositions of an interest in land must be in writing (s 2 of the Law of Property (Miscellaneous Provisions) Act 1989), the 'act of severance' by way of mortgage, sale or lease (if over three years) must be in writing and otherwise enforceable if it is to sever. This method requires an 'act' operating on one's own share, not an unenforceable intention to sever.

The result of such a severance is, of course, that the 'share' of the person severing passes to the person with whom he has contracted: for example, to the mortgagee or purchaser of the share. Necessarily, this must cause a tenancy in common with the remaining co-owners.

4.11.3 Where joint tenants agree to sever by 'mutual agreement'

The second *Williams v Hensman* (1861) method is that, if two or more joint tenants agree among themselves to terminate the joint tenancy, those agreeing are taken to have severed the joint tenancy and constituted themselves as tenants in common. Most importantly, this agreement need not take any specific form, and it need not be in writing. It need not be enforceable, and may be inferred from the surrounding circumstances. The point is simply that the fact of agreement severs the joint tenancy. For example, severance by this method may occur when the co-owners agree on the precise distribution of property on the breakdown of their relationship (*Re McKee* (1975)). However, the agreement must contemplate an intention to sever the joint tenancy (that is, the ownership), and not merely amount to an agreement as to the use of the property (*Nielson-Jones v Fedden* (1975)).

4.11.4 By mutual conduct

Mutual conduct is a flexible and shifting category that is intended to express the idea that severance may occur because the joint tenants, by their conduct in relation to each other, have demonstrated that the joint tenancy is terminated (*Williams v Hensman* (1861)). Although very similar to mutual agreement, the point here is that the parties have not agreed to sever – formally or informally – but have so acted that it is clear that the continuance of a joint tenancy would be inconsistent with their intentions. There are many possible examples of mutual conduct, but the most common include physical partition of the land so that each co-owner is barred from the other's portion, the writing of mutual wills and negotiations between the joint tenants as to disposal of the property. The last of these is somewhat controversial, for it is difficult to see why a failed severance under mutual agreement (for example, because the co-owners disagree about the value of the land) can nevertheless amount to a successful severance under mutual conduct because of severance negotiations. This, however, is the clear inference of Lord Denning's judgment in *Burgess*. Essentially, the matter will turn on the facts of each case and whether the court is prepared, as a matter of policy, to extend the circumstances in which severance is possible. The degree of hardship caused by the operation of the right of survivorship might well be relevant in that calculation, as the courts favour severance if this preserves the 'share' of a deceased co-owner for their family.

CO-OWNERSHIP

The nature and types of concurrent co-ownership

'Concurrent co-ownership' of property describes the simultaneous enjoyment of land by two or more persons. Since 1 January 1926, co-ownership of property will either be by way of a *joint tenancy* or *a tenancy in common*. In a joint tenancy, each co-owner is treated as being entitled to the whole of the land and there are no distinct 'shares'. It is characterised by the right of survivorship and the four unities (unity of possession, interest, title and time (PITT)). A tenancy in common exists when two or more people own an 'undivided share in land', giving unity of possession but where no other unities are necessary and where there is no right of survivorship.

The effect of the Law of Property Act 1925 and the Trusts of Land and Appointment of Trustees Act 1996

Before 1926, it was possible for a joint tenancy and a tenancy in common to exist in both the legal and equitable estate in the land. However, after 1925, it is now impossible to create a tenancy in common at law. The legal owners of co-owned property must be joint tenants of the legal estate. They will hold the land as 'trustees of land' for the persons entitled in equity (ss 34 and 36 of the LPA 1925; ss 4 and 5 of the TOLATA 1996). Co-ownership of the equitable interest may be by way of either a joint tenancy or a tenancy in common.

The equitable interest: joint tenancy or tenancy in common?

First, if the unities of interest, title or time are absent, a joint tenancy in equity cannot exist. Secondly, if the original conveyance to the co-owners stipulates that they are 'joint-tenants' or 'tenants in common' *of the beneficial or equitable interest*, this is normally conclusive as to the nature of their co-ownership in equity. Thirdly, if 'words of severance' are used, then a tenancy in common will exist in equity. Fourthly, failing any of the above, 'equity follows the law' and there will be a joint tenancy of the equitable interest (as there must be of the legal) unless the co-owners are business partners, co-mortgagees or where they as purchasers have provided the purchase money in unequal shares.

The nature of the trust of land: the effect of the Trusts of Land and Appointment of Trustees Act 1996

The trustees hold the legal title for the benefit of the equitable owners (who may be themselves), but it is the legal owners who have powers equivalent to those of an absolute owner to deal with the land (s 6 of the TOLATA 1996). These powers can be restricted by the document establishing the trust or by order of the court (s 14 of the TOLATA 1996) and must be exercised in conformity with the TOLATA regime. The trustees may delegate powers to a beneficiary, except the power to conduct an overreaching transaction. The trustees are not under a duty to sell the land (as was the case with the old trust for sale). Any person interested in the trust of land may apply to the court under s 14 of the TOLATA 1996 (replacing s 30 of the LPA 1925) for an order affecting the land, including an order for sale. The powers of the trustees, including sale, may be made subject to the consent of a specified person (for example, a beneficiary), but only in limited circumstances. Providing the trustees are two or more in number and are in agreement and are not subject to a protected consent requirement, and that the equitable rights are overreachable, a sale will overreach the equitable interests, sweeping them off the land and into the purchase money so that they do not bind the purchaser.

The advantages of the trust of land as a device for regulating co-owned land

By abolishing tenancies in common at law, the LPA 1925 has ensured that there is but one title to investigate: the legal joint tenancy. The number of potential legal joint tenants is limited to a maximum of four (irrespective of the number of equitable owners). The right of survivorship diminishes the inconvenience and cost if a legal joint tenant dies. If there are two or more trustees of the land, the purchaser may usually ignore all the equitable owners because of statutory overreaching. The court's powers under s 14 of the TOLATA 1996 prevents co-owned land becoming inalienable. The TOLATA 1996 gives concrete rights to the equitable owners to possess and enjoy the fruits of the land, subject to the possibility of overreaching.

The disadvantages of the trust of land as a device for regulating co-owned land

There may be disputes between the legal owners as to whether a sale or mortgage, etc, should take place or whether the land should be retained for the benefit of the equitable owners. The problem is greater if the trustees' powers are subject to the consent of some other person, although disputes may be resolved by application to the court under s 14 of the TOLATA 1996. The powerful effect of overreaching may effectively destroy an equitable owner's valuable rights. The ability to prevent overreaching through the imposition of a consent requirement is of limited value only. The trustees' duty to consult the beneficiaries is likely to offer little practical protection. In cases of bankruptcy, it is very likely that the land will be sold, despite any objections by the equitable owners.

The position of a purchaser who buys co-owned land: overreaching or not?

If a purchaser buys co-owned land from two or more legal owners (that is, there are two trustees) the equitable interests are transferred to the purchase money and the purchaser obtains the land free from their rights (overreaching). If the purchaser buys the property from a single trustee only, then the purchaser cannot rely on overreaching to protect him from the rights of the equitable owners: he *may* be bound by them according to the normal rules of registered and unregistered conveyancing.

The position of the equitable owners when overreaching occurs

If overreaching has occurred, the fundamental rule is that the equitable owners have no claim against the purchaser (which includes a mortgagee) to remain in possession of the land, *City of London Building Society v Flegg* (1988). In order to protect the equitable owner in this position, the Law Commission offered various devices for consideration, none of which were practical or sensible. In any event, it is important to see this 'problem' in perspective. Under the TOLATA 1996, the trustees' power to sell or mortgage may be made subject to the consent of another person. In registered land, this will prevent overreaching if the consent requirement is registered as a restriction against the title (assuming consent is not given!) and in unregistered land a purchaser will not be able to overreach if he has actual notice of the consent requirement.

The question of possession: who has a right to occupy?

All the legal owners have a right to occupy the property unless there is something specific to the contrary in the document establishing the trust of land. A purely equitable owner has a right to occupy under s 12 of the TOLATA 1996, although this may be excluded or made conditional in the limited circumstances specified in s 13 of the TOLATA 1996.

The payment of compensation for exclusive use

Under s 13 of the TOLATA 1996, a co-owner enjoying exclusive use of the land (that is, where the other or others are excluded) can be required to pay compensation for such use. This had been the position under the old trust for sale (*Re Pavlou* (1993)).

The express creation of co-ownership

Any land may be deliberately conveyed to two or more people. In such circumstances, the persons to whom legal title is transferred will be the legal owners (joint tenant trustees) and, in the absence of any statement to the contrary, they will also be the equitable owners. This conveyance may also expressly declare who are the equitable owners and the nature of their ownership and this is conclusive for those parties (*Goodman v Gallant* (1986)).

Creation of co-ownership even though the legal title is in one name only

The legal owner (A) may expressly declare in writing (s 53(1) of the LPA 1925) that he holds the land on trust for the claimant (B) or, more usually, a person may claim an equitable interest through the operation of resulting or constructive trusts, viz:

(a) a resulting trust arises where the claimant has contributed to the purchase price of the property, either initially or by way of mortgage payments. Also, they may have made financial contributions to the cost of running the household, the value of which may have enabled the legal owner to pay the purchase price of the property, although this 'indirect' method is disputed. The size of the claimant's share will either be directly related to the proportion of the purchase price she has paid or be calculated according to the actual agreement of the parties;

(b) a constructive trust arises where the legal owner makes an express oral promise to, or express oral agreement with, the claimant that they 'own' the property or have a share in it, provided this is relied on by the claimant to their detriment. The size of the share may be equivalent to the interest that was promised or agreed or calculated by reference to the whole course of dealings between the parties.

Severance

Severance is the process of turning an equitable joint tenancy into an equitable tenancy in common, usually in order to avoid the effect of the right of survivorship. (A legal joint tenancy cannot be severed.) Severance occurs either by statutory written notice under s 36(2) of the LPA 1925; or by the act of a co-owner operating on his own share (for example, mortgaging it); or where the joint tenants decide to sever by 'mutual agreement'; or where an intention to sever is manifested by the 'mutual conduct' of the joint tenants.

CHAPTER 5

SUCCESSIVE INTERESTS IN LAND

5.1 What is successive ownership of land?

In the previous chapter, we examined one way in which two or more persons could share in the ownership of land: viz, the simultaneous enjoyment of land by two or more people under the law of concurrent co-ownership. There is another method by which two or more people can have 'ownership' rights over land at the same time, albeit that (unlike concurrent co-ownership) only one of them is entitled to immediate physical possession of the property. This is the law relating to successive ownership of land, whereby one person has an estate in the land for life and another, or others, have rights which 'fall into' possession after the life interest has ended. For example, it was once quite common for property to be left to one person for their life, then to another, then to another, and so on, as where Blackacre is left to A for life, with remainder to B for life, remainder to C in fee simple. In such a case, A has a life interest in possession (and is known, somewhat confusingly, as the 'life tenant'), B has a life interest in remainder (and will be the life tenant when A dies) and C has a fee simple in remainder (and will become the absolute owner on the death of A and B). The reason for creating successive interests in land was primarily to 'keep land in the family' by limiting its ownership to successive heirs (for example, my son, my son's son, etc), although it could also be used for business or commercial arrangements.

5.2 Successive interests: in general

The Trusts of Land and Appointment of Trustees Act (TOLATA) 1996 has had a profound impact on the law relating to successive interests in land. Prior to the Act, there were two methods of creating successive interests: first, under a settlement (or strict settlement, as it is known) governed by the Settled Land Act (SLA) 1925; and secondly, under a trust for sale governed by the Law of Property Act (LPA) 1925. However, now that the TOLATA 1996 has come into force (1 January 1997), the picture has changed dramatically. The TOLATA 1996 changes fundamentally the way in which successive interests can, in future, be created (that is, as from 1 January 1997), with the express aim of simplifying the law and making dealings with land subject to life interests more transparent. The principal effects of the TOLATA 1996 are as follows:

(a) it has not been possible to create any new strict settlements since 1 January 1997. The concept has been abandoned for all new successive interests (s 2). The obvious consequence is that no new land can be made subject to the regime of the SLA 1925, and, over time, the influence of this creaking statutory regime will diminish;

(b) existing strict settlements will remain effective and be governed by the SLA 1925 (s 2) as will resettlements of existing settled land. Inevitably, however, much existing settled land will fall into absolute ownership (that is, all the life interests will terminate on the death of the life tenants), and the land will cease to be 'settled land'. Note, however, that if the 'old' settlement is perpetuated by the creation of new life interests *before* the termination of the existing settlement, the land continues to be 'settled land' and remains subject to the SLA 1925. If, by way of contrast, the settlement does indeed terminate, and no land or heirlooms remain subject to it, any subsequent attempt to create a life interest in that land really is a 'new' creation, and will be governed by the TOLATA 1996;

(c) all new attempts to create successive interests in land must take effect under the rubric of the 'trust of land' (largely replacing the trust of sale) as specified in the TOLATA 1996 (ss 4 and 5). However, even though all 'new' successive interests will be governed by the TOLATA 1996, and most will be 'pure' trusts of land, it remains possible to create expressly a 'trust for sale' to regulate successive interests on or after 1 January 1997. Yet, as noted in Chapter 4, even if the settlor chooses to use a trust for sale as the device for regulating successive interests, it will still be governed by the TOLATA 1996, and the practical differences between it and a 'pure' trust of land are minimal. (For example, the definition of a 'trust of land' includes a trust for sale of land: s 1 of the TOLATA 1996.) It is very doubtful whether many (indeed any?) express trusts for sale will be created after December 1996 as, under the TOLATA 1996, very little would be gained;

(d) for those *existing* successive interests not governed by the SLA 1925 – being those created deliberately as 'trusts for sale' – TOLATA 1996 will now apply and they will be governed by the 'trust of land' rubric. If the successive interest trust for sale has been created expressly, technically, it will continue to be a 'trust for sale', albeit subject to the TOLATA 1996. If the trust for sale arose by operation of statute, it will be converted into a 'pure' trust of land. In fact, the practical differences between the concept of a 'pure' trust of land and a 'trust for sale' trust of land are likely to prove minimal: the important point is that the successive interest is governed by the TOLATA 1996.

5.2.1 Successive interests under the Trusts of Land and Appointment of Trustees Act 1996

As we have seen in the previous chapter, the TOLATA 1996 abolished the concept of the trust for sale and replaces it with the trust of land. Furthermore, as noted above, the Act also ensures that all future successive interests shall take effect as trusts of land under the TOLATA 1996 rubric. In fact, the great majority of the provisions of the TOLATA 1996 will be more applicable to cases of successive ownership of land than for concurrent co-ownership (Chapter 4).

This is because, in cases of successive ownership, it is likely (indeed, almost inevitable) that the trustees of the land will be completely different persons from the person who is to occupy the land for life (the life tenant), or the persons who are entitled in remainder should the life tenant die. The trustees may well be a bank or independent advisers, and the life tenant will be the person most intimately connected with the land – say, the eldest son of the settlor (he who created the successive interests). Necessarily, in such typical cases of successive interests, the life tenant will usually wish to occupy the land (not the trustees: see s 12 of the TOLATA 1996), and the life tenant may be exactly the person who should exercise the powers given to the trustees under the TOLATA 1996 in order to manage the land effectively – hence the trustees' ability to delegate their powers under s 9 of the TOLATA 1996. The trustees will hold a 'watching brief', and allow the tenant for life to use the land as befits his limited ownership. To sum up then, for successive interests created on or after 1 January 1997 and for those previously existing as 'trusts for sale', the legal regime governing control and use of the land is that found in the TOLATA 1996. The principal features of this regime are as follows:

(a) first, as noted above, it will not be possible to create new strict settlements of land and the entailed interest is abolished (s 2 and Sched 1). All future successive interests will operate under the umbrella of the trust of land. Existing settlements will remain valid. All successive interests by way of trust for sale are converted into trusts of land. The net effect of this reform is that there is to be one set of rules governing the creation and operation of successive interests, the only exception being pre-1 January 1997 strict settlements which will continue to operate under the SLA 1925 until expiry;

(b) secondly, the doctrine of conversion is abolished, effective for all new and nearly all existing trusts of land (s 3). The doctrine of conversion was an ancient property law doctrine applicable to certain property concepts whereby the interests of the persons entitled (for example, in our case, the life tenant) were treated not as interests in the relevant land, but as interests in the proceeds of sale of that land. Hence, the rights were technically 'personalty' and not 'realty'. Thus, a will leaving 'my personal property' to X, would actually pass the interests so converted, even though they *looked* like interests in land. Its abolition means, in effect that the interests of persons under the trust of land (including expressly created trusts for sale) are to be regarded as interests in the land, rather than its monetary equivalent. As is the case with concurrent co-ownership (Chapter 4), this is more a recognition of reality than a change likely to have wide ranging effects. The exception is for trusts for sale created by a will of a person dying before 1 January 1997 for the simple reason that such a testator may have ordered his affairs precisely on the basis that the doctrine of conversion was applicable;

(c) thirdly, the legal title to the land will be vested in the trustees and they will have all the powers of an absolute owner: s 6(1) of the TOLATA 1996.

The life tenant and persons entitled in remainder will have equitable interests in the land. However, the trustees' powers are given in virtue of their status as trustees and consequently are subject to the general equitable jurisdiction in relation to the exercise of trustees' powers. More specifically, the trustees may delegate certain powers to the life tenant (or other person) and their powers may be restricted by the instrument that establishes the trust (see generally ss 6–9 of the TOLATA 1996). Given that trusts concerning successive interests are usually created deliberately and with considerable formality, it is likely that the trustees will intend from the outset to delegate powers of management of the land to the tenant for life, including the power of sale. However, only the trustees can give a valid receipt for purchase money, hence preserving their role in overreaching;

(d) fourthly, the trustees must consult with the persons interested in the successive interests, both the life tenant and persons entitled in remainder. They should give effect to their wishes in so far as is consistent with the purposes of the trust of land (s 11. This raises similar issues to those considered in relation to concurrent co-ownership considered in Chapter 4);

(e) fifthly, the trustees' powers may be made subject to the consent of the equitable owners (for example, the life tenant, persons entitled in remainder), but only if stated in the instrument creating the trusts (ss 8 and 10) or if imposed by the court under a s 14 of the TOLATA 1996 application. This may have consequences when a sale is proposed. Given the formality attending creations of successive interests, it is quite likely that consent requirements will be imposed. In this respect, it is worth noting that it is quite difficult for successive interest trusts of land to be created accidentally, although this can sometimes be the result of a successful claim of constructive trust or proprietary estoppel, as contemplated by *Ungarian v Lesnoff* (1990) (see Chapter 4, constructive trust) and *Dent v Dent* (1996) (see Chapter 9, proprietary estoppel);

(f) sixthly, the successive interest trust of land is subject to the same overreaching machinery as concurrent co-ownership trusts of land. This is because the interests of the life tenant and persons entitled in remainder are equitable interests, and the legal title is held by the trustees, for example, where Z Bank plc holds land on trust for A for life, remainder to B. Necessarily, on sale of the land, it is the trustees who will have to transfer the legal title and it will be the beneficiaries (for example, life tenants) who are susceptible to being defeated by a purchaser from the trustees under the overreaching machinery. If the overreaching process is successful, the equitable interests will take effect in the purchase money: for example, the tenant for life will receive the income from the capital sum for life, balance to the person entitled in remainder on the death of that life tenant. This works in the same way as for concurrent co-ownership, considered in Chapter 4. However, should overreaching not occur (as in a rare case of there being only one trustee of a *successive* interest trust for land), whether these equitable interests bind the purchaser is determined by the application of normal principles of registered or unregistered conveyancing. In registered land, the interests of the beneficiaries, under a TOLATA 1996 successive interest trust, can be protected as either a minor interest or as an overriding interest (of course, assuming no overreaching). In unregistered land, such an interest cannot be a land charge (s 2 of the Land Charges Act 1972), so may take effect against a purchaser according to the doctrine of notice (assuming no overreaching). In essence, the position is the same as with concurrent co-ownership interests considered in the previous chapter, and the ability of the trustees to overreach is subject to the same considerations as those prevailing for concurrent trusts of land (see Chapter 4), including issues as to the effectiveness of consent requirements;

(g) seventhly, in addition to the overreaching provisions, the purchaser of land subject to a successive trust of land is given protection should the trustees sell the land in breach of their functions, or in breach of the provisions of the TOLATA 1996 (see s 16 of the Act). In general terms for unregistered land, the answer depends on the particular provision violated by the trustees. In some cases (for example, violation of the duty to consult), it seems that the purchaser will obtain a good title, assuming overreaching. In these circumstances, the remedy of the beneficiaries lies against the trustees personally. In other cases, (for example, non-compliance with a consent requirement), the purchase will obtain a clean title, assuming overreaching, providing he did not have actual notice of the relevant limitation (s 16 of the TOLATA 1996). In registered land, it is assumed that the limitation on the trustees' powers (if any) will be entered on the register of title by way of restriction, thus preventing any disposition by the trustees unless the limitation is complied with. Necessarily, this will prevent a purchaser buying the land at all unless the restriction is complied with. If for some very unusual reason (for example, a solicitor's failure to act properly), the limitation on the trustees powers is not entered on the register, it seems likely that a purchaser will still obtain a clear title free of such interests if overreaching occurs. Although this result has been contested (see Chapter 4), it is consistent with the purposes of the legislation. If overreaching does not occur, then the normal rules concerning the bindingness of third party rights in registered land would prevail;

(h) eighthly, the tenant for life has a right to occupy the property (s 12). The persons entitled in remainder may have a right to occupy (see s 12(1)(a) and (b) and s 12(2) of the TOLATA 1996), but this would almost certainly be restricted under s 13. Compensation may be ordered for exclusive use of the land by one co-owner, for example, the life tenant might be ordered to pay a sum equivalent to the market rent of the land, or some proportion thereof;

(i) lastly, any person with an interest in the land can make an application to the court under s 14 for a variety or orders – for example, sale, no sale, override consent requirement, impose consent requirements. The criteria specified in s 15 do not apply in cases of bankruptcy, see s 335A of the Insolvency Act 1986.

5.3 Successive interests under the old regime: the strict settlement

As is now clear, in general terms, the law of strict settlements will apply only to those successive interest trusts created before the entry into force of the TOLATA 1996. Necessarily, this means that the complicated rules of the SLA 1925 will become less important. They are discussed below. Points of comparison with the regime of the TOLATA 1996 1996 should be kept in mind during this analysis.

The 'strict settlement' is not a creation of the 1925 property legislation and, indeed, one of the reasons for the SLA 1925 was to reform and regulate the pre-1926 rules which had previously governed the creation and operation of successive interests in land. That said, it is to the SLA 1925 that we must look for a comprehensive statement of the pre-TOLATA 1996 law. Unfortunately, the SLA 1925 – and the substantive law – are quite complicated, and it is not an accident that the strict settlement was, for many years, rarely deliberately created or that it has now been abolished for new successive interests.

In general terms, a 'strict settlement' exists when land is left on trust (not being a trust for sale) for someone for life, with remainder to another, perhaps also with provision by way of rentcharges for the payment of a regular income to someone else (for example, the widow of the 'settlor', that being the person who created the settlement). However, this is a simplified definition, and ss 1 and 2 of the SLA 1925 define 'settled land' in much more precise terms. Thus, according to the SLA 1925, and bearing in mind that this is not effective after the TOLATA 1996, settled land was either:

(a) land 'limited in trust for any persons by way of succession'; or

(b) land 'limited in trust for any person in possession' for an entailed interest (that is, a fee tail, now abolished – TOLATA 1996), for an infant, for a determinable fee, or for a fee simple subject to an executory limitation; or

(c) land limited in trust for any person for an estate that was contingent upon the happening of any event; or

(d) land which was charged by way of a family arrangement with the payment of any sums for the benefit of any persons (for example, *Re Austen* (1929)).

Importantly, land which was subject to 'an immediate binding trust for sale' (s 1(7) of the SLA 1925) is excluded from the definition of settled land and falls outside the SLA 1925. Such land is already governed by the LPA 1925 and the TOLATA 1996 and now takes effect behind a trust of land.

There is no denying that this appears to be complicated, but the essential point to remember is that settled land is land where the estate of the owner in possession is 'limited' in some way. Thus, either the owner's interest is limited to his life, or is tied to the happening of an event, or is charged with the payment of money.

5.3.1 The essential characteristics of settled land

Settled land is land held on trust. Consequently, there will be 'trustees of the settlement', and beneficiaries under the settlement. These beneficiaries may be the owner of a life interest and those persons entitled in remainder, that is, after the life interest has expired. The settlement will have been created by the settlor, by deed, and this deed will usually identify the trustees. Under the SLA 1925, a range of persons are given statutory powers to deal with the land and it is important to remember that the major purpose behind the grant of these powers is to ensure that the land itself can be freely dealt with: in other words, that the land is alienable and does not get tied up in the settlement. As with concurrent co-ownership, if the land is sold, the rights and interests of the beneficiaries will be transferred to the purchase money via the mechanism of overreaching.

5.3.2 The specific attributes of settled land

The person under the settlement who is of full age, and entitled to immediate possession of the settled land (or the whole income from it), is generally regarded as the 'tenant for life' (s 19 of the SLA 1925).

The tenant for life is holder of the legal estate in the land, and he holds that legal estate on trust for the beneficiaries under the settlement (ss 4 and 107 of the SLA 1925). In the great majority of cases, this tenant for life is also the person entitled to an equitable life interest in the property. In other words, the tenant for life often has two roles: holder of the legal estate in the land and owner of an equitable, but limited, ownership, such as a life interest. It is no accident that the person in possession of the land should have the legal title. Before 1925, that legal title could be vested in several trustees, or split up among several beneficiaries, and this made dealing with settled land a painful process. Under the SLA 1925, the legal title is vested solely in the tenant for life, for they are the person in immediate possession of the land, and they are the person who may best judge how to deal with it.

The tenant for life exercises most of the important statutory powers to deal with the settled land. These are found in Pt II of the SLA 1925 and effectively place the tenant for life in control of the land, and it is in his hands that the power to manage it for the best interests of all the beneficiaries is to be found. Thus, the strict settlement was ideally suited to 'family' property arrangements, where the present occupier of the land could have been expected to manage it for the good of the family with, of course, the ability to deal with the land (and sell it) if the need should arise.

There are also 'trustees of the settlement' and, although they rarely hold the legal title to the land, they exercise general supervisory functions over the settlement (*Wheelwright v Walker* (1883)). It is their responsibility to ensure that the rights and interests of all the beneficiaries under the settlement are protected, especially if the tenant for life misuses his statutory powers. The identity of the trustees is determined according to s 30 of the SLA 1925, although they will usually be named as such in the trust deeds.

If the person with the statutory powers chooses to sell the settled land, the interests of the beneficiaries are overreached *if* the purchase money is paid to the trustees of the settlement (who must be two in number, or a trust corporation), or into court. If overreaching occurs, the purchaser need not concern himself with the equitable interests, because these take effect in the purchase money: the 'curtain principle'. The purchaser obtains a clean and unencumbered title to the land. If overreaching does not occur, the tenant for life cannot make a good title to the purchaser, and the purchaser may be bound by the equitable interests according to the provisions of the SLA 1925.

5.3.3 The creation of strict settlements under the Settled Land Act 1925

Under the SLA 1925, all strict settlements must be created by two deeds: a 'trust instrument' and a 'principal vesting deed' (ss 4 and 5 of the SLA 1925). The trust instrument declares the details of the settlement, appoints the trustees of it, and sets out any powers conferred by the settlement that are in addition to those provided automatically in the Act. The principal vesting deed is less comprehensive and describes the settled land itself, names the trustees, states the nature of any additional powers and, most importantly of all, declares that the settled land is vested in the person to whom the land is conveyed (the tenant for life) on the trusts of the settlement. The principal vesting deed is, in one sense, the statement of ownership of the tenant for life and it is with this that any purchaser will be concerned, not least because the equitable interests detailed in the trust instrument will be swept off the land by overreaching.

5.3.4 The position of the tenant for life and the statutory powers

As indicated above, the tenant for life is given statutory powers to deal with the land. These powers are subject to various controls, usually overseen by the trustees of the settlement, in order to prevent the tenant for life from taking advantage of his dominant position. Certain controls are specific to certain powers, and these are noted below where appropriate; furthermore, the tenant for life is trustee of his powers and must have regard to the interests of the other beneficiaries when he exercises them (s 107 of the SLA 1925):

(a) the tenant for life has power to sell the settled land, or to exchange it for other land (s 38 of the SLA 1925). However, he must obtain the best price that can be reasonably obtained and a court will take action to ensure this (*Wheelwright v Walker (No 2)* (1883)). This power is subject to the written notice procedure, as considered below, 5.3.5;

(b) the tenant for life has power to grant and accept leases of the land, although, for certain specific types of lease, the duration of the lease which the tenant for life may grant is limited (ss 41 and 53 of the SLA 1925). This power is also subject to the notice procedure;

(c) the tenant for life may mortgage or charge the land in order to raise money for specific purposes, these generally being purposes which would benefit the land *per se*, rather than any individual owner (s 71). This power is also subject to the notice procedure;

(d) the tenant for life may grant options over the land, including granting a person an option to purchase the land, or an option to purchase a lease (s 51). This power is also subject to the notice procedure;

(e) the tenant for life has various ancillary powers in relation to the settled land. This includes the power to dispose of the principal mansion house (s 65 of the SLA 1925), the power to cut and sell timber (s 66 of the SLA 1925), the power to compromise claims concerning the settled land (s 58 of the SLA 1925), and the power to sell and purchase chattels and family heirlooms (s 67 of the SLA 1925). These powers are subject to the tenant for life obtaining, variously, the consent of the trustees of the settlement or the leave of the court;

(f) the tenant for life may effect any other transaction for the benefit of the settled land under order of the court (s 64 of the SLA 1925);

(g) the trust deeds of the settlement may expressly confer additional powers on the tenant for life.

5.3.5 The role of the trustees of the settlement in regulating the powers of the tenant for life

It has been indicated already that a major role of the 'trustees of the settlement' is to act in a general supervisory function in order to safeguard the rights of all persons entitled to an interest in the land. In addition to this, the most important powers of the tenant for life are subject to the provisions of s 101 of the SLA 1925. Under s 101, a tenant for life who intends to make a sale, exchange, lease, mortgage, or charge in respect of the land, or to grant an option over it, must give written notice to each of the trustees by registered post, and to the solicitor for the trustees, of his intention to exercise one of these powers. Each notice must be posted not less than one month before the sale, mortgage, etc, and, if there are currently no trustees of the settlement, these powers cannot be exercised (*Wheelwright v Walker* (1883)).

These provisions are designed to ensure that the trustees are aware of all proposed major dealings with the land and are ready to activate the overreaching mechanism where appropriate. However, although at first sight this notice procedure appears perfectly adequate to protect all beneficiaries, the SLA 1925 itself weakens this protection considerably. Thus, a trustee is under no obligation to interfere with a proposed dealing with the settled land of which he has notice (*England v Public Trustee* (1967)) and, except for the power to mortgage or charge, the tenant for life may give notice of a general intention to exercise these powers, rather than specific notice on each occasion (s 101(2)). Furthermore, the trustees may, in writing, waive the notice requirement, or accept less than one month's notice (s 101(4)) and, importantly, a person dealing with the tenant for life in good faith is not required to inquire whether these procedural safeguards have been observed (s 101(5)).

5.3.6 The fiduciary position of the tenant for life

According to s 107 of the SLA 1925, the tenant for life is trustee of his statutory powers for those entitled under the settlement, and 'shall' have regard to their interests when exercising those powers. This is meant to give further protection to those entitled to either the land or its monetary equivalent after the current tenant for life has departed. It has some practical consequences, albeit of a limited nature. For example, if the tenant for life sells the settled land, he must sell as fairly as a trustee would sell, which, effectively means for the best price reasonably obtainable paying due regard to the interests of the people entitled in remainder (*Wheelwright v Walker* (1883)). Moreover, the tenant for life cannot accept and keep a payment for exercising the powers because, as a trustee, he is under a duty not to profit from his trust (*Chandler v Bradley* (1897)). However, once again, the protection against a dishonest tenant for life is quite shallow, for it is clear that a court will not invalidate a sale simply because the tenant for life sells the property for a bad motive, or even if the tenant for life is simply uninterested in managing the land (*Cardigan v Curzon-Howe* (1885)).

5.3.7 Attempts to restrict the powers of the tenant for life

It should be apparent from the above that the tenant for life really is in control of the settled land, and that the statutory powers he is given are not subject to serious control either by the trustees of the settlement or under the general law of trusts. Consequently, there is a temptation for settlors to attempt to control or restrict the tenant for life in the exercise of his powers by inserting some express limitation clause in the deeds of the settlement. Unfortunately, this cuts against the philosophy of the SLA 1925 which was designed to prevent just this sort of control being exercised over the settled land by the 'dead hand' of the settlor. Therefore, according to s 106 of the SLA 1925, any provision inserted in a settlement which purports or attempts to forbid a tenant for life to exercise a statutory power, or any provision which attempts, tends or is intended to induce the tenant for life not to exercise those powers, is void, as in *Re Patten* (1929). Likewise, in *Re Orlebar* (1936), the court discussed a so called 'residence condition', which stipulated that the tenant for life should lose his interest under the settlement if he ceased to occupy the land, and said that there would be no forfeiture of that interest if he left the land because of the exercise of a statutory power (although not if he left for another reason).

Obviously, s 106 is a very powerful statutory provision and it is largely effective to prevent settlors avoiding the policy of the SLA 1925 by special drafting of the settlement. However, in *Re Aberconway* (1953), a majority of the court held that, if that which might be lost to the tenant for life through such a provision was not a benefit to him, s 106 did not apply to make that provision void, although according to the dissenting voice of Lord Denning anything which even 'tended' to restrict the tenant for life in the exercise of his powers was void. Indeed, Lord Denning's view does seem more consistent with the overall policy of the Act, and with the words of s 106 itself. It is echoed in s 104, whereby any contract entered into by the tenant for life himself not to exercise a statutory power is void.

5.3.8 Protection for the beneficiaries

In a very general sense, the beneficiaries under the settlement are protected by both the notice procedures discussed above, the general supervisory role of the trustees of the settlement, and the overreaching machinery, especially if all they are concerned with is the income which the land may generate rather than the land itself.

More importantly, a very powerful provision is found in s 13 of the SLA 1925. As noted above, each settlement will be constructed via two deeds: the trust instrument and the vesting deed. Under s 13, if no vesting deed has been executed in favour of the tenant for life, any proposed dealing *inter vivos* by him with the legal estate operates only as a contract to carry out that transaction: it does not transfer the legal title to the prospective purchaser. In other words, in the absence of a vesting deed, dealings with the legal title are paralysed, except in four specified cases, the most important of which is a sale, etc, to a purchaser of a legal estate without notice of the absence of the vesting deed. Simply put, the absence of a vesting deed makes it difficult for the tenant for life to deal with the land. However, if he sells that land in violation of the settlement to an innocent purchaser (as most will be), that purchaser will obtain good legal title to the land. Once a vesting deed has been executed, s 13 no longer applies, and the beneficiaries must fall back on s 18 of the SLA 1925.

Under s 18 of the SLA 1925, once a vesting deed has been executed, and until the settlement is discharged, any transaction which is not 'authorised' by the SLA 1925 or other statute is void. Thus, any sale or mortgage, etc, by the tenant for life outside his statutory powers is ineffective to convey legal title to the land, and operates only to convey the tenant for life's own equitable interest (*Weston v Henshaw* (1950)).

5.3.9 Protection for the purchaser of settled land

Once again, in a general sense, the purchaser of settled land is protected by the overreaching machinery. He need be concerned only with the vesting deed and can rely on the interests of the beneficiaries being overreached. However, of course, things can, and do, go wrong. To meet this situation, s 110 of the SLA 1925 provides that a purchaser who deals in good faith with the tenant for life is, vis à vis the beneficiaries, deemed to have paid the best price and to have complied with all the requirements of the Act. Although it is sometimes thought that this provision sits uneasily with s 18 (which voids all unauthorised transactions), it seems that s 110 is concerned with matters of detail, not of principle. Thus, s 110 will not protect a purchaser if the transaction with the tenant for life is wholly unauthorised (s 18), but will protect him if there are omissions of detail in an authorised transaction (*Re Morgan's Lease* (1972)).

5.3.10 The overreaching machinery

Equitable interests under strict settlements are capable of being overreached on a sale of the settled land (s 2 of the LPA 1925). If successful, overreaching will confer legal title on a purchaser free of all equitable interests under the settlement. Of course, no legal rights are capable of being overreached and with three minor exceptions (annuities, limited owner's charge, general equitable charge), neither are any equitable interests created prior to the settlement. As with all overreaching, the capital purchase money must be paid to at least two trustees (of the settlement) or a trust corporation. Failure to overreach may result in the purported transaction being void or the equitable interests binding the purchaser under the normal rules of registered or unregistered conveyancing save that equitable interests under a SLA 1925 settlement of registered land cannot be overriding interests – s 86(2) of the LRA 1925. Usually, such rights (in registered land) will be protected by the entry of a restriction on the register of title.

5.3.11 The duties of the trustees of the settlement

The supervisory duties of the trustees of the settlement, and their role in regulating the tenant for life in the exercise of his statutory powers, have been mentioned already. In addition to this, the SLA 1925 gives the trustees other responsibilities, not least, receipt of the capital sum in order to facilitate overreaching. More specifically, the trustees may actually act as 'statutory owner' (with all the powers of a tenant for life) if there is no tenant for life, or the tenant for life is an infant and, under s 24 of the SLA 1925, the court may authorise the trustees to exercise the powers of the tenant for life (in his name) if the tenant has ceased to have a substantial *interest* in the land, or has refused (but not merely neglected) to exercise those powers (*Re 90 Thornhill Road* (1970)).

5.4 The trust of land

The second method of regulating successive interests in land was the trust for sale. Although trusts for sale *expressly* created before or after 1 January 1997 may continue to exist in name, they will take effect under the TOLATA 1996. Further, any such trusts which had been or will be imposed by statute will become the 'pure' trust of land, subject to an identical TOLATA 1996 regime. Consequently, in terms of pre-1997 law, the 'other' method of creating a trust for successive interests (the old trust for sale) comes under the new TOLATA 1996 regime. This has been discussed above, and reference also should be made to Chapter 4.

5.5 A comparison between the old strict settlement under the Settled Land Act 1925 and the new Trusts of Land and Appointment of Trustees Act 1996 regime

As noted at the outset of this chapter, pre-1997 existing successive interest trusts for sale, and all new attempts to create successive interests in land, will take effect under the TOLATA 1996. This is regardless of whether they take effect as the 'pure' trust of land (likely for all new trusts), or whether they retain their 'trust for sale' status, having been created as such expressly. Again, as noted above, the difference between the two is minimal, as it is the provisions of the TOLATA 1996 that are important and these apply equally. In order to appreciate more fully the difference that the obligatory application of the TOLATA 1996 will make to the law of successive interests, a comparison with the 'old' strict settlement of the SLA 1925 is appropriate:

(a) settled land is governed by the complicated provisions of the SLA 1925. The trust of land under the TOLATA 1996 is relatively easy to understand and operate (and this includes expressly created trusts for sale). The abolition of the strict settlement for new successive interests should mean less litigation and less cost;

(b) the strict settlement was ideally suited to keeping land 'in the family', especially where the tenant for life may have wished to occupy the land and consequently refused to exercise his power of sale. This was perfectly legitimate, even if those entitled on his death saw the value of their prospective interests dwindle. The new machinery can ensure occupation by interested persons (that is, the tenant for life), but also has the flexibility to ensure that land is sold if this is in the best interests of every equitable owner (see s 14 of the TOLATA 1996);

(c) under a strict settlement, the tenant for life has legal title and is in effective control of the land. Under the TOLATA 1996, the trustees have legal title, and have all the powers of an absolute owner. They will control the land unless they choose to delegate to the person with the life interest or other person. They will not divest themselves of legal title unless the land subject to the trust is sold;

(d) the tenant for life under the SLA 1925 is constrained by the fact that his powers and the legal estate are held on trust. Moreover, certain powers are subject to notice procedures, consent of the trustees of the settlement, etc. The trustees under the TOLATA 1996 are obliged to consult the beneficiaries (for example, person with life interest), and should endeavour to give effect to his wishes. But, they are not bound to do so. Under the TOLATA 1996, the trustees may have delegated their powers irrevocably, and may be subject to consent requirements;

(e) on the death of a life tenant under a strict settlement, the legal estate can be transferred only by means of the expensive and time consuming process of obtaining a vesting deed. On the death of a trustee of land under the TOLATA 1996, legal title simply accrues to the remaining trustees under the right of survivorship. No cost, no documents and no fuss;

(f) the position of a purchaser of land subject to a strict settlement was not always clear, but was generally quite favourable. Under the TOLATA 1996, a purchaser may be bound by equitable interests if overreaching does not occur.

SUCCESSIVE INTERESTS IN LAND

What is successive ownership of land?

Successive ownership of land occurs when one person has an estate in the land for life and another (or others) has (have) rights which 'fall into' possession after the 'life interest' has ended. There are two ways in which land can be held subject to successive interests. First, for successive interests created before 1 January 1997, a settlement (or 'strict settlement') may be used. Such land is called *settled land* and falls within the machinery of the SLA 1925. Secondly, for successive interests created on or after 1 January 1997, the TOLATA 1996 requires that a trust of land be used. No new strict settlements can be created after this date, save for resettlements of existing settled land.

The strict settlement and settled land

A 'strict settlement' will exist in a number of (complicated) circumstances, but the most common are where land is 'limited in trust for any persons by way of succession' or where land which is charged by way of a family arrangement with the payment of any sums for the benefit of any persons.

The essential characteristics of settled land

The person under the settlement who is of full age and entitled to immediate possession of the settled land (or the whole income from it) is generally regarded as the 'tenant for life' (s 19 of the SLA 1925). The tenant for life is holder of the legal estate and holds that estate on trust for the beneficiaries under the settlement (ss 4 and 107 of the SLA 1925). The tenant for life exercises most of the important statutory powers to deal with the settled land. These effectively place the tenant for life in control of the land. There are also 'trustees of the settlement' and they exercise general supervisory functions over the settlement. Where the person with the statutory powers chooses to sell the settled land, the interests of the beneficiaries are overreached *if* the purchase money is paid to the trustees of the settlement (who must be two in number or a trust corporation) or into court.

The position of the tenant for life and the statutory powers

The tenant for life will usually have various powers to deal with the settled land, including the power to sell it, grant a lease of it and mortgage it for specific purposes. These powers are subject to the consent of the trustees of the settlement or the leave of the court, although the tenant for life may effect any other transaction for the benefit of the settled land under order of the court (s 64 of the SLA 1925). The trusts of the settlement may expressly confer additional powers on the tenant for life. Under s 106 of the SLA 1925), any provision inserted in the settlement which purports or attempts to forbid a tenant for life to exercise a statutory power, or any provision which attempts, tends or is intended to induce the tenant for life not to exercise those powers, is void.

The role of the trustees of the settlement in regulating the powers of the tenant for life

Under s 101 of the SLA 1925, a tenant for life who intends to make a sale, exchange, lease, mortgage, or charge in respect of the land, or to grant an option over it, must give written notice to each of the trustees by registered post and to the solicitor for the trustees of his intention to exercise one of these powers.

The fiduciary position of the tenant for life

Under s 107 of the SLA 1925, the tenant for life is trustee of his statutory powers for those entitled under the settlement and 'shall' have regard to their interests when exercising those powers.

Protection for the beneficiaries

In addition to the notice procedure, the general supervisory role of the trustees of the settlement and the overreaching machinery, the beneficiaries are protected by ss 13 and 18 of the SLA 1925 that can paralyse dealings with the land in certain circumstances.

Protection for the purchaser of settled land

Section 110 of the SLA 1925 provides that a purchaser who deals in good faith with the tenant for life is, vis à vis the beneficiaries, deemed to have paid the best price and to have complied with all of the requirements of the Act. This is concerned with matters of detail and s 110 will not protect a purchaser if the transaction with the tenant for life is wholly unauthorised (s 18).

The overreaching machinery

Equitable interests under strict settlements are capable of being overreached on a sale of the settled land (s 2 of the LPA 1925). No legal rights are capable of being overreached.

The trust of land and the TOLATA

The TOLATA 1996 regulates all successive interests of land (except resettlements) created on or after 1 January 1997. Legal title is vested in the trustees who have all the powers to deal with the land. The life tenant and others entitled will have equitable interests. The trustees may delegate their powers (except the power to overreach) to any person and may well give some powers to the person in occupation of the land, usually the tenant for life. The trustees must consult the beneficiaries before dealing with the land, but only in limited circumstances will they have to obtain the consent of the beneficiaries before exercising their powers. The tenant for life (and other beneficiaries) has a right to occupy the land, although this can be excluded. Usually, only the tenant for life will occupy. A sale (including a mortgage) by the trustees will overreach the equitable owners, providing the conditions for statutory overreaching are met. Any person interested in the trust of land may apply to the court under s 14 of the TOLATA 1996 for an order concerning the land.

CHAPTER 6

LEASES

6.1 The nature of a lease

The leasehold is one of the two estates identified in s 1 of the Law of Property Act (LPA) 1925 as capable of existing as either a 'legal' or 'equitable' interest. As we shall see, whether any given lease is legal or equitable will depend primarily on the way in which it is created. However, irrespective of whether a leasehold is legal or equitable, there is no doubt that it is one of the most versatile concepts known to the law of real property. Even the terminology of leases reflects the many purposes to which they may be put. The 'term of years', 'tenancy', 'sublease' and 'leasehold estate' are all terms in common use, and all of them describe the existence of a 'landlord' and 'tenant' relationship. For example, a 'lease' or 'term of years' is most often used to describe a commercial or long term letting, whereas the description 'tenancy' is used for residential or short term lets. This variety does not mean that different substantive rules apply to different types of lease (although this may be the case where a statute applies only to one kind of lease), but it does indicate the importance that the leasehold plays in the world of commercial and residential property management. In this respect, three fundamental features of the leasehold should be noted at the outset.

First, the leasehold allows two or more persons to enjoy the benefits of owning an estate in the same piece of land at the same time: the freeholder will receive the rent and profits, and the leaseholder will enjoy physical possession and occupation of the property. Indeed, if a 'subtenancy' (also known as an 'underlease') is created, being where a shorter lease is carved out of the 'headlease', the number of people enjoying the land or its fruits increases further. For example, if a freeholder (A) grants a 99 year lease to B, and B grants a 50 year subtenancy to C, then A receives rent from B, B receives rent from C and C enjoys physical possession of the land. In theory, there is no limit to the number of underleases that can be created out of a freehold estate, and each intermediate person will be the tenant of their superior landlord and the landlord of their own tenant. It is the ability of the leasehold to facilitate this multiple enjoyment of land that gives it its unique character. It allows the landlord to generate an income through rent (and so, land may be an investment vehicle), while, at the same time, the tenant 'buys' an estate in land through the payment of that rent.

Secondly, it is in principle inherent in the leasehold estate that both the landlord and tenant (and all subtenants) have a proprietary right in the land (but see the discussion of *Bruton v London and Quadrant Housing Trust* (1999), below). Thus, the tenant owns the lease, and the landlord owns the 'reversion expectant on the lease' (that is, the right to possession of the property when the lease ends). Importantly, both of these proprietary rights can be sold or transferred after the lease is created. The tenant may sell his lease to a person who becomes the new tenant (an assignee of the lease), and the landlord may sell his reversion to a person who becomes the new landlord (an assignee of the reversion). Again, the assignees of the lease and reversion may assign their interests further. The result is that the current landlord and tenant under a lease may be far removed from the original landlord and tenant who actually negotiated its creation. Nevertheless, as explained below, the landlord and tenant currently 'in possession' may well be bound by the terms of the lease as originally agreed. Figure 1 represents this diagrammatically.

Figure 1

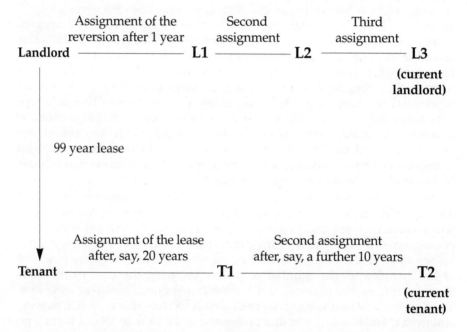

Thirdly, all leases will contain covenants (or promises) whereby the landlord and tenant promise to do, or not to do, certain things in relation to the land. These may either be 'express covenants', as where they are agreed between landlord and tenant and written deliberately into the lease, 'implied covenants', being covenants read into the lease as a matter of law (for example, the repairing covenant implied in certain leases by s 11 of the Landlord and Tenant Act 1985) or 'usual' covenants being those that are not expressly mentioned but are so common in the landlord and tenant relationship that they are taken to be part of the lease (for example, the tenant's obligation to pay rent under an equitable lease: *Shiloh Spinners v Harding* (1973)). Typical examples of express covenants are the landlord's covenant to repair the buildings and the tenant's covenant to pay rent or not to carry on a trade on the premises. All these types of covenant are enforceable between the original landlord and tenant and, as we shall see, also between assignees of the lease or reversion. The particular rules concerning the enforceability of leasehold covenants are discussed below, 6.4, but the important point is that the ability to make rights and obligations 'run' with the land is a special feature of the landlord and tenant relationship. It is the reason why the leasehold estate is a particularly useful investment vehicle because the freeholder can generate an income while, at the same time, preserving the value of the land through properly drafted covenants (for example, that the tenant must repair, may not keep pets, etc), which will bind the original tenant *and* any subsequent assignees. Moreover, given that both the benefit of a leasehold covenant (the right to enforce it) and its burden (the obligation to observe it) can run with the land, the use of a leasehold with appropriate covenants can achieve what covenants affecting freehold land cannot: that is, that even positive obligations can be made to run with the burdened estate: see Chapter 8.

6.2   The essential characteristics of a lease

There are various definitions of a lease, both in statute (for example, s 205 of the LPA 1925) and in common law, but one of the most commonly cited is that of Lord Templeman in *Street v Mountford* (1985): viz, that the essential qualities of a lease are that it gives a person the right of exclusive possession of property, for a term, at a rent. These three conditions are commonly regarded as the *indicia* of a leasehold, irrespective of the purpose for which the estate is created and have been affirmed many times in a residential context (*Aslan v Murphy* (1989)) and a commercial context (*Vandersteen v Angus* (1997)). These three indicia will be examined in turn.

6.2.1   Exclusive possession

A lease is an estate in the land; it signifies a form of 'ownership' of the land for a stated and defined period of time. Yet, there are many other ways in which a person may enjoy a limited right to use or occupy land owned by another person and it is sometimes necessary to distinguish these relationships from the leasehold estate. For example, a person may be given a 'licence' to occupy the land of another which, in many ways, might resemble a lease (for example, the occupier pays a regular 'occupation fee', and a defined period of occupation is agreed). However, a licence is a mere personal right, binding only the parties that created it (*Lloyd v Dugdale* (2001)). A lease, on the other hand, is properly regarded as a proprietary interest in the land itself and it may be assigned to, and become binding on, any subsequent owner of the reversion. Moreover, 'leases' fall within the statutory regulatory machinery of the Rent Act 1977 and the Housing Act 1988, so restricting the ability of landlords to remove tenants and set rent; licences do not. There are other differences too. For example, a tenant may sue any person in trespass (including his landlord), but a licencee enjoys only a very narrow right (*Manchester Airport v Dutton* (1999); a tenant may sue in nuisance, a licencee may do so only in exceptional circumstances (*Hunter v Canary Wharf* (1996)); and only a landlord is entitled to the old feudal remedy of distress for rent or may avail himself of the remedy of forfeiture (and hence only a tenant may claim 'relief'). In fact, in years past, these differences, particularly the absence of statutory protection and rent control for licencees (as opposed to tenants) prompted landowners (be they themselves leaseholders or freeholders) to attempt to draw up agreements with potential occupiers of the land that give mere licences and not leases. In most cases, this has been attempted by seeking to deny the grant of 'exclusive possession' to the occupier, thereby removing a vital element in the creation of a lease. Consequently, a series of cases in the House of Lords and Court of Appeal have sought to draw a legal and practical distinction between a lease and a licence, and this battle has been fought largely over the concept of 'exclusive possession'. Indeed, although legislative changes have made the distinction between a lease and a licence less critical (for example, the removal of rent control and security of tenure under the Housing Acts), these cases still provide the basic tools for making the distinction.

As a basic proposition, a lease will exist when the occupier of land has been granted exclusive possession of the premises. This is a question of fact, to be decided in each case by reference to the surrounding circumstances, the course of any negotiations prior to the grant of the right of occupation, the nature of the property and the actual mode of occupation of the occupier. Further, the landowner cannot avoid granting a lease by merely calling the arrangement between the parties 'a licence', even if this is expressly stated. Labels are not decisive. Generally, it is not the parties' intentions (whether expressly stated or not) that are relevant, but the substance of the rights they have created by their agreement (*Street v Mountford* (1985); overruling *Somma v Hazlehurst* (1978) on this point).

However, there are certain exceptional situations where the occupier of land will have exclusive possession of the property but, for special reasons, no lease will exist. These are cases where the grant of exclusive possession is referable to some other *bona fide* relationship between the parties. Examples include a mortgagee going into possession of the property under the terms of a mortgage, usually where the borrower cannot repay the loan (Chapter 10), occupancy of the purchaser under an enforceable contract for the sale of the land (*Bretherton v Paton* (1986)), and where the occupation is based on charity (see, for example, *Gray v Taylor* (1998)) or friendship, when there is no intention to create legal relations between the owner and the occupier (*Marcroft Wagons v Smith* (1951)). These exempted categories were explained at length by Lord Denning in *Facchini v Bryson* (1952) and a good example is *Norris v Checksfield* (1991), where the occupier of a cottage with exclusive possession was held to be a 'service occupier' (and, hence, a licensee). A 'service occupier' is a person who occupies property for the better performance of his duties under a contract of employment with the landowner. Although such an occupier may have exclusive possession of the property, that occupation feeds off their employment contract and does not exist because of the existence of the landlord and tenant relationship as in *Carroll v Manek* (1999) where a hotel manager was held to have a licence of a hotel room (despite being in exclusive possession) because the possession was entirely referable to this employment relationship. The effect is, then, that as well as having only a personal right in the land, the exclusive possession of the employee must end when the employment ends.

According to Lord Templeman in *Street*, the practical effect of the principle that an occupation agreement is to be assessed according to its substance, not its label, is that a genuine licence can exist in only very limited circumstances. In fact, apart from the *Facchini* exceptions, Lord Templeman's view is that an occupier of premises must be either a 'tenant' or a 'lodger'. This is another way of saying that the only genuine occupation licence that can exist is that held by a lodger. In law, a lodger is someone who receives services and attendance from the landlord, such as room cleaning or meals. Moreover, as *Markou v Da Silvaesa* (1986) illustrates, a mere promise by the landowner to provide such services is not sufficient to generate a lodging agreement (that is, licence): they must actually be provided. What this means, then, is that it should be a relatively straightforward task to distinguish between a lease and a licence: if the occupier receives 'board and lodging', he holds a mere personal licence. Otherwise, he must be a tenant, unless one of the exceptional situations exists. Unfortunately, things are never this simple, for if it is true that an occupier is *either* a lodger or a tenant, this means that no other kind of 'occupation licence' can exist. There would be no intermediate category of licensee who, while not a lodger, is still not a tenant. Obviously, this has far reaching consequences for it restricts the options open to a landowner when seeking to make use of his property. It is the triumph of property law over freedom of contract, and it is precisely this legal straitjacket that cases subsequent to *Street* found difficult to accept. Indeed, many of the apparently inconsistent decisions of the Court of Appeal that followed *Street* have resulted from attempts to identify some middle way, some form of occupation that can still give rise to a licence, but where the occupier is not a lodger. For example, *Hadjiloucas v Crean* (1988) and *Brooker Estates v Ayers* (1987), both decisions of the Court of Appeal quite soon after *Street*, are of this type. In fact, although the primacy of the tenant/lodger distinction has been preserved by the House of Lords in cases such as *Antoniades v Villiers* (1990), *Westminster CC v Clarke* (1992) and by the Court of Appeal in *Aslan v Murphy* (1989), there has been an acceptance that property rights, or rights to use property, are not as black and white as the tenant/lodger distinction suggests. Necessarily, this has resulted in a certain refinement of the principles, and some other guidelines have emerged.

It is now clear that a licence (as opposed to a lease) may exist in cases where two or more persons occupy the same property, as in shared houses. It is not that the persons occupying the property under a 'multiple occupancy agreement' *cannot* be leaseholders, rather it is that to be leaseholders of the entire property the 'four unities' must be present, so as to support a joint tenancy of the leasehold estate (*AG Securities v Vaughan* (1988)). Therefore, the issue turns on the nature of the multiple occupancy agreement. For example, if four people occupy a four bedroomed house, but each sign a different agreement, on different days and for different rents, there can be no 'exclusive possession' of the *entire* premises, because there is no unity of interest, title, or time. The house, as a whole, cannot be held on a leasehold, because the necessary conditions for a joint tenancy of this estate do not exist. Of course, each occupier may have a lease of his individual room, with a licence over the common parts, but this is very different from one jointly owned leasehold of the whole premises. Note, however, that while it is perfectly understandable and indeed practical that no joint leasehold should exist in respect of a property occupied by a shifting population of previously unrelated persons (for example, house sharing in London), the same considerations do not apply where the 'multiple' occupancy is that of a romantically linked couple who, for all intents and purposes, are living in the property together, not as separate individuals. In such cases, as explained below, the court might well regard the existence of a multiple occupancy licence agreement as a deliberate and artificial attempt to avoid artificially the grant of a joint leasehold interest.

The cases also suggest that there are certain types of public sector landlords who may be able to grant licences in circumstances where a private landlord could only grant leases. Examples are *Westminster CC v Basson* (1991), *Ogwr BC v Dykes* (1989), and the House of Lords' decision in *Westminster CC v Clarke* (1992). In these situations, the landowners may be able to deny exclusive possession to the occupiers (and hence deny a lease) because to do otherwise would be to hinder them in the exercise of their statutory housing duties. In other words, the denial of exclusive possession with all that this entails, is necessary if local authorities and the like are to be able to carry out their duty to accommodate the homeless and provide temporary accommodation to the needy. Such landlords should be able to grant personal licences in order to be able to manage their housing stock more effectively without being 'caught' by the greater obligations owed by landlords to their tenants. Seen in this light, the privileged position of public sector landlords is justified by policy rather than principle, but, of course, that does not make it any less sensible. A similar view was taken in *Gray v Taylor* (1998), where one ground for denying that the occupier of a charity almshouse was a tenant was that it would be inconsistent with the duty of the particular trustees of the charity to have granted a tenancy and with it, a measure of residential security.

Importantly, however, this view of the *Westminster* cases (that it is the identity of the landlord in these cases that is the decisive factor in drawing the lease/licence distinction) has been challenged. In *Bruton v London and Quadrant Housing Trust* (1999), the House of Lords were considering the status of Mr Bruton who held a property on an express 'licence' from the Trust. The Trust itself held a licence from the freeholder, Lambeth LBC, and was acting in support of Lambeth's housing functions. In deciding that Mr Bruton held a lease (on which see immediately below), Lord Hoffmann noted (*obiter*) that the law does not accept that the identity or type of landlord is relevant in determining the existence of a lease or licence. However, as the earlier cases demonstrate, this may well be going too far, at least in the sense that the identity of the landlord can help to establish whether the giving of a licence to an occupier (as opposed to a lease) was a genuine response to the unique circumstances of a case rather than an attempt to avoid the grant of a lease *per se*. So, the fact that Westminster Council had statutory housing functions must impact on the genuineness of its attempt to give some of its occupiers 'mere' licences, just as in *Mehta v Royal Bank of Scotland* (1999) where the Court of Appeal decided that a hotel occupier had 'only' a licence as against the hotel owners (as *per* his agreement) because this was the only sensible interpretation of the relationship between the particular parties. In fact, as discussed below, *Bruton* is a case that raises other concerns when considering the distinction between a lease and a licence.

As mentioned, in *Bruton* the claimant contended that he held a lease from the Housing Trust on the basis that he enjoyed exclusive possession. However, the Trust itself held only a licence from the freeholder, not because of some clever draughtsmanship by the freeholder, but because any grant of a lease by Lambeth LBC (the freeholder) would have been *ultra vires* its powers under s 32 of the Housing Act 1985. Naturally (one might think) the Trust resisted the claim that Bruton held a lease on the simple ground that because it (the Trust) held no estate in the land (no lease), it could not grant such an estate in the land to Mr Bruton. *Nemo dat quod non habet*: a person cannot grant what they do not own. This was accepted by the Court of Appeal but, somewhat surprisingly, was rejected by the House of Lords. According to Lord Hoffmann, giving the leading judgment and deciding in favour of a lease for Mr Bruton, the test of whether an occupier held a lease was the 'exclusive possession' test of *Street*. Bruton had exclusive possession, so he had a lease. Unfortunately, this deceptively simple (and, with respect, simplistic) reasoning has far reaching consequences. It means, as acknowledged by Lord Hoffmann, that a lease is not always a proprietary right in the land. Apparently, it is a state of affairs between 'landlord' and 'tenant' and whether it is also proprietary in the sense of being capable of binding third parties can depend on the circumstances in which the 'lease' arises. To put it another way, apparently there is in English law the 'normal' proprietary lease that has been with us for centuries and also the 'non-proprietary lease' being a 'lease' between the parties, but not so counted for other purposes. It is an understatement to say that this muddies the waters. The decision in *Street* itself is premised on the assumption that a lease is proprietary and that is why it must be distinguished from a licence. To take the *ratio* of *Street* and apply it to *Bruton* in the manner suggested by Lord Hoffmann does great violence not only to established principles of property law but goes against the very purpose of Lord Templeman's judgment in the earlier case. No doubt, the decision in *Bruton* was convenient in that it enabled Mr Bruton to compel the Trust to perform the repairing obligations that may be implied into a 'lease' under s 11 of the Landlord and Tenant Act 1985. On the other hand, the 'non-proprietary lease' is a strange creature in English property law and, we might suggest, it already has a name: that is, it is a licence! Of course, where the law develops from here remains to be seen. It may well be that *Bruton* will come to be regarded as decided 'by reference to its own special facts' and that it is not taken as authority for the destruction of one of the most fundamental distinctions connected with the use of land: that is, the distinction between proprietary leases and personal licences.

There is, then, some uncertainty as to the extent to which a *bona fide* intention to grant only a licence, in circumstances where the need to do so is manifest and genuine, permits the landowner to deny the occupier a proprietary lease.

In similar vein, Lord Oliver in *Antoniades v Villiers* (1990) suggests that there may be circumstances where a landlord can *genuinely* reserve to himself a right to make use of the premises that they have given over to an occupier and, if such use is made, no exclusive possession will be given and a licence will result; for example, if a landowner grants occupation of her house to a student for £50 per week, but reserves a right (subsequently used) to enter at any time and make use of the study, dining room, etc. In effect, this is no more than a restatement of the distinction between exclusive *possession* and exclusive *occupation*: the former establishing the legal relationship of landlord and tenant, the latter describing a factual situation, devoid of proprietary effect. However, the ability of a landowner to reserve a right to himself which effectively destroys the grant of exclusive possession is controversial as it appears to offer landowners a way out of the rigors of *Street v Mountford* (1985). For that reason, it must constitute a rare exception to the *Street ratio*, and the 'pretence' rule (discussed below) may invalidate most attempts by land owners to achieve such an outcome. In any event, this 'exception' would not be applicable if the right reserved by the landowner was consistent with the grant of a lease. For example, a landowner may reserve the right to enter the premises, in order to inspect and carry out repairs, but such a right actually confirms the grant of a tenancy rather than denies it, for this is just the sort of right a landlord would expect to have under a lease.

Finally, as just noted, all attempts by the landlord to deny the grant of exclusive possession are subject to the court's powers to ignore 'pretences' (or 'sham devices'). According to *Antoniades v Villiers* (1990), a 'pretence' exists where a clause in an agreement for the occupation of land is inserted into that agreement deliberately in order to avoid the creation of the lease that would otherwise arise and where *either* party do not intend to rely in practice on the clause. A pretence may be established from an examination of the surrounding circumstances of the case and may be confirmed by the parties' subsequent practice. For example, in *Antoniades*, an unmarried couple signed separate agreements for the occupation of what was clearly going to be their joint home and these agreements gave the landlord certain rights over the property which were unlikely to be enjoyed in practice (for example, the right to nominate another occupier). This was an attempt by the landlord to avoid the grant of a tenancy by artificially destroying the 'four unities' necessary to give the couple a joint tenancy of the leasehold and by reserving to himself some power over the property. This was held to be a pretence, created only to deny artificially the grant of exclusive possession. Hence, the parties held the property under a lease.

6.2.2 For a term certain

Another essential ingredient in a lease is that the exclusive possession granted to the tenant must be for a defined and certain period of time: for example, one year, one month, seven years, 99 years, etc. This means not only that the lease must start at a clearly defined moment, but also that the length of the term granted must be certain. At the commencement of the lease, it must be possible to define exactly the maximum duration of the lease, even if it is possible to end the lease at some time before this. So, a lease for 3,000 years is perfectly valid, even if the lease contains 'break clauses' entitling the landlord and tenant to terminate the lease by notice on, say, every 10th anniversary. Any lease, or rather any intended lease, that fails to satisfy this condition is necessarily void, because it does not amount to a 'term certain'. Of course, in the great majority of cases, this condition is easily satisfied, as in the above example, because the landlord and tenant will state clearly the duration of the lease. However, problems can arise where the term of the lease is set by reference to some other criteria, such as the happening of an uncertain event. For example, in *Lace v Chandler* (1944), a lease for the duration of the Second World War was held void as being of uncertain maximum duration. In recent years, the principle of 'time' or 'term' certain has been under attack, and there was an attempt to accept as leases certain arrangements which, on a proper construction, could not be said to create a certain term. So in *Ashburn Anstalt v Arnold* (1989), an arrangement whereby a tenant occupied property indefinitely until the landlord gave three months' notice was held to be a lease on the ground that the term could be rendered certain by action of one of the parties. In reality of course this does contradict the rule that a lease must be certain *at the date* of its commencement and it came as no surprise when the House of Lords in *Prudential Assurance v London Residuary Body* (1992) reaffirmed the rule that a leasehold term must be certain from the outset. Consequently, it is not enough that an uncertain term can, in fact, be rendered certain by action of either the landlord or the tenant after the lease has commenced. This is a significant and welcome return to the orthodox position. Both landlord and tenant will know the maximum duration of their obligations and it will be easier to place a monetary value on both lease and reversion should either wish to assign their rights to a purchaser.

6.2.3 Periodic tenancies

In a great many cases concerning residential property, a tenant may occupy premises and pay a regular sum in rent to the landlord, but there may not be an express agreement (written or oral) regulating the occupation. In these circumstances, a tenancy of a certain duration will be presumed from the facts. Thus, if money is paid weekly in respect of a week's occupation, a *periodic tenancy* of one week will be presumed. Likewise, if rent is paid with reference to a monthly or quarterly period, a monthly or quarterly periodic tenancy will result. Obviously, if a further weekly, monthly or quarterly payment is made, the lease will continue for a further period. In this sense, the lease can continue indefinitely and the total period of the tenancy will not be known in advance. However, although this appears to give rise to a lease of uncertain duration, in fact there is a succession of periodic tenancies, all of which are of a certain term; that is, one week after one week, or one month after one month, and so on. The validity of periodic tenancies was confirmed by *Prudential*, with the court explaining that there is a clear conceptual distinction between a succession of certain periods with simple uncertainty about how many more periods there will be (a periodic tenancy), and a 'term' that, from its outset, is defined by reference to uncertainty (for example, a tenancy 'until the good weather ends'). As discussed below, because the great majority of periodic tenancies are for a period of three years or less they will be legal interests. For example, the rent is unlikely to be calculated by reference to a period any longer than a quarter, and yearly periodic tenancies are in practice the longest 'periods' under this rule.

6.2.4 Statutory provisions concerning certain terms

There are a number of statutory provisions which are related to the principle of 'time certain' and whose general effect is to convert uncertain periods into certain terms or to invalidate certain types of arrangement. Thus:

(a) a lease for the duration of the life of any person, or which is due to end with expiry of any life, or on the marriage of the lessee, for a rent or a premium (all uncertain terms) is converted into a lease for 90 years, subject to determination (that is, ending) if the death or marriage occurs before this (s 149(6) of the LPA 1925). So, a lease of a cottage granted to me by my parents 'until I marry', for £60 per week (rent), or for an initial capital sum of, say, £45,000 (a premium), will take effect as a lease for a certain period of 90 years, determinable when (if) I marry;

(b) a lease which is perpetually renewable is converted into a lease for 2,000 years (Sched 15, s 145 of the Law of Property Act (LPA) 1922). So, a lease for 40 years, containing a clause whereby the tenant has the right to renew the lease for a further 40 years at the expiry of every period is perpetually renewable, and will take effect as a lease for 2,000 years. This, of course, is tantamount to the grant of a freehold. Note, however, that a lease for 40 years that is renewable only for one further period of 40 years is not perpetually renewable and takes effect in the normal way;

(c) a lease which is intended to start more than 21 years after the instrument which creates it is void (s 149(3) of the LPA 1925). So, if Z, by contract with X dated 1 January 2000, attempts to grant a lease of land to start after 1 January 2021, the contract and all rights arising from it (including the intended lease) are void. The commencement of the lease is postponed for longer than the law allows.

6.2.5 Rent

One of the main motives for the letting of property may well be the desire to generate income through the payment of rent. Even where the tenant pays a large premium or fine (a capital sum) at the start of the lease, there is usually provision for a ground rent payable annually. Indeed, as noted above, Lord Templeman, in *Street v Mountford* (1985), included 'rent' as part of the definition of a tenancy. However, strictly speaking, the existence of a lease does not depend on a provision for the payment of rent. Section 205(1)(xxvii) of the LPA 1925 provides that a term of years means a 'term of years ... whether or not at a rent'. As it happens, certain types of leases (such as those within the Rent Acts and early Housing Acts) must be supported by rent in order to qualify for statutory protection and this is why Lord Templeman in *Street* refers so explicitly to 'rent', that being a Rent Act case. Yet, as *Ashburn Anstalt v Arnold* (1989) makes clear, a lease may exist where there is no rent payable. Of course, in reality, the existence of an obligation to pay rent as an adjunct to a lease is so likely that, in the absence of an express promise by the tenant or an express exclusion of rent, a covenant by the tenant to pay rent will be readily implied from the words of a deed. Moreover, although the landlord and tenant can *deliberately* exclude the rent obligation while still creating a lease, an explicit exclusion of rent (or other clear evidence that rent is not to be paid) may suggest that the parties did not intend to create a lease at all. Necessarily, this will depend on the peculiar facts of each case, but the absence of a rent obligation, if not counteracted by the existence of any of the other hallmarks of a lease (for example, a repairing obligation), can indicate that no landlord and tenant relationship was intended. In such cases, the occupier may have a mere licence. Note, however, that, as discussed above, the fact that the parties choose to describe the periodic payment as an 'occupation fee', a 'licence fee', or some such similar phrase, does not prevent it in law amounting to 'rent'. Again, it is a matter of substance, not form.

Finally, it is a common misconception that rent has to be in monetary form. It can be in goods, services, or payable in kind. The only clear requirement is that the amount of rent must be capable of being rendered certain. Thus, in *Bostock v Bryant* (1990), the obligation to pay fluctuating utility bills (gas, electricity, etc) could not be regarded as rent, being an ever changing sum. On the other hand, an annual rent of 'a peppercorn' or 'five tons of flour' is perfectly acceptable.

6.3   The creation of legal and equitable leases

The existence of a 'term certain', the granting of exclusive possession, and (subject to the reservations just discussed) the payment of rent, are the hallmarks of a tenancy. Of course, in most cases, the parties will have agreed a web of other rights and obligations extending beyond acceptance of this bare legal framework: for example, the lease may contain covenants to repair, options to renew the lease, obligations relating to the use of the premises and the like. Generally, the more complicated or extensive these other matters, the more likely it is that the 'lease' itself will be embodied in a formal document, such as a deed or written instrument. Moreover, while there are very few legal rules concerning the precise words or phrases which must be used to create a valid lease or obligations therein (although certain 'precedents' or standard wordings have been developed), there are a number of legal formalities which must be observed before the arrangement agreed by the parties will be enforced as a lease by the courts. These 'formality' requirements generally are required by statute. They relate to the manner in which a lease may be created, rather than to what a lease must contain. In essence, they are the embodiment of a legislative policy that seeks certainty about dealings with land. So, these statutory rules determine whether an arrangement between owner and occupier that otherwise satisfies the inherent requirements of a lease can nevertheless be enforced as a lease and, if it can, whether the lease so created is legal or equitable.

6.3.1   Introductory points

A lease is a legally binding agreement between landlord and tenant. As such, the creation of a lease amounts to both a contract between them *and* the creation of a proprietary right that exists beyond the mere contract. It can give rise to contractual remedies (such as an action for damages), but it can affect 'third parties' to whom the reversion or lease is assigned. Furthermore, in many cases, the creation of a lease will occur in two stages: the conclusion of a 'contract to grant a lease' between prospective landlord and tenant, and the later execution of the contract by the 'grant' of the lease by deed. This is important in understanding how equitable leases are created. However, even where a lease is created without first concluding a separate contract to grant it (for example, the parties simply execute a deed or agree to a written lease), the lease itself will always amount to a contract between them. So, 'the lease as a contract' refers either to an aspect of the landlord and tenant relationship (its contractual aspect), or to the manner in which the lease was created originally.

6.3.2   Legal leases

The creation of legal leases depends on rules laid down by statute and, as with all legal rights, there is a premium on formality:

(a) leases for three years or less that give the tenant an immediate right to possession of the land without the payment of an initial capital sum (that is, a premium) will be legal whether created orally, by written contract, or by deed (ss 52(2)(d) and 54(2) of the LPA 1925). Into this category will come many residential or domestic leases, and, significantly, most 'periodic tenancies' created in the way described above, 6.2.3. This is simply because the 'period' for which rent is paid and accepted will usually be three years or less (for example, a week, month, quarter, etc);

(b) leases for more than three years, and those of three years or less that do not fall within (a) above (for example, where a premium *is* charged), are legal only if created by deed (s 52(1) of the LPA 1925). A 'deed' is, in essence, a more formal written document and, prior to the Law of Property (Miscellaneous Provisions) Act (LP (Misc Prov) A) 1989, such a document had to be 'signed, sealed and delivered' before it could be regarded as 'a deed'. Now, by virtue of s 1 of that Act, a document is a deed if it declares itself to be such (for example, it says 'this is a deed made between X and Y'), it is signed as a deed, and is witnessed as a deed by one other person. The execution of a deed remains a relatively formal process, although, given that most leases by deed are drawn up by solicitors or licensed conveyancers, the creation of a deed is straightforward and now relatively inexpensive. Note also that in due course it will be possible to execute a 'deed' in relation to registered land in electronic form. This will be no less a deed than its paper counterpart and will necessarily satisfy the rules relating to the creation of legal leases (s 91 of the Land Registration Act (LRA) 2002).

If the lease is to take effect in land of unregistered title, the grant by deed (where required) is all that is needed to convey the legal leasehold estate to the tenant (from the date specified in the deed) – save where the execution of the lease triggers compulsory registration of title (see Chapter 2). Moreover, following the general rule that 'legal rights bind the whole world', a legal lease will bind automatically any subsequent purchaser or transferee of the land out of which it is created (that is, of the reversion).

Currently, a deed is required to create a legal lease of registered land in exactly the same circumstances as unregistered land. However, if the legal lease is over 21 years, etc, under s 19(2) of the LRA 1925 it must be entered for registration with its own title number at the appropriate district office of the Land Registry: that is, it must be substantively registered in its own right. Pending such registration, the lease operates to convey only an equitable estate to the tenant, because registration is required to perfect the legal title: *Brown and Root v Sun Alliance* (1995). It should be remembered, however, that as the very great majority of these long legal leases will have been negotiated and executed with professional advice, there is every likelihood that they will be appropriately registered. If they are not, they take effect as equitable leases, and this can have some unforeseen consequences: for example, where leasehold covenants are limited expressly to pass only with legal title, but the current tenant has only an equitable estate due to a failure to secure substantive registration (*Brown and Root*). We should also note that, whereas at present the requirement is that legal leases over 21 years should be registered with their own title in registered land, the LRA 2002 will lower this to leases of over seven years when it enters into force (s 4(c)(i) of the LRA 2002). In fact, the Act gives power to alter this period further and the ultimate aim is that all legal leases of over three years should become registrable estates. Similarly, the LRA 2002 will eventually make important changes to the circumstances in which legal leases can exist at all. Currently, legal leases are created by deed and then – if required – entered on the register of title. When the electronic conveyancing provisions of the LRA 2002 come into full effect, a registrable legal lease will not actually exist until it is electronically entered on the register, whether created by deed or not (s 93 of the LRA 2002).

As far as the effect of legal leases on third parties in registered land is concerned (that is, purchasers, etc, of the reversion), then the current position is that:

(a) legal leases for 21 years or less are overriding interests (s 70(1)(k) of the LRA 1925) (*City Permanent Building Society v Miller* (1952)). Consequently, they bind subsequent purchasers and transferees of the reversion automatically. Necessarily, when the LRA 2002 reduces the length of leases which must be substantively registered in their own right to those above seven years, there will be a corresponding change in the length of leases that can amount to overriding interests. This category will then encompass legal leases of seven years or less (Scheds 1 and 3 to the LRA 2002);

(b) as noted above, legal leases created for more than 21 years, and existing legal leases which are assigned when there is more than 21 years left to run, currently are registrable as titles in their own right and clearly will bind a purchaser or transferee of the reversion for their duration if so registered. If they are not so registered, they will take effect as equitable leases only. Even then, they may still enjoy protection against third parties in the manner appropriate to equitable leases. Once again, there will be corresponding changes when the relevant provisions of the LRA 2002 come into force. Thus, legal leases above seven years which are not registered in their own right (when they should be) will take effect as equitable leases and might obtain protection in the manner suitable to equitable leases. More importantly, however, when electronic conveyancing comes into full effect it may not be possible to create a registrable legal lease without an electronic entry on the register and so it will not be possible for such leases (that is, of over seven years) to take effect as 'equitable' leases or anything else proprietary (s 93 of the LRA 2002).

6.3.3 Equitable leases

While it is true that the LP (Misc Prov) A 1989 simplified the requirements for the execution of a deed, nevertheless many leases are created in the absence of a deed. The majority of these are for three years or less and qualify as legal interests however created. It is unusual for a lease of over three years' duration to be created without the use of a deed – primarily because the parties routinely use lawyers who proceed to execute the lease by deed without first concluding a contract – but it does occur. There are a number of reasons for this: if a contract is used, the parties may be content to rely on it rather than execute a deed, or the parties may not use professionals and so not realise that a deed is required at all. In such cases – that is, a lease of over three years not executed by deed – if there is a written contract (or a written record of an agreement that can be treated as if it were a contract), the parties may be taken to have created an equitable lease. In simple terms, an equitable lease arises from an enforceable contract between landlord and tenant to grant a lease, but where no grant of a lease has in fact occurred. There are a number of distinct steps in this process:

(a) the contract between prospective landlord and tenant must be enforceable, viz, the contract must in writing, containing all the terms and signed by both parties (s 2 of the LP (Misc Prov) A 1989, replacing s 40 of the LPA 1925 (which allowed oral contracts if supported by acts of part performance)). In this connection, 'written contract' means either a written document clearly expressed to be a contract, or a written record of agreement that the law is prepared to treat as a contract. A good example of the latter is where A and B set down in writing the terms on which A will let her house to B. A and B may not intend to take any further steps to create the lease, perhaps believing they have done all that is necessary, but their written agreement will be treated as a 'written contract to grant a lease', so as to give rise to an equitable lease. Note also, as in the case of deeds, it will become possible in due course to create an enforceable contract electronically (the intended s 2A of the LP (Misc Prov) A 1989. This will have the same effect as its paper counterpart;

(b) the remedy of specific performance must be available, should either party to the contract actually wish to enforce it and compel the grant of a legal lease (*Coatsworth v Johnson* (1886)). Specific performance will be available if:

- the person seeking to enforce the contract has given valuable consideration; and

- damages would be an inadequate remedy (as they nearly always are with contracts for land); and

- the person seeking to enforce the contract comes to equity with 'clean hands', that is, there is no reason why the remedy should be denied.

If all of these conditions are fulfilled – which will be true in most cases – a court of equity will treat the unenforced (but enforceable) contract to grant the legal lease as having created an equitable lease between the parties on the same terms as the potential (but ungranted) legal lease (*Walsh v Lonsdale* (1882)).

The contract/lease analysis is the usual way in which an equitable lease comes into existence. However, it is also possible for an equitable lease to arise out of the operation of the doctrine of proprietary estoppel. Proprietary estoppel leases will arise where the 'landlord' has promised some right to the 'tenant' in writing *or* orally (for example, that they may have a lease), and this is relied on by the prospective tenant to his detriment. The court may then 'satisfy' the estoppel by giving the promisee a tenancy, albeit an equitable one created orally (see generally *Taylor Fashions v Liverpool Victoria Trustees* (1982)). Such a situation will be rare, but cannot be discounted completely. It is discussed in more detail in Chapter 9. For now, the important point is that proprietary estoppel may result in the generation of an equitable lease out of a purely oral agreement. Similarly, if a party to an agreement seeks to use s 2 of the LP (Misc Prov) A 1989 as a vehicle for unconscionable conduct – for example, by pleading that the contract is not in writing and so not valid when that very person had assured the other party that the contract need not be written – the agreed lease might be enforceable under a constructive trust or property estoppel: see *Yaxley v Gotts* (1999).

The above principles concerning the creation of equitable leases apply whether the land is registered or unregistered. However, bearing in mind that one of the main purposes of the 1925 reforms was to bring clarity to dealings with equitable interests in land, it is not surprising that the effect of an equitable lease on a third party (that is, a purchaser of the reversion from the current landlord) differs according to whether title has been registered.

In unregistered land

(a) Equitable leases that arise from enforceable contracts are registrable as class C(iv) land charges ('estate contracts'). Consequently, they must be registered against the appropriate name of the estate owner (that is, the freeholder or superior leaseholder) in order to bind a purchaser of a legal estate in the land. Failure to register voids the interest against such a purchaser. This can mean the ejection of the equitable tenant if the superior interest is sold (*Hollington Bros v Rhodes* (1951)). Of course, even an unregistered equitable lease is binding against a non-purchaser (for example, adverse possessor, devisee under a will, donee of a gift), or against someone who purchases only an equitable interest. Importantly, these rules mean that there is no protection for an equitable tenant in unregistered land merely because they occupy the land. This should be contrasted with the position in registered land.

(b) Equitable leases arising from proprietary estoppel may not be registrable as land charges at all, and would bind a subsequent transferee of the reversion through the doctrine of notice (*Ives v High* (1967)).

In registered land

(a) Equitable leases can be minor interests protected by notice or caution. If so registered, they will bind subsequent purchasers of the reversionary interest (assuming the caution is upgraded to a notice). Under the LRA 2002, equitable leases will become protectable by the entry of the new form of notice, usually the 'consensual' form, having been created deliberately between registered proprietor and tenant.

(b) However, most equitable leases will be overriding interests and automatically binding against a subsequent purchaser. This is because the equitable tenant will almost certainly be a person 'in actual occupation' of the land within s 70(1)(g) of the LRA 1925. Here, then, is virtually automatic protection for the equitable tenant in registered land, for the tenant need do nothing – except remain in occupation – to be secure. In this regard, the position initially will remain the same under the LRA 2002, save that the equitable tenant will have to be in 'actual occupation' within the refined definition of Scheds 1 and 3 to the LRA 2002. Eventually, however, as with many other rights in registered land, it may not be possible to create an equitable lease at all until an electronic entry is made on the register of title by notice (s 93 of the LRA 2002). As with the position of legal leases described above, leases that are currently equitable and protected by 'actual occupation' will not exist at all *if* they are required to be completed by electronic registration.

It will be appreciated from the above that the circumstances in which an equitable tenancy can arise can be distinguished from those concerning the creation of a legal lease by the *relative* informality of the former. However, in one set of circumstances this is not true: viz, the creation of a legal periodic tenancy where the 'period' is three years or less, as these may be 'legal' whether created by deed, in writing or orally. Consequently, it can happen that the same set of facts can presumptively give rise to either an equitable tenancy or a shorter, legal periodic tenancy. For example, in those cases where the equitable tenancy has sprung from a written contract (or a document taken to be a written contract), the tenant may well have entered the premises and be paying rent to the landlord. It is easy to see that this could be taken to have given rise to the creation of a periodic tenancy in favour of the occupier because of the payment/acceptance of rent. This periodic tenancy will usually be legal, as the period for which rent is paid and accepted will be three years or less. Potentially, then, there is a conflict between the equitable lease arising from the enforceable written contract (which will be of the same duration as the original intended lease), and the implied short term, legal periodic tenancy. According to *Walsh v Lonsdale* (1882), the equitable lease will prevail (despite the problems encountered by equitable leases, see below, 6.3.4), not least because it will contain all the terms originally found in the contract between the parties and be of longer certain duration. Of course, if the equitable lease does not arise (for example, because of a failure to conclude an enforceable contract, or where the contract is not specifically enforceable), the implied legal periodic tenancy can take effect to provide some comfort for the tenant.

6.3.4 The differences between legal and equitable leases

As noted above, legal and equitable leases are created in different ways, with legal leases generally requiring more formality. In a similar vein, the existence of an equitable lease depends on the availability of the remedy of specific performance of the enforceable contract out of which it arises. (Note: estoppel leases are rare.) The following further points of difference should also be noted.

Currently, equitable leases are potentially very vulnerable to a sale of the freehold or leasehold estate out of which they are created. So, a purchaser of the land may not be bound by an existing equitable lease according to the rules of registered and unregistered conveyancing. However, as noted, the problem is likely to be more acute in unregistered land where there is no protection *per se* for the rights of occupiers. Currently, legal leases do not suffer from this problem and are fully protected in registered and in unregistered land. Significantly, however, the entry into force in full of the electronic conveyancing provisions of the LRA 2002 may produce a curious effect for land of registered title. If it becomes the case that certain legal leases and equitable leases must be 'completed' by electronic entry on the register (s 93 of the LRA 2002), they will not exist at all as proprietary rights until such registration even if 'created' by deed or written contract. Of course, neither will they be capable of binding a purchaser if they are not so registered. This illustrates very clearly that the brave new world of electronic conveyancing under the LRA 2002 is going to affect fundamentally the way we think about legal and equitable proprietary rights in registered land.

As we shall see below, 6.5, the ability of covenants in leases granted before 1 January 1996 to 'run' to (that is, bind) purchasers of the tenant's interest (the lease) depends on the existence of 'privity of estate' between the claimant and defendant. As a general principle, 'privity of estate' exists between the current landlord and the current tenant of a legal lease only. Thus, the lack of privity of estate in equitable leases makes it difficult for all leasehold covenants to bind purchasers of the lease. Fortunately, the position is different for equitable leases granted on or after 1 January 1996 because of the Landlord and Tenant (Covenants) Act (LTCA) 1995.

As demonstrated in Chapter 7, easements may be created by s 62 of the LPA 1925 on the occasion of a conveyance by deed of an estate in the land, either freehold or leasehold. In other words, this section applies only to legal leases, so a tenant under an equitable lease cannot claim the benefit of any potential s 62 easements.

Finally, when the tenant under an equitable lease first enters into the lease, he is 'only' a purchaser for value of an *equitable* estate in the land. Consequently, the tenant is not a purchaser of a legal estate so as to avoid being bound by those equitable rights in unregistered land that still depend on the doctrine of notice for their validity against purchasers. Neither could such a tenant avoid being bound by an unregistered Class C(iv) or Class D land charge, both of which are void only against a purchaser of a legal estate (see Chapter 3).

6.4 Leasehold covenants

Nearly all leases contain 'covenants' whereby the landlord and tenant promise each other to do, or not to do, certain things in relation to the land and its environment. For example, the landlord may promise to keep the premises in repair and the tenant may promise not to use the premises for any trade or business. Necessarily, these covenants are binding between the original landlord and the original tenant – being contained in a deed or binding contract to which they are party – and they can be enforced by either of them using a suitable remedy. However, one of the great advantages of the leasehold estate is that these covenants are *capable* of running to both purchasers of the original landlord's reversion and to purchasers of the original tenant's lease. In other words, both the right to sue on the leasehold covenants, and the obligation to perform them, can be passed on to successors in title of the original parties.

Figure 2

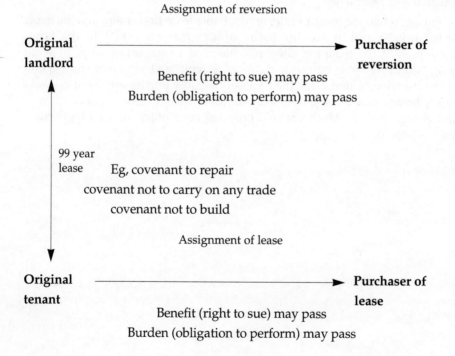

6.4.1   The separate nature of the 'benefit' of a covenant and the 'burden' of a covenant

In order to understand the law of leasehold covenants, it is first necessary to appreciate that the right to sue on a covenant (the benefit) and the obligation to perform or observe a covenant (the burden) must be treated separately. For example, it may well be true for pre-1996 leases (see below for the relevance of the date) that the current tenant under a lease (not being the original tenant) has the benefit of covenants, but is not subject to the burden of them: that is, the tenant has the right to enforce a covenant, but cannot be compelled to observe any obligation the lease imposes. Consequently, in any 'real life' problem, there are always two distinct questions to be answered, viz:

(a) has the benefit of the particular covenant in issue run to the claimant?; and

(b) is the defendant subject to the burden of it?

Only if both of these questions can be answered positively can there be an action 'on the covenant' between claimant and defendant.

6.4.2   Two sets of rules concerning the enforceability of leasehold covenants

The rules relating to the enforceability of leasehold covenants have undergone a radical transformation in recent years. As we shall see, the common law/pre-1996 statutory rules were unsatisfactory in many respects and prompted the Law Commission to propose wholesale reform of the law of leasehold covenants (Report No 174). Although the Law Commission's proposals were not enacted as originally conceived, they did provide the impetus for reform. After much consideration and consultation, a Private Member's Bill was presented to Parliament and this became the LTCA 1995. This reforming statute applies to all leases – legal and equitable – that are granted on or after 1 January 1996, and it establishes a code for determining the enforceability of leasehold covenants in all such leases. However, for leases granted before 1 January 1996, the old common law/statutory rules still apply, save only that ss 17–20 of the 1995 Act operate retrospectively and apply to them. In due course, the 1995 Act and cases decided under it will come to govern the great majority of leases. For now, however, it is necessary to be aware of both the pre-1996 principles and those of the 1995 Act. This is all the more important when we remember that many pre-1996 leases will have been granted for terms in excess of 90 years and will have decades left to run.

6.5 Rules for leases granted before 1 January 1996

These rules are found in both common law and statute. They are complicated, often inconsistent, and may produce injustice. They were ripe for reform.

6.5.1 Liability between the original landlord and original tenant: the general rule

In any action on a leasehold covenant between the original landlord and the original tenant in a pre-1996 lease, *all* covenants are enforceable. This is simply because the liability of these original parties to the lease is based squarely in contract: viz, the contract between them, which is also the lease. Liability is said to be based on 'privity of contract'. Importantly, as noted, *all* covenants are enforceable, whether or not they relate to the leasehold land or to a personal obligation undertaken by either party. For example, between the original parties, a tenant's covenant to provide the landlord with a free pint of beer (personal) is just as enforceable as a landlord's covenant to repair the premises (proprietary).

6.5.2 The continuing liability of the original tenant throughout the entire term of the lease

The fact that the liability of the original tenant is founded in contract has important consequences. Even though the original tenant may assign (that is, sell or transfer) his lease to another, he will remain liable on the leasehold covenants in a pre-1996 lease throughout the entire term of the lease (*Allied London Investments Ltd v Hambro Life Assurance Ltd* (1984)). This liability will be enforceable by whomsoever has the benefit of the covenants. So, if the current tenant violates any of the covenants (for example, the covenant to pay rent), the landlord may look to the original tenant to perform the covenant (pay the rent), even though the original tenant may have actually left the land many years ago and had nothing to do with the breach. A typical example is where the original tenant took a lease in, say, 1950, but the current tenant (say, the fifth assignee) defaults on the rent in 2002. The original tenant remains liable for this rent, despite having parted with possession years before and in ignorance of the identity of all assignees apart from the very first to whom he assigned. It should come as no surprise that this continuing liability attracted considerable criticism and, as we shall see, it has been abolished by the 1995 Act for tenancies granted on or after 1 January 1996. For tenancies granted prior to the Act, the original tenant remains liable throughout the term of the lease, subject only to the following exceptions and mitigating factors:

(a) the liability of an original tenant will not continue after an assignment of a perpetually renewable lease (Sched 25, s 145 of the LPA 1922);

(b) the contract/lease between the original landlord and original tenant may stipulate expressly that the tenant's liability is to end when the lease is assigned. This is rare. It depends on the original tenant having, and using, a dominant bargaining position. It can occur on a more widespread scale when there is an oversupply of premises for rent, such as during a recession in the commercial property market;

(c) the original tenant will not be liable for breaches of covenant committed by an assignee where the original term of the lease has been statutorily extended under the Landlord and Tenant Act 1954 (and, by analogy, under the Housing Act 1988) and the breach occurs during the statutory extension (*City of London Corp v Fell* (1993)). This is because the original tenant's liability is to be construed, as a matter of contract, as relating to the term as originally agreed, and not to the subsequent legislative extension of that term. The counterargument – that the original parties should have contemplated the risk of a statutory extension when they signed the lease – was not accepted in *Fell*;

(d) the original tenant will not be liable if a subsequent assignee of the lease and landlord agree to surrender the old lease and carry out a 'regrant' of the lease on new terms. Simply put, the 'original' lease has ended and the original tenant's liability with it. In most cases, this surrender and regrant will be explicit, but it can be presumed if current landlord and tenant so vary the terms of the 'old' lease that, in reality, it ceases to exist. This is a more extreme version of the principle noted below, that an original tenant may not be liable if subsequent tenant and landlord vary the terms of individual leasehold covenants (*Friends Provident Life Office v British Railways Board* (1996));

(e) if the original tenant is made liable on a covenant through the actual breach of that covenant by an assignee, the original tenant under a pre-1996 tenancy may have a right to recover any damages or rent paid by them under an indemnity obligation. A right to claim an indemnity may be in the form of an express or implied obligation undertaken by an assignee of the original tenant, and any subsequent assignee, to reimburse any monies paid by the original tenant where the actual acts of default are attributable to that assignee. An indemnity obligation can take one of three forms:

- each assignee in turn may have made an express covenant of indemnity with their assignor, promising to indemnify the assignor in respect of liabilities arising post-assignment. So, a 'chain' of indemnity covenants may exist, stretching from original tenant to current tenant. If, then, the original tenant is forced to pay, he may claim an indemnity from his assignee, who may pass that liability to their assignee, and so on until the current (and defaulting) tenant is reached. As can be seen, however, a chain of indemnity is only as strong as its weakest link and the original tenant may find that the chain is broken before the defaulting tenant is reached;

- in the absence of an express indemnity covenant, the original tenant may be able to rely on the covenant of indemnity that is implied under s 77 of the LPA 1925. However, this covenant may – and often is – expressly excluded by the terms of the original lease;

- the original tenant may be able to rely on an action in 'restitution' (once known as 'quasi-contract') against the person (that is, the defaulting tenant) whose liability has been discharged by the original tenant (*Moule v Garrett* (1872)) but, of course, only to the extent that the defaulter was actually liable. This will occur where it can be shown that the defaulting tenant has been unjustly enriched at the expense of the original tenant and so will be required to reverse the unjust enrichment. It has been held that an express exclusion of the s 77 indemnity covenant does not also exclude the implied indemnity available under *Moule v Garrett* (*Re Healing Research Trustee Co* (1992));

(f) the original tenant will not be liable for any increased rent resulting from a variation of the terms of the lease. In the case of variations effected on or after 1 January 1996, s 18 of the LTCA 1995 applies. This is one of those sections of the 1995 Act that applies to all tenancies, and it means that the original tenant's liability for rent cannot be increased by any variation to the lease after it has been assigned. Note, however, that the original tenant escapes liability only for the *increased* rent attributable to the variation. Further, s 18 does not affect the operation of rent review clauses. So, if a tenant's rent is increased because of the effect of a rent review clause that was a term of the original lease (for example, a clause that says the rent may be adjusted every five years in line with inflation), the original tenant is liable for this increased rent if the current tenant defaults, because this increase is contemplated by the lease itself. It matters not that the increased rent may be far in excess of what the original tenant paid when he actually occupied the premises, because the increase has not been caused by a variation to the terms of the lease, but by the lease itself. A 'variation' (that is, a change in rent for which the original tenant is not liable under s 18) is where the current tenant and current landlord effectively alter the terms of the lease between themselves and it is quite right that the original tenant should not be liable for any increased rent flowing from this later agreement to which he is not a party.

Indeed, such is the common sense embodied in s 18 that the court in *Friends Provident Life Office v British Railways Board* (1996) (followed in *Beegas Nominees Ltd v BHP Petroleum Ltd* (1998)) had already decided, prior to the entry into force of the LTCA 1995, that privity of contract meant privity to the original contract, and not some later variation of it. As it turns out, then, s 18 of the LTCA 1995 was not actually needed. This means that no original tenant will be liable for an increased rent due to a variation, even if that variation occurred before 1 January 1996 and the entry into force of the LTCA 1995;

(g) under s 17 of the 1995 Act, although a pre-1996 original tenant's liability continues throughout the term of the lease, a landlord may only enforce a liability for a fixed charge (for example, rent, service charge or liquidated damages for breach of covenant) by serving a statutory notice (a 'problem notice') within six months of the charge becoming due. For pre-1996 tenancies where a fixed charge is already owed, a landlord must serve a notice within six months of the Act coming into force (which was 1 January 1996) if he wishes to recover rent owed from the original tenant. Failure to serve a notice relieves the original tenant of all liability. This is another aspect of the 1995 Act that applies to all tenancies. It means that an original tenant must now be informed of his potential liability within six months of it becoming due, otherwise the landlord cannot recover from him. Moreover, as noted immediately below, the payment by an original tenant of a fixed charge in consequence of a problem notice gives the original tenant certain rights in relation to the land which he may utilise in an attempt to recover the sum paid;

(h) if an original tenant is served with a problem notice under s 17 of the LTCA 1995 and pays the charge in full (for example, the rent owed), the original tenant becomes entitled to the grant of a lease of the property (called an 'overriding lease') (s 19 of the LTCA 1995). This effectively inserts the original tenant back into the property, so enabling him to deal with it in the hope of recovering some of the money paid out. This is the third provision of the 1995 Act that applies to pre-1996 tenancies. The tenant (or their guarantor) called on to pay the 'fixed charge' (who may be the original tenant or, under the new law, a tenant liable under an authorised guarantee agreement (AGA) (see below, 6.6.2)) may opt for an overriding lease within 12 months of making the payment, and this overriding lease itself is either a pre-1996 or post-1996 tenancy, depending on the nature of the lease which it overrides. It contains the same covenants as the overridden lease, except covenants 'expressed to be personal'. This right to call for an overriding lease against the landlord claiming payment of the fixed charge is itself a Class C(iv) land charge, or minor interest requiring registration, but cannot be an overriding interest (see ss 19 and 20 of the LTCA 1995). As noted above, the effect of accepting an overriding lease (which has nothing to do with 'overriding interests') is to insert the original tenant back into the property. Thus, he becomes the tenant of the current landlord but also the landlord of the defaulting tenant. Consequently, the original tenant who takes an overriding lease can then pursue action against the defaulting tenant to recover the monies they have paid: for example, suing in damages or forfeiting the lease and then assigning it for value to another person.

Finally, for completeness, we should note that the problem notice/overriding lease system applies when the original tenant is liable for a 'fixed charge'. So, the original tenant's liability under other covenants, such as the covenant to repair, remains unaltered unless and until that liability is crystallised by a liquidated damages clause (a clause fixing the amount of damages in advance of a breach).

6.5.3 The continuing rights and obligations of the original landlord throughout the term of the lease

As with the original tenant, the original landlord remains liable on all the leasehold covenants throughout the term of the lease, even after assignment of the reversion (*Stuart v Joy* (1904)), and even to assignees of the tenant if they have the right to enforce the covenants (*Celsteel v Alton (No 2)* (1987)). (This position is modified for tenancies granted on or after 1 January 1996, and is discussed below, 6.6.3.) In similar fashion, as a matter of principle, the ability of the original landlord under a pre-1996 lease to sue for breaches of covenant should remain for the full duration of the lease. However, if and when the landlord assigns the reversion, he will, in effect, pass the benefit of covenants (the right to sue) to the assignee. As we shall see, the effect of s 141(1) of the LPA for pre-1996 leases is to transfer the benefit of all proprietary leasehold covenants to the assignee and, following *Re King* (1963), this operates to transfer the original landlord's right to sue the assignee even if that right exists in respect of a breach of covenant occurring before assignment. So, if in 1989 L has the right to sue T for (say) non-payment of rent, an assignment of the lease by L to L1 in 1990 will pass not only L's right to sue on the benefit of leasehold covenants from thenceforward, but also L's accrued right to sue T for the rent owed in 1989. If L wishes to retain this right, it will have to be reconveyed back explicitly by L1 to L at the time of the assignment (*Kataria v Safeland* (1997)).

6.5.4 The assignment of the lease to a new tenant for pre-1996 leases

The question here is whether the benefit *and* burden of any of the covenants in the lease made between the original landlord and the original tenant can 'run' with the land automatically when the lease is assigned. In simple terms, do the leasehold covenants (benefit and burden) pass automatically to a new tenant on assignment of the lease? In essence, this depends on two factors (*Spencer's Case* (1583)):

(a) does 'privity of estate' exist between the landlord and tenant so as to allow enforcement of the covenants?; *and*

(b) do the covenants 'touch and concern' the land?

6.5.5 The claimant and defendant must be in 'privity of estate'

It is intrinsic to the enforcement of leasehold covenants under pre-1996 tenancies by, and against, the assignee of the lease (the new tenant) that he must stand in the relation of 'privity of estate' with a landlord who is also subject to the benefits and burdens of the covenants. In general terms, privity of estate exists where the claimant and defendant in an action on a leasehold covenant currently stand in the relationship of landlord and tenant under a legal lease. This can be broken down into two parts:

(a) the claimant and defendant must stand in the relationship of landlord and tenant. Hence, there is the potential for privity of estate between the original landlord and an assignee of the lease, between an assignee of the reversion and the original tenant, and between assignees of the reversion and the lease while they are sharing the estate in the land. Significantly, however, there is no privity of estate between a landlord and a subtenant, as they are not *each other's* landlord and tenant. So, the simple point is that, in order for the benefit and burden of leasehold covenants to run to an assignee of the original tenant, that assignee must be 'the tenant' of the landlord who is suing/being sued;

(b) the claimant and defendant must be landlord and tenant under a legal lease. Despite some *dicta* to the contrary (for example, Lord Denning, in *Boyer v Warby* (1953)), it is reasonably clear that 'privity of estate' can exist only in respect of a legal lease. This means not only that the original lease must be legal in character (for which, see above), but also that an assignment of the reversion and/or the lease (as the case may be) must be in the form prescribed for legal interests, that is, by deed (s 52 of the LPA 1925). In this respect, it is important to note that, even if the original lease is created as a legal estate without the need for a deed (that is, it is under three years, etc), if the 'legal' character of it is to be maintained, any assignment of it must be effected by deed (*Julian v Crago* (1992)). The insistence that privity of estate can exist only when the assignee tenant and his landlord are tenant/landlord under a legal lease may seem strange. In truth, it is an historical anomaly generated by the now defunct distinction between courts of law and courts of equity. Nevertheless, it is a distinction at the heart of the pre-1996 law. In fact, it is also important to remember that those leases of long duration, where it is important to have an effective web of transmissible leasehold covenants (for example, a 999 year lease of an office block), will usually be legal in character (having been created by deed), and will be assigned in proper fashion because of the involvement of property professionals. For leases granted on or after 1 January 1996, the same rules apply to legal and equitable leases and this distinction has been swept away.

6.5.6 The covenant must 'touch and concern' the land

In order that the benefit and burden of a leasehold covenant can pass to an assignee of the lease, it is not enough that the tenant stands in a relationship of privity of estate with the claimant/defendant landlord under a legal lease. In addition, for pre-1996 tenancies, only those covenants which 'touch and concern' the land are capable of being enforced by, and against, the assignee of a lease. The purpose of this requirement is to distinguish 'proprietary' covenants from merely 'personal' covenants. Proprietary covenants are those which attach to the land and affect its use, while personal covenants are those which were intended to confer an individual benefit on the original tenant alone. In practice, it can be difficult to distinguish between those covenants which do, and those which do not, 'touch and concern' the land, although considerable help has been provided by the guidelines put forward by Lord Oliver in *Swift Investments v Combined English Stores* (1989). Although this test is not to be applied mechanically (that is, each case depends on its own facts), it is of considerable assistance. In determining the nature of a covenant, the following points are to be considered:

(a) could the covenant benefit *any* owner of an estate in the land as opposed to the particular original tenant (indicates a proprietary covenant)?;

(b) does the covenant affect the nature, quality, mode of user or value of the land (indicates a proprietary covenant)?;

(c) is the covenant expressed to be personal?

Examples of covenants which, by this test, would touch and concern the land are covenants to repair, covenants restrictive of use of the premises (for example, not to carry on a trade or business, not to grow trees over a certain height), covenants not to assign or sublet without consent and, of course, the tenant's covenant to pay rent. Covenants imposing an obligation to pay money have, in the past, caused some concern, but it is now clear from *Swift* that a 'monetary covenant', which underpins the performance of covenants which touch and concern the land, will itself 'touch and concern'. For example, a covenant by a third party promising to underwrite the performance of the covenants (a 'surety covenant') does touch and concern so that it may be enforced by a person other than the original party to whom it was made, *Swift*. Note, however, the strange position with one covenant that appears to 'touch and concern' the land but is in fact treated differently. A landlord's covenant to renew the lease (that is, to give the tenant a new lease at the tenant's option when the old lease expires through time) clearly fulfils the *Swift* test, but it is not capable of being passed (that is, binding a new landlord) under leasehold covenant rules. Following *Phillips v Mobil Oil* (1989), such covenants fall to be treated as typical third party interests under the Land Charges and Land Registration Acts. Hence, in unregistered land, the tenant must ensure that the covenant to renew is registered as a Class C(iv) land charge if it is to bind a purchaser of a legal estate in the land (that is, a new landlord under a legal lease), and, in registered land, the covenant should be registered as a minor interest (and equivalent provision under the LRA 2002), unless it can take effect as an overriding interest under s 70(1)(g) as a right of a person (the tenant) in actual occupation of the land (and equivalent provision under the LRA 2002). This anomalous position is now well established (that is, conveyancers know about it) and has been continued under the system for post-1996 leases.

To sum up then, if the covenants touch and concern the land, they may be enforced by, or against, an assignee of the lease (a new tenant) by or against a landlord with whom the tenant then stands in the relationship of privity of estate under a legal lease or legal assignment thereof.

6.5.7 Special rules

As noted above, even if the assignee of the lease is liable under the leasehold covenants, the liability of the original tenant under a pre-1996 tenancy continues throughout the entire term and, given that this is a primary liability, a landlord may resort to him immediately without resort to the assignee. Hence, it is always in the original tenant's interest to ensure that any assignee of the lease is able and willing to fulfil all covenants. In contrast, the liability of an assignee of the lease extends only to breaches committed while the lease is vested in them. Therefore, an assignee is not liable for breaches of covenant committed before assignment of the lease (*Grescot v Green* (1700)), unless these are of a continuing nature. Likewise, there is no liability for breaches committed after the lease has been assigned (*Paul v Nurse* (1828)). Also, under pre-1996 tenancies, the original tenant is able to sue for breaches of covenants committed while he is in possession of the property, even though the lease may have been assigned subsequently (*City and Metropolitan Properties v Greycroft* (1987)). The same is probably true for all subsequent assignees. Finally, in contrast with the position of original landlords, we may note that an original tenant does not lose the right to sue for breaches of covenant occurring before assignment.

6.5.8 The assignment of the reversion to a new landlord under pre-1996 tenancies

The question to be considered here is the mirror image of that considered above, viz, whether an assignee of the reversion (the 'new' landlord) is able to enjoy the benefits of the covenants in the original lease and whether he is subject to the burdens they impose. However, although the issue is the same, the relevant conditions are slightly different from those surrounding assignment of the lease, primarily because of the intervention of statute.

6.5.9 Section 141 of the Law of Property Act 1925: the benefit of the original landlord's covenants

For pre-1996 tenancies, s 141(1) of the LPA 1925 provides that an assignment of the landlord's reversion carries with it the benefit (the right to sue) of all covenants which 'have reference to the subject matter of the lease'. In essence, this is a statutory transfer of the benefit of all covenants which 'touch and concern' the land (*Hua Chiao Commercial Bank v Chiaphua Investment Corp* (1987)). Note that this means that the benefit of all 'touching and concerning' covenants are transferred to an assignee of the reversion, irrespective of whether privity of estate exists, although, of course, the defendant in an action must still be liable on the covenants and privity of estate may be necessary to establish this. It also means (because of the clear words of the section) that the 'new' landlord acquires the right to sue in respect of breaches of covenant that occurred before assignment and that the 'old' landlord loses this right (see *London and County (A and D) Ltd v Wilfred Sportsman Ltd* (1971)). The test of covenants which have 'reference to the subject matter of the lease' (that is, touch and concern) is that specified by Lord Oliver in *Swift*. In practical terms, then, the transfer of the benefit of all proprietary covenants to an assignee of the landlord is a simple matter: statute ensures that they pass automatically with the lease. Note that under the new rules, s 141(1) has no application to tenancies granted on or after 1 January 1996. It is replaced by a provision having wider effect.

6.5.10 Section 142 of the Law of Property Act 1925: the burden of the original landlord's covenants

For pre-1996 tenancies, s 142(1) of the LPA 1925 provides that an assignment of the landlord's reversion carries with it the burden of (the obligation to perform) all covenants which also 'have reference to the subject matter of the lease'. In essence, this is a statutory transfer of the burden of all covenants which 'touch and concern' the land. Again, this means that the obligation to perform these covenants passes to an assignee of the reversion, irrespective of privity of estate, although the claimant (for example, the current tenant) may need to plead such privity in order to prove that the benefit of the covenant has run to him. In this respect, the *Swift* test of 'touching and concerning' is again relevant, although, as discussed below, some problems have emerged. Note that under the new rules, s 142(1) has no application to tenancies granted on or after 1 January 1996.

Again, then, in practical terms, the position for pre-1996 leases is relatively simple: the burden of all proprietary covenants passes to an assignee of the reversion automatically. However, for reasons that are not particularly clear or convincing, there are some exceptions:

(a) it is clear that a landlord's covenant to renew the lease at the tenant's option when the original term expires does 'have reference to the subject matter of the lease' and hence is capable of being enforced against assignees of the reversion (*Simpson v Clayton* (1838)). However, according to *Beesly v Hallwood Estates* (1960) and *Phillips v Mobil Oil* (1989), the burden of this covenant does not pass automatically on assignment of the reversion, despite the clear words of s 142(1) of the LPA 1925. According to the judge in that case, such a covenant is registrable as a Class C(iv) estate contract in unregistered land, and must be so registered in order to bind the assignee of the reversion: it will not pass automatically. This does seem a strange decision, and has been roundly criticised as being inconsistent with s 142. Indeed, in *Armstrong and Holmes v Holmes* (1993), the judge criticised *Hallwood* and pointed out that it had been disproved of by the Court of Appeal in *Greene v Church Commissioners* (1974). However, even under the new regime, these covenants will continue to be registrable (s 3(6)(b) of the LTCA 1995). Note that, in registered land, if the burden of such a covenant cannot pass automatically under 'leasehold covenant rules' (as *Mobil Oil* implies), it will (happily) constitute an overriding interest under s 70(1)(g) of the LRA 1925 (and equivalent provision of the LRA 2002) and be binding on the assignee of the reversion because the tenant who can enforce it will be in actual occupation of the land to which the covenant relates;

(b) in contrast to a surety covenant which underpins the performance of leasehold obligations (see above (*Swift*)), a covenant by the landlord to repay a deposit given by the tenant does not 'touch and concern' and cannot, therefore, be enforced against an assignee of the landlord who actually received the money under a tenancy granted before 1 January 1996 (*Hua Chiao Commercial Bank*). This changes for tenancies under the LTCA 1995;

(c) a landlord's covenant to sell the freehold to the tenant does not 'touch and concern' the land, and cannot be enforced against an assignee of the reversion (*Woodall v Clifton* (1905)). It is not entirely clear why this covenant should be regarded as personal, whereas the landlord's covenant to renew the lease is regarded as proprietary. Again, this will change for tenancies under the LTCA 1995.

6.5.11 Special rules

As noted above (and in contrast to the position with the original tenant), the ability of the original landlord to sue for breaches of covenant ceases after assignment of the reversion, even if the breach was committed before that assignment. This is because s 141(1) of the LPA 1925 transfers all rights to the assignee whenever they accrue (*Re King*).

Secondly, the liability of an assignee of the reversion ceases when he assigns the lease to another assignee. However, it is uncertain whether an assignee of the reversion is liable for breaches of covenants committed by the original landlord before assignment. As a matter of principle, it would seem that he should not be so liable, but *dicta* in *Celsteel v Alton* (1985) suggest otherwise.

Thirdly, the benefit and burden of leasehold covenants under pre-1996 tenancies pass to the assignee of the reversion by statute, not by the doctrine of privity of estate. Therefore, benefits and burdens pass, and may be sued on, in circumstances where there is no privity of estate, as in equitable leases/equitable assignments, or where the assignee of the reversion sues the original tenant even though the original tenant had never been *that* assignee's tenant (for example, because the lease was assigned before the reversion) (*Arlesford Trading v Servansingh* (1971)).

Fourthly, rights of re-entry are special rights reserved by a landlord to 're-enter' the property and end the lease as a result of a tenant's breach of covenant. Importantly, every assignee of the reversion of a pre-1996 tenancy obtains the benefit of this right if it was included in the original lease (s 141 of the LPA 1925), and every tenant will be subject to the right of re-entry even if they are not actually liable on the covenants which have been broken (*Shiloh Spinners v Harding* (1973)). The position will be the same under the new regime (s 4 of the LTCA 1995). Finally, by way of confirmation of the special position of rights of re-entry, we can note *Kataria v Safeland plc* (1997). In that case, the reversion was assigned together with a right of re-entry, but the 'old' landlord was granted by contract the right to recover rent owed prior to the assignment (that is, the parties contracted out of *Re King* (1963)). The new landlord was not owed rent but, nevertheless, was permitted to enforce his right of re-entry because rent was owing on the land and the right of re-entry stands separately from the covenants that it underpins.

6.5.12 Equitable leases and equitable assignments of legal leases

As far as pre-1996 tenancies are concerned, all that has been said above about the running of leasehold covenants to successors in title of the original landlord and original tenant apply when both the original lease was legal and the assignment of it was made in the way appropriate to legal interests, that is, by deed. If, however, the original lease is equitable, or if a legal lease is imperfectly assigned (by written contract, not deed), then for pre-1996 tenancies, different considerations apply, primarily because, as explained above, 'privity of estate' does not exist under equitable leases or equitable assignments of legal leases.

6.5.13 The original landlord and tenant

As noted above, most equitable leases arise from a specifically enforceable contract between the prospective landlord and prospective tenant. Consequently, the original parties are bound in contract to perform all the obligations of the lease, even those which are purely personal in nature.

6.5.14 The assignment of the reversion of an equitable lease to a new landlord

The intervention of statute means that, where the reversion of an equitable lease is assigned (or a legal reversion is imperfectly assigned), the absence of privity of estate does not seriously prejudice the equitable assignee's position. This is because ss 141 and 142 of the LPA 1925 apply to the benefits and burdens of the original landlord's covenants, irrespective of the nature of the lease in which they are contained. Therefore, for pre-1996 tenancies, by virtue of s 141(1) of the LPA 1925, the assignee of the reversion of an equitable lease will be entitled to enforce all leasehold covenants (the benefit) which 'have reference to the subject matter of the lease' (that is, 'touch and concern'). Likewise, under s 142(1), the obligation to perform similar covenants (the burden) will pass to the assignee. In short, the position is very similar to that operating for legal leases granted prior to 1 January 1996.

However, for a pre-1996 tenancy, the position is not quite as straightforward as first appears. In order for the passing of the 'benefit' or 'burden' to have any practical meaning, the landlord must have someone to sue, or someone who can sue him. If the land is still held by the original tenant, there is no problem, as this will be the original contracting party and he will be bound by the terms of the lease. But, if the tenant has also assigned the equitable lease, two further issues must be resolved. First, does the lease *itself* bind the purchaser of the reversion, so that the new landlord takes the land subject to the equitable tenancy? This falls to be determined by the normal rules of registered or unregistered conveyancing (see Chapters 2 and 3). Secondly, and more importantly, before the new landlord can actually rely on the leasehold covenants or be accountable under them, it is also necessary to show that the assignee of the equitable tenant is subject to the burden, or enjoys the benefit of those covenants (as the case may be). For pre-1996 tenancies, this turns on the rules discussed below.

6.5.15 The assignment of the equitable lease to a new tenant

The ability of the benefit or burden of the original tenant's covenants in a pre-1996 tenancy to run with the assignment of an equitable lease (or an imperfect assignment of a legal lease) is complicated. The first point is that, traditionally, this situation lacks the necessary 'privity of estate' and so *Spencer's Case* (1583) does not apply and the covenants cannot pass automatically. However, it is well established that the *benefit* (but not the burden) of any contract can be expressly assigned. Consequently, an equitable tenant is perfectly free to transfer the benefit of every covenant (including personal ones) to the assignee expressly when the lease is itself assigned. Indeed, this is normal conveyancing procedure, and has the consequence that most equitable assignees will have the right to enforce the original tenant's covenants against whomsoever is subject to their burden. The reason is, quite simply, that the original contracting party has passed the benefits under the contract (the right to sue) to the person to whom he has also assigned the lease.

Unfortunately, however, there are no parallel rules concerning the passing of the burden of the original equitable tenant's leasehold covenants. In fact, as *Purchase v Lichfield Brewery* (1915) illustrates, an equitable assignee of the lease may not be liable to perform any of the original tenant's covenants, including the obligation to pay rent. This is the combined effect of the rule that no privity exists between landlord and tenant under an equitable lease (or equitable assignment of a legal lease), so leasehold covenants cannot pass automatically, and the rule that burdens of a contract cannot be assigned, so preventing the express *inter partes* transfer of leasehold obligations. So, while benefits may run under an equitable lease, and the new tenant may sue the landlord (because of *inter partes* assignment), the landlord cannot sue the tenant. Obviously, this can cause considerable hardship to the landlord who may find the value of his reversion substantially diminished through an assignment of the lease over which they had no control and where the land is now possessed by a tenant whom they cannot control. Consequently, a number of alternative, or 'indirect', methods of enforcing the burden of leasehold covenants against equitable assignees of the lease have been developed. These are considered below. For the most part, they will be redundant for tenancies granted on or after 1 January 1996 because of the statutory magic of the LTCA 1995.

In *Boyer v Warby* (1953), Denning LJ held that the burden of leasehold covenants which 'touched and concerned' could pass to the assignee of a lease for three years or less (which is legal without a deed), even though the assignment itself was not by deed. On one view, this could be taken to mean that the principle of *Purchase* has been overruled, and that burdens (and so benefits) can pass automatically, as with legal leases. However, this wide interpretation is very doubtful, and no conclusive reasoning was given other than that 'law' and 'equity' were now fused. Unfortunately, this merely assumes what it has to prove. In other words, *Boyer* should be limited to its own facts: viz, the lease was originally legal, even though not made by deed (being for three years or less), and its assignment without deed was treated (without justification) as an effective transfer of the legal estate, so preserving the required 'privity of estate' necessary to make leasehold covenants run.

Secondly, even if the covenants themselves are not binding on the equitable assignee, they can be enforced against that assignee indirectly by means of a right of re-entry (forfeiture clause) in the original lease. As we shall see, the right of re-entry allows a landlord to recover premises after a breach of covenant and thereby end the lease. Such rights of re-entry stand alone, and may be relied on by a landlord if a covenant is broken, even though the covenant itself was not binding on the tenant (*Shiloh Spinners v Harding* (1973)), or, indeed, even if a previous landlord enjoys the personal right to enforce the covenant, as in *Kataria v Safeland plc* (1997). This may seem odd, because the right of re-entry is usually seen as a remedy for breach of covenant and thus appears to require that a covenant has been broken by the person subject to the remedy of forfeiture. However, land law is more inventive than this. A proprietary ('touching and concerning') leasehold covenant attaches to the land, even though the current tenant as an equitable assignee may not be bound by it. Consequently, if actions take place on the land which contravene the covenant, the covenant has been broken. Admittedly, direct action against the defaulting tenant is not possible (for example, no damages), but action against the land is. So, if the landlord has the benefit of a right of re-entry, the landlord can 're-enter', take possession and bring the lease to an end. Although there are statutory controls on the exercise of the right of re-entry (see below, 6.7.5), it will be appreciated that the possibility of re-entry is very persuasive in ensuring that the tenant does, in fact, observe the leasehold covenants. Would the tenant be happy to lose his lease through forfeiture or instead actually perform the leasehold obligations? We must note, however, that the efficacy of this indirect enforcement method is constrained by the following requirements: first, that a right of re-entry must first exist and its benefit have been passed to the current landlord (this is most likely); secondly, that the leasehold covenant is proprietary in nature; and thirdly, that the tenant is bound by the right of re-entry, even though not bound by the actual covenants. This last restriction operates differently, depending on whether the land is registered or unregistered. In unregistered land, rights of re-entry in an equitable lease are not land charges and are binding on a tenant (and any other person in possession) according to the doctrine of notice. A tenant will be deemed to have notice of all terms of the original lease, including the right of re-entry, and hence the condition is satisfied easily. In registered land, the right of re-entry is likely to bind automatically under the express provision in s 23(1)(a) of the LRA 1925 (or the LRA 2002 equivalent).

Thirdly, even though the landlord and equitable assignee do not stand in a relationship of privity of estate, any 'restrictive covenants' (that is, those preventing the assignee of the lease from doing something on the land) may be enforced by virtue of the principle of *Tulk v Moxhay* (1848). This is discussed more fully in Chapter 8 (the law of freehold covenants), but in essence the rule in *Tulk v Moxhay* (1848) permits the enforcement of any restrictive proprietary covenant against a person in possession of the land over which the covenant takes effect. This may be an adverse possessor, freeholder or, as here, an equitable tenant. So, if an equitable lease contains a restrictive covenant and the benefit of that covenant has passed to the current landlord (as is most likely: s 141(1) of the LPA 1925), that covenant can be enforced against the equitable tenant by means of an injunction preventing any continuation of the activity which is prohibited (for example, the tenant may not carry on a trade or business). The conditions are that the covenant is proprietary ('touches and concerns'), that it has become attached to the land (achieved through s 79 of the LPA 1925; see Chapter 8) and that it is binding on the tenant. In unregistered land, the restrictive leasehold covenant cannot be a land charge, and so will be binding according to the doctrine of notice (*Dartstone v Cleveland Petroleum* (1969)). Again, the tenant will be deemed to have notice of all covenants contained in the lease. In registered land, the restrictive covenant will be binding because of the effect of s 23(1)(a) of the LRA 1925 (or the equivalent under the LRA 2002).

Fourthly, it may be possible to argue that a new legal tenancy comes into existence between the landlord and the equitable assignee when the assignee pays rent and this is accepted. Such a periodic tenancy will usually be legal (because it will be for three years or less, no formality required) and leasehold covenants will be directly enforceable. However, it is not clear why the covenants implied into the 'new' legal periodic tenancy between landlord and equitable assignee should be the same as those contained in the original equitable lease, and there remains the difficulty that the parties will have intended and believed that their relations are governed by the old equitable lease, not some new artificial creation.

Finally, it may be possible to *imply* new contractual obligations on the part of the equitable assignee in favour of the landlord which will then create a direct contractual nexus between the parties. This is similar to the above situation, except that now, only new obligations are being created, not a whole new lease. The circumstances in which this implication may be made are a matter of some debate and much will depend on the circumstances in which the assignee has taken the lease. Proprietary estoppel may come to the aid of the landlord, although it may be difficult to prove that simple denial of the benefit of covenants is unconscionable enough to give the landlord his remedy. Of course, if the equitable assignee enters into new *express* covenants directly with the landlord, then these are enforceable as a matter of contract. In fact, the possibility of new, direct covenants between the intended assignee and the landlord is a real option if the landlord has the right to refuse/withhold consent to assignment of the lease. In such a case the insistence on new direct covenants between assignee and landlord may be the price extracted for the landlord's agreement to the assignment.

The efficacy of these methods of enforcement should not be underestimated. The threat of re-entry, the enforcement of restrictive covenants by injunction and the ability of the landlord to extract new direct covenants can prove just as effective in ensuring that the equitable assignee observes the leasehold covenants as would have been the case had the covenants passed automatically. Consequently, the 'new' statutory rules of the LTCA 1995, discussed below, 6.6, should not be seen as directed primarily at the 'evils' associated with equitable leases. These 'evils' can be countered and usually are.

6.5.16 The position of subtenants

As was indicated at the very outset of this chapter, a tenant may create out of their interest a 'shorter' tenancy for another person. The original tenant under the 'headlease' then becomes the landlord of his own tenant, often called the subtenant. Of course, the subtenancy may contain its own covenants and, often, these will be identical to those contained in the headlease. However, it may well happen that it is the subtenant (the actual occupier) of the land who so acts as to cause a breach of a covenant which was made between the original landlord and original tenant. An example is where the original tenant has promised not to carry on any trade or business, but then a sublet is established, and the subtenant does just that. Once again, the head landlord has a problem, as he or she does not stand in the relationship of privity of estate with the subtenant and cannot enforce leasehold covenants against him directly. There are, however, a number of possibilities that may effectively assist the landlord in this situation, assuming that the current tenant is not personally prepared to act against the subtenant under the contract (that is, the sublease) that exists between the tenant and subtenant:

(a) the head landlord may enforce a right of re-entry against the current tenant. This is because, in absolute terms, the acts of the subtenant have factually caused a violation of the covenant which the tenant owes to his landlord. Hence, the landlord has at his disposal the remedy of forfeiture. As is explained below, successful forfeiture of the tenancy automatically terminates the subtenancy. Necessarily, this is an effective, but drastic, remedy. It results in the landlord having no tenant and hence no income from the land unless a new lease can be arranged. It may not be a remedy of first choice;

(b) the head landlord may be able to use the *Tulk v Moxhay* rules to enforce restrictive covenants directly against the subtenant. The situation is effectively the same as that discussed in relation to the position of equitable assignees and subject to the same limitations, both legal and practical;

(c) the subtenant may enter into direct covenants with the head landlord. These can again be enforced directly as a matter of contract. Likewise, the landlord may be able to insist that these covenants are entered into as a condition of his consent to such subtenancy, if that power has been retained in the lease between the landlord and tenant.

6.5.17 The Law Commission and proposals for reform

Prompted by some of the uncertainties, inconsistencies and perceived injustices of the pre-1926 law, the Law Commission proposed (in Report No 174) a number of changes to the law of leasehold covenants. The Law Commission believed that the continuing liability of the original tenant throughout the entire term of the lease both distorted the public perception of the nature of the landlord and tenant relationship (that is, that liability is co-extensive with possession), and caused unwarranted and unfair hardship to tenants who found themselves liable to perform repairing or other obligations undertaken some time ago and now broken by some tenant over whom they had no control: for example, where the tenant in breach was the third or fourth assignee. Consequently, they proposed that when a tenant assigned a leasehold interest, he should be released automatically from all liability in respect of any future breaches of the covenants. The only exception would be where an assignment by the tenant was conditional on the landlord's consent, in which case the landlord could impose a condition whereby the original tenant would guarantee the performance of the covenants by the immediate assignee. However, any continuing liability imposed in this manner could not extend beyond one assignment and it would truly be a guarantee, so that the landlord would have to look to the assignee first in the event of any breach.

Somewhat surprisingly, however, the Law Commission did not feel it necessary to protect the landlord from continuing liability under his covenants. Thus, under the original proposals, a landlord would remain liable for breaches of covenant committed by his successors unless he served a notice on the tenant indicating his desire to be released. Should the tenant disagree with the proposed release, the matter would be resolved in court, with the landlord seeking to establish that it would be reasonable to release him from continuing responsibility. In similar fashion, originally, there was no proposal to change the current effect of s 141 of the LPA 1925 whereby a landlord who assigns the reversion loses the right to sue for beaches of covenant, even if they have been committed while he was the landlord (that is, the rule of *Re King* (1963)).

The Law Commission also proposed a much more radical reform: the abandonment of the requirement of 'touching and concerning' as the touchstone for the transmissibility of the benefits and burdens of leasehold covenants. As we shall see, this has now been done, even though most of the problems with the 'touching' principle appear to have been generated more by the fact that it is difficult to define in advance what the concept of 'touching and concerning' requires, rather than by an analysis of whether the rationale behind the requirement is still compelling.

6.6 The new scheme: the law applicable to tenancies granted on or after 1 January 1996; the Landlord and Tenant (Covenants) Act 1995

The Law Commission's proposals generated much public interest and resulted eventually in the presentation of a Private Member's Bill to Parliament. It may seem surprising that such a 'technical' item of legislation should be presented to Parliament under the cumbersome Private Member's Bill procedure instead of being guided through smoothly as an uncontroversial government Bill. In fact, opposition to the Law Commission's proposals by landlords' pressure groups, such as the British Retail Consortium, and pressure on the legislative timetable, meant that the Private Member's Bill procedure was, at the time, the only hope of securing reform of leasehold covenant law. Even then, the strength of this opposition, when combined with the absence of government protection, nearly destroyed the Bill and did result in the new Act being much more of a compromise between tenants' and landlords' interests than was envisaged originally by the Law Commission. As we shall see, one view of the legislation is that the improvement in the position of tenants secured by the LTCA 1995 is effectively countered by the corresponding advantages secured for landlords, at least in respect of commercial leases.

The LTCA 1995 came into force on 1 January 1996. Save for those sections of the Act, mentioned above, that apply to all tenancies, the Act will regulate the transmission of the benefit and burden of leasehold covenants in all new tenancies granted *on or after* that date. Consequently, for such tenancies, reference must be made to the Act to determine whether a landlord or tenant is bound by, or may enforce, leasehold covenants relating to the land demised in the lease (*Oceanic Village v United Attractions* (2000)).

6.6.1 General principles of the 1995 Act

First, the Act applies to tenancies granted on or after 1 January 1996, and it applies in the same way to legal and equitable tenancies. The old rules that differentiated between these types of lease are no longer relevant (s 28(1) of the LTCA 1995).

Secondly, the tenant (whether original or an assignee) is released automatically from the burden of leasehold covenants when he assigns the tenancy (s 5 of the LTCA 1995), subject only to the possibility that he might be required to guarantee performance of the leasehold covenants by the next (but only the next) immediate assignee (s 16 of the LTCA 1995). There is an exception for assignments made in breach of covenant, or assignments made by operation law, when the assigning tenant remains liable (s 11(2)).

Thirdly, the original landlord is not released automatically from the burdens of leasehold covenants, but may serve a notice on the tenant applying for such release (s 6). Release will then occur if the notice is not answered within a specified time, or if the landlord's application to the county court in the event of objection by the tenant is successful (s 8). A landlord assigning this reversion in breach of covenant, or by operation of law, cannot serve such a notice (s 11(3)). Note, however, that a successful notice relieves the original landlord from liability under 'landlord' covenants. It does not relieve liability under personal covenants which, because they are expressed to be personal (see below) have not passed to the assignee: *BHP Petroleum v Chesterfield Properties* (2001)

Fourthly, the rule, that covenants must 'touch and concern' the land, or 'have reference to the subject matter of the lease', before the benefits and burdens can pass to assignees of the lease or the reversion, is abolished (ss 2 and 3).

Fifthly, the benefit and burden of all leasehold covenants pass automatically to assignees of the lease and the reversion so that an assignee may enforce, and will be subject to, any covenant contained in the lease (s 3). There is no need to show 'privity of estate', and ss 141 and 142 are no longer applicable. There is automatic annexation of all leasehold covenants to the premises comprised in all leases and reversions. Only those covenants that are positively expressed to be personal, or that are not actually binding on the assignor, or that do not relate to the premises subject to the lease (ss 3(1)(a) and 3(2)) will not so pass. Note, also, that, unlike the 'old' law, the transfer of the benefit of a covenant to an assignee of the landlord does not deprive the assignor of the right to sue in respect of breaches occurring before the assignment, so reversing *Re King* (1963) for 'new' leases (s 24(4)).

Sixthly, the provisions relating to problem notices and overriding leases, discussed above, also apply to tenancies falling under the Act. For example, if an assigning tenant is called on to pay a sum under his guarantee of the next immediate assignee's liability, then a notice must be served within the proper period (six months from the liability arising) for the guarantee to be enforceable. Likewise the guarantor has the option of securing an overriding lease.

6.6.2 The tenant's position in more detail

The 1995 Act has modified considerably the position of tenants under leasehold covenants. The two most important reforms are the rule that tenants are released from the burden of all covenants when they assign the lease, and the rule that the benefit and burden of covenants will pass to an assignee of the lease. Gone are the worries about the continuing liability of an original tenant throughout the entire term of the lease, but no longer does a landlord have to prove 'privity of estate' and 'touching and concerning' before he can enforce leasehold covenants against a tenant in possession. All current tenants under post-1995 legal or equitable leases will be bound by the leasehold covenants. For example, an assignee under an equitable lease will be bound to carry out the original tenant's covenant to repair, even though no privity of estate exists with the current landlord. Similarly, the original tenant will be released from this liability, save only that he may have been required to enter an authorised guarantee agreement (AGA) to guarantee performance of the obligation by the tenant to whom he assigns.

Although the Act has entered into force, and applies to leases granted on or after 1 January 1996, case law remains scarce. The statute itself is well drafted, but the diverse use of the leasehold estate is sure to generate unforeseen difficulties and anomalies. It will be some time yet before the precise operation of the statute is clear. What follows, then, is an outline of the effects of the legislation on both a legal and equitable tenant under a lease to which the statute applies. Note that the statute says nothing about the position of subtenants: a subtenant takes a new lease from his landlord (to which, of course, the Act will apply separately) and is not an assignee.

First for consideration is the principle encapsulating one of the fundamental motives for the legislation: that the original tenant and all subsequent tenants will be released from the obligation to perform the covenants (and lose the right to enforce them) on assignment, provided that such assignment is not itself in breach of covenant, or otherwise excluded by operation of law (ss 5 and 11 of the LTCA 1995).

Necessarily, the release of the original tenant from liability on assignment deprives the landlord of an effective remedy if the tenant currently in possession defaults on the lease. For this reason, a landlord may require the current tenant to enter into an Authorised Guarantee Agreement (AGA) as a condition to an assignment of the lease (s 16). Such an agreement will oblige the assigning tenant to be guarantor of the tenant's leasehold covenants for the next immediate assignee. So, if T wishes to assign to T1, the landlord may be able to require T (usually by means of a covenant, or as a condition annexed to the landlord's agreement to the assignment) to guarantee the performance of the covenants by T1. Such an agreement may only operate as a guarantee for the next assignee; so, on an assignment by T1 to T2, T's guarantee agreement is discharged. This procedure is a necessary counterbalance to the release of the tenant on assignment, and was proposed by the Law Commission in its original report. The circumstances in which a landlord may require a current tenant to enter into an AGA as a condition to consent to assign are found in s 16(3) of the 1995 Act, being: where the lease contains a covenant by the tenant not to assign without the landlord's consent; and where the landlord gives such consent on condition that an AGA is concluded; and where the AGA is, in fact, concluded, in order to satisfy the landlord's condition. As a starting point, the landlord cannot withhold consent to the proposed assignment on the grounds that he wishes the tenant to enter into an AGA, unless the insistence on an AGA is reasonable in the circumstances (s 16(3)). However, for commercial leases, if the tenant's refusal to agree to an AGA is made an express ground on which the landlord may refuse consent to assign, the landlord's insistence on an AGA cannot be challenged on the grounds of reasonableness, and not even if the landlord imposes additional conditions such as that the assignment (with AGA) may be made only if the assignee meets some other objective criteria – such as that the company must have a certain level of capital reserves, or is publicly quoted, or is fully insured, or is backed by appropriate guarantees (s 22 of the LTCA 1995 (amending s 19 of the Landlord and Tenant Act 1927)).

Although these provisions appear complicated, the crucial point is that if a lease granted on or after 1 January 1996 contains a promise by the tenant not to assign without the landlord's consent, and the landlord requires an AGA before he will give such consent, the assigning tenant will be required to enter an AGA in order to assign if that is reasonable or, for commercial leases, if the need for an AGA was stated expressly as a condition on which consent to assignment could be refused by the landlord. It should also be noted that, if the tenant has promised by covenant to give an AGA on assignment, that promise will bind all future assignees under the new scheme as a transmissible leasehold covenant: thus, all assignees may be required to give an AGA for the person to whom they wish to assign. Note also that if a landlord seeks to enforce an AGA against the last immediate tenant, the 'problem notice' procedure of s 17 is applicable, so that the guaranteeing tenant will be given at least six months notice of a liability and the potential to claim an overriding lease under s 18 of the LTCA 1995. So to sum up this point, although landlords have lost the right to sue the original tenant, all professionally drafted leases will contain a provision enabling a landlord to impose an AGA on the assigning tenant, and that obligation will bind each assignee in turn as a 'running' leasehold covenant. The landlord retains a second defendant (the guarantor/immediate assignor) as compensation for losing the original tenant as second defendant. Seen as such, it is clear that the Law Commission's aim of relieving the original tenant of continuing liability has been achieved at the price of transferring that liability 'down the chain' of assignments to each assigning tenant in turn. Undoubtedly, this is fairer, but it should not be thought that the 1995 Act has diminished to any great extent the totality of rights available to a landlord when default occurs.

Secondly, and as a corollary, the other major effect of the LTCA is that assignees of the current tenant will acquire the benefit and burden of all leasehold covenants relating to the demised premises, save only that benefits and burdens of covenants that are 'expressed to be personal to any person' will not pass (s 3(6)(a) of the LTCA 1995). Again, however, this does not deprive the assignor of the right to sue for pre-assignment breaches, so reversing *Re King* (1963) (s 24(4) of the LTCA 1995). As noted above, the decision to ensure that the benefit and burden of all leasehold covenants relating to the demised premises pass on assignment was taken in response to concerns over the adequacy of the 'touching and concerning' test. Under the new law, it appears that we need not attempt to differentiate between 'proprietary' and 'personal' covenants, because all pass unless 'expressed to be personal' (*BHP Petroleum v Chesterfield Properties* (2001)). It is not at all clear that this was a wise reform because the distinction between obligations attaching to the land (for example, 'the tenant must repair') and obligations attaching only to the person (for example, 'the tenant must walk the landlord's dog') is at the heart of property law: see, for example, the distinction between leases and licences. If it is argued that very few 'personal' covenants are found in leases anyway, so implying that making all covenants run will cause little practical hardship, surely that also demonstrates that the occasions for applying the allegedly fickle 'touching and concerning' test were also rare and caused little practical hardship! In fact, much will turn on how the courts interpret the statute when it says that a covenant which '(in whatever terms) is expressed to be personal' will not run. There is the possibility that a court will take the view that a covenant is 'expressed to be personal' which says, either, 'this is personal', or which is manifestly personal in substance although the judgment in *BHP Petroleum v Chesterfield Properties* suggests that the personal nature of a covenant must be expressly declared and, importantly, is conclusive. If so, we will need rules about what is personal in substance and may find ourselves back at the feet of the 'touching and concerning' test, whatever the Law Commission intended. Note, also, that the Law Commission felt unable to change the rule that covenants to renew required separate registration in order to bind an assignee of the reversion: the *Mobil Oil* principle remains intact (s 3(6)(b) of the LTCA 1995).

6.6.3 An assessment of the landlord's position

The landlord may, at first, appear to have lost most by the passing of this new Act. After all, the original landlord is not automatically released from performance of his covenants, but must serve a notice on the tenant requesting this, and the landlord has lost the right to sue the original tenant throughout the term of the lease. However, as intimated already, all is not as it seems.

First, the benefit and burden of all landlord's covenants will pass automatically to an assignee of the reversion, unless expressed to be personal and with the exception of the landlord's covenant to renew the lease at the tenant's option (*Mobil Oil* and *BHP Petroleum*). With the passing of the benefit and burden of all the tenant's covenants – even to an equitable tenant/assignee – every landlord can now be certain of having a remedy against the tenant in possession of the land. Although landlords acting against assignees of equitable leases did have ways of ensuring that leasehold obligations were observed (see above, 6.5.15), the simplification of the rules concerning enforceability brought about by the Act is a definite advantage for landlords. Secondly, the ability to require the assigning tenant to enter into an AGA, and the fact that, if this requirement is itself imposed by covenant, it will require the same of all subsequent assignees of the lease, places the landlord in a strong position – the more so in commercial leases, where there is no reasonableness requirement. Thirdly, the problem notice procedure is tiresome, but will not hinder a careful landlord. The landlord – or, more realistically, his legal advisers – will simply have time limits to observe, and this is already a common feature of the landlord and tenant relationship. Moreover, if the tenant called to account under the AGA chooses to take up the option of an overriding lease, this is unlikely to disturb the landlord: after all, the landlord knows that the tenant under the overriding lease is solvent, as they have just paid the sum demanded! Fourthly, the benefit of a landlord's right of re-entry is automatically annexed to the land, thus giving all assignees of the reversion the opportunity to forfeit the lease if the current tenant defaults (s 4), or, indeed, if there is any default on a covenant affecting the land irrespective of whether the covenant binds the defaulter (as above, 6.5.5; and see *Kataria v Safeland plc* (1997)).

6.6.4 To sum up

It is tempting to shy away from the law of leasehold covenants because of its complexity. Admittedly, this is understandable when dealing with the law applicable to tenancies granted before 1 January 1996 where the old common law/statutory rules still hold sway, and where it is vital to distinguish between different types of covenant and different types of landlord and tenant. However, for leases granted on or after 1 January 1996, the position is relatively simple:

(a) all leasehold covenants relating to the demised premises bind assignees of the landlord and tenant (including equitable lessees/assignees) unless expressed to be personal (and excluding the covenant to renew). There is no need to worry about 'touching or concerning', privity of estate, or ss 141(1) and 142(1) of the LPA 1925. The same is true of the benefit of such covenants;

(b) an original tenant is released from liability throughout the term of the lease, but an original landlord must serve a notice requesting such release;

(c) a landlord can require the assigning tenant to guarantee the next immediate assignee's performance of covenants by means of an AGA (but only the next immediate assignee), and can enforce this liability subject to the problem notice/overriding lease procedure. If the tenant specifically promises by covenant in the original lease to give an AGA, that promise will bind all assignees of the lease just as any other leasehold covenant, so that assignees must give an AGA before *they* assign;

(d) restrictive covenants will continue to bind subtenants, subject to registration requirements under the *Tulk v Moxhay* rules (s 3(5) and (6) of the LTCA 1995).

6.7 The landlord's remedies for breach of covenant

After having established that a particular landlord has the right to sue on a covenant *and* that the particular defendant tenant is subject to the burden of it, the next matter is to consider the nature of the remedies available to the landlord. These will be considered in turn, although there is no doubt that the remedy of forfeiture is the most important for our purposes.

6.7.1 Distress

The remedy of distress allows a landlord to enter the land of his tenant and seize goods found there in order to sell them for the purpose of paying any arrears of rent. It is a feudal remedy, grounded in self-help, and is available only to a landlord proper, and not a licensor (*Ward v Day* (1864)). It requires no court proceedings and perhaps that is why there are many restrictions on the exercise of the remedy of distress, both common law and statutory. For example, distress must be levied between sunrise and sunset, entry must not be forcible (unless the landlord has already gained entry and is forcibly ejected: *Khazanchi v Faircharm* (1998)), certain goods are exempt, especially the tenant's 'tools of the trade' and goods in actual use. Likewise, a subtenant's property may not be seized by a head landlord, although an innocent stranger's goods may be seized, subject to the right of the owner to claim their return. Importantly, resort to distress by the landlord is a clear affirmation of the continuation of the landlord and tenant relationship and, therefore, excludes the remedy of forfeiture (which seeks to end that relationship). Action by way of court proceedings to recover arrears of rent also precludes distress. The Law Commission has proposed the abolition of this remedy although this is resisted by landlords' interest groups precisely because of its utility in difficult situations: for example, when a landlord anticipates a tenant's bankruptcy and acts to seize goods in anticipation.

6.7.2 Action for arrears of rent

The landlord can enforce the covenant to pay rent by bringing an action to recover arrears of rent either in the High Court or county court, depending on the amount owed. By virtue of s 19 of the Limitation Act 1980, a maximum of six years' rent may be recovered in this way. The limitation also applies to guarantors of the tenant's promise to pay rent (*Romain v Scuba* (1996)). It often happens that one reason why a tenant has not paid rent is a real (or perceived) failure by the landlord to perform his covenants, often the landlord's covenant to repair. Usually, leasehold covenants are not interdependent, so that non-performance by the landlord of his obligations is not an excuse for non-performance by the tenant. For example, the landlord's failure to honour his promise to repair is not usually a lawful reason to withhold rent, and the tenant can be vulnerable to landlord's remedies for non-payment of rent unless the tenant can show that the withheld rent was actually used to pay for repairs for which the landlord was liable, and which fell due after the disrepair occurred. Note however, if the landlord does bring in an action for recovery of rent, a tenant may claim to 'set off' a sum representing damages for breach of covenant, unless such right is expressly excluded (*Lee-Parker v Izzet* (1971)). Thus, although the tenant has broken his covenant (and importantly opened himself to other remedies), the result can take account of the context of the claim.

6.7.3 Action for damages

The landlord may sue for damages for breach of every covenant other than the covenant to pay rent. Except in the case of covenants to repair, the measure of damages will be that necessary to put the landlord in the same position as if the covenant had not been broken. By virtue of the Landlord and Tenant Act 1927, damages for a tenant's breach of a covenant to repair are limited to the amount by which the landlord's interest (the reversion) has diminished in value through the lack of repair, and although this may be the amount necessary to carry out proper repairs (*Jones v Herxheimer* (1950)), there is a very real likelihood that the amount will be less than this, due to uncertainties about how much the reversion really has declined in value (*Crewe Services and Investment Corp v Silk* (1997)). Note, also, that for leases of seven years or more (with at least three years left to run), the procedure relating to 'notices' set down in the Leasehold Property (Repairs) Act 1938 must be followed before a claim in damages can be made (see below with reference to forfeiture).

6.7.4 Injunction and specific performance

At the discretion of the court, a landlord may obtain an injunction to prevent the breach of a restrictive covenant by the tenant: as where the landlord secures an injunction against the keeping of animals on the land contrary to covenant. However, the orthodox view is that a landlord cannot obtain specific performance of the majority of tenants' covenant (an exception is a covenant to build), as this would generate problems about how the court could supervise the tenant in execution of the covenant, as well as raising general issues of equity and fairness. So, in *Co-op Insurance Society v Argyll Stores* (1997), the House of Lords refused to order specific performance of a tenant's covenant to keep open retail premises for a specified time. Likewise, *Hill v Barclay* (1811) was thought to be clear authority that a landlord could not obtain specific performance of a tenant's repairing obligation, even though in fact this point was not critical to the decision in the case. Yet, in a novel judgment, Lawrence Collins QC (sitting as a deputy judge of the High Court) held in *Rainbow Estates v Tokenhold* (1998) that a landlord could obtain specific performance of a tenant's repairing obligation in special and exceptional circumstances, particularly where the landlord had no other remedy and the court's order could be defined with precision and, hence, was capable of supervision. It now appears that this has become the new orthodoxy (in the sense that it has not been judicially disapproved), but we might wonder why a landlord who has failed to include a right of re-entry in the lease, or a right to enter and repair and recover the costs from the tenant, should be sent the lifeboat of an order for specific performance. It might be thought that these 'exceptional' circumstances were all the landlord's own making.

6.7.5   Forfeiture

By far the most powerful weapon in the armoury of the landlord in the event of a breach of covenant is the remedy of forfeiture. In principle, this remedy is available for breaches of all covenants, including the covenant to pay rent, and the effect of a successful forfeiture of the lease is to bring the lease to an end. It is a remedy which can result in the tenant's estate in the land being terminated, even if the loss to the landlord consequent upon the breach is small, and even if the ejection of the tenant will give the landlord a windfall gain (by reacquiring the unencumbered freehold) out of all proportion to that loss. The drastic consequences of a successful forfeiture have always attracted the attention of the courts, and it is not surprising that both the opportunity to forfeit and the effect it has on the tenant are now strictly controlled by statute. In fact, the Law Commission has proposed wholesale reform of the law of forfeiture in its reports on termination of tenancies (Report No 142, 1985; Report No 221, 1994; and Report No 254, 1998) and other changes may occur if the Commonhold and Leasehold Reform Bill (2001) becomes law.

6.7.6   General considerations

In general terms, in order for forfeiture to be available at all, the lease must contain a *right of re-entry*. This is a stipulation that the landlord is entitled to re-enter the premises should the tenant fail to observe his covenants. All professionally drafted leases will contain such a right, and one will be implied in all equitable leases (*Shiloh Spinners v Harding* (1973)). By s 4 of the LTCA 1995, the benefit of the landlord's right of re-entry will pass automatically to assignees of the reversion for a legal or equitable lease. Subject to what will be said below about statutory safeguards, the existence of a right of re-entry gives the landlord two potential paths to a successful forfeiture. First, the landlord may physically re-enter the property by obtaining actual possession of it; a typical example being the changing of locks, providing this demonstrates an unequivocal intention to take possession. So, in *Charville Estates Ltd v Unipart* (1997), the landlord's entry to carry out works which the tenant had covenanted (but failed) to undertake was not a physical re-entry, and the lease remained alive, permitting the landlord to continue to claim rent; and, in *Cromwell v Godfrey* (1998), there was neither evidence of a manifest intention to forfeit, nor the retaking of possession. Secondly, and more frequently, a landlord may seek to exercise his right of re-entry through an action for possession brought against the tenant in the courts. At one time, a landlord had a free choice about which path to take, but this is now modified by statute, mainly to protect the tenant from an overzealous landlord. Thus:

(a) the enforcement of a right of re-entry in a residential lease 'while any person is lawfully residing in the premises' must take place through court action (s 2 of the Protection From Eviction Act 1977). Any attempt physically to re-enter such premises is without legal effect and will result in criminal liability;

(b) likewise, even if the lease is non-residential (or otherwise outside the scope of s 2, above), it is only *peaceful* physical re-entry that is permitted and effective, and the landlord must avoid committing offences under the Criminal Law Act 1977. The use or threat of violence for the purpose of gaining entry, when there is someone on the premises opposed to the entry, may be a criminal offence and render the forfeiture ineffective;

(c) furthermore, after the decision in *Billson v Residential Apartments* (1992), even a lawful physical re-entry may be set aside some time later if the tenant applies for 'relief' from forfeiture (see below, 6.7.7).

The net result of these provisions is that physical re-entry is *possible* only when the tenant is holding the premises under a business lease *and* those premises are unoccupied; further, it may not be *desirable* even then, due to the court's willingness to grant relief from forfeiture after such physical re-entry has occurred.

6.7.7 Forfeiture for non-payment of rent

Forfeiture of the lease for the tenant's non-payment of rent stands apart from forfeiture for breaches of other covenants, although both physical re-entry and an action for possession are available. In all cases, there must be a right of re-entry (forfeiture clause) in the lease, and the landlord must make a formal demand for rent unless the forfeiture clause dispenses with the need for such a demand (most do), or the rent is six months or more in arrears and there are insufficient goods available for distress (s 210 of the Common Law Procedure Act 1852). Clearly, these are not burdensome conditions. Following that, the landlord may proceed to forfeit the lease either by physical re-entry, or action in the High Court or county court (depending on the amount of rent in arrears). However, in all cases, the general rule applies that the 'law leans against forfeiture'. Thus, in suitable circumstances, a tenant will be granted 'relief from forfeiture' if he pays all the rent due plus all costs within the appropriate time, as detailed below.

In the *High Court*, a tenant has a statutory right under s 212 of the Common Law Procedure Act 1852 to have the possession proceedings 'stayed' (stopped) if he pays all the rent due plus costs before the date of the judgment against him, although this right is available only if at least six months' rent is in arrears. Furthermore, even if the landlord has obtained and executed a possession order, the tenant may apply for relief if he then pays all arrears and costs, providing that the application is made within six months of the possession order being executed (s 210 of the Common Law Procedure Act 1852) and the premises have not been let to a third party. Further, in those cases where this statutory relief is not available, the tenant may fall back on the High Court's general equitable jurisdiction to grant relief from forfeiture if the tenant pays all outstanding amounts (*Howard v Fanshawe* (1895)), and this may be useful where the tenant seeks relief more than six months after the landlord has regained possession (*Thatcher v CH Pearce* (1968)).

In the *county court*, a tenant has a right to stay the possession proceedings on the payment of arrears and costs at any time up to five days before the trial (s 138(2) of the County Courts Act 1984). Further, the county court will postpone execution of a possession order for four weeks (or more if warranted), during which time a tenant has an automatic right to relief on payment of outstanding amounts (s 138(3) of the County Courts Act 1984). Obviously, because the tenant in these circumstances has a right to have the proceedings stayed, it is important to know what sums must be paid to secure relief. Clearly, these include all the landlord's costs and it is now clear, following *Maryland Estates v Joseph* (1998), that the amount of arrears is calculated up to the date for possession specified in the court order and not the earlier date on which the tenant was served with the summons for possession. This is perfectly consistent with the concept that a lease remains in existence up until such time as it is actually forfeited, being when the landlord has taken possession and all hopes of relief from forfeiture are gone (*Ivory Gate Ltd v Spetale* (1998)). In the normal course of events, failure to pay by the date specified in the order will bar the tenant from further relief, and the landlord's possession order becomes enforceable, save only that a tenant may apply for *discretionary* relief within six months of the landlord taking possession under the court order (s 138(9A) of the County Courts Act 1984).

If the landlord lawfully re-enters physically (that is, without a court order), the High Court has a discretionary power to grant relief under its inherent equitable jurisdiction (*Howard v Fanshawe* (1895)) although only in favour of someone entitled to claim possession of the land by virtue of a legal or equitable proprietary right (*Bland v Ingrants Estate* (2001)). The county court also has a discretionary jurisdiction to grant relief in the event of physical re-entry although it is founded on statute. It exists only if the application for relief is made within six months of the re-entry occurring (s 139(2) of the County Courts Act 1984).

6.7.8 Principles for granting discretionary relief for non-payment of rent

It will be apparent from the above that there are circumstances in which the tenant may claim relief from forfeiture as of right. Where these circumstances exist, relief must be ordered and comprise those cases, in either the High Court or county court, where the tenant pays all necessary sums before the landlord recovers possession. However, in those cases where the *right* to relief does not arise, there remains the court's discretionary jurisdiction. Whether the source of this discretion be the statutory jurisdiction of the High Court or county court, or the inherent jurisdiction of the former, the cases illustrate clearly that 'the law leans against forfeiture' and a court will grant discretionary relief if at all possible, even in some cases where the landlord has re-let the premises (for example, *Bank of Ireland Home Mortgages v South Lodge* (1996)). The underlying rationale for this generosity is the simple point that the purpose of forfeiture in 'rent cases' is to secure the sum owed, and once this has been achieved, forfeiture is no longer appropriate and relief should be granted (*Gill v Lewis* (1956)). This means that it will be rare for a tenant offering full payment within the period in which relief can be claimed to be denied that relief, even if they are a persistently late or bad payer, even if the breach was wilful, and even if prospects for payment of future rent appear bleak. Moreover, it is now clear that this generosity should extend to all covenants aimed at securing a liquidated sum from the tenant. So, in *Khar v Delbounty* (1996), the landlord claimed to forfeit for non-payment of quantified service charges, and although this was a 's 146 case' (that is, not a rent case: see below, 6.7.9), the court held that the same principles of generosity should apply as would in rent cases and the tenants were granted discretionary relief.

6.7.9 Forfeiture for breach of covenants other than to pay rent

In all cases where the landlord is seeking to forfeit the lease because of breach of covenant, other than a breach of the covenant to pay rent (which includes a covenant to pay a service charge if the lease declares that the charge is to be treated as rent: as was *not* the case in *Delbounty*), the procedure specified in s 146 of the LPA 1925 must be strictly followed. Also, of course, the lease must contain a right of re-entry. Section 146 requires a landlord to serve a 'notice' on the tenant which must:

(a) specify the breach of covenant of which complaint is made;

(b) request compensation for breach of covenant if desired and also advise the tenant of their rights under the Leasehold Property (Repairs) Act 1938 if appropriate;

(c) request that the breach of covenant be remedied, if that is possible; and

(d) if the forfeiture is in respect of a service charge (not being a charge to be treated as rent), the landlord must inform the tenant of the safeguards introduced by s 81 of the Housing Act 1996, which, in effect, prohibit forfeiture for non-payment of a service charge unless the amount has been agreed between the parties or settled by a leasehold valuation tribunal.

This procedure is designed to give the tenant every opportunity to remedy the alleged breach of covenant and to avoid the serious consequences of forfeiture. Indeed, any attempt to forfeit the lease in violation of these provisions is void (*Billson v Residential Apartments* (1992)). Note also that under the provisions of the Commonhold and Leasehold Reform Act 2002 (not yet in force), a landlord will not be permitted to serve a 's 146 notice' unless the facts on which it is based have previously been determined by application to a Leasehold Valuation Tribunal (LVT) or are agreed. This is designed to prevent landlords threatening forfeiture on inadequate grounds as a means of coercing tenants. After the service of a 's 146 notice', the landlord *may* be able to proceed to forfeit the lease, either by a court action for possession, or by physical re-entry (if that is available). However, whether the landlord can, in fact, proceed to forfeit, and how long they must wait before doing so after the service of the notice, depends on whether the specified breach of covenant is 'capable of remedy'.

The s 146 notice must request that the breach of covenant be remedied if that is possible. If the covenant is capable of remedy (that is, it is 'remediable'), then the landlord must give the tenant 'a reasonable time' (for example, three months) to effect such remedy, and will not be allowed to forfeit during this period. Of course, if the tenant then remedies the breach of covenant, the question of forfeiture no longer arises, although there may be claims for damages for past breaches. If, however, the covenant is not capable of remedy, then the landlord may proceed to forfeit relatively quickly (possibly immediately, but normally after 14 days (*Scala House and District Property Co Ltd v Forbes* (1974)), again by action or physical re-entry.

Necessarily, it is vital to know whether the covenant is 'capable of remedy', as this will dictate both the contents of the s 146 notice and the speed with which the landlord may proceed to forfeit, if at all. The basic test of remediability was put forward in *Expert Clothing Service and Sales Ltd v Hillgate House Ltd* (1986), which in essence recognised that a covenant was 'capable of remedy' if the *damage* the breach had caused could be rectified. Thus, breaches of most positive covenants can be remedied (*Expert Clothing*) because the tenant can do that which they have not done, for example, by carrying out repairs. Conversely, it is commonly thought that breaches of negative covenants are more likely to be incapable of remedy, thus permitting early forfeiture. This may well be true in cases where the breach is 'once and for all', such that doing the prohibited action is irrecoverable: an example is breach of a covenant against subletting (but, see the doubts about such breaches in *Bass Holdings v Morton Music Ltd* (1988)); likewise, with a breach that taints the land, so that no amount of effort on the part of the tenant can remedy the stigma, as where, in breach, a tenant opens a sex shop (*Dunraven Securities v Holloway* (1982)), or keeps a brothel (*Kelly v Purvis* (1983)). Yet, it is not simply the case that breaches of all restrictive covenants should be regarded as incapable of remedy, for if the breach is 'ongoing and continuous', the tenant can effect a remedy by ceasing the prohibited activity (*Cooper v Henderson* (1982)), as where the tenant remedies breach of a covenant against keeping pets, by no longer keeping them. Moreover, in *Savva and Savva v Hussein* (1996), the Court of Appeal held that there was nothing in logic to differentiate between positive and negative covenants in this regard because the *Expert Clothing* test required that each breach of covenant be taken on its own merits. So, in that case, breach of a covenant against alterations was not, in principle, incapable of remedy.

Having surmounted the hurdle of remediability, the landlord may proceed to forfeit by an action for possession or by physical re-entry. However, the tenant still has the ability to apply for relief from forfeiture, as stipulated in s 146 of the LPA 1925. In general terms, a tenant has the right to apply for relief from forfeiture, either in an action for possession by the landlord, or by an independent application to the court. Indeed, one purpose of the s 146 notice is to alert the tenant to the possibility of forfeiture and the opportunity to apply for relief. Relief from forfeiture will be granted if the tenant has performed the covenants, or if the court considers that it would be just and reasonable to allow the lease to survive despite the breaches of covenant (*Shiloh Spinners v Harding* (1973)). Several matters will be relevant in determining whether relief should be given: for example, the drastic effect that a successful forfeiture has *per se*; the value of the lease when compared with the damage caused by the breach; the seriousness or triviality of the breach, whether the landlord has re-let the premises to an innocent third party (a tendency to deny relief, but see *Delbounty* and *Bank of Ireland Home Mortgages v South Lodge* (1996), where relief was granted with special provision for the innocent third party now in possession); whether the breach was wilful, negligent or innocent; and the past performance of the tenant in performing the covenants. Importantly, relief will not be refused just because the tenant breached a negative covenant, or because the breach was itself irremediable as in *Mount Cook Land v Hartley* (2000) where poorly behaved tenants were given relief after breaking a covenant against subletting. Under s 146(4) of the LPA 1925 (and probably the wider s 146(2) – *Escalus Properties v Robinson* (1995)) a subtenant or mortgagee of the original tenant may also apply for relief from forfeiture, even though the breaches of covenant were committed by the tenant, as in *Bank of Ireland Home Mortgages v South Lodge* (1996), where relief was granted to the tenant's mortgagee.

Availability of relief when the landlord proceeds to forfeit by an action for possession

The position here is effectively governed by s 146 of the LPA, as interpreted by the House of Lords in *Billson v Residential Apartments* (1992). As that case makes clear, an action for possession will be the normal method by which the landlord attempts to forfeit the lease. A tenant may apply for relief as soon as the landlord serves a s 146 notice and up to the moment at which the landlord actually recovers possession under an order of the court (that is, the moment when the order is executed). Thus, although the landlord is subject to a claim for relief after the court has granted the order, prompt action to enter into possession will defeat relief once and for all (*Rogers v Rice* (1892)). In most cases, the denial of a right to claim relief under s 146 where forfeiture has been by court proceedings and the landlord has actually recovered possession causes little hardship. It also encourages landlords to use the courts for forfeiture, because the same restriction does not apply to forfeiture by peaceful re-entry (below). However, there will always be cases where a tenant will wish to apply after the landlord has executed the possession order, and, indeed, such is quite possible if it is a tenant's mortgagee claiming late relief, having been unaware of the forfeiture proceedings. This potential cause for hardship has generated some discussion as to whether the court's inherent equitable jurisdiction to grant relief has survived the enactment of s 146. The strongest authority is against the survival of such a jurisdiction (*Smith v Metropolitan City Properties* (1986)), but it has been asserted *obiter* (*Abbey National Building Society v Maybeech Ltd* (1985)) and academically. Technically, *Billson* leaves the matter open to argument, and although the legislative intention probably was the removal of the inherent jurisdiction in non-rent cases, no doubt a 'hard case' would find a court open to persuasion. In *Bland v Ingrants Estate* (2001), the court (uncontroversially) noted the existence of an inherent jurisdiction in respect of non-payment of rent but said nothing about such a jurisdiction in non-rent cases.

Availability of relief when forfeiture is by physical re-entry

Prior to *Billson*, forfeiture by re-entry held some attractions for a landlord in that it was thought that the tenant had lost all rights to apply for relief once the landlord had actually entered the premises. So, for example, a landlord who was forfeiting for breach of an irremediable covenant might serve a s 146 notice and physically re-enter and terminate the lease, all within the space of 14 days. In *Billson*, however, the House of Lords adopted a purposive approach to s 146 and held that a landlord was 'proceeding to forfeit' within that section, so giving the tenant a right to apply for relief, even if he (the landlord) had actually entered on the land. Consequently, a tenant who suffers physical re-entry may apply for relief against a landlord in possession of the property for a 'reasonable time' after that possession has occurred. Necessarily, this will make the possession of a landlord who has physically re-entered somewhat fragile, and liable to be defeated by a claim for relief, although it is unlikely that relief will be granted if the landlord has since transferred the land to an innocent third party. In other words, the decision in *Billson* encourages landlords to forfeit leases by action in the courts, as no relief is available then, when the landlord has finally secured possession under a valid court order.

Waiver

A landlord attempting to forfeit the lease must ensure that he has not waived the right to forfeit the lease for the tenant's breach of covenant. The essence of the matter is that there will be a waiver of forfeiture if there is any act which amounts to an affirmation of the continuing validity of the lease, as this is inconsistent with forfeiture. In the typical case, waiver will exist where a landlord has knowledge of a prior breach of covenant and then does an act which manifests an intention to regard the lease as still in existence (*Matthews v Smallwood* (1910)). The most obvious example is where the landlord, or his duly authorised agent, accepts or demands rent after the breach of covenant has occurred, providing that he also knew (or ought to have known) of that breach (*David Blackstone v Burnetts* (1973)). This principle is applied strictly, as the courts are astute to ensure that the landlord does not gain the double advantage of forfeiture and rent recovery: after all, the purpose of forfeiture in rent cases is the payment of rent, and with such payment, forfeiture abates (*Gill v Lewis* (1956)). So, a 'without prejudice' demand for rent does not preserve forfeiture, and the landlord has the relevant degree of knowledge if he is aware that a breach has occurred, even if he did not know the legal consequences of such a breach. However, it remains true that all cases are decided on their own facts, and, for example, in *Yorkshire Metropolitan Properties v CRS Ltd* (1997), the landlord's demand for payments towards insurance costs did not amount to a waiver. Similarly, a landlord's express or implied waiver relates only to a particular breach of covenant, and not to any future breaches. Thus, a waiver of a breach of a restrictive covenant may be taken as a waiver of only the initial breach, and not any continuing breach.

Breaches of repairing covenants

All that has been said so far about forfeiture for breach of covenants other than to pay rent applies in equal measure to breaches of the tenant's covenant to repair, save that the tenant is given additional protection because of the propensity of some landlords to use minor breaches of repairing covenants as a means of ending an otherwise valid lease. Under the Leasehold Property (Repairs) Act 1938, the landlord must serve the s 146 notice in the normal way, but this triggers the tenant's right to serve a 'counter-notice' claiming the protection of the 1938 Act. If this counter-notice is served, the landlord may not forfeit the lease without the permission of the court, and such permission may be given only if one of the grounds specified in s 1(5) of the 1938 Act is established. The Leasehold Property (Repairs) Act applies to leases of seven years or more that have at least three years left to run.

It will be appreciated that the landlord will resort to forfeiture in cases of serious and sustained breach of covenant, and that this can have serious consequences for the tenant. Indeed, given that a forfeiture against the tenant will automatically cause the end of the interest of a subtenant and mortgagee (unless their own applications for relief are successful), it is vital that the procedure specified in s 146 of the LPA 1925 is followed and that any person thereby prejudiced should apply for relief in good time.

6.8   The tenant's remedies for breach of covenant

The tenant's remedies for breach of covenant by the landlord are less extensive than those of the landlord and are based on the normal contractual remedies available to any person who has suffered loss by reason of a breach of a binding legal obligation. Importantly, breach by the landlord of his covenants does not generally entitle the tenant to ignore their own obligations under the leasehold covenants (the covenants are *not* interdependent), subject only to the limited right to deduct future rent payments, as noted below.

6.8.1   Damages for breach of covenant

The tenant may sue the landlord for damages at common law for any breach of covenant which causes loss, and the measure of damages is that which puts the tenant in the same position as if the breach had not occurred (*Calabar v Stitcher* (1984)). In the context of damages for breach of the landlord's repairing obligations, this means the tenant should be compensated for the loss of comfort and convenience which they would have enjoyed had the repairs been undertaken. This can sometimes be reflected in a reduction in rent, having regard to the diminution in the value of the tenancy (*Wallace v Manchester CC* (1998)).

6.8.2   Action for an injunction

The tenant may sue for an injunction to stop a continuing or threatened breach of covenant by the landlord. As with all equitable remedies, this lies at the discretion of the court.

6.8.3   Action for specific performance

It is clear that the tenant may claim specific performance of a landlord's covenant where this is consistent with the supervisory jurisdiction of the court. Such an order has been granted to enforce performance of a landlord's repairing covenant (*Jeune v Queens Cross Properties* (1974)) and particular covenants such as the landlord's covenant to employ a resident porter (*Posner v Scott-Lewis* (1986)). Under s 17 of the Landlord and Tenant Act 1985, there is a statutory jurisdiction to order specific performance of a landlord's repairing covenant in respect of a dwelling house. This position should be contrasted with that of the landlord where, until recently, a landlord was denied the reciprocal right specifically to enforce the tenant's repairing obligations.

6.8.4 Retention of future rent

Following *Lee-Parker v Izzet* (1971), if the landlord is in breach of a covenant to repair, the tenant may carry out the necessary repairs and deduct the cost thereof from *future* payments of rent. However, the tenant must be careful not to withhold rent already due, as this will trigger liability to the landlord and perhaps the remedy of forfeiture. In similar vein, if the landlord is in breach of a repairing covenant, and the tenant therefore refuses to pay rent, the tenant may 'set off' any damages they would have received for the landlord's breach if the landlord should bring an action for arrears of rent. It is only in these two limited circumstances that performance of the tenant's covenants (that is, to pay the full rent) are modified in the face of a breach of covenant by the landlord.

6.9 Termination of leases

There are several ways by which the landlord and tenant relationship may come to an end. When it does, possession of the land reverts to the freeholder or other person (for example, headlessee) entitled on expiry of the term.

6.9.1 By effluxion of time

The most obvious way in which a lease will end is when the contractual term has expired. However, some leases may give the tenant the right to extend the lease at the end of the initial period and, of course, this must be honoured. Likewise, the tenant may be able to claim a statutory extension of the tenancy under the Landlord and Tenant Act 1954 (business tenancies), Agricultural Holdings Act 1986, or the Rent Act 1977 or early Housing Acts (residential tenancies).

6.9.2 By forfeiture

As above.

6.9.3 By notice

Leases sometimes give either or both the landlord and tenant the right to terminate the lease before the end of the contractual period by giving 'notice' to the other party. These 'break clauses' are common in long leases and are intrinsic in periodic tenancies. Importantly, if a lease is held by two persons as joint tenants, the notice of only one of them is required to terminate the tenancy, irrespective of the other's wishes (*Hammersmith and Fulham LBC v Monk* (1992)) and the giving of such notice is not a 'function relating to land' within s 11 of the TOLATA 1996 so as to require any tenant who is also a trustee to consult any beneficiary before giving notice (*Brackley v Notting Hill Housing Trust* (2001)). However, it should be remembered that the essence of a periodic tenancy is that it is implied from the circumstances surrounding the occupation, thus, in the case of a periodic tenancy, the continued occupation of the remaining tenant and acceptance of rent by the landlord will generate a new periodic tenancy with a sole tenant only (*Burton v Camden LBC* (1997)). Also, a notice to quit given by a tenant will automatically terminate any subtenancies which that tenant may have carved out of their own interest (*Pennell v Payne* (1995)), except if the tenant's notice to the landlord to quit is, in effect, merely a mechanism by which the tenant and landlord adopt to terminate the tenancy by mutual agreement. In such cases, the 'notice' amounts to a surrender of the head tenancy, with the consequence that any subtenancy is not thereby terminated (*Barrett v Morgan* (1998)). Obviously, in order to determine whether a subtenancy has survived, it is crucial to know whether the tenant's actions amount to a true notice to quit (subtenancy determined), or a consensual surrender to the landlord (subtenancy not determined). This, in turn, will depend on evidence as to the intentions of the parties and the circumstances in which the notice was given.

6.9.4 By merger

The tenant may acquire his landlord's interest in the land and thereby 'merge' the lease and reversion, as in *Ivory Gate v Spetale* (1998).

6.9.5 By surrender

The tenant may surrender his lease to their landlord, and, if accepted, this will terminate the lease. Surrender may be either express or implied by operation of law, this being an example of estoppel (*Mattey v Ervin* (1998)), but in either case, there must be an intention to terminate the lease (*Charville Estates Ltd v Unipart* (1997)). As noted above, a surrender, being a consensual act between landlord and tenant, will not thereby determine any subtenancies.

6.9.6 By enlargement

Under s 153 of the LPA 1925, a tenant of a lease of more than 300 years, of which at least 200 years are left to run, has a right, in some circumstances, to enlarge their leasehold interest into the freehold.

6.9.7 By disclaimer

A lease may come to an end because the tenant denies the landlord's superior title to the land, and thereby disclaims the lease.

6.9.8 By frustration

Since the decision in *National Carriers Ltd v Panalpina* (1981), it has been accepted that the normal law of frustration of contract applies to leases. Thus, a fundamental change of circumstance after the commencement of the lease may so alter the rights and obligations of the parties that the original lease (contract) between them in no sense represents their original bargain, and is frustrated.

6.9.9 By repudiatory breach of contract

Somewhat illogically, although leases could be frustrated, the availability of the other great contractual remedy of repudiation of the lease, because of a fundamental breach of covenant (contract) by the other party, was once not readily accepted in English law. However, in *Hussein v Mehlman* (1992), the High Court has taken the first steps to recognise this remedy, on the ground that there is no reason in principle why leases should be regarded as different from other types of contract and the availability of repudiatory principles has been confirmed in *Chartered Trust v Davies* (1997). This may well prove a valuable 'remedy' for a tenant as it could provide a method by which a tenant can 'terminate' a lease because of a landlord's refusal to perform critical leasehold covenants. As will be apparant from the above, no such right exists under the 'pure' law of landlord and tenant as there is *no* tenant's right of forfeiture. So it is that contract law may come to a tenant's aid.

LEASES

The nature of a lease

The leasehold allows two or more persons to enjoy the benefits of owning an estate in the land at the same time. Both landlord and tenant retain a proprietary right in the land and both of these proprietary rights can be sold or transferred after the lease has been created. All leases will contain covenants (or promises) whereby the landlord and tenant promise to do – or not to do – certain things in relation to the land. These rights and obligations may 'run' with the land on a transfer of the lease or of the landlord's 'reversion'. The essential qualities of a lease are that: (a) it gives a person the right of exclusive possession of land; (b) for a certain term; (c) at a rent (*Street v Mountford* (1985)), although the last of these is not strictly necessary as a matter of law. Leases may be legal or equitable.

The creation of legal and equitable leases

As a general rule, legal leases must be created by deed. Currently, in registered land, leases for over 21 years, even if created by deed, will not take effect as a legal estate until registered with their own title number. This will change to leases over seven years in the LRA 2002. Leases for three years or less that take effect immediately in possession where the tenant does not pay an initial capital sum will be legal, however created (orally, in writing or by deed). Most periodic tenancies are legal leases under this exception.

As a general rule, equitable leases must derive from a written contract (or written document equivalent to a contract). This written agreement will create an equitable lease if it is specifically enforceable (as most are). As an exception, an equitable lease can be generated purely orally via the principles of proprietary estoppel.

Leases in registered and unregistered land

Currently, in registered land, legal leases for 21 years or less are overriding interests, s 70(1)(k) of the LRA 1925 and legal leases created for more than 21 years are registrable as titles in their own right. (If they are not so registered, they will take effect as equitable leases only.) Appropriate changes will result when the 'trigger' is reduced to seven years. Equitable leases can be registered currently as a minor interest by notice or caution, although most equitable leases will be overriding interests and automatically binding against a subsequent purchaser because the equitable tenant will be a person in 'actual occupation' of the land, within s 70(1)(g) of the LRA 1925 (or LRA 2002 equivalent).

In unregistered land, a legal lease will bind automatically any subsequent purchaser or transferee of the estate out of which it is created. An equitable lease arising from an enforceable written agreement is registrable as a Class C(iv) land charge (and void against a purchaser if not so registered). Estoppel equitable leases probably bind a subsequent transferee of the freehold land through the doctrine of notice.

For registered land, rules concerning electronic conveyancing may mean that certain types of lease do not exist at all until requested.

The differences between legal and equitable leases

Legal and equitable leases are created in different ways. Equitable leases are potentially very vulnerable to a sale of the freehold or leasehold estate out of which they are created. For leases granted before 1 January 1996, leasehold covenants will 'run' with the land in a legal lease more easily than in an equitable one. For leases granted on or after 1 January 1996, leasehold covenants will 'run' in legal and equitable leases identically, thanks to the LTCA 1995. Easements may be created by s 62 of the LPA 1925 on the occasion of a grant of a legal lease only. The equitable tenant is a purchaser for value of an *equitable* estate in the land and, therefore, cannot be a purchaser of a legal estate so as to avoid being bound by those equitable rights in unregistered land that still depend on the doctrine of notice. Neither could an equitable tenant in unregistered land avoid being bound by an unregistered Class C(iv) or Class D land charge, both of which are void only against a purchaser of a legal estate.

Leasehold covenants in leases granted before 1 January 1996

In any action on a leasehold covenant between the original landlord and the original tenant, *all* covenants are enforceable: liability of these original parties is based in *contract*. Both original parties will remain liable on the leasehold covenants throughout the entire term of the lease, even after they have assigned their interests. The liability is to any person having the right to enforce the covenant. The position of an assignee of the lease (that is, the tenant's interest) depends on whether 'privity of estate' exists between the landlord and tenant so as to allow enforcement of those covenants which 'touch and concern' the land. The position of an assignee of the reversion is governed by the application of s 141 and 142 of the LPA 1925. 'Privity of estate' does not exist in respect of assignees of an equitable lease (although the original parties remain bound in contract). Consequently, although the benefits and burdens of leasehold covenants will be passed to the assignee of the reversion in an equitable lease (because ss 141 and 142 of the LPA 1925 still apply), the benefits and burdens will not pass automatically to an assignee of the tenant.

Note 1

An assignee of an equitable lease may obtain the benefit (but not the burden) of the covenants by express assignment, but the lack of privity of estate means that the burdens cannot run.

Note 2

There may be indirect enforcement of the burdens of leasehold covenants against an equitable assignee. For example, by use of the landlord's right of re-entry and the rules relating to restrictive covenants.

Note 3

Subtenants do not stand in privity of estate with the head landlord, so are treated vis à vis that landlord in the same manner as equitable tenants. A subtenant is in privity with his or her own immediate landlord.

Leasehold covenants in leases granted on or after 1 January 1996: the Landlord and Tenant (Covenants) Act 1995

The LTCA 1995 applies to all leases granted on or after 1 January 1996 whether legal or equitable. The original tenant is released from liability under leasehold covenants on assignment, subject only to the possibility of guaranteeing the next immediate tenant's performance of the covenants under an authorised guarantee agreement (AGA). The original landlord is not automatically released on assignment, but may apply to the court for such release. The rule that covenants must 'touch and concern' the land in order to run to new landlords and tenants is abolished. *All* covenants will run unless they 'are expressed to be personal'. By statute, the benefit and burdens of leasehold covenants pass automatically to assignees of the landlord and the tenant without the need to show privity of estate or to rely on ss 141 and 142 of the LPA 1925. A tenant is liable on the leasehold covenants only while in possession of the land, subject only to the possibility that he may be required to guarantee performance of the covenants by the next immediate assignee under an AGA. The rules concerning the imposition of AGAs are very favourable to landlords, particularly landlords of commercial premises. The obligation to enter an AGA can be made to run to every tenant if it is included as a covenant in the lease.

Note 1

The provisions of the LTCA 1995 relating to 'problem notices' to enforce liability against a tenant not in possession (for example, under an AGA) apply to leases granted before 1 January 1996. Hence, the procedure is applicable to the enforcement of original tenant liability in pre-1996 leases. The same is true of the provisions relating to overriding leases.

The landlord's remedies for breach of covenant

- The remedy of distress allows a landlord enter the land of his tenant and seize goods found there in order to sell them for the purpose of paying any arrears of rent.

- The landlord can enforce the covenant to pay rent by bringing an action to recover arrears of rent either in the High Court or County Court depending on the amount owed.

- The landlord may sue for damages for breach of every covenant other than the covenant to pay rent.

- At the discretion of the court, a landlord may obtain an injunction to prevent the breach of a restrictive (negative) covenant by the tenant. It may now be possible to get specific performance of a tenant's repairing obligation.

- The most powerful weapon in the armoury of the landlord in the event of a breach of covenant is the remedy of forfeiture. The lease must contain a *right of re-entry*. Re-entry may be by peaceful physical re-entry or through court action, although the former is not possible in all cases. Forfeiture for non-payment of rent depends on the landlord making a formal demand for rent and the court not being prepared to grant the tenant relief from forfeiture under its various inherent and statutory jurisdictions. Forfeiture of the lease because of a breach of any other covenant is governed by s 146 of the LPA 1925. After the service of a 's 146 notice', the landlord *may* be able to proceed to forfeit the lease either by physical re-entry or by a court action for possession. The tenant may apply for relief from forfeiture, as stipulated in s 146 of the LPA 1925, whether the re-entry is by court order or by physical re-entry. Also, a landlord attempting to forfeit the lease must ensure that they have not waived the breach, so losing the right to forfeit for that particular breach.

The tenant's remedies for breach of covenant

The tenant's remedies for breach of covenant are: to sue the landlord for damages at common law; to sue for an injunction to stop a continuing or threatened breach of covenant by the landlord; to sue for specific performance of the landlord's covenants, particularly the landlord's covenant to repair; to deduct the cost of carrying out the landlord's repairs from future payments of rent. The law of contract may also provide remedies in 'frustration' or repudiatory breach.

Termination of leases

The landlord and tenant relationship may come to an end in several ways: by effluxion of time (the term ends); by forfeiture; by serving notice if the lease contains a break clause; by merger with the superior estate out of which it is carved; by surrender to the landlord; by enlargement into the superior estate; by disclaimer; by frustration; by repudiatory breach of contract.

CHAPTER 7

THE LAW OF EASEMENTS

7.1 The nature of easements as interests in land

Easements are incorporeal hereditaments. They comprise certain rights which one landowner may enjoy over the land of their neighbour. Common examples are the right of way and the right of light, but easements are not limited to these two ancient rights: the right to use a neighbour's land in connection with the movement of aircraft (*Dowty Bolton Paul Ltd v Wolverhampton Corp (No 2)* (1976)), the right to park on land and cross it with shopping trolleys (*London and Blenheim Estates Ltd v Ladbroke Retail Parks Ltd* (1992)) and the right to the enjoyment of lighting and exit signs (*Bratt's Ltd v Habboush* (1999)) are more recent examples. As we shall see, the 'definition' of an easement cannot be expressed in simple terms – it is a recipe of many ingredients – but, at the outset, it is vital to realise that every easement will involve two separate pieces of land.

First, an easement confers a benefit on the *dominant tenement* (that is, benefited land) enabling the owner for the time being of that land to use the easement, for example, to walk across a neighbour's land, or to receive light. Secondly, an easement places a burden on the *servient tenement* (that is, burdened land), requiring the owner for the time being of that land to suffer the exercise of the easement, for example, to allow a neighbour to walk across it, or not to interfere with the passage of light to a neighbour. Moreover, as implied in the above, the easement confers a benefit and burden *on the land itself*, so that in principle it may be enjoyed or suffered by any subsequent owner of the dominant or servient land. In other words, the easement is not merely personal to the persons who originally created it. It is a proprietary interest in land, so that (subject to the rules of registered and unregistered conveyancing) the benefit of it passes with a transfer of the dominant tenement and the burden of it passes with a transfer of the servient tenement.

7.2 The essential characteristics of an easement

The essentially proprietary nature of an easement, which allows its benefit and burden to be passed to whomsoever comes to own an estate in the land, means that care must be taken in defining the types of right that may be recognised as an 'easement'. For example, if too many rights, or rights which are vague and uncertain, can amount to easements, the owner of the servient tenement might find the use and enjoyment of his own land seriously disrupted. Conversely, if the law recognises too few easements, or is stagnant in the face of economic and social change, it would be impossible for the owners of dominant tenements to safeguard the value and amenity of their property. A balance has to be struck. The law of easements must accommodate the needs of the dominant tenement, while at the same time ensuring that the servient tenement does not become overburdened and inalienable, all in the context of a modern society. For this reason, there are established criteria for determining whether an alleged right is capable of amounting to an easement (*Re Ellenborough Park* (1956)), although it is also clear that these encompass a certain amount of judicial discretion. These four 'essential characteristics' of an easement are taken from the judgment of Evershed MR in *Re Ellenborough Park* (1956), itself an adoption of the criteria put forward by Cheshire in *Modern Real Property* (7th edn). They represent the distillation of much case law, but they are not to be treated as if they were a statute.

7.2.1 There must be a dominant and a servient tenement

First, there must be a dominant and a servient tenement. This criterion lies at the very heart of the nature of an easement. Easements are rights which exist for the benefit of one piece of land and are exercised over another. This means that there must be land that is benefited (the dominant tenement), and land that is burdened (the servient tenement). In technical terms, the easement cannot exist 'in gross' (*Hawkins v Rutter* (1892)) and both the dominant and servient land must be identifiable at the time the easement is created. The creation of easements for land not yet identified is not possible (*London and Blenheim Estates* (1993)). This is one area where easements differ from *profits à prendre*, which, while always being a burden on some land, may be enjoyed by a person who owns no land himself (see below, 7.13).

7.2.2 The separation of the dominant and servient tenement

Secondly, the creation and continued existence of an easement is dependent on the dominant and servient tenements being owned or occupied by different persons. An easement is essentially a right in another's land, for example, to walk over it, or to enjoy the passage of light across it. For that reason, the dominant and servient tenements must not be both owned and occupied by the same person (*Roe v Siddons* (1888)). Moreover, should the dominant and servient tenements come into the ownership and possession of the same person, any easement over the servient land will thereby be extinguished: a person cannot have an easement against themselves. Note, however, that there is nothing to stop a tenant enjoying an easement over land retained by the landlord, and vice versa, because, in that situation, the land is not owned *and* occupied by the same person (*Wright v Macadam* (1949); *Bratt's Ltd v Habboush* (1999)). In the landlord and tenant situation, both parties own an estate in the land to which the benefit and burden of the easement can be attached. However, should the occupier be only a licensee (see Chapter 9), no easement can be created between him and the licensor, since a licensee owns no estate in the land. Finally, if the dominant and servient tenements come into the same occupation, but not also the same ownership, the easement is suspended for the duration of the common occupation and may be revived thereafter (*Canham v Fisk* (1831)).

7.2.3 The alleged easement must accommodate the dominant tenement

Thirdly, the alleged easement must accommodate (that is, benefit) the dominant tenement. This is an important requirement as it makes it clear that easements are rights which attach *to land* and not to persons. Thus, any alleged easement must confer a benefit on the land as such, and not merely on the person who currently owns the land.

The general idea is that the easement must benefit the user of the land, the value of the land or the mode of occupation of the land (like the idea of 'touch and concern' in restrictive covenants), but there are no set criteria for judging whether an alleged easement is of a sufficiently proprietary nature and each case must be decided on its own facts. The following guidelines give a flavour of what is required, but they may wilt in the face of peculiar or special facts:

(a) the servient tenement must be sufficiently proximate (that is, near) to the dominant tenement to be able to confer a benefit on it (*Bailey v Stevens* (1862)). For example, only in unusual circumstances can an alleged right of light over land that does not border the alleged dominant tenement actually be said to 'benefit' that tenement. Of course, the two tenements need not be adjacent, or share a common boundary, to satisfy this requirement, but in general, the more physically separate the two properties, the less likely it is that a court would regard an alleged easement over one as benefiting the other. For example, it would be difficult to establish a right of way over Blackacre in favour of Whiteacre when the two plots are at opposite ends of the village;

(b) the alleged right must not confer a purely personal advantage on the owner of the dominant tenement. For example, in *Hill v Tupper* (1863), the owner of a canal granted the plaintiff the right to put pleasure boats on the canal for profit, but this was held to be a personal advantage, not a right attaching to the plaintiff's land. It was not sufficiently connected with that land so as to amount to an easement. However, it is a mistake to think that *all* rights which confer a commercial or business advantage on the alleged dominant tenement cannot be easements. It is not the commercial nature of the right that is important, but whether the commercial advantage endures for the land or for the person who owns it. So, in *Moody v Steggles* (1879), it was accepted that there could be an easement to hang a pub sign on neighbouring land because this benefited a trade or occupation so closely connected with the dominant tenement that it could be said to benefit the land as such. Likewise, in *London and Blenheim Estates Ltd v Ladbroke Retail Parks Ltd* (1992), it was accepted that a right to park on adjoining land and to walk across it with shopping trolleys was capable of existing as an easement for the benefit of the dominant tenement on which there was a supermarket. If it were true that easements could not accommodate a commercial activity on the dominant land, then much of their usefulness would dissipate. Consequently, the issue is not whether a commercial use is being facilitated by the easement, but whether the alleged easement is so disconnected with the land that the benefit would disappear if the *current* owner of the dominant tenement departed;

(c) it is unlikely that a right which confers a purely 'recreational user' on the dominant tenement will be accepted as an easement. For example, a right to wander over open countryside or parkland would probably not be accepted as an easement. Given that the law of easements exists to enhance the social and economic value of land, by giving benefits and imposing burdens on the land as such, it is not appropriate for the provision of public amenities. However, the point to remember is that only a *pure and undefined* recreational use is suspect, so, in *Re Ellenborough Park* (1956) itself, a defined right to enjoy an enclosed private park was capable of existing as an easement because the park was created for the very purpose of enhancing the utility of the few private houses which had access to it. The law of easements can accommodate recreational use that confers a benefit in clear and defined circumstances, especially if it enhances the value of the dominant land (for example, allowing use of a swimming pool on neighbouring land), but it cannot be used to provide benefits for the public at large, or for ill defined recreational uses (for example, the right to ramble).

7.2.4 The alleged easement must 'be capable of forming the subject matter of a grant'

Fourthly, the alleged easement must be capable of forming the subject matter of a grant. This is an all-embracing criterion and one where the court enjoys considerable discretion in deciding whether any right is capable of being an easement. Technically, the point is that every easement must be *capable* of being expressly conveyed by deed (even if it is created in some other way): it must 'lie in grant'. What this means in practice is that there are certain types of right which previous case law has suggested are intrinsically unsuitable for inclusion in the list of easements as they could not have been 'granted'. Necessarily, this is a flexible and often illusive criterion. Note, however, that previous case law is not always decisive or consistent and each situation must be judged on its merits bearing in mind the context in which the easement is said to exist. The following points, being guidelines only, arise from the case law:

(a) an easement cannot exist unless there is a capable grantor, that is, somebody legally competent to create an easement (being the person in possession of an estate in the intended servient tenement). For example, no easement can exist where the purported grantor is a limited company having no power to grant easements under its Articles of Association;

(b) likewise, an easement cannot exist unless there is a capable grantee, that is, somebody in whose favour an easement may be legally granted (being the person in possession of an estate in the intended dominant tenement);

(c) all rights that are capable of forming the subject matter of a grant must be sufficiently certain, and this applies just as much to alleged easements as to other proprietary rights. In the case of an easement, the right must be capable of clear description and precise definition, principally so that the servient owner (and any purchaser from him) may know the extent of the obligation. For example, in *Re Aldred* (1610), a right to a good view could not exist as an easement, as a 'good view' was simply too indefinite. Similarly, there is no easement of privacy (*Browne v Flower* (1911)) and no easement to receive light generally as opposed to a right to receive light through a defined window. Given the proprietary status of easements – that is, that they may endure through changes in ownership of both the dominant and servient tenements – this requirement of exactness is no surprise. Easements affect land both as a benefit and a burden, and so it is vital to ensure that the scope of the right granted and the burden of the obligation imposed is clear and unambiguous;

(d) for a right to be capable of being an easement, it must be within the general nature of rights recognised as easements. This is where there is room for manoeuvre in the definition of easements. It is apparent that 'the general nature' of an easement is not cast in stone and may change over time as the use and occupation of land changes. Most importantly, this requirement does not mean that new easements will not be recognised; rather, it is that a court must be satisfied that the alleged easement will not affect the future use and enjoyment of the servient tenement in an unwarranted manner. For example, it is unlikely that a court will recognise new easements that require the servient tenement owner to spend money (*Phipps v Pears* (1965)). Easements are designed to allow the owner for the time being of the dominant tenement to gain an advantage from the servient land, rather than imposing positive obligations on the servient tenement owner. The recognised exception to this is the 'easement of fencing', whereby the servient tenement owner is required to maintain a boundary fence (*Crow v Wood* (1971)). Further, a court will only reluctantly allow an easement which gives the dominant tenement owner a right to prevent the servient tenement owner from doing something on their own land (*Phipps*). Such obligations may unduly restrict the servient owner in the use of their own land, and they fall more properly within the realm of restrictive covenants. However, some traditional easements do have this effect, as where the easement of light effectively prevents the servient owner from building on parts of his land. Again, a court is reluctant to recognise an easement which gives the dominant tenement owner exclusive occupation of the servient tenement. An easement is a right over the servient land for a defined purpose; it is not equivalent to a right of ownership of that land. For example, in *Copeland v Greenhalf* (1952), no easement could exist to store tools of the trade on the servient land, in *Grigsby v Melville* (1974), a right of storage in a cellar could not be accepted and in *Hanina v Morland* (2000) the alleged right to use the flat roof of neighbouring land could not be an easement because it was equivalent to ownership. However, following *London and Blenheim Estates Ltd v Ladbroke Retail Parks Ltd* (1992), it is now clear that it is a question of degree in each case whether the dominant rights are so extensive as to prevent them being recognised as easements. So, in that case, a right to park on the servient land could exist as an easement, even if charges were made for parking, provided that exclusive occupation was not given. And in *Newman v Jones* (1982), it was held that a right to park in the same defined space in a car park could not be an easement (see similar doubts in *Saeed v Plustrade* (2001)), although there could be an easement to park generally on a piece of land. Similarly, in *Batchelor v Marlowe* (2001) a right to park several cars by way of storage would not be an easement by analogy with *Copeland*. Indeed, this flexible approach is manifest in some of the earlier cases. In *Wright v Macadam* (1949), the tenant successfully claimed an easement of storage of coal in a small part of the landlord's coal shed. On one view there is little to distinguish between this case and *Copeland* and *Melville*, other than to say that the court in *Macadam* believed that the tenant deserved the right claimed.

It is apparent, then, that flexibility is inherent in the *Ellenborough* conditions, especially in the fourth criterion and it would be unfortunate if the development of the law of easements was circumscribed by too exacting and rigorously applied conditions. In other words, courts also appreciate that 'the categories of easement are not closed' and 'modern' rights have been recognised as appropriate to the time in which the issue arises: for example, an easement to use a letterbox was recognised in *Goldberg v Edwards* (1950), and an easement to use a clothes line passing over another's land was accepted in *Drewell v Towler* (1832).

7.2.5 Public policy

Public policy is not mentioned expressly in *Re Ellenborough Park* (1956) as a factor in deciding whether a right may exist as an easement. In any event, as noted above, that case attempted to define the intrinsic characteristics of an easement, rather than laying down comprehensive rules about when the courts would accept that a specific easement existed. To put it another way, the *Ellenborough* conditions tell us when a right is *capable* of being an easement, they do not necessarily tell us when that right will be recognised as an easement in a specific case. However, we must proceed with considerable caution when suggesting that considerations of 'public policy' may mean that a right which qualifies in principle as an easement will not be recognised as such in a concrete case. Rarely are questions of 'public policy' openly discussed in the cases. It is more likely that a court will refuse to recognise an easement for failure to comply with one of the *Ellenborough* rules than for explicit public policy grounds, even if this would have been justified. Yet, the flexible nature of the *Ellenborough* conditions means that there is always scope for judicial discretion and public policy. For example, in *Hill v Tupper* (1863), it may well have been against the public interest for a particular individual to have exclusive rights to a waterway, and the absence of any similar problem in *Moody v Steggles* (1879) might explain the acceptance of a 'commercial' easement in that case.

7.3   Legal and equitable easements: formalities

As with some other proprietary rights, an easement may be either legal or equitable (s 1 of the Law of Property Act (LPA) 1925). Essentially, the matter turns on the manner in which the easement has been created or, more precisely, whether the proper formalities for the creation of a legal easement have been observed. If they have not, the easement is likely to be equitable, subject to any formality rules relating to the creation of equitable interests. These various formality requirements are to be found both in statute and common law. Furthermore, the legal or equitable status of an easement currently is fundamental to understanding how the benefit of an easement passes with a transfer of the dominant tenement and how the burden passes with a transfer of the servient tenement; that is, how easements affect third parties. This, in turn, must be considered in the context of registered and unregistered conveyancing.

7.4   Legal easements

In order for an easement to be a legal interest, there are a number of essential conditions that must be met. These appear to be quite complicated, but it must be noted that they are satisfied in the great majority of cases. Normal conveyancing practice on the transfer of land usually ensures that the appropriate formalities are completed.

An easement can qualify as a *legal interest* only if it is held as an adjunct to a fee simple absolute in possession or as an adjunct to a term of years, s 1 of the LPA 1925. Quite simply, this means that an easement is only capable of being a legal interest if it is attached to a dominant tenement which is held under a normal freehold or leasehold. Of course, most are. (Easements held for other periods, for example, with a life interest or fee tail, must be equitable, although they are quite rare.) Secondly, and more importantly from a practical point of view, easements are only legal if they are created by statute, by deed or registered disposition, or by the process of prescription (long user). All other easements created by different means, even if held for a legal freehold or legal leasehold, must be equitable (if they exist at all).

7.4.1 Easements created by statute

Occasionally, an Act of Parliament may determine that a local authority, a corporation, or even a private individual shall be entitled to the benefit of an easement. Such easements will be legal. Note, however, that creation by statute *does not* refer to the creation of easements by the action of s 62 of the LPA 1925 (on which, see below). Here, we are concerned with specific easements deliberately created by a specific Act of Parliament.

7.4.2 Easements created by prescription

Easements created by the process of prescription are also legal. Prescription signifies the acquisition of a right by long use, for example, where a person has enjoyed a right of way for many years. Prescription is discussed in more detail below, but for now we may note that prescription takes three forms: common law prescription, 'lost modern grant' and prescription under the Prescription Act 1832.

7.4.3 Easements created by deed/registered disposition

The great majority of legal easements are created by deed (in the case of unregistered land), or by registered disposition entered on the register of titles (in the case of registered land). Easements created by this method are necessarily encompassed in a formal document (the deed or registered disposition) and rightly are regarded as legal rights. Indeed, the manner of their creation by formal documents ensures that their existence is easily discoverable by a prospective purchaser of the servient land. As we shall see below, the creation of legal easements by deed or registered disposition may occur in a wide range of circumstances, and may be either express or implied. Note, however, that whether the easement is *expressly* or *impliedly* created by a deed or registered disposition does not affect its quality as a legal interest.

7.5 Equitable easements

Easements held for periods less than a fee simple absolute in possession or a term of years (leasehold) *must* be equitable. They are not included in the definition of legal estates and interests found in s 1 of the LPA 1925. However, most easements are created for these two estates, and the equitable quality of an easement more usually derives from the fact that the easement has not been created in the manner appropriate for the creation of legal rights. Consequently, an easement will be equitable even if held for a legal freehold and leasehold if it is not created by statute, nor by prescription, nor by deed/registered disposition, provided that either: the easement is embodied in a written contract which equity regards as specifically enforceable (s 2 of the Law of Property (Miscellaneous Provisions) Act (LP (Misc Prov) A) 1989 and *Walsh v Lonsdale* (1882)); or the easement is created by proprietary estoppel. These two alternative conditions are the 'formality' requirements for the creation of equitable interests and mean that the easement must be created in writing, or fall within the limited exception of easements generated by proprietary estoppel. If even these more relaxed formality requirements for the creation of equitable easements are not met, then the right to use the neighbour's land cannot be regarded as an easement at all. It may then amount to a licence to use land, but licences lack proprietary status and are personal to the parties that create them (see Chapter 9).

To expand on the criteria for the creation of equitable easements further, under s 2 of the LP (Misc Prov) A 1989, a contract for the creation of an interest in land (for example, an easement) must be in writing incorporating all the terms and be signed by both parties, if it is to be enforceable. So, rather as is the case with equitable leases, if the parties have entered into a written agreement (that is, instead of a deed or registered disposition) which creates an easement, and if this agreement can be regarded as specifically enforceable under *Walsh v Lonsdale* (1882), a court of equity will treat the contract as having been performed (even though it has not), and an equitable easement will be the result.

In addition, while it is no longer true that mere oral agreements as such can create equitable easements (because of the need for writing under s 2 of the LP (Misc Prov) A 1989) an equitable easement may be created through the process of proprietary estoppel (see Chapter 9). Thus, as in *Ives v High* (1967), an oral promise, relied on by the promisee to their detriment, may generate an equitable easement against the promisor if it would be unconscionable to deny it. Prior to the entry into force of the 1989 Miscellaneous Provisions, easements could be created by oral contract if supported by 'acts of part performance' under s 40 of the LPA 1925, as in *Thatcher v Douglas* (1996). Section 40 is now repealed, and mere oral contracts (that is, where no estoppel is involved) cannot create equitable rights.

Thus, to sum up, equitable easements are those easements which do not qualify as legal easements, provided that they are either embodied in a specifically enforceable written contract (oral contracts are not sufficient), or in the exceptional situation of proprietary estoppel.

Under the LRA 2002

The manner in which legal or equitable easements can be created will necessarily change under the proposals contained in the Land Registration Act (LRA) 2002. As mentioned elsewhere, an essential part of these proposals is that for many proprietary rights, their creation will occur simultaneously with their registration (assuming registered land) and that this will be done electronically. This will have the following consequences. First, that pending entry into force of the electronic system in full, it will be possible to make a deed or a written contract electronically. The electronic deed or written contract will need to be effected in a prescribed manner, the details of which are not yet certain. However, the important point is that such electronic deeds and written contracts will have the same effect as their 'material' counterparts. An electronic deed will create legal easements and an electronic written contract will create equitable easements and, at first, these will exist alongside their 'traditional' counterparts. Secondly, and more profoundly, the LRA 2002 envisages that eventually an expressly created easement will not exist at all until entered on the register of the servient land and that this entry must be done electronically (see s 93 of the LRA 2002). Hence, when the full system of the 2002 Act comes into force, it will not be possible to create easements in registered land at all by a material (that is, non-electronic) deed or written contract: easements will exist only if entered on the register and this will only be capable by electronic entry. In that (still distant time) deeds and written agreements will create nothing at all!

7.6 The significance of the distinction between legal and equitable easements in practice: easements and purchasers of the dominant or servient tenement

The most important reason for distinguishing between legal and equitable easements is because of the effect that easements may have on subsequent purchasers of the dominant and servient tenements. We have noted that easements are proprietary: the benefit of the easement is capable of running with the dominant tenement, and may be enforced by any owner for the time being of an estate in that tenement; and the burden of the easement is capable of running with the servient tenement, and may be enforced against any owner for the time being of an estate in that tenement. (Note, also, that persons present on the servient land with no estate – such as adverse possessors and licensees – can be compelled to permit enjoyment of the easement (though they cannot create one) precisely because the easement binds the land, not simply the people occupying it.) As with other interests in land, whether an easement does in fact run with the land depends crucially on its legal or equitable status *and* the mechanics of the systems of registered and unregistered land. In practice, it is usually a potential purchaser of the servient tenement that is most concerned with this issue, simply because it is they who will have to allow the dominant tenement owner to exercise the easement. After all, the existence of a binding easement may well affect a purchaser's view of the desirability or value of the servient land.

7.6.1 Registered land

With regard to registered land, the *benefit* of an easement becomes part of the dominant tenement and automatically passes to a purchaser or transferee of it. This is so whether the easement is legal or equitable. In fact, in practice, the register of title of a dominant tenement often may note the existence of the benefit of a legal easement, but this is not necessary to ensure that the benefit has run (see ss 5, 20 and 23 of the Land Registration Act (LRA) 1925).

By way of contrast, the purchaser of the servient land (that is, of the land burdened) will be obliged to allow the exercise of the easement in the following circumstances:

Legal easements

The great majority of legal easements will be registered against the title of the servient land (because of the way they were created) and will, therefore, be binding against a subsequent purchaser of it. Indeed, no easement created after first registration of title may be 'legal' unless it appears on the register of titles, and so this condition is easily satisfied. Further, legal easements created before first registration of title are classed as overriding interests under s 70(1)(a) of the LRA 1925, and are also binding. The effect of these provisions in practice is that legal easements will be binding on a subsequent purchaser of the servient tenement in registered land.

Equitable easements

The original scheme of the LRA 1925 envisaged that the great majority of (if not all) equitable easements would need to be registered as minor interests if they were to bind the purchaser of the servient tenement. Consequently, *if* registration is required, but not achieved, the equitable easement will be void against a purchaser for value of the servient land. It will, of course, remain enforceable (even if not registered) against other persons, such as adverse possessors, and those who received the land by way of gift. Importantly, however, according to *Celsteel v Alton* (1986), as followed by the Court of Appeal in *Thatcher v Douglas* (1996), equitable easements which are 'openly exercised and enjoyed' can also be overriding interests under s 70(1)(a) because of the effect of Rule 258 of the Land Registration Rules. Although this approach has been criticised, the underlying rationale of both cases is that the equitable easement was not expressly or clearly created and, therefore, the person supposed to register it may have been unaware of its existence. In such cases, the owner of the dominant tenement at the time of the creation of the equitable easement may not understand that they have an easement, and so cannot (at least on one view) be expected to protect it by registration. It may be only fair in such circumstances that the easement is classified as an overriding interest and automatically binding. If this is the correct implication to be drawn from *Celsteel* (and not everyone would agree that it is) it is not certain that *all* equitable easements can be brought within s 70(1)(a). Indeed, many commentators would argue that, at best, the two decisions justify the inclusion of only non-expressly created equitable easements within s 70(1)(a). For expressly created equitable easements, the owner of the dominant tenement must, by definition, know of the existence of his right and should not be permitted to sidestep the requirement to register it as a minor interest. Note, also, that it may be possible for an equitable easement to be an overriding interest under s 70(1)(g) of the LRA 1925, but only if the person entitled to enforce the easement is in 'actual occupation' of the *servient* land. Although this is possible in theory, it is unlikely in all but the most unusual circumstances. For example, the requirement of s 70(1)(g) is not satisfied simply because the dominant tenement owner uses the easement (for example, walks across the servient land). This is not 'occupation' of the servient land so as to elevate the equitable easement to an overriding interest. Nevertheless, despite these reservations, the Court of Appeal in *Saeed v Plustrade* (2001) indicate that the owner of a dominant tenant in respect of a right to park, may have been 'in actual occupation' of the parking space so as to generate an overriding interest against a purchaser of the servient tenement. In fact, counsel for Plustrade conceded this point and so the result may be regarded as *obiter* and not fully argued.

Under the LRA 2002

The effect of easements on purchasers of the servient tenement of registered land has not escaped the attention of the LRA 2002. As indicated above, there will come a time when all expressly created easements over registered land will not exist unless entered on the register electronically and this will necessarily ensure that they are binding against any purchaser or possessor of the servient land. Apart from this, the Act provides first that all legal easements shall override (that is, be an 'overriding interest' against) a first registration of title to the land, being where the land is put on the register for the first time (Sched 1 to the LRA 2002). Such legal easements will thus bind the first registered proprietor and all later transferees. Secondly, that with respect to transfers after first registration (that is, registrable dispositions) as where the first registered proprietor of the servient land sells it to someone else, the Act again envisages that legal easements expressly created by the registered proprietor will not take effect at law until entered on the register and consequently must be so entered in order to take effect against a purchaser. Consequently, the only legal easements that will be overriding if created after first registration will be those generated by prescription and those impliedly granted (that is, by necessity, common intention, *Wheeldon v Burrows* (1879) and s 62 of the LPA 1925: see below, 7.9). Even then, not all of these impliedly granted legal easements will override a registrable disposition (although they would take effect against a first registered proprietor). Excluded from overriding status (except against a first registered proprietor) are legal easements which are in some sense unknown or unused. Finally, equitable easements will not be overriding at all, either against a first or subsequent registered proprietor (*Celsteel v Alton* (1986) is reversed).

Perhaps a summary may be helpful:

- all legal easements expressly or impliedly granted will override a first registration: that is, be binding as an overriding interest on the first registered owner;

- after first registration, expressly granted legal easements must be entered on the register to exist at law and so cannot be overriding. In fact, they are protected by such entry;

- after first registration, impliedly granted legal easements may be overriding against a purchaser provided they are either known to the purchaser, or are patent on a reasonably careful inspection of the servient land, or have been exercised within one year before the sale to the purchaser, or are entered on the special register maintained under the Commons Registration Act 1965;

- equitable easements will no longer be overriding at all against any registered proprietor, so *Celsteel v Alton* (1986) will be reversed. Such easements will either have been protected as a land charge in unregistered land so be entered on the register when the land is first registered, or if expressly created after first registration will need to be protected by an entry on the register of title (by a notice) in similar fashion to the current 'minor interests' protection;

- because eventually all expressly created easements will not exist until entered on the register, expressly created legal easements will be entered on the title and expressly created equitable easements will be protected by a notice in the equivalent of the minor interest section of the register. Impliedly created legal easements will be overriding as above (that is, if known, used etc), and impliedly created equitable easements will require protection by means of a notice against the title (that is, as with the current minor interests).

7.6.2 Unregistered land

With regard to unregistered land, the *benefit* of both legal and equitable easements becomes part of the dominant tenement and automatically passes to a purchaser of it. The position is identical to that in registered land. Once again, questions concerning the *burden* of the easement are best considered by separating legal and equitable easements:

Legal easements

As with all legal rights in unregistered land (except the *puisne* mortgage: see Chapter 3), legal easements 'bind the whole world'. They are automatically binding on a purchaser of the servient land, who must allow the owner of the dominant tenement to exercise it.

Equitable easements

Most equitable easements are Class D(iii) land charges under the Land Charges Act 1972. As such, they must be registered in order to bind a subsequent purchaser for money or money's worth of a legal estate in the land. If they are not registered as Class D(iii) land charges, they will be void against such a purchaser, but will remain enforceable against others (for example, a squatter) (*Midland Bank v Green* (1981)). The single exception to this seems to be equitable easements created by proprietary estoppel. According to Lord Denning in *Ives v High* (1967), equitable easements created by estoppel are not within the statutory definition of Class D(iii) land charges, apparently because that category includes only those equitable easements which could once have been legal but are rendered equitable by the 1925 legislation. Estoppel easements are, of course, purely equitable, and always will be. Therefore, equitable estoppel easements will be binding against a purchaser of the servient land according to the old 'doctrine of notice'. This means that an equitable estoppel easement will be valid against everyone except a *bona fide* purchaser for value of a legal estate in the servient land who has no notice (actual or constructive) of the easement.

7.7 The creation of easements

We have noted above that currently there are various ways in which a legal or equitable easement may come in to existence. To sum up, they are:

(a) by statute (legal);

(b) by prescription (legal);

(c) by deed or registered disposition (legal);

(d) by a specifically enforceable written contract, not amounting to a deed or registered disposition (equitable);

(e) by estoppel (equitable).

The creation of easements by statute is not common, and prescription is considered below, 7.10. The operation of the doctrine of proprietary estoppel is considered in Chapter 9, where it will be seen that the emergence of an easement is only one way that a court might choose to 'satisfy' the estoppel. The operation of proprietary estoppel is not restricted to the creation of easements but is a general doctrine that is best considered separately.

The following section therefore considers the creation of easements by deed, registered disposition or written contract. However, although the use of one of these three methods of creating an easement may give rise to a different quality of easement (that is, legal or equitable), it should be appreciated that all three will operate against the same factual background. Whether the parties to a transaction choose a deed, a registered disposition or a written contract to carry out their intentions will depend on the nature of the land (unregistered or registered) and their own appreciation of the needs of the situation at the time. What is important, therefore, is to analyse the factual scenarios in which easements may be created, and only after that ascribe a legal or equitable status to the easement thereby created. This, in turn, will depend on the actual method chosen by the parties. To put it another way, these three methods of creating easements (deed, registered disposition, written contract) simply reflect the level of formality desired by the parties: they are not intrinsically different. What is important is the different factual situations (excluding statute, prescription and estoppel) in which easements may be created. These are described immediately below.

7.8   Express creation

Easements may be created expressly, either by express *grant* or express *reservation*.

7.8.1   Express grant

An easement is expressly granted when the owner of the potential servient tenement gives (that is, grants) an easement over that land to the owner of what will become the dominant tenement. This may occur in two principal ways:

(a) where the servient and dominant tenements are already in separate ownership and the servient tenement owner grants an easement over his land to his neighbour; for example, where A grants B (a neighbouring landowner) a right of way over A's land. This is not very common (see *CP Holdings v Dugdale* (1998) for a recent example), but, if the grant is by deed or registered disposition (as the case may be), the easement will be legal, and if it is by enforceable written contract, the easement will be equitable;

(b) where land is owned by a potential servient owner and he then sells or leases a piece of that land to another, the potential servient owner may include in that sale/lease a grant of an easement to the purchaser. The land remaining in the vendor's possession becomes the servient tenement and the piece sold/leased becomes the dominant tenement. The vendor has granted an easement over his own land along with the sale/lease of the dominant part and the easement is mentioned expressly in the conveyance of the dominant part to the purchaser. If that conveyance is by deed or

example, no easement of way will be allowed where it is merely inconvenient to use another route, as in *Re Dodd* (1843). Indeed, we must remember the alleged dominant tenement owner (that is, the vendor) had it in his power expressly to reserve an easement when he sold part of his land. Consequently, the law 'leans against' the vendor, and the claimant will have to discharge a heavy burden of proof before the court will agree that an easement of necessity should be implied in his favour.

7.9.2 Implied by common intention: grant and reservation

Easements may be impliedly incorporated into sales of land, either in favour of the purchaser (grant), or in favour of the vendor (reservation), if this is required to give effect to the common intention of the parties. The result of such a doctrine is identical to the implied grant and reservation of easements by necessity, considered above, except that the easement does not have to be *necessary* for the use of the land, merely in the joint contemplation of the vendor and purchaser at the time of the sale (*Pwllbach Colliery v Woodman* (1915)). Clearly, the acceptance of such a doctrine facilitates the implied creation of easements in a much wider range of circumstances than that of 'necessity'. Indeed, it appears that all that is required is proof that the intended (but omitted) easement was in the contemplation of both parties when the land was sold. In fact, those cases commonly cited as examples of 'common intention' may perhaps be justified on a pure necessity basis (for example, *Wong* (1965)), and there are precious few examples of the creation of easements on this basis in practice. Nevertheless, despite these doubts, the case of *Stafford v Lee* (1993) in the Court of Appeal does apply *Pwllbach* on a clear 'common intention' approach. According to Nourse LJ, in *Stafford*, an easement by common intention can exist if there was a common intention between vendor and purchaser as to some definite user of the land, and if the easement is necessary to give effect to that intention. So, in *Stafford*, the plaintiff (the purchaser) wished to build a house on his own land, when the only practical access for construction purposes was over the defendant's land. As the land had been sold to the plaintiff with a view to the construction of a house, an easement of way for the purpose of construction was held to have been granted. Similarly, in the admittedly exceptional case of *Peckham v Ellison* (1998), an easement of way was held to be impliedly reserved in favour of the vendor on the basis of common intention. It is clear, however, that the implied creation of easements by way of common intention is not lightly presumed, more so in cases where it is alleged to be reserved in favour of the vendor. So in *Chaffe v Kingsley* (1999), the Court of Appeal refused to impliedly reserve an easement by way of common intention, distinguishing *Peckham* on the ground that the alleged easement was too unspecific and imprecise to justify such a step. It seems then that creation by common intention is possible, but not always permissible. After all, we must not forget that if the alleged easement was so crucial to the parties' common intention, why was it not expressly inserted in the relevant conveyance?

7.9.3 Easements implied under the rule in *Wheeldon v Burrows*: grant only

The rule in *Wheeldon v Burrows* (1879) may appear complicated at first, but it is only a variant of the situation considered above, as where a person sells/leases part of his land and expressly grants to the purchaser an easement for the benefit of the part sold, burdening the part retained. The difference is that, under *Wheeldon*, the easement is not *expressly* granted, but is deemed to be implied into the sale of the land. Note, however, that easements may only be *granted* by this method, that is, granted for the benefit of the land sold to the purchaser (dominant tenement), to take effect over the land retained by the vendor (servient tenement). They may not be reserved for the benefit of the land retained, as confirmed in *Peckham v Ellison* (1998).

The rule in *Wheeldon* provides that, where a person transfers part of his land to another, that transfer impliedly includes the grant of all rights in the nature of easements (called 'quasi-easements') which the vendor enjoyed and used prior to the transfer for the benefit of the part transferred, providing that those rights are either 'continuous and apparent' or 'reasonably necessary for the enjoyment of' the part transferred.

As we know, no easement can exist where the dominant and the servient tenement are owned and occupied by the same person. However, it often happens that a landowner will use one part of his land for the benefit of another, as where a landowner walks across a field to get to his house. These are 'quasi-easements', because they would have been easements had the plots been in different ownership or possession. Thus, under the rule in *Wheeldon*, if the owner of the entire land sells or leases the 'quasi-dominant' part of his land (being the land benefited by the right: in our example, the house), the purchaser is taken to have been impliedly granted the right previously used for the benefit of that part (in our case, a right of way over the retained field). The purchaser's land then truly becomes the dominant tenement, and the land retained by the vendor (in our example, the field) is truly now the servient tenement.

The conditions for the application of the rule are as follows:

(a) the rule can be expressly excluded, as where a vendor stipulates that the only easements granted to the purchaser are those expressly mentioned in the sale or lease. However, as *Millman v Ellis* (1996) shows, the express grant of a lesser (but similar) easement does not exclude the implied grant of a wider easement. So, in that case, the express grant of an easement of way over a road did not exclude the implied grant, under *Wheeldon*, of an associated easement of way over an adjoining layby. It seems then that the exclusion of the *Wheeldon* rule must itself be clearly made in the grant of the dominant land. Thus, in *Hillman v Rogers* (1998), the express grant of an easement to cross a road did not exclude the implied grant of a right of way over the road under *Wheeldon*. Likewise, and contrary to the earlier *Wheeler v JJ Saunders* (1995), an obligation placed on the servient owner by the same conveyance to fence the land (possibly implying that no right of way across it could exist) did not *always* provide the 'contrary intention' necessary to exclude *Wheeldon* and, despite the apparently contradictory obligation on the servient owner to fence, he was also taken to be subject to a right of way;

(b) secondly, only those rights which are *capable* of being easements within the *Ellenborough* criteria may become easements by operation of the *Wheeldon* rule. This is self-evident: if a right is not capable of amounting to an easement, it is irrelevant how it is created. Such a right will be a licence;

(c) the rule applies to those quasi-easements that are used by the owner of the whole land for the benefit of the part sold prior to the lease or sale. It does not appear to be enough that some other person used the quasi-easement, save only if this other person can be regarded as the original owner's agent or *alter ego*. So, if the owner of land always flew by helicopter to his house, but all visitors approached the house by walking across his adjoining field, it is doubtful whether sale of the house to a third party would carry with it an easement of way over the field: the right alleged to be an easement was not used by the owner of the common part for the benefit of the land sold. It would be otherwise if any of those using the field could be regarded as the owner's agent, *alter ego*, or with his permission, as in *Hillman v Rogers* (1998), where the owner of the whole land had given permission for others to use the right of way created subsequently;

(d) the quasi-easement must have been either 'continuous and apparent' or 'necessary for the reasonable enjoyment' of the part granted. These are almost certainly alternatives, although some cases give the impression that both are required (for example, *Millman*, but not *Rogers*). This may be because, in the majority of cases, the alleged easement is indeed 'continuous and apparent' as well as 'necessary for the reasonable enjoyment' of the dominant part.

A quasi-easement is 'continuous and apparent' if it is visible on inspection of the servient land over which it exists, or so obvious that its use for the benefit of the part sold is beyond doubt. In *Millman*, the fact that the layby was covered in tarmac was evidence that it was used as part of a right of way and was proof that it was 'continuous and apparent'. Similarly, the passage of light through a defined window would be continuous and apparent, even though the window itself is the only outward sign. Moreover, 'continuous' does not mean 'in continuous use', in the sense that the owner continuously used the right now alleged to be an easement (for example, there is no need to walk over the field every day). Rather, it is that the right was constantly *available* for use by the owner and was, in fact, used when appropriate.

The alternative requirement, that the quasi-easement must be 'necessary for the reasonable enjoyment' of the dominant part, often causes greater problems. Strictly speaking, the requirement is *not* that the easement is 'necessary' for the enjoyment of the land – these are not easements of necessity. Rather, it is that the easement is necessary for the 'reasonable enjoyment' of the land. The emphasis is on reasonable enjoyment, not necessity. In *Millman*, therefore, the fact that use of the layby as part of the easement of way made access to the property considerably safer was enough to establish its contribution to the reasonable enjoyment of the land. By no stretch of the imagination was this layby actually 'necessary' in order to access the land; it merely facilitated its reasonable use. However, in *Wheeler v JJ Saunders* (1995), decided before *Millman*, and also in the Court of Appeal, it was held that a proposed easement of way was not 'necessary for the reasonable enjoyment' of land because other access to the property existed. While, on a simple view, this could be correct – that is, the existence of other access can mean that the proposed easement of way adds nothing to the reasonable enjoyment of the land and is not, therefore, 'necessary' for its reasonable enjoyment – the judgment in *Wheeler* comes close to equating this criterion with the much stricter test for easements of necessity. This is unfortunate, as the rationale for the two methods of easement creation are different. Easements of necessity do not depend ultimately on the express or implied intentions of the parties but are 'granted' in order to ensure that use of land can be maximised: it is almost policy based. Easements created by *Wheeldon* are much more clearly rooted in the parties' intentions as demonstrated by their actions prior to sale of the dominant part. The decision in *Wheeler* was subjected to close analysis in *Hillman v Rogers* (1998), and this later case makes it clear that 'necessary for reasonable enjoyment' should not be equated with 'necessity';

(e) note, also, that if the original landowner grants the quasi-dominant part to X, and, at the same time, grants the quasi-servient part to Y, the rule in *Wheeldon* operates to give X an easement over Y's land, as in *Swansborough v Coventry* (1832) and *Hillman v Rogers* (1998). In other words, the rule will operate for simultaneous transfers of the prospective dominant and servient parts. So, if A (original landowner) walks across a field to get to his house, and then sells the house to X and the field to Y, X enjoys the right of way across Y's land. In respect of Y, this is *not* a case where the burden of an *existing* easement is passing to Y and so questions of registration are irrelevant. This is a case of a new easement being created over Y's land, so Y is, in fact, the first owner of the servient tenement. For the purposes of this principle, transactions will be regarded as 'simultaneous' if clearly part of a design to deal with all of the land (*Hillman v Rogers* (1998)).

As in the case of easements of necessity and common intention, the character of the easement implied by *Wheeldon v Burrows* (1879) follows the character of the document into which it is implied. So, a sale or lease of the dominant part by means of a deed (or registered disposition in registered land) means that the easement will be legal, and a sale or lease of the dominant part by enforceable written contract (as in *Borman v Griffiths* (1930)) means that the easement will be equitable. Finally, although the rule in *Wheeldon* does appear complicated, it is a relatively common way in which easements are created and, as we have seen from *Millman*, a vendor needs to be astute to exclude its operation. It is premised on the simple view that a person (the vendor) cannot 'derogate from their grant' when transferring land. In the absence of clear words to the contrary, a vendor transfers land with all the rights attaching to it, even if this means that 'new' easements are created over his retained land.

7.9.4 Easements implied under s 62 of the Law of Property Act 1925: grant only

The final method by which easements may be impliedly created arises because of the effect of s 62 of the LPA 1925. Once again, the situation in which this occurs is where an owner of land sells or leases part of it to another, and that sale or lease impliedly carries with it certain easements for the benefit of the part sold, burdening the part retained. In this respect, the operation of s 62 is similar to *Wheeldon v Burrows* (1879), especially as easements may only be granted to the purchaser (not reserved for the vendor) by this method. However, as we shall see, there are some crucial differences between the creation of easements via s 62 and their creation under the rule in *Wheeldon*.

At first glance, s 62 of the LPA 1925 appears to have only little to do with easements. The material part says that:

> ... a conveyance of land shall be deemed to include and shall by virtue of this Act operate to convey, with the land, all buildings, erections, fixtures ... liberties, privileges, easements, rights, and advantages whatsoever, appertaining or reputed to appertain to the land, or any part thereof ...

So, in simple terms, if a landowner has two or more plots of land and then conveys by deed one of those plots to a purchaser, the purchaser will be granted, by the automatic action of s 62 of the LPA 1925, all those rights that were previously enjoyed with the land. This is straightforward enough, but s 62 is a powerful statutory provision. Its importance lies in the fact that it will convert into easements (for the benefit of the land sold, to the burden of the land retained) all those rights which were previously enjoyed for the benefit of the land sold (or leased), even though, prior to sale, they were merely 'precarious'; that is, were exercised over the land now retained by the vendor only by virtue of his permission, and not as of right. An example will be given shortly, but note first, the conditions which must be fulfilled before s 62 can create new easements in favour of the purchaser:

(a) s 62 of the LPA 1925 applies only to sales or leases that are made by 'conveyance', and a conveyance is defined in the LPA 1925 as a deed/registered disposition. In other words, s 62 will create easements only when the sale or lease to the purchaser is made by a deed or registered disposition as the case may be, not when it is made by written contract. Consequently, s 62 creates only legal easements;

(b) the operation of s 62 can be excluded by clear words in the conveyance to the purchaser. Most professionally drafted conveyances will exclude s 62, as this prevents the vendor of land creating new easements burdening any land which they might retain;

(c) like *Wheeldon*, only those rights which are intrinsically capable of being easements may be impliedly created by virtue of s 62. So, even though the 'right' over the land which is then turned into an easement by a conveyance under s 62 is not yet an easement (because, for example, the landowner gave merely a limited, temporary permission), it must fall within the nature of easements to be so created. A mere permission to park a car can turn into an easement of way by s 62 (as in *Hair v Gillman* (2000)), but a mere permission to play football somewhere on the land never can;

(d) most importantly, and in complete contrast to the rule in *Wheeldon*, it is essential for the operation of s 62 that the plots owned by the vendor were in separate occupation before the sale or lease by deed (what is called 'prior diversity of occupation') (*Sovmots v Secretary of State for the Environment* (1979); following *Long v Gowlett* (1923)). What this means in practice is that, before the potential dominant tenement is sold, different persons must have been occupying that land and the land retained by the vendor (the potential servient tenement). Effectively, this means that the vendor will have been occupying the potential servient land and the potential dominant tenement will have been occupied by his tenant or licensee. Indeed, usually, this tenant or licensee will be the person who then purchases or leases the property by deed/registered disposition and obtains the easement under s 62, but it is not essential that this be so (as in *Hillman v Rogers* (1998)) provided that such diversity did exist.

If these conditions are fulfilled, and a conveyance by deed/registered disposition is made (for example, a sale, a lease, a renewal of a lease), the purchaser will be impliedly granted as legal easements those rights which were previously enjoyed for the benefit of the land sold.

It will be appreciated from the above explanation that the operation of s 62 is dependent on the existence of the proper factual background and the fulfilment of appropriate legal formalities (a deed or registered disposition). It is also important to remember that, once again, this is the creation of an easement where none existed before: it is not the purchase of already burdened land by the purchaser and so questions of registration are not relevant. The following example demonstrates how s 62 operates in practice.

7.9.5 An example of the creation of easements by s 62 of the Law of Property Act 1925

A owns two houses, one of which she occupies herself and one of which she lets by lease or licence to B (therefore the land is in 'prior diversity of occupation'). A allows B to walk over the garden of the house she occupies as a short cut to the road. A then grants a new lease by deed to B (or sells him the house). The effect of s 62 of the LPA 1925 is to turn the mere permission to walk over the garden into an easement of way. An easement has been implied into the conveyance of the land from A to B. Note, also, the result would be the same if B had vacated the property and A had conveyed it by deed to X: then X would have been impliedly granted the same easement with and for the benefit of the land he had purchased. The crucial elements in this easement creation are:

(a) that both plots of land were owned by the vendor originally (A), but that there was diversity of occupation (A and B). The status of B (tenant or licensee) prior to the 'easement creating' conveyance is immaterial;

(b) that A then sells that part of the land which enjoys the benefit of the right by a conveyance (transfer of a legal estate) without excluding s 62. The sale will often be to B (the person previously on the land), but may be to a completely new person; and

(c) that the 'precarious' right is inherently capable of being an easement because s 62 of the LPA 1925 may only generate easements where the previous right is capable of being an easement. Consequently, B now owns dominant land, and A owns servient land.

As you will see on reading s 62 of the LPA 1925, it has many uses, but the creation of easements by implied grant is one of its most startling. Obviously, a vendor of land that has been occupied by some other person prior to the sale must be very careful not to grant new easements in favour of a purchaser. For example, in *Goldberg v Edwards* (1950), a licensee enjoyed a limited access by permission over her landlord's land, and when a new tenancy by deed was granted to her, that permissive right was transformed into an easement (see also *Wright v Macadam* (1949)) and in *Hair v Gillman* (2000), the vendor inadvertently granted a legal parking easement to a former tenant when she purchased the freehold of what became the dominant land.

7.9.6 A comparison between the rule in *Wheeldon v Burrows* and s 62 of the Law of Property Act 1925

The circumstances in which *Wheeldon v Burrows* (1879) and s 62 operate are superficially so similar that they are often regarded as interchangeable (as in *Hillman v Rogers* (1998)). This is a mistake. Section 62 and the rule in *Wheeldon* operate against the same factual background, but the conditions on which they depend are so different in detail as to make them virtually mutually exclusive:

(a) *Wheeldon* operates where the common vendor was in occupation of all the land before the sale of the dominant part and he (or his alter ego) used the potential easement. Section 62 operates where the land was in separate occupation (albeit single ownership) before the sale of the dominant part, and the right was enjoyed by the other occupier against the owner;

(b) *Wheeldon* creates easements only where the right is 'continuous and apparent', or 'necessary for the reasonable enjoyment of the land'. Section 62 has no such limitation;

(c) *Wheeldon* can imply easements into a legal or equitable sale or lease and may, therefore, create legal or equitable easements. Section 62 operates only where the sale or lease is by deed and can create only legal easements;

(d) both *Wheeldon* and s 62 of the LPA 1925 can be excluded by clear words in the conveyance of the alleged dominant tenement.

7.10 Easements resulting from prescription

Another method of creating easements is by 'prescription'. To be more precise, we should say easements are 'generated' by prescription, rather than 'created', because 'prescription' is more a process than a deliberate act. In general terms, 'prescription' occurs when the owner of what will be the dominant tenement establishes long use of a 'right' over what will be the servient land. If, then, the 'right' so used is capable of being an easement (that is, if the *Ellenborough* conditions are satisfied), the long use can mature into an easement proper. All easements created in this fashion will be legal. As we shall see, the period for which the use must be established may vary from case to case (depending on which of the three 'methods' of prescription is used), but the essential point is that easements generated by prescription are easements created through the very use of the right itself. So, if the owner of Pinkacre has walked across Blueacre for the required period of time in the appropriate circumstances, an easement of way by prescription (long use) may be established.

Before going on to consider the conditions for the acquisition of an easement through prescription, it is important to appreciate the basis of this doctrine. After all, it seems strange that one person can acquire a powerful right over their neighbour's land in the absence of any written document or express grant of the right. In fact, the rationale for prescription is a subtle one. The essential point is that the fact of long use of the 'right' by the owner for the time being of the dominant tenement, gives rise to a presumption that a grant of the right was actually made. This is so even though there clearly is no grant at all. In this sense, prescription is not 'adverse' to the owner of the servient tenement, for the fact of long use is taken to be conclusive evidence of the servient owner's grant of the right. Unlike the law of adverse possession (Chapter 11), the owner of the dominant tenement is taken to have acquired the easement through the acquiescence of the servient owner. Also, again unlike the law of adverse possession, the effect of a successful prescriptive claim is to create a new right for the dominant tenement owner, not merely to extinguish the rights of the owner on whose land the long use occurs. Consequently, the law of prescription is sometimes known as the law of 'presumed grant': the grant of the easement is presumed in favour of the dominant tenement owner from the fact of long use.

7.10.1 General conditions for obtaining an easement by prescription

As mentioned already, there are three 'methods' or 'routes' to a successful claim of prescription. They are: common law prescription; common law prescription under the rules of 'lost modern grant'; and prescription under the Prescription Act 1832. However, these methods are not inherently different, but simply describe the three different ways by which the person claiming the prescriptive right may establish that the long use was, indeed, long enough to mature into an easement. All three take the same common thread, that long use presumes a grant of the easement in favour of the dominant tenement. Therefore, the following sections discuss the general conditions for establishing an easement by prescription and, where the different methods have different requirements, this will be noted.

7.10.2 Easements of prescription lie in fee simple only

Although it may now appear to be somewhat anomalous, the origin of prescriptive easements is that they are presumed to 'lie in grant', meaning that they are presumed to have arisen by a grant from the fee simple owner of the servient tenement (absolute in possession) to the fee simple owner of the dominant tenement (absolute in possession). Consequently, easements of prescription are always legal, and always attach to the fee simple estate: they are 'permanent' in the same sense that a fee simple is permanent. There can be no easement by prescription in favour of, or against, a leaseholder or an estate that exists in equity only, such as a life interest (illustrated by *Kilgour v Gaddes* (1904)). This has certain consequences that limit the circumstances in which a prescriptive easement can arise:

(a) the long use must be by a fee simple owner of the dominant tenement. This is not necessarily a serious problem, because if the dominant land is possessed by a tenant, the tenant's use of the alleged easement (that is, by walking across a neighbour's land) can be held to be on behalf of the landlord, that is, on behalf of the fee simple owner. So, providing that the tenant is not asserting that the alleged easement should endure only for so long as the tenancy, this requirement can be met, as explained in *Hyman v Van den Bergh* (1907);

(b) the long use must be against a fee simple owner of the servient tenement. This is the converse of the above and means that easements by prescription cannot exist against tenants (however long their lease) or any equitable estate holder. Moreover, there are further difficulties here, because if the long use commences at a time when a tenant is on the alleged servient land, this is conclusive evidence that the fee simple owner cannot be presumed to have granted the easement. To put it another way, use of the right against the tenant of the fee simple owner does *not* amount to use against the fee simple owner. In such cases, there can be no easement by prescription against the fee simple owner (they are not in possession), nor against the tenant (simply because they are not the fee simple owner) (as discussed in *Pugh v Savage* (1970)). Note, however, that there is no objection if the fee simple owner is in possession at the commencement of the long use, but subsequently leases the land to a tenant (*Pugh*). This is because at the time the long use started it is possible to presume that the grant was made by the fee simple owner. This has the odd effect that a claimant to an easement by prescription may assert that the long use started at a later date than that acknowledged by the servient owner *if*, at the later date, the fee simple owner was back in possession of the land after the termination of an earlier lease;

(c) the above rules have additional practical implications. It is impossible for a tenant to claim a prescriptive easement against his own landlord and vice versa. If L (landlord) occupies Plot 1, and leases Plot 2 to T (tenant), T can never claim an easement of prescription against L, and L can never claim an easement by prescription against T. In either case, the fee simple owner cannot be presumed to have granted an easement against himself. Likewise, if L leases both plots to different tenants, the tenants cannot claim an easement by prescription against each other, since neither is a fee simple owner;

(d) it has been confirmed, in *Simmons v Dobson* (1991), that the above limitations apply to both common law prescription proper and common law prescription under 'lost modern grant'. In principle, they should apply in the same measure to prescription under the Prescription Act 1932. However, it seems that the words of this statute may have modified the position. Thus, if the 40 year period of the Act is applicable (see below, 7.11.3), it may well be that objections based on the lack of a fee simple owner fall away. This is because, under s 2 of the Act, a claim to an easement based on 40 years' use (without consent) is said to become 'absolute and indefeasible', and, according to *Wright v Williams* (2001), this is enough to oust objections based on (at least) the lack of a fee simple servient owner. (Note, this appears to have been doubted in *Davies v Du Paver* (1953).) Likewise, under s 3 of the Act, it is clear that claims to easements of light do not have to fulfil all the common law conditions.

One of the consequences is that there is no objection, if relying on the Prescription Act 1832, to prescriptive easements of light in favour of, or against, land held for the leasehold or life interests. Under the Prescription Act 1832, a tenant may acquire an easement of light by prescription against his landlord (and vice versa), and two tenants of the same landlord may acquire such easements for and against each other.

7.10.3 Use must be 'of right', so as to presume the grant

A second general requirement for the acquisition of an easement by prescription is that the long use must be 'as of right'. To some extent this is circular. An easement is only truly 'a right' after it has been acquired, but in order to be generated by prescription, the requirement is that the long use must already be 'as of right'! What is meant, then, is that the dominant tenement owner's use of the servient tenement owner's land must be in the character of a use as of right, and not be explicable for any other reason. As is sometimes said, the use must be *nec clam* (without secrecy), *nec vi* (without force) and *nec precario* (without permission) (*Solomon v Mystery and Vintners* (1859)).

Use without secrecy

No easement can be acquired by prescription unless it arises in circumstances where a grant can be presumed. Consequently, a secret, hidden use by the owner of the alleged dominant tenement is not sufficient because it demonstrates that no grant can be presumed: a grant presumes a degree of awareness on the part of the servient owner. In practice, this now means that prescriptive easements can be generated only if the use has been 'open' – that is to say, 'of such character that an ordinary owner of land, diligent in the protection of his interests, would have, or must be taken to have, a reasonable opportunity of becoming aware' of the use (*per* Romer LJ in *Union Lighterage Co v London Graving Dock Co* (1902)). For example, the wearing of a path on the servient land, or the open use of an existing path, are not secret, but the hidden discharge of water onto a neighbour's land would be.

Use without force

No easement can be acquired by prescription if the owner of the alleged dominant tenement must use 'force' to accomplish the use. Again, the need to use force shows that no grant can be presumed. 'Force' in this situation means either forcible assertion of the use (for example, breaking down a fence), or continued use in the face of protests by the alleged servient owner. The latter is a forcible assertion of a use, even though no violence is used. A typical example of use 'with force' is continued use after the alleged servient owner has threatened to take, or has taken, legal proceedings (provided, of course, that this does not occur *after* the completion of the period of use sufficient to establish the prescriptive claim).

Use without permission

As we have seen, the acquisition of an easement by prescription assumes the grant of a right to the dominant tenement. The crucial matter, then, is the servient tenement owner's acknowledgment of the dominant tenement owner's 'right' to the use, not the servient owner's consent to it. The servient owner must acquiesce in the right, not give his permission for the use, because 'consent' implies that the dominant owner has no right. Consequently, evidence that the alleged servient owner has consented to the use, perhaps by giving a licence, will bar a prescriptive claim, as in *Hill v Rosser* (1997). Necessarily, however, the line between acquiescence (the claim succeeds) and consent (the claim fails) is a thin one. Generally speaking, the servient owner cannot argue that their mere knowledge of the use amounts to implied consent so as to defeat the claim (*Mills v Silver* (1991)), and the dominant and/or servient owner's belief that consent has been given, when it has not, does not defeat prescription (*Bridle v Ruby* (1989)). A good checklist for determining whether the use has been without consent (but with acquiescence), and, therefore, may generate a prescriptive easement, is provided by Fry J in *Dalton v Angus and Co* (1881), viz:

(a) is there a use of the servient owner's land?;

(b) is there an absence of a strict right to carry on the use?;

(c) does the servient owner have knowledge (actual or constructive) of the use?;

(d) does the servient owner have the ability to stop the use, either practically or legally?;

(e) has the servient owner abstained from stopping the use for the period required for a successful prescriptive claim?

If these can be answered positively, the prescriptive claim is likely to succeed, although one must be wary of dismissing claims simply because they fail to meet these criteria in some small way. Finally, it is in the nature of many prescriptive easements that they start out as being exercised with the servient owner's consent and then cease to be consented to at a later date, for example, where a neighbour is given permission to walk across land for one month, but continues after that time. If it can be established that the use became without consent, the prescriptive claim can succeed, with the period of use being calculated by reference to the moment the consent ended.

A limited exception

As we have seen above, claims to easements of light under s 3 of the Prescription Act 1832 do not have to fulfil all the common law conditions. A further consequence is that the long user does not have to be 'as of right', in the sense just discussed. Therefore, under the Act (but only the Act), easements of light may be established even if it is clear that the servient owner was consenting to the right of light.

7.10.4 Use must be in the character of an easement

This is an obvious condition because, after all, we are discussing the generation of a proprietary right that will affect the dominant and servient tenements, irrespective of who later owns the land. Thus, no 'easement' by prescription can arise unless the 'use' itself satisfies the inherent characteristics of an easement. For example, no easement to wander over land can arise by prescription, because such a right can never be an easement and no prescriptive easement of drainage for the benefit of 'higher' over 'lower' land can exist, because the drainage is natural and not in the way of a right which the owner of the lower land could ever have prevented – *Palmer v Bowman* (1999). Again, if both the dominant and servient tenements have come into common ownership at some time during the period of long use, there may be difficulties in establishing a prescriptive claim. In such cases, there is a union of the two tenements, and a landowner cannot have a true easement against himself. The period of long use would, therefore, be terminated and would have to recommence if the tenements later separated. It is also the case that long use may mature into an easement by prescription only if the use is lawful: easements may not exist for purposes contrary to the criminal law or statute, and no servient owner can be presumed to grant one. So, a prescriptive claim to an easement to walk across land where that is a criminal offence (for example, Ministry of Defence land) cannot succeed.

7.11 Methods of establishing an easement by prescription

As indicated at the start of this section, there are three recognised varieties of prescription: prescription at common law; prescription at common law utilising the doctrine of 'lost modern grant'; and prescription under the Prescription Act 1832. We have seen, also, that the inherent nature of a prescriptive claim is the same under all three methods, save that prescription under the Prescription Act 1832 has less rigid requirements in matters of detail, due to the wording of that statute. In fact, when it comes to making a prescriptive claim, the owner of the potential dominant tenement may rely on any, or all three methods. This illustrates more than anything their common origin. As we shall see, the methods differ essentially in the way in which the claimant must establish the long use and the length of time he must have used the 'right' before it can mature into an easement proper. In essence, the methods are about how the long use is to be proven, not primarily about the quality of the long use. In all three methods, even though the period of long use required for a successful claim can vary, the claimant must establish that the use has been 'continuous' throughout the relevant period.

'Continuous user' (sometimes referred to as 'continuity of user') does not mean that the claimant must use the 'right' incessantly, never stopping. It denotes, rather, that there is a regular, consistent use of the right for the relevant period, commensurate with the nature of the right. This means that 'regular' use will be a question of fact. The exercise of a right of way might be 'continuous' in one case if it is exploited only two or three times a year but, in another set of circumstances, monthly use might be required. Again, some easements are, by nature, more obviously exercised 'continuously' – such as an easement of way – while others (an easement to enter and cut obstructing trees) are not. The continuity of some easements is often completely hidden – as with the easement of support offered by a wall on the servient owner's land. Likewise, unimportant inconsistencies in the long use cannot defeat a claim, as where the route of a path deviates over time, or a replacement sign is hung in a slightly different position on the servient owner's land. Assuming, then, that the claimant can establish that he is a continuous user, what period of time is necessary to propel this into an easement proper?

7.11.1 Prescription at common law

At common law, long use could mature into an easement if it could be shown to have occurred since before 'legal memory'. According to the Statute of Westminster 1275, legal memory was fixed (arbitrarily) at 1189, so a claim of prescription could succeed at common law if it could be shown that the use existed before then. Obviously, this was well nigh impossible, so it became accepted that use for 20 years raised a presumption that use commenced before 1189 (as explained in *Dalton v Angus* (1881)). Unfortunately, however, this did not mean that 20 years' use generated a prescriptive easement. It remained the case that the claim could be defeated by any evidence that the use could not, in fact, have started before 1189. So, for example, a claim to a right of light, even if used for 150 years, could be defeated by showing that the building so benefited was built 'only' in the year 1190. The ease with which an alleged servient owner can defeat the 20 year presumption effectively ensures that this form of common law prescription is hardly ever successful.

7.11.2 Prescription at common law: lost modern grant

The doctrine of lost modern grant developed as an antidote to the manifest deficiencies of 'pure' common law prescription. In fact, this doctrine is really no more than a fictional gloss on the old common law rules. As we know, the rationale for prescription is a presumed grant of the right by the servient owner. Under 'lost modern grant', the law assumes that 20 years' use of the right is conclusive evidence of such a grant being made by the servient owner. The grant is 'modern', because it is assumed to have been made at some time after 1189, and it is 'lost', because it cannot now be produced – of course, it does not actually exist, but this is the convenient fiction. Stripped of its trappings, the doctrine means that 20 years' continuous use by the owner of the dominant tenement is sufficient to establish an easement by prescription (*Dalton v Angus* (1881)). This is so even if the servient owner produces evidence that no grant had been made – which, of course, is true. Indeed, it seems that the one way in which the servient owner can defeat the claim (apart from the absence of other requirements mentioned above, 7.10.2–7.10.4) is if he shows that the servient owner who is assumed to have made the grant (that is, the owner at the commencement of 20 years' use) was legally incompetent at the time, being a minor or lunatic. Even then, although there is authority to support this limitation (*Oakley v Boston* (1976)), it seems strange to deny a prescriptive claim on the ground that the person supposed to have made the fictitious grant was unable to do so, when everybody knows that he never made the grant at all. Why is legal incapacity a bar, when actual non-existence of the grant is not? Be that as it may, the doctrine of lost modern grant is sufficient in most cases to ensure that long use, as of right, matures into an easement.

7.11.3 The Prescription Act 1832

The Prescription Act 1832 is not a replacement for the common law (especially lost modern grant), and, considering some of its mystifying language, this is just as well. It is intended to bolster the common law principles, supplementing them, where necessary, with the general aim of making it easier to establish an easement by prescription. It is doubtful whether it does this, but that is its purpose. The Act divides easements into two classes: easements of light and all other easements.

All easements except easements of light

Under s 2 of the Act, a period of 20 years' use is sufficient to establish a prescriptive claim, provided that the 'right' was enjoyed 'without interruption' for that period (for example, the successful claim of way in *Denby v Hussein* (1999)). Evidence that the 'right' was not enjoyed, or lacked some other quality, in the period *before* commencement of the 20 years, cannot defeat the claim. Moreover, an interruption by the servient owner during the 20 years is sufficient to defeat the claim only if the alleged dominant owner tolerated the interruption for one year or more. However, the Act does not remove the need to satisfy the conditions for prescription *during* the 20 year period. Thus, any inability to meet the common law conditions during the 20 years' use is fatal to the claim. Finally, there is a further practical limitation in that the alleged dominant owner cannot pick any 20 years' use: the 20 years' use must be calculated by reference to the 20 years immediately prior to 'some suit or action'. This has the unfortunate consequence that no easement of prescription can arise if, say, the use has been enjoyed for 100 years, but no 'suit or action' is brought, or if the easement was enjoyed for 200 years in conformity with the common law conditions, but at some time in the last 20 years before a suit, one of the common law conditions was not met (for example, the dominant and servient tenements came into common ownership).

In contrast to this, s 2 provides as an alternative that 40 years' use without interruption ensures that the right is 'absolute and indefeasible' unless exercised with the consent of the servient owner. This effectively eases the conditions imposed by s 2 for 20 years' use. It remains the case (with the same problems) that the 40 years' use must be that which is immediately prior to a 'suit or action', and the same principles of 'interruption' apply. However, because 40 years' use makes the right 'absolute and indefeasible', it seems that it does not matter that someone other than the fee simple owner (for example, a tenant) was in possession of the land at the start of the period, provided the period is completed. On the other hand, the remaining common law conditions appear to apply, save only that if the servient tenement's consent is given at the start of the use (or possibly the start of the 40 year period – the Act is unclear), it must be in writing or by deed to negate the prescriptive claim. The issue of 'consent' occurring at any other time during the 40 years is determined by reference to the common law.

Easements of light

Under s 3 of the Act, use of light for a period of 20 years (probably that period prior to any 'suit or action' – again, the Act is unclear) 'without interruption' becomes 'absolute and indefeasible' unless the servient owner consents in writing or by deed. In particular, there is no provision in s 3 that preserves the conditions of the common law, so uninterrupted use for 20 years without written consent will mature into an easement even if there is some defect that would have defeated a common law claim. Note, however, that there can be 'an interruption' of light for the purposes of s 3 by the alleged servient owner without that owner actually physically blocking the light. The servient owner can take steps to register a notice in the local land charges register as provided by the Rights of Light Act 1959. This notice acts in law as an interruption and may prevent the acquisition of a right of light under s 3. Its purpose is to remove the need for the erection of numerous anti-light structures by potential servient owners as the end of a 20 year period approaches.

7.12 The extinguishment of easements

Given that an easement is essentially a right enjoyed by one landowner over the land of another, it is vital to its existence that the dominant and servient tenements are in separate ownership or occupation. Thus, the most common reason why easements cease to exist is that the dominant and servient land comes into the ownership *and* possession of the same person. Note that there must be unification of both ownership and possession, for it is perfectly possible for a tenant to enjoy an easement against their landlord and vice versa (for example, *Wright v Macadam* (1949)), although, as just noted, one such cannot be generated through prescription. Importantly, there is no statutory mechanism by which a person may apply for the judicial termination of an easement, unlike the position with restrictive covenants. Consequently, failing extinguishment through unification of the tenements, easements may only be terminated by a release of the easement by the current owner of the dominant tenement (express or implied through conduct), by abandonment (mere non-use is not abandonment – *Benn v Hardinge* (1992)), or by a specific Act of Parliament. Equitable easements may also become void and unenforceable against subsequent purchasers of the servient tenement by reason of a failure to register (if required) in registered or unregistered land. The Law Commission proposes to undertake a review of easements in the medium future and so the LRA 2002 does not contain specific proposals going to the substance of easement law, save where this affects land of registered title and the effect of easements on purchasers of registered land. The LRA 2002 effectively reduces the opportunities for easements to be overriding interests.

7.13   A note on *profits à prendre*

Profits à prendre are often considered alongside easements, not least because they also give rights over land belonging to another. The essential nature of a profit is that it is a proprietary right to enter upon another's land and take for oneself the profits of the land. For example, the profit of piscary entitles a person to enter another's land and take fish, likewise with the profits of turbary (turf) and estovers (wood). Profits may also be legal or equitable, although it is worth noting that currently, in registered land, *all* profits are overriding interests (s 70(1)(a) of the LRA 1925). Again, with the possible exception of the rule in *Wheeldon v Burrows* (1879), profits may be created in the same ways as easements. However, there is one important difference that is worthy of note. Whereas an easement can exist only if there is a dominant and a servient tenement, a profit may exist 'in gross', that is, it exists over servient land, but the person entitled to the benefit of it does not have to own land of their own. The burden of a profit attaches to land (hence its proprietary status), but the benefit may be held by any person, or, indeed, any number of persons. Profits can be commercially important, as with profits of piscary in salmon-rich waters. For this reason, the LRA 2002 enables legal profits to be registered with their own title (s 3 of the LRA 2002).

THE LAW OF EASEMENTS

The essential characteristics of an easement

The traditional criteria for determining whether a right amounts to an easement are found in *Re Ellenborough Park* (1956):

- there must be a dominant and a servient tenement (easements cannot exist in gross);

- the dominant and servient tenements must be owned or occupied by different persons;

- the alleged easement must accommodate (that is, benefit) the dominant tenement, meaning that the servient tenement must be sufficiently proximate (that is, near) to the dominant tenement; the alleged easement must not confer a purely personal advantage on the owner of the dominant tenement; the alleged easement must not confer a purely 'recreational user' on the dominant tenement;

- the alleged easement must 'be capable of forming the subject matter of a grant', meaning that an easement cannot exist unless there is a capable grantor; an easement cannot exist unless there is a capable grantee; an easement cannot exist unless the right is sufficiently definite; the right must be within the general nature of rights recognised as easements;

- public policy may also be relevant, though not mentioned in *Re Ellenborough Park* (1956).

Legal and equitable easements: formalities

An easement can qualify as a legal interest only if it is held as an adjunct to a freehold or leasehold estate and if it is created by statute, by prescription or by deed (unregistered land) or registered disposition (registered land).

Easements held for less than a freehold or leasehold must be equitable. Even easements held for these estates will be equitable if not created properly. In that event, the easement may be equitable, provided it is embodied in a written contract or instrument that equity regards as specifically enforceable or it arises orally through proprietary estoppel.

The significance of the distinction between legal and equitable easements in practice: third parties

In registered land, the benefit of an easement becomes part of the dominant tenement and automatically passes to a purchaser, whether legal or equitable. The burden of a legal easement in registered land currently will either be registered against the title of the servient land or be an overriding interest under s 70(1)(a) of the LRA 1925. It will bind a purchaser of the servient land. In order for an equitable easement to bind a purchaser of the servient land, the easement must either be registered as a 'minor interest' or, if 'openly exercised and enjoyed' it will amount to an overriding interests under s 70(1)(a) (*Celsteel v Alton* (1986) and Rule 258 of the Land Registration Rule).

In unregistered land, the benefit of an easement becomes part of the dominant tenement and automatically passes to a purchaser, whether legal or equitable. The burden of a legal easement in unregistered land will 'bind the whole world'. The burden of an equitable easement in unregistered land must be registered as a Class D(iii) land charge under the LCA 1972 in order to bind a purchaser, save that estoppel easements bind according to the doctrine of notice.

The LRA 2002 makes changes to the way legal easements take effect in registered land. Most will be entered against the title of the servant land, but those legal easements impliedly created will in many cases (but not all) be overriding interests. Equitable easements will have to be entered on the register.

The express creation of easements

An easement may be expressly granted by the potential servient owner to the potential dominant owner: for example, where the servient and dominant tenements are already in separate ownership and a grant is made, or where land is owned by a potential servient owner, and he then sells or leases a piece of that land to another and includes an express grant in the sale.

An easement may be expressly reserved by the potential dominant owner when that owner sells or leases a piece of that land to another and includes in that sale a reservation of an easement for themselves.

Note

That the easement is legal or equitable depending on the character of the document in which it is contained. A legal conveyance creates a legal easement and transfer of an equitable estate creates an equitable easement.

The implied creation of easements

Necessity

An easement may be impliedly granted, and occasionally impliedly reserved, because of necessity, as where the land sold (grant) or land retained (reservation) would be useless *without* the existence of an easement in its favour.

Common intention

An easement may be impliedly incorporated in a sale of land either in favour of the purchaser (grant) or exceptionally in favour of the vendor (reservation) if this is required to give effect to the common intention of the parties.

Wheeldon v Burrows (grant only)

Where a person transfers part of their land to another, that transfer impliedly includes the grant of all rights in the nature of easements (called 'quasi-easements') which the vendor enjoyed and used prior to the transfer for the benefit of the part transferred, providing that those rights are either 'continuous and apparent' or 'reasonably necessary for the enjoyment of' the part transferred.

Implied under s 62 of the Law of Property Act 1925 (grant only)

If a landowner has two or more plots of land and then conveys, by deed, one of those plots to a purchaser, the purchaser will be granted, by s 62 of the LPA 1925, all of those rights that were previously enjoyed with the land. This is so even if before the sale the 'rights' were enjoyed purely by permission and not as of right. Section 62 applies only to sales by deed or registered disposition and creates only legal easements.

Note

In cases of implied creation, the easement is legal or equitable depending on the character of the document into which it is implied.

Easements by prescription

Prescription occurs when the owner of what will be the dominant tenement establishes long use of a 'right' over what will be the servient land. If, then, the 'right' so used is inherently capable of being an easement, the long use can mature into an easement proper. All easements created in this fashion will be legal. The period for which the use must be established will vary from case to case, depending on which of the three 'methods' of prescription is used.

General conditions for obtaining an easement by prescription

- Easements of prescription lie in fee simple only. There can be no easement by prescription in favour of, or against, a leaseholder or an estate that exists in equity only, such as a life interest. So, the long use must be by a fee simple owner of the dominant tenement and it must be against a fee simple owner of the servient tenement. It is impossible for a tenant to claim a prescriptive easement against his own landlord and vice versa (or against another tenant). These rules have been modified for claims made under the Prescription Act 1832.

- The use must be 'of right'. The long use must be *nec clam* (without secrecy), *nec vi* (without force) and *nec precario* (without permission).

- The use must be in the character of an easement, as satisfying the criteria of *Re Ellenborough Park* (1956).

Methods of establishing an easement by prescription

For all 'methods' of establishing an easement by prescription, the claimant must establish first that the use has been 'continuous' throughout the relevant period. The length of the required period varies with each method:

- prescription at common law. The use must have occurred since before 'legal memory', that being before 1189. Use for 20 years raises a presumption that use commenced before 1189, but the claim can be defeated by any evidence that the use could not, in fact, have started before then. Such claims hardly ever succeed;

- prescription at common law – lost modern grant. The law assumes that 20 years' use of the right is conclusive evidence of a grant of the easement being made by the servient owner. This means that 20 years' continuous user by the owner of the dominant tenement is sufficient to establish an easement by prescription, even if the servient owner produces evidence that no grant had ever been made – which of course is true;

- Prescription Act 1832. For all easements – except easements of light – a period of 20 years' use is sufficient to establish a prescriptive claim, provided that the 'right' was enjoyed 'without interruption' for that period. Alternatively, 40 years' use without interruption ensures that the right is 'absolute and indefeasible', unless exercised with the consent of the servient owner. For easements of light, a period of 20 years' use 'without interruption' becomes 'absolute and indefeasible', unless the servient owner consents in writing or by deed.

The extinguishment of easements

This can occur in a variety of ways. For example, the dominant and servient land may come into the ownership and possession of the same person; the dominant owner may 'release' the easement, expressly or impliedly through conduct; the easement may be terminated by Act of Parliament.

Profits à prendre

A 'profit' is a proprietary right to enter upon another's land and take for oneself one of the 'profits' of the land. Profits may be legal or equitable, although, in registered land, all profits are overriding interests (s 70(1)(a) of the LRA 1925). With the possible exception of the rule in *Wheeldon v Burrows* (1879), profits may be created in the same ways as easements. Note, however, that profits may exist 'in gross': that is, they may exist over servient land even if the person entitled to the benefit owns no land himself. Examples are the profit of piscary (to take fish), the profit of turbary (to cut turf) and the profit of estovers (to cut wood). Under the LRA 2002, legal profits will be capable of being registered with their own title.

CHAPTER 8

FREEHOLD COVENANTS

Freehold covenants represent yet another way by which one landowner may control or affect the use of neighbouring land. In some respects, the principles discussed below are similar to those seen in Chapter 6 (leasehold covenants) and Chapter 7 (easements), in that a binding freehold covenant both gives a benefit and imposes a burden on the relevant plots of land. In simple terms, 'freehold covenants' are, as their name implies, covenants (or promises) made between freeholders, whereby one party promises to do or not to do certain things on their own land for the benefit of neighbouring land. Thus, the owner of house No 1 may promise the owner of house No 2 not to carry on any trade or business on his (No 1's) land, or the owner of house No 3 may promise the owner of house No 4 not to build above a certain height. In these examples, the landowner making the promise on behalf of his land is the covenantor (where the burden lies), and the landowner to whom the promise is made is the covenantee and his land is where the benefit lies. As in these two examples, the great majority of covenants between freeholders are 'restrictive' (negative) in nature, in that they prevent a landowner from doing something on his own land, as opposed to requiring him to take positive action. Of course, that is not to say that 'positive' covenants cannot exist (for example, a covenant to pay for the upkeep of a boundary fence), but, as we shall see, the enforcement of a positive covenant between persons other than the original parties to it is extremely difficult. Consequently, much of the law in this area has concentrated on restrictive covenants, and many textbooks refer to this topic as 'the law of restrictive covenants'. Freehold covenants may be contrasted with 'leasehold covenants', the latter being a term of the lease made by the original landlord and original tenant and usually (but not necessarily) referring to the land that is the subject matter of the lease.

8.1 The nature of freehold covenants

The nature of freehold covenants can be analysed in the following way.

8.1.1 Positive and negative covenants

Covenants between freeholders may be either positive or negative in nature. Positive covenants require the owner of the burdened land to take some action on their own or adjoining property, usually requiring the expenditure of money: an example is a covenant to keep one's own property in good external repair in order to maintain the character of a neighbourhood. Negative or restrictive covenants require the owner of the burdened land to refrain from some activity on his own land: an example is a covenant not to carry on any trade or business perhaps because it is intended to preserve the residential character of a neighbourhood (for example, *Gafford v Graham* (1998)).

8.1.2 Covenants as contracts

Covenants are promises made by deed by one person to another to do, or more usually not to do, something on their own or adjoining land. The covenant is made between the *covenantor* and the *covenantee*. Covenants are binding and enforceable as a matter of contract law between the parties. Consequently, the covenantor must do, or refrain from doing, that which he promised (and, therefore, is subject to a burden), and the covenantee has the right to sue for performance of the covenant (and therefore enjoys a benefit).

8.1.3 Covenants as interests in land

Most importantly, covenants are proprietary interests in land. This means that they have the following attributes:

* **The covenantor's land: the burden of the covenant**

  It is clear from the above that the covenantor (he who made the promise) is under the burden of the covenant. He must refrain from doing something on his own land if the covenant is restrictive (negative), or he must carry out the terms of the promise if the covenant is positive. As we shall see, however, performance of this burden is not limited to the original covenantor, but may (if certain conditions are fulfilled) pass or run with the land itself. In other words, any person who subsequently comes into possession of the original covenantor's land may be subject to the burden of the covenant and be required to observe its terms. So, if Mr Smith, the owner of Pinkacre, covenants with Mr Jones, the owner of Blackacre, that he (Smith) will not carry on a trade or business on Pinkacre, it is perfectly possible for any future owner (or, indeed, mere occupier) of Pinkacre to be bound to observe the covenant, whether or not that new owner specifically agrees to the covenant. The burden of the covenant may 'run with the land'.

* **The covenantee's land: the benefit of the covenant**

  Likewise, there is no doubt that the covenantee (the person to whom the promise was made) has the 'benefit' of the covenant. He has the right to sue for performance of the covenant and may be awarded damages (for past breaches of covenant), an injunction (to prevent impending breaches of covenant), or a decree of specific performance (to compel performance of a positive covenant). Once again, in certain circumstances, this benefit may run with the land and pass to any subsequent owner of it, giving that person the right to sue for performance of the covenant and obtain the appropriate remedy. So, adopting the above example, if Mr Jones, the owner of Blackacre (the land having the benefit of the covenant) sells that land to another, the new owner may obtain the benefit of the covenant along with the land, and may sue the person now subject to the burden of it. As can be seen, this means that the landowners who are parties to 'an action on the covenant' may, or may not, be the original covenantor and original covenantee. Assuming the requisite conditions are satisfied (on which see below, 8.4–8.6), the parties can be the *current* owners of the burdened and benefited land.

- **The duality of benefit and burden**

  In practice, what we have just discussed is the proprietary nature of covenants: their ability to impose benefits and burdens on land in the sense that they may affect persons other than the original covenantor and original covenantee. In short, the covenant has been attached to the land itself. Obviously, in practice, the person claiming the benefit of a covenant usually will be the claimant, and the person allegedly subject to the burden usually will be the defendant. Indeed, it is important to realise that in all cases where a person is seeking to enforce a freehold covenant against another, it must be possible to show *both* that the benefit of the covenant has run to the claimant *and* that the burden has run to the defendant. In the following sections, we shall see that the rules or conditions for the transmission of the benefit and then the burden of a freehold covenant can be very different. However, the essential fact remains that, before any covenant can be enforced, it must be shown separately that the benefit has passed to the claimant (under the appropriate rules) and that the burden has passed to the defendant (under the appropriate rules). Without this duality, there can be no action 'on the covenant' (*Thamesmead Town v Allotey* (1998)).

8.2 The relevance of law and equity and the enforcement of covenants

The history of land law is replete with references to the differences between common law and equity and this is one area where the old distinctions still have relevance today. Historically, this distinction resulted from the different types of remedies available in a court of law or equity and particularly because of the latter's willingness to allow the covenant to 'run' with the land more easily. The distinction may have consequences today, although there is a tendency to downplay it, save where this is impossible. A good example being *Gafford v Graham* (1998), where the court observed that the defence of acquiescence should operate identically, whether the claimant was claiming suit at law or in equity.

8.2.1 Suing at law

If a person sues on a covenant at law, he will be claiming that the defendant is subject to the burden of the covenant at law and should pay damages. If successful, the claimant has a right to damages, which the court cannot refuse. As we shall see, the circumstances in which a remedy lies at law (that is, for damages) are narrower than the situations in which a remedy lies in equity.

8.2.2 Suing in equity

As noted above, a court of equity would always act to mitigate the harshness of the common law, and this is now reflected in the rules concerning freehold covenants. Consequently, not only is it easier to enforce a covenant in equity, but the range of potential defendants is much greater because the burden of a covenant runs with the land much more freely than at law. Moreover, because enforcement of the covenant is in equity, equitable remedies are available, although unlike remedies at law they are subject to the discretion of the court and may be withheld in an appropriate case. These remedies are the injunction (for restrictive covenants) and the decree of specific performance (for positive covenants). Finally, if the claimant sues in equity (for example, because a remedy at law is not available), then the normal principles of registered and unregistered land come into operation. These will be considered below, but for now, the point is that a restrictive covenant may need to be registered (in registered and unregistered land) to be enforceable against certain kinds of defendant.

Thus, in any concrete case involving the enforcement of freehold covenants, there are always two issues of primary importance:

(a) has the benefit of the covenant run to the claimant in law or equity?; and

(b) has the burden of the covenant also passed to the defendant in law or in equity?

Note that, if the claimant is suing in equity, he must establish that the burden has passed to the defendant in equity. Likewise, if the claimant is suing at law, he must establish that the defendant is subject to the burden at law.

8.3 The factual context for the enforcement of freehold covenants

As the heading to this chapter makes clear, the rules about to be discussed operate when one freeholder has the right to enforce a covenant against another freeholder. Also, at the risk of repetition, there is no doubt that the benefit and the burden of certain types of covenant may *in principle* be transferred on a sale of either or both of the benefited and burdened freehold land. However, it is not only in actions between freeholders that these rules may be relevant. In fact, they may be applicable between any claimant and defendant who do not stand in a relationship of 'privity of contract' or 'privity of estate' under a tenancy granted before 1 January 1996 (on which, see Chapter 6). Consequently, as well as regulating actions on the covenant between freeholders, these rules also will be relevant when a landlord seeks to enforce a covenant contained in a lease against a subtenant and where a landlord seeks to enforce a leasehold covenant against a person who has taken only an equitable lease or an equitable assignment of the lease under an assignment taking effect on or before 1 January 1996. For equitable leases/assignments taking effect after 1 January 1996, the Landlord and Tenant (Covenants) Act 1995 may ensure the enforcement of restrictive covenants against the owner or occupier of land (ss 3(5) and 3(6)) (see Chapter 6). Finally, the rules may also be relevant where the claimant is seeking to enforce a restrictive covenant (but not a positive one) against someone who has no estate in the land, for example, a squatter.

8.4 Principle 1: enforcing the covenant in an action between the original covenantor and the original covenantee

A covenant is a legally binding contract between the covenantor and the covenantee. As such, the covenantee may sue the covenantor for damages at law for breach of contract or, in appropriate circumstances, obtain one of the equitable remedies of injunction or specific performance. This is straightforward, and is a reflection of the 'privity of contract' that exists between the original covenantee and original covenantor. However, because the benefits and burdens of certain types of covenants are transmissible to subsequent purchasers of both the original covenantor's and original covenantee's land, a number of different situations must be identified.

8.4.1 Both original parties in possession

If the original covenantor and original covenantee are still in possession of their respective land, the matter is relatively straightforward. *All* covenants are enforceable and the covenantee may obtain damages, an injunction (to prevent breach of a restrictive covenant), or specific performance (to ensure compliance with a positive covenant) against the covenantor. This is a matter of contract. For example, in an action between original covenantor and original covenantee, the claimant can enforce a covenant to maintain a boundary fence and a covenant prohibiting the carrying on of a trade or business on the land. Both positive and negative covenants are enforceable between the original parties.

8.4.2 After the original covenantor has parted with the land

If the original covenantor has parted with the land which was subject to the covenant, he remains liable on all the covenants to whomsoever has the benefit of the covenant. This is because of the contractual nature of the covenant. In most cases, a claimant will desire the covenant to be enforced in the sense of actually enforcing the substance of the obligation (that is, making sure the covenant is actually performed) and so will take action against the person currently in possession of the burdened land. Consequently, a remedy against the original covenantor who is no longer in possession of the land is of little use, unless this is the only person against whom there is a realistic chance of recovering more than nominal damages.

8.4.3 After the original covenantee has parted with the land

If the original covenantee has parted with the land which had the benefit of the covenant, he *may* still be able to enforce a covenant against whomsoever has the burden of it. However, when suing at law (that is, claiming damages), this right will almost certainly have been given up due to an express assignment of the right to sue to the new owners of the benefited land (see below, 8.8.2). In addition, when suing at equity (that is, for an injunction or specific performance), the court is likely in its discretion to refuse to grant an equitable remedy to an original covenantee who no longer is in possession of the benefited land, because, in reality, such a person suffers no loss (*Chambers v Randall* (1923)).

8.4.4 Defining the original covenantee and convenantor

It goes without saying that it is vital to be able to determine exactly who is an 'original' covenantor or covenantee, particularly if either is still in possession of the land and so able to sue effectively and easily. Usually, of course, this is quite simple, they being the parties to the deed of covenant and identified as such on paper, having signed the deed under witness: as where the deed recites that 'Mr Smith, freehold owner of Pinkacre, hereby covenants with Mr Jones, freehold owner of Blackacre', and both sign the deed in the presence of a witness. However, it is possible under s 56 of the Law of Property Act (LPA) 1925 to extend the range of original covenantees (but not covenantors) beyond those persons who are actually parties to the deed. By virtue of s 56, a person may enforce a covenant (that is, be regarded as an original covenantee), even if they are not actually a party to it (that is, have not signed it under witness), provided that the covenant was intended to confer this benefit on the person as a party and they are existing and identifiable at the date of the covenant (*White v Bijou Mansions* (1938)). What this means in practice is that far more people may have the right to the benefit of a covenant as an original covenantee (which may then be transmitted on a sale of *their* land) than simply the person who signs their name to the deed, providing only that the deed does not purport to confer these benefits on 'future' owners of land or persons who cannot be identified. A good example is where A covenants with B 'and the present owners of Plots 1, 2 and 3' not to carry on any trade or business on his (A's) land. Here, A is the original covenantor, B is an original covenantee and party to the deed, and the owners of Plots 1, 2 and 3 are also original covenantees, by virtue of s 56. Thus, the 'benefit' of the covenant is enjoyed originally by four persons, each of whom may pass that benefit with their land if the conditions discussed below are satisfied. Note, however, that it now seems established that s 56 only has this effect when the persons identified in the covenant as being entitled to its benefit are intended to be treated as *parties*, not simply additional persons to whom the benefit has been given (*Amsprop Trading Ltd v Harris Distribution* (1996)). This is a fine distinction, and although it can be crucial (as in *Amsprop*), the difficulty can be avoided by careful drafting. Simply put, the point is that s 56 is intended to ensure that specific, identifiable persons are treated as parties to the covenant, and is not intended to confer the benefit of the covenant on hoards of landowners simply because they fall within the literal ambit of a particularly boldly drafted covenant.

8.5 Principle 2: enforcing the covenant against successors in title to the original covenantor – passing the burden

One of the great steps forward in English property law was the transformation of freehold covenants from purely personal obligations governed by the law of contract to proprietary obligations governed by the law of real property (*Tulk v Moxhay* (1848)). What this means in simple terms is that, *if* the various conditions discussed below are satisfied, a covenant can be enforced not only against the original covenantor, but against anyone who comes into possession of the land burdened by the covenant (that is, the land over which the covenant operates). Obviously, this might be a severe limitation on the uses to which the burdened land can be put by a successor in title to the original covenantor (for example, if the land is subject to a covenant against business use, as in *Re Bromor Properties* (1995)), and so it is not surprising that there are strict limitations defining the precise circumstances in which the burden of a covenant may 'run' with the land.

First, it is not possible for the burden of *any* covenant at all to run at law. There can be no claim at law against a successor to the original covenantor. However, as noted above, equity is not as strict as the common law and it is possible for the burden of some covenants to run with the land in equity. In short, if a burden is to run at all, it must be in equity. This has its own consequences, in particular, that a claimant relying on the equitable claim takes the risks associated with the enforcement of all equitable rights over land. These are dealt with below, but encompass the rule that the award of a remedy is discretionary (even if the burden has actually run to the defendant) and that the covenant must have been registered appropriately in the systems of registered and unregistered land.

Secondly, even in equity, it is not the burden of every covenant that is capable of passing on transfer of the covenantor's land. The rule is simple – some would say simplistic – and is that only the burden of restrictive covenants are capable of passing (*Hayward v Brunswick Building Society* (1881); *Thamesmead Town v Allotey* (1998)). This means that it is not possible for the burden of a positive covenant to be enforced against a successor to the original covenantor, and so only the original covenantor can be liable on positive covenants. For example, if the original covenantor and owner of plot X has made a covenant with the owner of plot Y (the original covenantee) not to carry on a trade or business and a covenant to maintain a fence, if then plot X is sold to a third party, the new owner could be liable on the covenant restricting use, but cannot be liable on the covenant to maintain the fence. Positive burdens cannot pass. This is vitally important. What it means in practice is that, as soon as the land has passed out of the hands of the original covenantor, only restrictive covenants can be enforced against the land. Indeed, the claimant may well have the benefit of both positive and restrictive covenants, but the defendant can only be liable for breaches of the restrictive ones. Despite some criticism of this rule, there is no doubt that it remains the law. The rule has been reiterated by House of Lords in *Rhone v Stephens* (1994) and applied (albeit with considerable reluctance) by the Court of Appeal in *Thamesmead Town*. In both cases, there was distinct judicial criticism of the rule, but the fact that conveyancing practice has developed around it (and because of it!), and the reluctance of the House of Lords to intervene, means that it can be changed only by Act of Parliament. This course of action was urged strongly by the Court of Appeal in *Thamesmead Town* but there is little hope of legislation in the near future, despite the fact that the burden of positive leasehold covenants is easily transmissible (especially for leases granted on or after 1 January 1996: see Chapter 6), and even though the Law Commission has argued persuasively that the burden of positive obligations should run (see Law Commission, Report No 127). For now, it remains vital to be able to distinguish between those freehold covenants that impose on the covenantor an obligation to act (positive), and those that impose an obligation to refrain from acting (negative).

In a sentence, then, it is *possible* for the burden of a restrictive covenant made between freeholders to run in equity. Whether, in fact, the burden of such a covenant has so run depends then on the fulfilment of the following conditions.

8.5.1 The covenant must touch and concern the land

It is axiomatic that only freehold covenants which relate to the use or value of the land should be capable of passing with a transfer of it. The law of property is generally concerned with proprietary, not personal, obligations. Consequently, only the burden of freehold restrictive covenants which 'touch and concern' the land are capable of being transmitted. There is one possible exception to this rule, being cases where a landlord attempts to enforce a leasehold restrictive covenant against a subtenant. Such parties do not stand in either privity of contract or privity of estate, so, as noted above, the 'freehold covenant rules' are applicable. However, according to s 3(5) of the Landlord and Tenant (Covenants) Act 1995, a restrictive covenant contained in a lease (but only in a lease) 'shall' be capable of being enforced against any owner or occupier of the land, subject to requirements of registration (see below, 8.5.5–8.5.6). There is nothing in this section that requires a leasehold restrictive covenant to 'touch and concern' the land, and it may be that this requirement has been abolished (possibly accidentally?) in those cases where the burden of leasehold restrictive covenants is being enforced under the 'freehold covenants' rules. However, there is no doubt that, for restrictive covenants not contained in a lease, the requirement of 'touching and concerning' still applies (see, for example, *Robins v Berkeley Homes* (1996)) and, given that the *Tulk v Moxhay* (1848) principle is applicable most frequently in disputes concerning freeholders, the importance of the requirement remains. In essence, whether any particular restrictive covenant does 'touch and concern' will depend on the facts of each case, but, like the position with pre-1996 leasehold covenants (Chapter 6), a general test has been laid down by Lord Oliver in *Swift Investments v Combined English Stores* (1989), viz, could the covenant benefit *any* owner of an estate in the land as opposed to the particular original owner; does the covenant affect the nature, quality, mode of user or value of the land, and is the covenant expressed to be personal? These conditions will determine whether the restrictive covenant 'touches and concerns' the land and should be applied with reference to the mass of case law on this point. Perhaps the safest route for a conveyancer when attempting to ensure that a covenant 'touches and concerns' is to follow the advice of Wilberforce J in *Marten v Flight Refuelling* (1962) that a covenant which *expressly* states that it is imposed for the purpose of benefiting land will normally be taken by the court as being capable of doing so. Assuming, then, that this hurdle has been cleared, the remaining conditions must be met.

8.5.2 The covenant must be restrictive or negative in nature

As noted above, it is vital that the covenant be restrictive or negative in nature and this bears repetition. Importantly, this is a question of substance, not of form, and it is irrelevant how the covenant is actually worded (as in *Tulk v Moxhay* itself, where a covenant to keep land as an open space was rightly held negative in substance: not to build). The essence is that a covenant is negative if it prevents the landowner from doing something on his own land. Typical examples include a covenant not to carry on any trade or business, a covenant not to build and a covenant not to sell certain types of product. A covenant which compels the owner of land to spend money on his property will usually be regarded as positive, and hence unenforceable against successors to the original covenantor. As before, a covenant to maintain a boundary fence is a good example (see also *Rhone v Stephens* (1994)).

8.5.3 The covenant must have been imposed to benefit land of the original covenantee

The next condition is that, at the date of the original covenant, the covenant must have been imposed on the burdened land in order to benefit or protect land owned by the original covenantee (*Whitgift Homes Ltd v Stocks* (2001)). In other words, the covenant must have been made to benefit *land* and if there is no benefit or no such land, the covenant is unenforceable. In the language of easements, there must be a 'dominant tenement' which could benefit from this restrictive covenant (*London and South Western Railway v Gomm* (1882)). Note that this condition is satisfied if the covenant was made to benefit the estate of a lessor or mortgagee, and there are statutory exceptions in favour of local authorities under the Town and Country Planning Acts. So, contrary to the general rule, a restrictive covenant may be enforced against a landowner by a local authority, even if they (the authority) did not own land at the time of the covenant. A common reason why there may have been no land owned by the covenantee which was intended to benefit from the covenant at the time it was given, is the simple one that the original covenantee may not have retained any such land at the time the covenant was made. So, if Smith sells Blackacre to Jones, and in the sale Jones (as original covenantor) covenants with Smith (as original covenantee) not to build on Blackacre, the burden may run to Jones' successors in title only if Smith retained some land at the time the covenant was executed (*Formby v Barker* (1903)). If Smith sold everything at that time (that is, he kept no portion of Blackacre), he remains the original covenantee, but has no benefited land, and so the burden cannot pass to successors of the original covenantor.

8.5.4 The burden of the restrictive covenant must be intended to run with the land

A further important condition is that the burden of the restrictive covenant must have been intended to run with the land of the original covenantor. That is, there must be evidence to establish that the 'burden' was intended to be proprietary, not personal. This is not difficult to establish because, in the absence of a contrary intention, the burden of a restrictive covenant is deemed to be attached to the land by virtue of s 79 of the LPA 1925. According to s 79(1) of the LPA 1925:

A covenant relating to any land of the covenantor ... shall, unless a contrary intention is expressed, be deemed to be made by the covenantor on behalf of himself, his successors in title and the persons deriving title under him.

By virtue of this section, the burden of a covenant is deemed to be made by the original covenantor on behalf of himself and all future owners of the land, thereby annexing the burden of the covenant to that land because of an intention that it shall run (*Tophams Ltd v Earl of Sefton* (1967)). The burden may then become enforceable against such successors. A 'successor' is someone with a legal or equitable estate in the land (*Mellon v Sinclair* (1996)) and, for restrictive covenants only, includes any person in occupation of the land without an estate, such as an adverse possessor (s 79(2) of the LPA 1925). Of course, this statutorily assisted annexation of the burden occurs 'unless a contrary intention appears', and it is clear that the covenant does not have to recite specifically that s 79 is inapplicable to exclude its effect (*Re Royal Victoria Pavilion, Ramsgate* (1961)). A 'contrary intention' will 'appear' from the instrument creating the covenant if there is anything in it indicating that successors in title or assigns of the original covenantor would not be bound, as in *Morrells v Oxford United FC* (2000) where s 79 was found to be excluded by the whole tenor of the arrangement between the parties. Clearly, whether s 79 of the LPA 1925 is so excluded is a matter of construction, and so the safest course for someone wishing to exclude statutory annexation of the burden would be to say so in clear terms in the deed of covenant.

The fifth and final condition which must be satisfied before the burden can be enforced against a successor to the original covenantor arises because such burdens are enforced only in equity. In short, restrictive covenants are treated as equitable interests in another's land, and, in consequence, must comply with the rules of registered and unregistered conveyancing relating to such interests.

8.5.5   In registered land

In registered land, if the person against whom the restrictive covenant is being enforced is registered as proprietor of the burdened land under the Land Registration Act (LRA) 1925, the covenant *must* be registered as a minor interest against that burdened land in order to be binding (s 20 of the LRA 1925), unless one of the two exceptions noted below apply. Of course, most transferees of the burdened land will be registered as title holders in this way and most restrictive covenants will have been protected by registration at the time they were created. However, if the restrictive covenant is not registered as a minor interest, it is void and unenforceable forever. Note, however, that even a covenant which is not protected as a minor interest can be binding against:

(a) someone who is registered as proprietor, but who was not a purchaser of the burdened land for valuable consideration: for example, the donee of a gift, a devisee under a will or a squatter; or

(b) someone who purchases only an equitable interest in the land: for example, an equitable tenant.

The position will remain substantially unaltered under the Land Registration Act 2002.

8.5.6   In unregistered land

If the person against whom the restrictive covenant is being enforced is a purchaser of a legal estate in the burdened land for money or money's worth, the covenant *must* be registered against the name of the original covenantor as a Class D(ii) land charge under ss 2(5) and 4(6) of the Land Charges Act (LCA) 1972. Of course, most transferees will be purchasers of this type and most covenants will be registered. However, if the restrictive covenant is not registered in this way, it will be void and unenforceable forever. Note, however, that even an unregistered restrictive covenant can be binding against:

(a) someone who is not a purchaser: for example, the donee of a gift, the devisee under a will or a squatter; or

(b) someone who does not give 'money or money's worth': for example, the recipient of land under the marriage consideration; or

(c) someone who purchases only an equitable estate: for example, an equitable tenant.

To conclude, then, the burden of a restrictive covenant may run in equity to successors of the original covenantor if certain conditions are met. In the great majority of these cases, the conditions will be met, and the only live issue is likely to be whether the covenant was appropriately registered. Assuming that it was – and the other conditions are satisfied – the burden runs and the defendant is liable. Even then, the award of equitable remedies is discretionary, and the claimant may not get what he asked for (see, for example, *Thamesmead Town*: damages instead of the desired injunction). In the worst possible scenario for the claimant, the court might decide that he has behaved so inequitably that neither an injunction nor damages should be awarded, despite the fact that the burden of the covenant has run to the defendant.

8.6   Principle 3: passing the benefit of a covenant to successors in title to the original covenantee

As indicated at the beginning of this chapter, in all cases where it is proposed to enforce a covenant, it must be possible to show both that the defendant has the burden and that the claimant has the benefit of the covenant. There must be correlative rights and obligations. Before dealing with the matter in detail, a number of preliminary points relating to the passing of the benefit should be noted.

First, the benefit of a covenant may be passed at law or in equity (unlike the burden, which passes only in equity). The conditions for the transmission of the benefit in equity are slightly easier to satisfy than those needed to pass the benefit at law. Also, the benefit of both positive *and* restrictive covenants may pass at law and in equity.

Secondly, however, given that only the burden of restrictive covenants may pass, and then only in equity, in practice the claimant usually pleads that the benefit has also passed in equity (as explained in *Gafford v Graham* (1998)). This will give us our claimant (benefit) and defendant (burden) suing in equity. The passing of the benefit of covenants at law and the passing of the benefit of positive covenants are relevant practically only when the claimant is suing the original covenantor as this is the only person liable in such cases.

8.6.1 Passing the benefit of positive and negative covenants at law

To reiterate, passing the benefit of positive and negative covenants at law will be relevant only when the claimant – the successor to the original covenantee – is claiming the benefit of such covenants in order to sue the original covenantor. If any other person is the defendant, the claimant must sue in equity, and on a restrictive covenant, as it is only the burdens of these that are capable of passing. With that practical limitation in mind, the conditions for the passing of the benefit of a freehold covenant at law are as follows:

(a) first, the covenant must 'touch and concern' the land of the original covenantee (*Rogers v Hosegood* (1900)). In other words, the covenant must relate to use of the land, and not be merely personal in nature. The test of 'touching and concerning' is the same as that for pre-1996 leasehold covenants, viz: whether the covenant could benefit any estate owner as opposed to the particular original covenantee; whether the covenant affected the nature, quality, mode of user or value of the land; and whether the covenant was expressed to be personal (*Swift Investments v Combined English Stores* (1989));

(b) secondly, the claimant must have a legal estate in the land, although, by virtue of s 78 of the LPA 1925, the claimant does not have to have the *same* legal estate as the original covenantee. Thus, the original covenantee may have been the freeholder, but the claimant will succeed even if they have 'only' a legal lease. Importantly, however, *any* occupier (including a squatter) may enforce the benefit of a restrictive covenant. This is because s 78 of the LPA 1925 deems 'the owners and occupiers for the time being' to be successors in title for the purpose of enforcing restrictive (but *not* positive) covenants. This mirrors the position in respect of the burden of restrictive covenants (see s 79(2) of the LPA 1925, above, 8.5.4);

(c) thirdly, the benefit of the covenant must have been annexed to a legal estate in the land, either expressly or by implication. A covenant may be annexed expressly by words which make it clear that the covenant is for the benefit of certain land, or words which make it clear that the covenant is intended to endure for successive owners of the land (for example, where a covenant is with the 'heirs and successors of X, the owner for the time being' of Plot 2). In either case, however, the land must be readily identifiable, and capable of benefiting from the covenant (*Re Gadd's Transfer* (1966)), and this must be possible at the time the covenant is executed, rather than the (later) time when the title to which it relates (that is, on which the benefit is conferred) is presented for registration (*Mellon v Sinclair* (1996)). This has the happy side effect that the benefit of a freehold covenant still annexes to the estate in the land even if the first owner of the benefited land (that is, the original covenantee) delays or forgets to apply for registration as proprietor. This is to be contrasted with the unhappy side effect produced by *Brown and Root v Sun Alliance* (1996) in the law of leasehold covenants, where lack of registration of the lease seriously disrupts the timing of passing of the leasehold covenant (Chapter 6).

A covenant will be assumed to benefit land where it affects the value, method of enjoyment or mode of user of the land to which it is annexed. Importantly, however, as well as express annexation, a covenant may be annexed by virtue of s 78 of the LPA 1925, as discussed in *Federated Homes v Mill Lodge Properties* (1980) and *Whitgift Homes v Stocks* (2001). According to the Court of Appeal in *Federated Homes*, s 78 of the LPA 1925 has the effect of statutorily annexing the benefit of every covenant – both positive and negative – to each and every part of the land. The only conditions are that the land is capable of benefiting from the covenant and that the land can be readily identified from the deed. However, even then, it is clear that it is permissible to use extrinsic evidence to establish the precise scope of the benefitted land, as illustrated by *Whitgift Homes* (2001). In practice, this means that, unless a contrary intention is clearly shown (*Roake v Chadha* (1984)), the benefit of most covenants will now be annexed to the covenantee's land and be available to a purchaser of it, or part of it. This appears to be a significant development, for the effect of the *Federated Homes* decision is to ensure that the benefit of covenants will attach to each and every part of benefited land, and (subject to the other conditions) will run to successors in title of the original covenantee, even if the original benefited land is subsequently sold off in parts. So, if X (original covenantor) covenants with Y that no trade or business is permitted on X's land, the benefit of that covenant will attach to each and every part of Y's land, and subsequent purchasers of the whole, or part, will obtain the benefit of it (for example, *Robins v Berkeley Homes* (1996)). If we then imagine that Y is a property developer, selling off individual plots on a housing estate, the wide impact of this interpretation of s 78 seems obvious as apparent from very similar facts in *Whitgift Homes* (2001). However, although much has been written about *Federated Homes*, for example, whether s 78 of the LPA 1925 was ever intended to have this magic effect – it is not at all clear that the interpretation has had much effect on the practical realities of freehold covenant disputes. In most cases, the covenant will have been drafted expressly to permit annexation, expressly to exclude it (at least after *Roake v Chadha* (1984)) or to provide for express assignment of the benefit (see below, 8.6.2). This means that practical impact of *Federated Homes* will be felt most readily in those less frequent cases where the covenant is silent or ambivalent about its intended effect on purchasers of the benefitted land, in which case statutory annexation to each and every part will follow. *Whitgift Homes v Stocks* (2001) is just such a case, concerning a dispute over a housing development completed in the 1920s and 1930s and where statutory annexation was central to the question whether certain covenants were now enforceable.

If the above conditions are satisfied, the claimant, being a successor to the original covenantee, may sue at law any person who is subject to the burden of the covenants. However, in practice, because of the limited ability of burdens to pass and then only in equity, the defendant to an action on the covenant at law is going to be the original covenantor. No other person can be liable at law and the same is true if the covenant is positive.

8.6.2 Passing the benefit of covenants in equity

This brings us to consideration of the principles concerning the passing of the benefit in equity. The rules about to be discussed apply equally to positive and negative covenants, but (once again) because the burden of a positive covenant cannot run, the principles have developed primarily in the context of restrictive covenants and their enforcement against successors of the original covenantor. With that significant point in mind, there are a number of conditions to be satisfied in order to establish that the benefit of a covenant has passed in equity:

(a) first, the covenant must 'touch and concern' the land of the original covenantee (*Rogers v Hosegood* (1900)). This is identical to the position 'at law', discussed above. We might note, however, that if the claimant is trying to use the 'freehold' rules to enforce a leasehold restrictive covenant against, say, a subtenant or squatter (that is, *not* an *assignee* of the original tenant), it is arguable that the Landlord and Tenant (Covenants) Act 1995 has removed the 'touching and concerning' requirement for the restrictive covenant contained in a lease granted on or after 1 January 1996. So, for example, if the landlord is attempting to enforce a restrictive covenant prohibiting 'any occupier wearing brown shoes' – which clearly does not touch and concern – it is arguable that the benefit of this covenant runs to a new landlord because of the 1995 Act. We shall probably never know whether this is correct, because, in practice, it is unlikely that a landlord would ever wish to enforce such a clearly personal leasehold restrictive covenant against an occupier;

(b) secondly, the claimant must have a legal or equitable estate in the land of the original covenantee. Again, this is similar to the position 'at law', and by virtue of s 78 of the LPA 1925, the claimant does not have to have the same estate as the original covenantee. For example, the claimant may be the equitable tenant of the original covenantee. Moreover, it remains true that *any* occupier (including a squatter) may enforce the benefit of a restrictive covenant because s 78 of the LPA 1925 deems 'the owners and occupiers for the time being' to be successors in title for the purpose of enforcing restrictive (but *not* positive) covenants. It will be appreciated that this is particularly important given that a claim in equity will usually be to enforce a restrictive covenant against a successor of the original covenantor in a situation where the burden of a restrictive covenant may well have passed;

(c) thirdly, the benefit of the covenant must have been transmitted to the claimant in one of three ways:

- **annexation: express or implied**

The benefit of a covenant can be expressly annexed to the land in equity in exactly the same way as at law. Indeed, the same words will, in most cases, annex the benefit of the covenant at law and in equity simultaneously. Again, it is important that the words establish that the covenant is for the benefit of certain land, or make it clear that the covenant is intended to endure for successive owners of the land. This was not the case in the marginal decision in *Lamb v Midas Equipment* (1999), where the Privy Council held, on appeal from Jamaica, that a covenant to X and 'his heirs, executors, administrators, transferees and assigns' did not result in express annexation to the land but was meant to describe the covenantee personally. Moreover, the land must be readily identifiable at the time the covenant is executed (*Mellon v Sinclair* (1996)) and be capable of benefiting from the covenant, according to the general test laid down in *Re Gadd's Transfer* (1996). Once again, however, it is the effect of s 78 of the LPA 1925, as discussed in *Federated Homes*, that is most important here. According to s 78, '[a] covenant relating to any land of the covenantee shall be deemed to be made with the covenantee and his successors in title and the persons deriving title under him or them, and shall have effect as if such successors and other persons were expressed'. As noted above, originally this was thought to be a 'word saving' provision which simply ensured that 'successors', etc, were deemed to be included in the deed, but without doing away with the necessity of finding the relevant express intention to annex. Yet, as with annexation at law, Bridge LJ, in *Federated Homes*, makes it clear that the effect of s 78 (by including these words in the deed) is to annex automatically the benefit of the covenant to the covenantee's land. Again, of course, the land has to be readily identifiable from the deed (although extrinsic evidence may be produced to prove this: *Whitgift Homes*) and capable of benefiting from the covenant, but, if these conditions are satisfied, the benefit of the covenant is annexed to each and every part of the land. It will, therefore, be available to a purchaser of the whole or any part of it. Again, as noted, it does appear that 'automatic statutory annexation' can be avoided by an express contrary intention (*Roake v Chadha* (1984)), and the doubts expressed earlier about the practical impact of *Federated Homes* are equally applicable here. As a consequence of *Federated Homes*, some commentators have argued that the other two methods of passing the benefit of a covenant in equity are now much less important, although, as we shall see, the 'scheme of development' does give some additional advantages;

• **assignment: express or implied**

As an alternative to annexation, the claimant may rely on the general rule that the benefit of a contract may be assigned expressly to another. This means that it is perfectly possible for the original covenantee expressly to assign the benefit of a covenant at the same time as he transfers the land. Again, the land must be capable of benefiting from the covenant, and must be readily identifiable. It is important to note here that this is an assignment of the benefit of the covenant *inter partes*: it is not an annexation of the covenant to the land (*Marten v Flight Refuelling* (1962)). Theoretically, therefore, if the purchaser of the land, who has had the benefit of the covenant assigned to them, transfers the land again, there should be another assignment of the benefit to the second purchaser. So, if the benefit is to be transmitted with the land in perpetuity, a 'chain of assignments' appears to be necessary (*Re Pinewood Estates* (1958)). However, it may be that, if there has been an initial express assignment of the benefit, future transfers of the land will include an implied assignment of the benefit of the covenant to the purchaser under s 62 of the LPA 1925, although the view expressed in *Kumar v Dunning* (1989), that restrictive covenants are outside s 62, would negate this;

• **a scheme of development: a 'building scheme'**

A third alternative is to establish that the benefit of the covenant has passed in equity under a 'building scheme'. The ability of the benefit of covenants to pass under a 'scheme of development' derives from a rule based on 'common intention' and practicality. In simple terms, it allows a common vendor of land (such as a property developer or builder) to transfer the benefit of any covenants received by him from the purchasers of a plot of the land to every other purchaser of a plot of that land. Thus, it represents an attempt to create mutually enforceable obligations by giving the benefit of every covenant, made by every purchaser, to every other purchaser. (The burdens, of course, pass in the normal way if possible.) In itself, there is nothing unusual about a building scheme, as it is perfectly possible for a common vendor of land to transfer the benefit of covenants already made by previous purchasers (and, therefore, attaching to his remaining land) to subsequent purchasers of parts of it under the rules of annexation or assignment considered above. However, the advantage of a building scheme is that it allows the benefit of later purchasers' covenants to be annexed to the land *already* sold (that is, to that owned by previous purchasers), notwithstanding that this should not be possible because the covenantee (the builder) no longer owns *that* land. Thus, despite the fact that previous purchasers bought their land before later purchasers had made their covenants, the benefit of those later covenants still passes: the benefit of every covenant is available to all purchasers within the scheme of development, irrespective of the time of their purchase. For example, if Bloggs and Bloggs own 20 plots of land on which they have built houses, they can extract a covenant against business use from any person who buys a house, say, Mr A. The burden will follow the plot purchased by Mr A in the normal way, and the benefit will pass to all land then owned by Bloggs and Bloggs. When Bloggs and Bloggs sell a second plot to Mr B on the same terms, Mr B's land comes under a burden (that is, he is an original covenantor) and, because he has purchased part of the land that was owned by Bloggs and Bloggs at the time of their sale to Mr A, Mr B gets the benefit of Mr A's covenant. Alas, however, under the normal rules, Mr A cannot get the benefit of Mr B's covenant, because Mr A already has his land. A 'building scheme' ignores this problem of timing and permits the passing of the benefit of every purchaser's covenant to every other purchaser. It also permits benefits to pass even though on the occasion of a sale of the last plot, the covenantee (for example, Bloggs and Bloggs) no longer owns land to be benefitted. However, in order to generate this effect, it must be clear that the entire land was intended to fall within a common scheme of covenants, and be governed by similar rules.

The necessary factual conditions for a scheme of development were laid down in *Elliston v Reacher* (1908):

(a) there must be a common vendor;

(b) the land must be laid out in identifiable plots;

(c) the benefit of every purchaser's covenants must be intended to be mutually enforceable (that is, to pass to every other purchaser);

(d) the purchasers must have bought the land on condition that this was intended; and

(e) the area of the scheme must be well defined.

As ever, these conditions are not inflexible and, on one view, the *Elliston* conditions are not conclusive or mandatory, but merely evidence of a more general rule stemming from common intention. So, a 'scheme' has been accepted where there was no lotted plan (*Baxter v Four Oaks Properties* (1965) approved in *Whitgift Homes*), where there was no common vendor (*Re Dolphin's Conveyance* (1970)), where the property was laid out in sublots (*Brunner v Greenslade* (1971)), and even following the demerger of separate plots that had been 'joined' after the scheme had come into existence. However, recognition of a building scheme has been rightly refused when it was clear that each purchaser's covenants were different in substance, and, therefore, lacking the element of mutuality (*Emile Elias v Pine Groves* (1993)). More importantly, it is clear from *Whitgift Homes* that it is crucial for a building scheme that the area subject to it be defined with sufficient certainty – that is, sufficient certainty to ensure that all purchasers of plots know the extent both legally and physically of their mutual obligations. In that case, a housing development had been completed in the 1920s and 1930s and there was no doubt that a mutually enforceable scheme had been contemplated at the time the site was developed. However, there was real uncertainty as to the physical reach of the alleged scheme and although one could say that certain roads on the development may have been within a scheme, there were a number of areas where one could not be certain whether they were included or excluded. Consequently, a scheme could not operate even for those areas that appeared to have mutually enforceable obligations because there was fatal uncertainty as to the physical and hence legal reach of the alleged mutual obligations. No purchaser could be certain of the extent of his benefits and burdens. Finally, we should note, for the avoidance of doubt, that a successful 'building scheme' does not affect the running of the burden of covenants and if the obligations are to be truly mutually enforceable, the normal steps for transmitting the burden of restrictive covenants must be followed. Usually, this will mean registration of the covenants against the title of all purchasers. That said, however, it is also clear that the courts are very reluctant to disturb the 'local law' established by a building scheme and once one has been validly created, the courts will not readily refuse a remedy to a claimant seeking to enforce the benefit which he has been given. Neither will the Lands Tribunal readily agree to the discharge (that is, destruction) of building scheme covenants under the procedure laid down in s 84 of the LPA 1925: *Re Bromor Properties' Application* (1995); *Re Lee's Application* (1996).

8.7 Escaping the confines of the law: can the burden of positive covenants be enforced by other means?

The position, as it stands so far, can be summarised quite easily:

(a) the benefit of positive and negative covenants can run with the land at law or in equity;

(b) only the burden of negative covenants may run, and then only in equity;

(c) therefore, the great majority of disputes involve a triple claim that the benefit has passed in equity, that the covenant is negative and that the burden has passed in equity.

Naturally enough, this is not an entirely satisfactory position (as *Rhone v Stephens* (1994) and *Thamesmead Town* make clear), and there seems no reason why, in principle, the burden of positive covenants should not be able to run with the land. In fact, it is difficult to find such a restriction in *Tulk v Moxhay* (1848) itself, even though it appears firmly in later cases. Indeed, it is not unknown for the law to allow positive obligations, including those requiring expenditure of money, to pass as proprietary obligations – see for example the easement of fencing and (subject to human rights issues) the feudal chancel repair liability. Given that any such burden would need to be registered to be binding (as currently with negative burdens), any prospective purchaser of affected land would be well warned that they were accepting such a liability and could act accordingly (for example, walk away, offer a lower price, take out insurance). Nevertheless, be that as it may, the rule is that the burden of positive covenants cannot run and any claimant must sue the *original* covenantor in damages to have any remedy at all. This has led to the development of a number of indirect methods of enforcing positive covenants, none of which is entirely satisfactory.

8.7.1   A chain of covenants

A chain of covenants is very common in practice, although it only gives a remedy in damages. In essence, each purchaser of the burdened land covenants separately with their immediate predecessor in title to carry out the positive covenant. Thus, if the original covenantor is sued on the covenant, he (the original covenantor) will be able to recover any damages paid from the person to whom he sold the land (and who covenanted with him directly to perform the positive covenant), and so on down the chain. The well known defect is that the chain is 'only as strong as its weakest link', so that (for example) the death, insolvency or other circumstance affecting any person in the chain may render the device useless. After all, personal liabilities such as these are not as robust as proprietary obligations. A variation on this is to ensure that each successive purchaser of the burdened land covenants directly, at the time they purchase the land, with the person entitled to the benefit of the covenant. In *Thamesmead Town*, for example, the original covenantor had covenanted with the claimant (entitled to the benefit) to pay certain charges relating to the maintenance of the common parts of a housing estate. When the defendant purchased the land from the original covenantor, it was intended that he should then make a covenant with the claimant to like effect: in fact, the original covenantor had promised the claimant that, when they sold the land, they would require their purchaser to make such a covenant. This was, therefore, an attempt to create a series of covenants, with each new owner of the burdened land promising separately to pay the charge. It failed miserably because, when the defendant purchased the land, he was not asked to make this new covenant! Here, the chain broke the first time it was tested. Note, however, that if the land burdened is of registered title, it is possible to register a restriction against that title requiring the purchaser of the burdened land to enter into the positive covenant as a condition of the purchase. This would have been effective in *Thamesmead Town* to ensure that positive obligation was undertaken when the land was sold to a new purchaser. The entry of such a restriction is the most effective way of ensuring that positive burdens are undertaken by purchasers of the original covenantor's land.

8.7.2 The artificial long lease

As seen in Chapter 6, positive covenants in leases are quite capable of binding successive owners of the land. Thus, by artificially creating a long lease containing the desired positive covenant, and then 'enlarging' the lease into a freehold under s 153 of the LPA 1925, the positive covenant will bind successive owners of land, because the 'leasehold rules' remain applicable.

8.7.3 Mutual benefit and burden

It is a general principle of equity that a person who takes the benefit of a covenant must also share any burden inherent in it. Thus, if a landowner enjoys the benefit of a covenant to use a private road or sewer, they must also take the burden of the upkeep of the road or sewer. They may take the benefit of the covenant if they share its burden (*Halsall v Brizell* (1957)). Consequently, any later owner of the land will also be subject to the burden of the positive covenant, if they wish to enjoy the benefits it offers. The proper ambit of the 'benefit and burden' principle has been the subject of recent judicial consideration, and a number of uncertainties about its scope have now been resolved. In *Thamesmead Town*, the claimant alleged that the defendant was liable to pay maintenance charges (that is, liable to perform a positive covenant), because those charges related to facilities from which the defendant took a benefit. In fact, the charges related to two distinct 'benefits': a charge for the upkeep of roads and sewers, and a charge for the maintenance of common parts, such as walkways, open spaces, etc. The Court of Appeal decided that the benefit and burden rule allowed recovery of the charges in respect of roads and sewers, but not in respect of the 'general facilities'. In the court's view, a person could be liable for the burden of a positive covenant only if the burden was intrinsically related to the benefit gained. It was not enough that the documents of title said that a person *could* take a benefit from the land only if they accepted an attached burden: the mere linking of a benefit with a burden was insufficient. What was required was that the burden be the 'flip side' of the benefit: the burden had to be inherent in the benefit obtained. So, if a landowner wanted to use sewers and a private road, he had to pay for those sewers and that road – this was mutual benefit and burden, the mutuality being that the benefit and burden were simply two halves of the same coin. However, if a landowner was required to pay a sum towards the upkeep of open spaces, and this was linked on paper to the benefit of not having his neighbours carry on a trade or business, this was not mutual benefit and burden. The benefit would run, but the burden would not, because the burden was not inherently connected to the benefit: it was not mutual, but merely reciprocal. The benefit and burden rule allows the enforcement of a positive covenant if it conforms to 'if you want to use X, you must pay for it'; it does not allow the enforcement of a positive covenant in terms that 'I will give you X, if you will give me Y'.

This must be correct. Otherwise, careful drafting of covenants could utilise the 'benefit and burden' principle to circumvent almost entirely the rule against the transmission of the burden of positive covenants. What is not so clear is why the Court of Appeal in *Thamesmead Town* further limited the principle. In its view, a person was liable on the burden of a truly mutual positive covenant only if that person chose to exercise the corresponding benefit. The contrary view, that such a person is liable to the burden if they are entitled to the benefit, whether they use it or not, has much to commend it, for (as counsel for the claimant put it) it does not confuse the acquisition of a right with its exercise. In truth, the court were persuaded by this argument but felt compelled by authority to adopt the former view. So, for the present, the principle of mutual benefit and burden will permit the enforcement of a positive covenant when the burden is intrinsic in the benefit, and if the defendant has actually partaken of the benefit.

8.7.4 Construing s 79 of the Law of Property Act 1925

It has been noted that s 79(1) of the LPA 1925 is taken to annex the burden of restrictive covenants to land so that, other things being equal (for example, registration), the burden passes to a successor in title. In fact, a careful reading of s 79(1) reveals that it is not in terms limited to restrictive covenants, and there is nothing in the statute itself that prevents it being interpreted as annexing the burden of positive covenants as well. Indeed, the fact that it was felt necessary deliberately to confine the effect of s 79(2) to restrictive covenants (that is, those enforceable against adverse possessors), surely implies that the general s 79(1) is not so limited. Be that as it may, the argument is all but over. Section 79(1) has been interpreted narrowly for reasons of policy rather than necessity on the ground that it does not change substantive principles of law, but merely facilitates the passing of that which could already pass: that is, burdens of restrictive covenants.

All in all, of course, none of these devices are satisfactory and it would make far greater sense to allow the burden of positive covenants to run in much the same way as the burden of restrictive ones. This has been proposed many times, but unless there is a revolutionary House of Lords decision, the matter will have to wait for legislation, perhaps even that proposed by the Law Commission in its report on 'land obligations'. Pending that, the law of freehold covenants remains restricted: the benefit of any covenant can pass, in law or in equity; but only the burden of restrictive covenants can pass, and then only in equity.

8.7.5 Discharge and modification of restrictive covenants

As noted briefly, s 84 of the LPA 1925 contains a jurisdiction to discharge or modify restrictive covenants affecting freehold land. In fact, s 84(1) gives the court a useful power to declare whether any land is subject to the burden of a restrictive covenant – thus providing a simple method of determining whether a burden has 'run' – and s 84(2) gives the Lands Tribunal power to discharge or modify restrictive covenants. The power contained in s 84(2) is critical, for the enduring nature of restrictive covenants means that they can impose restrictions on the use of land that simply become outdated or even positively detrimental. For example, a restrictive covenant against building may impede the development of land for social housing or may obstruct the economic regeneration of a depressed industrial area. Conversely, one landowner may seek the discharge of a covenant against building, in order to build a second house in his capacious garden which he wants to sell for a large capital gain. In other words, the Lands Tribunal exercises a discretion under s 84 to discharge or modify covenants, albeit one confined by law and bounded by precedent, but, necessarily, each decision is unique.

Finally, we might reiterate something already discussed. If a covenant is to be enforceable, the claimant must have the benefit of it and the defendant must be subject to the burden. If it should happen that the burden of a covenant is passing and binding land, but that there is no person entitled to its benefit, then in practice the covenant has been rendered unenforceable and the owner of the burdened plot can proceed in safety to ignore the covenant.

FREEHOLD COVENANTS

Positive and negative freehold covenants

Covenants between freeholders may be either positive or negative. Positive covenants require the owner of the burdened land to take some action on his own property or property related to it, usually requiring the expenditure of money. An example is a covenant to pay for the upkeep of a private road. Negative (or 'restrictive') covenants require the owner of the burdened land to refrain from some activity on his own land. An example is the covenant against carrying on any trade or business on the land.

Covenants as contracts

Covenants are promises by one person to another contained in a deed to do, or, more usually, not to do, something on their own or related land. The covenant is made between the *covenantor* and the *covenantee* and is enforceable like any other contractual obligation between these original parties.

Covenants as interests in land

Covenants comprise both a benefit (the right to sue) and a burden (the obligation to perform). Both the benefit and burden may be 'attached' to the benefited and burdened land respectively so that they pass to later purchasers or transferees of it. Although the benefit and burden of each covenant may pass independently, before a covenant can be enforced in practice, the claimant must prove they have the benefit and the defendant must be fixed with the burden.

The relevance of 'law' and 'equity' and the enforcement of covenants

If a person sues on a covenant *at law*, he will be claiming that the defendant is subject to the burden of the covenant under the common law and should pay damages. The remedy is as of right. If a person sues on a covenant *in equity*, he will be claiming that the defendant is subject to the burden of the covenant under the rules of equity and susceptible to the discretionary equitable remedies of injunction and specific performance and to rules of registration. Note that, if the burden has passed to the defendant in equity, so must the benefit have passed to the claimant in equity.

Principle 1: enforcement between the original covenantor and the original covenantee

If the covenantor and covenantee are still in possession of their respective land, all covenants are enforceable and the covenantee may obtain damages, an injunction or specific performance (that is, may sue at law or in equity). If the original *covenantor* has parted with the land that was subject to the covenant, he remains liable on all the covenants to whomsoever has the benefit of them, although damages only are available because the covenantor has no land on which to perform the covenant. If the original *covenantee* has parted with the land that had the benefit of the covenant, he may still be able to enforce a covenant against whomsoever has the burden of it. However, at law, this right could easily have been given to another by an express assignment of the right to sue and, in equity, the court is likely in its discretion to refuse to grant an equitable remedy to such a claimant as he has no land to actually benefit. Note that it is important to identify exactly who are the *original* covenantees and covenantors, especially as this may go beyond the actual signatories to a deed: s 56 of the LPA 1925.

Principle 2: enforcement against successors to the original covenantor (passing the burden)

It is not possible for the burden of *any* covenant to run at law. In equity, the burden of restrictive covenants only may pass, providing:

- the covenant is restrictive in nature;

- the covenant touches and concerns the land (except possibly where the Landlord and Tenant (Covenants) Act 1995 applies to a leasehold covenant not enforceable under 'leasehold rules': for example, a subtenancy granted on or after 1 January 1996);

- at the date of the covenant, the covenant actually did confer a benefit on land owned by the original covenantee;

- the burden of the restrictive covenant must have been intended to have run with the land of the original covenantor: s 79 of the LPA 1925;

- in registered land, the covenant must be registered as a minor interest against the burdened land to bind a purchaser for value who becomes registered proprietor;

- in unregistered land, the covenant must be registered as a Class D(ii) land charge to bind a purchaser of a legal estate who gives money or money's worth;

- the claimant is granted a remedy by virtue of the court's discretion.

Principle 3: enforcement by successors to the original covenantee (passing the benefit)

The benefit of a both a positive and restrictive covenant may be passed at law or in equity. However, given that only the burden of a restrictive covenant may pass, and then only in equity, most practical examples concern the passing of the benefit of a restrictive covenant in equity. This will give us our claimant (benefit) and defendant (burden) in suit in equity.

If it is necessary to consider passing the benefit of a covenant *at law* (for example, the original covenantor may be the defendant), then:

- the covenant must 'touch and concern' the land of the original covenantee;

- the claimant must have a legal estate in the land, although not necessarily the same legal estate as the original covenantee. For restrictive covenants only, this may include an 'occupier', for example, a squatter: s 78 of the LPA 1925;

- the benefit of the covenant must have been annexed to a legal estate in the land either expressly or by implication: that is, by express words or by statute under s 78 of the LPA 1925.

In order to pass the benefit of a covenant *in equity*, then:

- the covenant must 'touch and concern' the land of the original covenantee;

- the claimant must have a legal or equitable estate in the land of the original covenantee, although not necessarily the same estate as the original covenantee. For restrictive covenants only, this may include an 'occupier' for example, a squatter: s 78 of the LPA 1925;

- the benefit of the covenant must have been transmitted to the claimant in one of three ways:

  (a) by *annexation*, express or implied. The benefit of a covenant can be expressly annexed to the land in equity in exactly the same way as in law, that is, by express words or by statute under s 78 of the LPA 1925;

  (b) by assignment: express or implied. Following the general rule that the benefit of a contract may be assigned to another, the original covenantee may expressly assign the benefit of a covenant at the same time as he transfers the land. For future sales of the land, an assignment of the benefit of the covenant may be implied by s 62 of the LPA 1925, subject to criticism in *Kumar v Dunning* (1989);

  (c) a scheme of development (building scheme). This allows the benefit of later purchasers' covenants to be passed to the land already sold by a common vendor (that is, to previous purchasers), notwithstanding that this should not be possible because the original covenantee (the common vendor) has already parted with the land. The conditions are that there must be a common vendor, the land must be laid out in definable plots, the benefit of every purchaser's covenants must be intended to be mutually enforceable (that is, to pass to every other purchaser), the purchasers must have bought the land on condition that this was intended and the area of the scheme must be well defined.

Devices that may allow the passing of the burdens of positive covenants in practice

These include:

(a) a chain of covenants;

(b) the artificial long lease;

(c) mutual benefit and burden;

(d) reinterpreting s 79 of the LPA 1925;

(d) restrictions on the title of registered land.

CHAPTER 9

LICENCES AND PROPRIETARY ESTOPPEL

9.1 Licences

In Chapters 7 and 8, we examined in some detail two important ways in which one person could enjoy certain rights over the land of another. In many respects, easements and freehold covenants were seen to be similar, especially where the effect on the 'servient' or 'burdened' land was restrictive. Moreover, both easements and restrictive covenants are proprietary in nature: they are interests in land which may 'run' with the land. They are not personal to the parties that created them. However, a moment's thought will also make it clear that easements and freehold covenants can cover only a small fraction of the situations in which one person may wish to use the land of another. For example, what is the position where I wish to park my caravan on my neighbour's land, or my children play football there? Again, what are my rights if I pay an entrance fee to go to a play or a film on someone else's land, or hire my neighbour's garden for the day for a party? All of these are activities undertaken on another person's land, but clearly they do not fall within the realm of easements or freehold covenants.

This is where the 'licence' has a role to play. 'Licences' are a third way in which a person may enjoy some right or privilege over the land of another, although, as we shall see, they are fundamentally different from both easements and freehold covenants.

9.2 The essential nature of a licence

Licences involve a permission from the owner of land, given to another person (who may or may not own land themselves), to use that land for some purpose. The permission (or 'licence') can be to do anything from attending a cinema (*Hurst v Picture Theatres Ltd* (1915)), to parking a number of cars (*Batchelor v Marlowe* (2001)), erecting an advertising hoarding (*Kewall Investments v Arthur Maiden* (1990)), running a school (*Re Hampstead Garden Suburb Institute* (1995)), using buildings as a social club (*Onyx v Beard* (1998)), or allowing children to play in your garden. They can even give a limited right of occupation (see, for example, the distinction between leases and licences in Chapter 6 (*Ogwr BC v Dykes* (1989)) and between licences and life interests in Chapter 5 (*Dent v Dent* (1996)). Indeed, the range of activities that can be covered by 'a licence' is virtually limitless simply because it is impossible to foresee all the circumstances in which one person may wish to use the land of another! With this in mind, the following points about licences should be noted:

(a) there are no formal requirements for the creation of a 'licence' as such, although occasionally a licence may depend on the fulfilment of conditions imposed by some other branch of the law: for example, an 'offer and acceptance' for contractual licences, or 'detrimental reliance' for licences created by proprietary estoppel. Licences may be created orally, in writing, or even be found in a deed or registered disposition. If a licence is contained in a deed/registered disposition, it is usually connected to, or in some way ancillary to, the proprietary right created by the deed/registered disposition. A good example is a conveyance of a house by deed from A to B, wherein B is given a personal right to park his car on land retained by A. As is obvious, however, where licences are found in formal documents (and sometimes where they are not!), there is always the danger that they will be confused with true proprietary rights, especially if the substantive right granted (for example, to park a car) is, in fact, capable of being either a licence or a proprietary right (for example, an easement);

(b) a licence is given by the owner of land (the licensor) to some other person (the licensee), permitting them to do something on the owner's land. They are classically defined, in *Thomas v Sorrell* (1673), as a permission to use land belonging to another which, without such permission, would amount to a trespass. As such, licences may cover any activity – long or short term – that may be undertaken on land. This versatility means that licences can arise in all manner of situations, and consequently it is crucial to be able to distinguish licences from leases, easements and freehold covenants, all of which also allow one person to use another's land but which have the essentially different quality of being proprietary;

(c) a licence may be given to any person for any lawful purpose, not only to someone who also owns land. In this respect, they are different from easements and most freehold covenants. There is no need for a 'dominant tenement'. So, using the example above, when A conveys land to B, he may grant a parking licence over his retained land to B (who is a landowner). But, A may also decide to give or sell a parking licence to X, a person with no land who simply wants somewhere to park his car;

(d) an orthodox view of licences is that they are not proprietary in nature. As Vaughan CJ makes clear in *Thomas v Sorrell* (1673), the traditional analysis of licences is that they 'properly passeth no interest nor alter or transfer property in any thing'. In other words, a licence is not an interest *in* land, but rather a right *over* land, one that is personal to the parties who created it (the licensor and licensee). As a consequence, the right conferred by a licence can be enforced only against the person who created it. It does not 'run' with the land, and unlike easements and freehold covenants, cannot be enforced against a purchaser of the land over which it exists. The licence is a matter of contract, not property law, and is incapable of binding third parties when the licensor transfers the 'burdened' land to a third party. So, assuming A has indeed granted a parking licence over his retained land to B, if A then transfers (by sale or gift) the 'burdened' land to P, P is under no obligation whatsoever to continue to allow B to park his car. The point is, simply, that a licence is incapable of binding land: it is personal to licensor and licensee. In recent years, this fundamental theoretical distinction between 'interests in land' and 'licences' has been unsuccessfully attacked, and we shall consider the matter in more detail when examining 'contractual licences' and so called 'estoppel licences'.

9.3   Types of licence

Although a licence to use land may be given for any lawful purpose, it is possible to classify types of licences according to the functions they serve, the circumstances in which they arise, or the way in which they are created. The following classification draws the traditional distinctions between different types of licence and will seek to answer the four most important practical questions concerning the operation of licences. These practical issues, rather than a rather artificial classification of licences, should be at the forefront of any discussion of the law relating to licences, viz:

(a) what is the nature of the licence and how is it created?;

(b) what are the obligations of the licensor to the licensee?;

(c) is the licence an 'interest in land'?;

(d) are there any circumstances in which a licence can 'bind' a third party: that is, can a person who purchases land over which a licence already exists ever be bound to give effect to that licence?

9.3.1   The bare licence

A bare licence is probably the most common form of permission which a landowner gives to another person to use his land. It is, in essence, permission to enter upon the land, given voluntarily by the owner, who receives nothing in return. The giving of the licence is 'gratuitous' in that it is not supported by 'consideration' moving from the licensee. There is no contract between the parties, merely a bare permission to do that which the landowner has allowed and which otherwise would be a trespass. Typically, such licences allow the licensee to carry on some limited activity on the licensor's land, as where permission is given to hold a garden party, or to deliver some previously ordered goods. Necessarily, these bare licences can be given in any shape or form, and many are oral or implied from the landowner's lack of objection to the activity taking place. It is also inherent in a bare licence that it lasts only for so long as the licensor wishes. Thus, the licensor may terminate the licence by giving reasonable notice to the licensee (*Robson v Hallet* (1967); *Re Hampstead Garden Suburb Institute* (1995)), and the licensee has no claim in damages or specific performance should this happen. Importantly, there is no doubt that a bare licence is *not* an interest in land: it is personal only to the original licensor and licensee. Such a licence *per se* is incapable of binding a third party and any person who subsequently acquires the licensor's land may disregard the bare licence with impunity.

9.3.2 Licences coupled with an interest (or 'grant')

This is a rather loose category of licences covering a range of activities that are grouped together because the licences are said to be 'coupled' with an interest in land or with the grant of an interest in land. As discussed in Chapter 7, a landowner may grant another person a *profit à prendre* over their land: that is, a right to take from it a natural resource, such as fish, wood or turf. Necessarily, in order to exercise this 'profit', the grantee must be able to enter upon the land and remain there for an appropriate time. This is achieved by means of a licence attached (or coupled) to the profit, as in *James Jones and Son v Earl of Tankerville* (1909). To some extent, of course, to call this a 'licence' at all is misleading for the licence is merely incidental and ancillary to the right which has actually been granted over the land (the profit). The licence merely facilitates the achievement of the primary purpose, it is not a purpose in itself. So where, as in the case of profits, the right granted is proprietary in nature (that is, an interest in land), the licence which attaches to it *appears* also to be proprietary, because it lives or dies with the profit. The licence will last for as long as the profit exists and will be enforceable against whomsoever the profit is enforceable against because it is an inherent component of the greater right. Likewise, should the grantee (and licensee) be unlawfully denied the right granted, the normal remedies will be available to prevent interference with it (injunction) or compensation (damages) for its denial. Note, however, that the licence only has these characteristics because it is coupled with a grant: it has no proprietary status of its own.

9.3.3 Contractual licences

Contractual licences are, in nature, similar to bare licences, with the important rider that contractual licences are granted to the licensee in return for valuable consideration. Two examples are the purchase of a cinema ticket and the 'occupation licence', discussed in Chapter 6. Simply put, there is a contract between the two parties, the subject matter of which is the giving of a licence to use land for a stated purpose. Crucially, therefore, contractual licences are governed by the ordinary rules of the law of contract, and like most contracts, do not need to be created with any particular formality. Indeed, although they are contracts concerning the use of land, they are not contracts for the disposition of an *interest in* land (they are not proprietary) and so need not meet the requirements of s 2 of the Law of Property (Miscellaneous Provisions) Act (LP (Misc Prov) A) 1989. They may be oral or written. Their important characteristics are discussed below.

9.3.4 Remedies and contractual licences

As these licences are founded in contract, both licensor and licensee may rely on the normal remedies for breach of contract in the event of a failure to carry out its terms. Thus, either party may sue for damages for breach of contract, although it is usually the licensee that needs such a remedy when the licensor fails to allow them to use the land. More importantly, it is now clear that an injunction or a decree of specific performance may be obtained by the licensee in appropriate circumstances. An injunction can be obtained to prevent the licensor from revoking the licence before its contractual date of expiry (*Winter Garden Theatre v Millennium Productions Ltd* (1948)), or a decree of specific performance may be awarded requiring the licensor to permit the activity authorised by the licence to take place (*Verrall v Great Yarmouth BC* (1981)). Indeed, the effect of the availability of these last two remedies can be to make the licence *de facto* irrevocable between the parties throughout the contractual period of the licence (for example, the theatre performance, the weekly occupation). In this respect, a contractual licence is vitally different from a bare licence and can assume the character of an unbreakable arrangement between the original parties lasting for the agreed duration of the licence. So, if A gives B a parking licence for three years, at £100 per year, this is a contractual licence of three years' duration. If A should then seek to deny the right, A may be liable in damages for breach of contract or held to the licence for the three years by injunction. Note, however, that if A breaks the contract because he has sold the land to P within the three years and simply has no land on which B can now park, A will remain liable in damages, but, of course, P cannot be subject to an injunction because the licence is not proprietary and cannot 'bind' a third party. The liability of P in these circumstances (if any) is discussed below, 9.3.7.

9.3.5 Licences as interests in land and their effect on third parties: purchasers of the licensor's land

The above is clear enough, for there is no reason why a contractual licence should not be *de facto* irrevocable between the original parties in the same way as many other contracts. However, as indicated above, there are lingering problems. For example, if A grants a contractual licence to B allowing B to park her caravan in his garden for five years, a court may well enforce this by injunction for five years against A. Yet, what if, after three years, A sells his land to P? Is P bound to give effect to the licence for two more years, or can P ignore it, even though A would have been bound? In other words, does the *de facto* irrevocability of some contractual licences between the original parties mean that a purchaser of the licensor's land is also bound to give effect to it for the remainder of the contractual term? In essence, this boils down to two very important questions: first, is a contractual licence an 'interest in land', so that it may bind a purchaser of land in the normal way appropriate to registered and unregistered land (that is, like easements)? Secondly, even if it is not an interest in land, can a contractual licence take effect against a purchaser of the licensor's land in any other way?

9.3.6 Are contractual licences interests in land (are they proprietary)?

The starting point for a discussion of this question must be the famous *dictum* in *Thomas v Sorrell* (1673) that a licence 'properly passeth no interest nor alters or transfers property in any thing'. This states that, as a matter of principle, a licence is merely personal between the parties and creates no interest in land that might be enforceable against a third person. Indeed, as much has been confirmed by the House of Lords in *King v David Allen and Sons, Billposting* (1916), which decided expressly that contractual licences could not bind third parties. Yet there have always been doubts about whether this orthodox view took account of the very many uses to which licences could be put. In particular, the spread of 'occupation licences' (see Chapter 6) meant that some licensees were occupying their homes under a 'mere' licence which, it would seem, could be defeated simply by a sale of the land from licensor to a new owner. For example, is it 'equitable' that a landowner could allow a person to occupy their property under a licence for an agreed period of (say) five years, but then one month later sell their land to P and thereby defeat the licence and turn the occupier onto the street? Of course, the licensee might well be able to claim damages for breach of contract from the licensor, but this is not the same as enjoying the benefits of occupation. Moreover, an injunction or specific performance could not be awarded once the land had been sold.

This was the problem before the courts, especially pressing in the case of occupation licences. In typical fashion, it was addressed squarely by Lord Denning in *Errington v Errington* (1952). In that case, Lord Denning regarded a contractual licence as binding on a third party who had received land under a will, her husband being the original licensor. His reasoning was that, as the licensee could restrain revocation of the licence by the licensor for its agreed duration (that is, by injunction), there was no reason why the licence could not continue against a third party in appropriate circumstances. The 'appropriate circumstances' seemed to be when the contractual licence was 'supported by an equity' (for this gave it a proprietary status), and an 'equity' would exist where it would be unjust to deny the continued existence of the licence. Unfortunately, however, all of this simply assumes that which must be established: that is, that contractual licences are *per se* interests in land that are *capable* of binding third parties. The question is not, *when* can a contractual licence bind a third party? It is, rather, is it *possible* that it can? If it is possible, then the circumstances when it can happen may be identified. If it is not possible, then the 'when' becomes irrelevant. Moreover, Lord Denning did not (and could not) explain why the House of Lords' decision in *King* could be ignored. Neither is Lord Denning's appeal to 'justice' very persuasive, because it may always be 'unjust' in one sense to deny the validity of a continuing licence against a purchaser of the licensor's land. It can be very 'unjust' for a landowner to be able to ignore an unregistered option, even though such options are proprietary interests, (for example, as *was* the case in *Midland Bank v Green* (1981)) but should we, therefore, abolish the Land Registration and Land Charges Acts? It might seem unjust to allow a purchaser of land to escape from a valid licence granted by the vendor, especially if he knew of its existence, but this possibility may be the very reason why the original owner gave 'a licence' in the first place, that is, to enable him to sell the land quickly and unburdened at a moment of his choosing. In other words, the very definition of, and the role for, 'licences', is that they are not interests in land.

However, even though Lord Denning in *Errington* did not explain why he was at liberty to ignore the House of Lords in *King*, there were a number of decisions involving the Court of Appeal and other courts which appeared to confirm that contractual licences should now be accorded the status of an interest in land. On one view, these cases can be explained on the simple basis that the courts thought that they were dealing with contractual licences when, in fact, the rights of the claimant were truly proprietary (maybe an easement, covenant or right of co-ownership). Naturally, such substantive rights, although mislabelled, should be binding on third parties and the error lay in calling them licences in the first place. Yet, be that as it may, on the question of principle (that is, can a licence ever be an interest in land?) the Court of Appeal, in *Ashburn Anstalt v Arnold* (1989), re-examined the matter afresh and reasserted the orthodox view. In that case, Fox LJ relied on the House of Lords' decisions in *King* and *National Provincial Bank v Ainsworth* (1965) to confirm unequivocally that licences were not interests in land. They were personal rights between licensor and licensee, and nothing more. Furthermore, in so far as *Errington* decided otherwise, it was *per incuriam* and could be explained on other grounds (for example, that there was an estate contract binding a non-purchaser, that there was a *Rosset* type equitable right of ownership, or that the purchaser was bound by an estoppel). Indeed, Fox LJ's judgment makes it clear that, *as a matter of principle*, licences are not interests in land and cannot bind third parties for that reason. This view has recently been confirmed with some force by Mummery LJ in *Lloyd v Dugdale* (2001) who notes that '[n]otwithstanding some previous authority suggesting the contrary, a contractual licence is not to be treated as creating a proprietary interest in land so as to bind third parties who acquire the land with notice of it'.

This latest view is, without doubt, a thoroughly orthodox and convincing approach to the problem and it serves to highlight the fundamental distinction between interests in land and purely personal interests, even those which just happen to relate to property. It is submitted that the contrary view now is virtually unarguable. In fact, now that the House of Lords has asserted that residential occupation usually gives rise to a lease, and not a licence (see *Street v Mountford* (1985)), some of the practical concerns about the non-binding status of licences have been removed. Indeed, if one takes Lord Wilberforce's definition of an interest in land, in *National Provincial Bank v Ainsworth* (1965), that:

> ... [b]efore a right or interest can be admitted into the category of property, or of a right affecting property, it must be definable, identifiable by third parties, capable in its nature of assumption by third parties and have some degree of permanence or stability ...,

it is obvious that licences *per se* have no claim to proprietary status (*Nationwide Anglia Building Society v Ahmed* (1995)). Of course, this does mean, as noted above, that courts must be very careful to categorise rights correctly. This is not always easy, but it is easier than floundering in the chaos created by dissolving the distinction between personal and proprietary rights (as witnessed by the decision in *Saeed v Plustrade* (2001) confusing contractual rights and easements).

9.3.7 Can the personal contractual licence take effect against a purchaser despite not being an interest in land?

Following the decision in *Errington*, a second, related attempt was made by Lord Denning's Court of Appeal to explain why a contractual licence could bind a purchaser of the licensor's land. In *Binions v Evans* (1972), a purchaser of land subject to what looked like a contractual licence, *expressly agreed* to purchase the land subject to that licence. The purchaser then sought to evict the licensee and he was prevented from doing so. In fact, two judges in the Court of Appeal actually decided that no licence was involved at all: rather, the occupier had a life interest (a true proprietary right) under a strict settlement which was protected under the Settled Land Act 1925 (Chapter 5). Lord Denning, however, took a different view, and decided that the purchaser was bound to give effect to the licence because he had purchased the land expressly subject to it. As Lord Denning explained it, the licensee was protected against eviction by the imposition of a constructive trust on the purchaser. Subsequent decisions, such as *Re Sharpe* (1980) have followed this reasoning. The net result is that the contractual licence takes effect against a purchaser because that *particular purchaser* is bound by a constructive trust. It will be apparent from this explanation that the words and deeds of the particular purchaser will be crucial here. Importantly, because the licence takes effect against the particular purchaser only, and then only because of his conduct, the licence has not become an interest in land. It still remains incapable of binding the land, even though it may take effect against one particular purchaser of it.

The 'constructive trust' idea was also re-examined by Fox LJ in *Ashburn Anstalt v Arnold* (1989) and he accepted that, in appropriate cases, a contractual licence may take effect behind a constructive trust and be enforceable against a purchaser. However, it was not enough that the purchaser simply *agreed* to buy the land subject to the licence (for that would be to repeat the heresy of *Errington* (1952)). Rather, the purchaser must have so conducted himself that it would be inequitable and unconscionable for the licence to be denied. An example would be where the purchaser promised to give effect to the licence, obtained the land from the vendor for a lower price in consequence, and then refused to honour the licence. Moreover, as Fox LJ makes absolutely clear, the licence is only protected behind a *personal* constructive trust binding on this particular purchaser because of his particular conduct: the licence has not thereby assumed the status of an interest in land. It 'takes effect' against a particular purchaser and, in strict terms, is not 'binding' on the land. So, if the first purchaser is bound to give effect to the licence by means of a constructive trust because of his conduct, but then sells the land to a second purchaser, the second purchaser takes free of the licence (it is only a personal right) unless he also becomes personally affected through unconscionable conduct.

The limits of this special intervention by equity have been examined recently by the Court of Appeal in *Lloyd v Dugdale* (2001) where among other things it was claimed that a purchaser of land was obliged to give effect to the claimant's otherwise void interest because of a personal constructive trust. It was clear that Mr Dugdale had some kind of interest in the property (possibly a proprietary one), but equally clear that he had neither registered it as a minor interest nor was he in actual occupation of the property so as to gain an overriding interest under s 70(1)(g) of the Land Registration Act (LRA) 1925. In such circumstances, his interest could not bind Lloyd (the purchaser) in the normal manner either because it was merely a personal interest or (more likely) that it was an unprotected property interest. Lloyd had, however, purchased the property apparently subject to such rights that Dugdale could claim. In rejecting the submission that Lloyd was thus bound by a personal constructive trust, Mummery LJ summarised the relevant principles thus: first, that even where a vendor has stipulated that the purchaser shall take the land subject to potential adverse rights, there is no general rule that a constructive trust shall be imposed on the purchaser to give effect to those rights; secondly, a constructive trust will not be imposed unless the court is satisfied that the purchaser's conscience is so affected that it would be inequitable to allow him to deny the claimant; thirdly, the critical question in deciding whether the purchaser's conscience is bound is to assess whether the purchaser has undertaken some new obligation, not merely offered to give effect to an obligation which will in any event bind him; fourthly, a contractual licence is not to be treated as creating a proprietary interest in land; fifthly, evidence that the purchaser has paid a lower price can indicate the acceptance of a new obligation; finally (and perhaps most importantly), 'it is not desirable that constructive trusts of land should be imposed on inferences from slender materials'. Clearly, this is an orthodox and, it is submitted, entirely cogent explanation of the relevant principles. It highlights the need to protect a claimant where appropriate but also reminds us that the courts will not side-step 'normal' property law principles by easy use of the constructive trust.

9.3.8 A summary

To summarise the above position regarding contractual licences. First, given that they arise through a binding contract, the availability of normal contractual remedies may make them irrevocable between the licensor and licensee for the agreed duration of the licence. Secondly, however, licences are not, as a matter of principle, interests in land. They are not proprietary and cannot be registered within the system of registered or unregistered land. If they are so registered (assuming they get past the scrutiny of the Registrar), the registration is of no effect, for it cannot confer a status that the right does not have. Note the similar view in *Nationwide v Ahmed* (1995) where it was held that a contractual licence cannot be an overriding interest under s 70(1)(g) of the LRA 1925, even if the licensee is in actual occupation. As licences, they cannot bind third parties who purchase the licensor's land. Thirdly, licences can 'take effect' against a particular purchaser if it is possible to impose a constructive trust. This can occur in limited circumstances, and is personal to the individual purchaser. It would not affect a second or third purchaser, because the licence takes effect against the first purchaser personally, not proprietarily. Finally, we must also note that, following the general rule that 'benefits' of a contract may be assigned (that is, transferred), the right to *enjoy* a contractual licence may be expressly transferred to another person by the original licensee. This is purely a matter of contract and has nothing to do with property law. So, if B enjoys a licence to park his car on A's land, B may transfer ('assign') that benefit to P expressly, providing that the licence does not expressly, or by implication, prohibit such assignment. In fact, the benefit of many licences is indeed declared to be available only to the original licensee and this is why many contractual licences like theatre and car park tickets are said to be 'non-transferable'.

9.3.9 Estoppel licences: the operation of proprietary estoppel

As we shall see in the discussion below, proprietary estoppel may be pleaded by any person claiming that they have an interest in land or a right to use land for some specific purpose. This claim arises from an assurance made to them, upon which they have relied to their detriment. This matter is considered in greater detail shortly, but it is a basic rule of the law of proprietary estoppel that the court may 'satisfy' the estoppel in any way it chooses, at least up to the maximum extent of the right assured to the claimant (*Orgee v Orgee* (1997)), and, as a minimum, in such a way as to do justice between the parties (*Crabb v Arun DC* (1976); *Jennings v Rice* (2002)). This may, in fact, result in the award of a 'licence' to the successful claimant, as may have occurred in *Binions v Evans* (1972) and *Bibby v Stirling* (1998). The same issues that are raised in connection with other licences are relevant here also, especially whether the 'estoppel licence' is an interest in land and whether it has any impact on third party purchasers of the land over which it is said to exist. However, these are large questions, which cannot be considered fully without an analysis of the nature of proprietary estoppel itself. For that reason, consideration of the nature of estoppel licences (and every other right created through the process of proprietary estoppel) must be deferred, see below, 9.7. Bearing that in mind, it is important to realise, in the context of licences, that the term 'estoppel licence' can describe rights arising in a number of different situations, not all of which have common attributes.

The first, and most usual, scenario for the existence of an 'estoppel licence' is where a person is already enjoying some access to another's land by means of a licence and then the owner makes some assurance (for example, that the right shall continue, or be enlarged) which is relied upon in such a way as to generate an estoppel in favour of the promisee. An example is where B enjoys a right to park his car on A's land for two years, and A then encourages B to believe that B can always park his car on the land, in reliance on which B turns down the offer of another permanent parking space elsewhere. It is obvious why this is called an estoppel licence – because it arose in the context of a pre-existing licence. However, this can be misleading. Clearly, as between the landowner (A) and the promisee (B), the effect of the estoppel is to prevent the former from going back on their promise: A is estopped from denying his assurance; in our example, the assurance of a permanent right. However, if A then sells the land to a purchaser, it is by no means clear that the purchaser will be bound to give effect to the estoppel. This depends crucially on the nature of proprietary estoppel itself, particularly whether it gives rise to, or is itself, an interest in land. Moreover, just because the estoppel arose out of a situation where a licence already existed, that does not mean that the 'right' generated by the estoppel is actually a licence. It could be a lease, or an easement, or some other proprietary right. In other words, an 'estoppel licence' as used in this scenario may not be a licence at all (it merely arose out of a licence situation), and, even if it is, its proprietary status and its ability to affect third parties depends on a wider question about the nature of proprietary estoppel.

Secondly, an estoppel licence may also arise when a landowner and the promisee had no previous arrangement concerning the land in question. Thus, it is perfectly possible for a landowner (A) to make an assurance to any person (B) that they shall enjoy some right over A's land, which is relied on in such a way as to give rise to an estoppel. It does not matter that they did not stand in any prior legal relationship. If then the court chooses to 'satisfy' the estoppel by awarding the claimant (B) a licence, an 'estoppel licence' in its purest form has been created. Moreover, it is a licence that has been created entirely informally – that is, by the oral promise of A – and, clearly, the landowner will be compelled to give effect to the licence for so long as the court orders (which may be the period that A had originally promised). An example is where A orally promises B that B can use A's land as a short cut, and, in reliance, B spends money improving access to A's land. However, whether this estoppel licence is binding on a third party purchaser of the 'burdened' land depends, again, entirely on the matter considered below, viz, whether 'proprietary estoppel' is, itself, an interest in land, so that once it has arisen it can bind third parties irrespective of how the court chooses to satisfy it.

The third scenario in which the term 'estoppel licence' may be used is where a landowner (A) grants a licence over her land to another person (B), but then sells the land to a purchaser (P), and P then assures B that they may continue to enjoy the licence. An example is where A has granted B a licence permitting B's children to play on A's land, A sells to P, P assures B that the children can continue to play, in reliance on which B purchases a new climbing frame to build on P's land. This will generate a new estoppel licence between P and B. Note that there is not an estoppel between A and B (merely the licence they had previously created), but there is an estoppel directly between P and B, due to the former's assurance to the latter. In consequence, it is important to realise that this is *not* an example of an existing licence (between A and B) becoming binding on a third party (P). It is the creation of a new licence by estoppel between two new parties (P and B). The estoppel licence (if that is how the court chooses to satisfy the estoppel) might be irrevocable by P, but whether it can be binding on a new purchaser (Z) depends, once more, on the crucial question about the nature of proprietary estoppel.

9.4   Proprietary estoppel

Land law is the study of proprietary rights, being estates or interests in land. Generally, when discussing the creation, operation or transfer of these rights, we have seen that a certain amount of formality is required. Usually, 'interests in land' can be created only by deed, registered disposition or a specifically enforceable written contract (or, in due course, electronic versions of the same). Similarly, a will is needed to transfer land on death and the absence of a valid will is usually fatal to a person's claim to own land that they allege has been promised orally during the deceased's life (*Yeo v Wilson* (1998)). Of course, there are exceptions to this, such as certain leases for three years or less (Chapter 6), or rights acquired through adverse possession (Chapter 11) or by prescription (Chapter 7), but the overall picture is clear enough. Further, the reason why formality is required is also obvious: proprietary rights become part of the land itself and may endure through successive changes in ownership of the land, so it is imperative that their existence and scope is certain and well defined. Of course, there is always a price to pay for certainty, especially if it is secured through the use of formality requirement. In land law, that price is flexibility, and, occasionally, fairness. A person may claim that they have a right in land, and it may be 'fair' or 'just' that this be recognised but, nevertheless, their right could be denied because it was not created with due regard to the formality requirements laid down by statute. Importantly, the LP (Misc Prov) A 1989 was passed in order to bring more clarity and more certainty to the creation and disposition of interests in land. In effect, s 2 of that Act replaced s 40 of the Law of Property Act (LPA) 1925 and abolished the doctrine of part performance (at least in terms of contract formation, but possibly not in other circumstances: *Singh v Beggs* (1996)). This Act deliberately sets out to require more formality for dealings with land than was the case under the old s 40 of the LPA 1925 (under which purely oral contracts could generate an interest in land if 'partly performed') and a direct consequence is that many more informal arrangements are now invalid, as with the informal mortgage by deposit of title deeds (*United Bank of Kuwait v Sahib* (1995)).

Fortunately, the difficulties that can flow from an over-rigorous reliance on formality are mitigated in English property law by the doctrine of proprietary estoppel. Proprietary estoppel is the name given to a doctrine or set of principles whereby an owner of land may be held to have conferred some right or privilege connected with the land on another person, despite the absence of a deed, registered disposition, written contract or valid will. Typically, the right or privilege conferred will arise out of the conduct of the parties, usually because of some assurance made by the landowner, which is relied upon by the person claiming the right. Consequently, proprietary estoppel is a mechanism whereby rights in, or over, land may be created informally. This can be important in two principal ways.

First, proprietary estoppel can provide a defence to an action by a landowner who seeks to enforce his strict rights against someone who has been informally promised some right or liberty over the land. For example, an action in trespass by the landlord can be met by a plea of estoppel, in that the landowner had assured the 'trespasser' that they could enjoy the right now being denied. The landowner is not permitted to plead the lack of formality in the creation of the defendant's rights if this would be inequitable. This is proprietary estoppel as a defence or shield.

Secondly, as indicated already in this chapter, proprietary estoppel can have a much more dramatic effect. There is no doubt that, if successfully established, it can generate new property interests in favour of a claimant. As is commonly stated, proprietary estoppel can be a sword in the hands of a claimant who has relied on an assurance by a landowner that they will be given some right or privilege over the land (*Crabb v Arun DC* (1976)). A court of equity will 'satisfy' the estoppel by awarding the claimant that right or interest which they deem appropriate, although the court will rarely, if ever, go beyond the maximum the claimant was informally promised (*Orgee v Orgee* (1997)). This means that proprietary estoppel can result in the creation of an interest in land without the need for any formality. It represents the creation of rights arising from the action of equity on an individual's conscience.

9.5 Conditions for the operation of proprietary estoppel

Proprietary estoppel has had a role in English property law for many decades, being another example of the intervention of equity to mitigate the consequences of lack of compliance with the formality requirements of the common law. At one time, the conditions for the operation of proprietary estoppel were fairly strictly drawn and these were codified by Fry LJ in *Willmott v Barber* (1880). The so called 'five probanda' of proprietary estoppel were:

(a) that the claimant must have made a mistake as to their legal rights over some land belonging to another; and

(b) that the true landowner must know of the claimant's mistaken belief; and

(c) that the claimant must have expended money or carried out some action on the faith of that mistaken belief; and

(d) that the landowner must have encouraged the expenditure by the claimant, either directly, or by abstaining from enforcing their legal right; and

(e) that the owner of the land over which the right is claimed must know of the existence of their own rights, and that these are inconsistent with the alleged rights of the claimant.

Obviously, these conditions are quite difficult to satisfy, but that is not surprising given that a successful claim of proprietary estoppel could have resulted in the creation of an interest in land that might have effectively destroyed the owner's title or his planned use of the land. However, social and economic changes in the late 20th century, combined with a tightening of the formality rules themselves (for example, s 2 of the LP (Misc Prov) A 1989), has meant that proprietary estoppel has assumed a new importance. As a reflection of this, the traditional criteria for establishing an estoppel have been largely abandoned and the modern tendency is to adopt a much more flexible approach. According to Oliver J in *Taylor Fashions v Liverpool Victoria Trustees* (1982), a claimant will be able to establish an estoppel if they can prove an assurance, reliance and detriment in circumstances where it would be unconscionable to deny a remedy to the claimant. This has confirmed that the emphasis in cases of proprietary estoppel has shifted away from an examination of the actions of the landowner and has become more focused on the behaviour of the claimant.

Before examining in more detail the conditions necessary to establish an estoppel, it is important to appreciate that it is not a universal remedy which can cure every defect in formality. If it were, there would be little point in having formality rules at all. As the court emphasised in *Prudential Assurance v Waterloo Real Estate* (1998) at first instance, estoppel is a drastic remedy and it is a major step for a court to award a claimant a proprietary right over another's land in the absence of due formality, even more so if the effect of the estoppel is to compel a transfer of ownership of the land itself. So, in *Taylor v Dickens* (1997), the claimant had been promised property in a will, but when the promise was not honoured, the court rejected the claim that the property should be transferred under proprietary estoppel; in *Evans v James* (2000) proprietary estoppel did not cure the absence of a valid contract between the parties relating to the transfer of land; in *Slater v Richardson* (1980), the claimants were unable to rely on estoppel having failed to observe the formalities of the Agricultural Holdings Act 1986; and in *Canty v Broad* (1995), the claimants, having failed to conclude a contract for the sale of land in accordance with s 2 of the LP (Misc Prov) A 1989, were unable to claim the land by estoppel (following *AG for Hong Kong v Humphreys* (1987)). By way of contrast, the claimant was partially successful in *Matharu v Matharu* (1994), using estoppel as a means to live in a property for the rest of her life; in *Wayling v Jones* (1993); *Gillet v Holt* (2000); *Jennings v Rice* (2002), the claimants established a right to particular land promised by the deceased, but not left by will; in *Bibby v Stirling* (1998) the claimant used estoppel to establish a right to use a greenhouse erected on the defendant's land; and in *Flowermix v Site Developments* (2000) a contract that was void for uncertainty (as to the extent of land concerned) was nevertheless effectively enforced by reliance on the estoppel rules. Of course, many of the cases where the plea of proprietary estoppel was unsuccessful can be explained on the basis that, say, the assurance was never made, or the detriment was never suffered or there was no unconscionability. However, to apply the *Taylor Fashions* criteria mechanically is to miss the point. Estoppel is available to cure absence of formality when, but only when, it would be unconscionable for the defendant to rely on the lack of formality to defeat the claimant. Unconscionability is at the heart of the doctrine (*Waterloo Real Estate* (1998); *Orgee v Orgee* (1997)). The existence of unconscionability is the reason why the lack of formality can be excused. This is examined in greater detail below, but it is mentioned at the outset to reinforce the message that a successful claim of estoppel is relatively infrequent, even though it is pleaded very frequently.

9.5.1 The assurance

Proprietary estoppel is a flexible doctrine that acts on the conscience of a landowner. Accordingly, the landowner must have made some kind of assurance to the claimant that either he would refrain from exercising his strict legal rights over his own land or, more commonly, that the claimant might have some right over that land. A typical example is where a landowner assures the claimant that 'you may live in my house' or 'use my land as a short cut'. Occasionally, the assurance can be much more dramatic, as where the landowner promises to bequeath property to the claimant on his death, as in *Wayling v Jones* (1993) and *Gillet v Holt* (2000).

Importantly, the form this assurance takes is irrelevant and often it is given orally or in the context of a written transaction that is not itself enforceable as a contract to transfer an interest in land (as apparently in *Flowermix*). Likewise, the assurance may be express (for example, *Salvation Army Trustees v West Yorkshire CC* (1981)), or implied, as where a landowner refrains from preventing the claimant using his land in a particular way (*Ramsden v Dyson* (1866)). Indeed, somewhat remarkably, it seems from *JT Developments v Quinn* (1991) that an estoppel can arise even though the assurance was given in circumstances where there was clearly no intention to create binding obligations between the parties, as where the parties had attempted to negotiate a contract governing use of the land, but had failed. Again, in *Lim Teng Huan v Ang Swee Chuan* (1992) and in *Flowermix*, a written, though unenforceable agreement was held to constitute the requisite assurance, with the consequence that the unenforceable agreement was indirectly given effect through the intervention of proprietary estoppel, even though this appears to be enforcing a contract that the parties have not put into effect properly through their own fault!

The *Lim Teng* case is, perhaps, the most extreme example of a very liberal approach to proprietary estoppel that developed in the years immediately following the tightening of the formality rules in the 1989 Law of Property (Miscellaneous Provisions) Act. In so far as it rejects unconscionability as an element of estoppel, it must be regarded with considerable suspicion. In more recent years, a restrained backlash against very liberal rules is apparent, and some cases (for example, *Matharu v Matharu* (1994)) appear to suggest that the narrow and ancient *Willmott v Barber* criteria should be used once again. In *Orgee v Orgee* (1997), Hurst LJ (who sat in *Matharu*) rejected this, and reiterated the modern approach of assurance, reliance and detriment. However, he did make it clear that a crucial element in determining whether an actionable assurance had been made was whether the defendant (that is, the landowner) had encouraged or acquiesced in the belief held by the claimant and on which the claimant then relied to his detriment. This assurance might be 'unilateral' in that it was offered freely by the landowner, but it may also arise from a mutual understanding between the parties about use of the land. This 'understanding' or unilateral 'promise' may be express or implied by conduct and it does not have to amount to active encouragement so long as it amounts to knowing acquiescence. This seems complicated, but the point is, simply, that a landowner can be held to have generated an estoppel in favour of the claimant only when the landowner knows (or ought to have known) that the claimant believes he has a right of the land and, by words or conduct, this is encouraged, or not dispelled. For example, if A promises B the right to park a car on A's land, but B takes this as a promise to give him the land, which belief is neither encouraged nor acquiesced in by A, no estoppel involving transfer of the land can arise (although a right to park the car might). So, in *Slater v Richardson* (1980), the defendants were wholly unaware of the claimant's belief and had done nothing to encourage it. Most definitely, this is not to say that the promise or 'understanding' must amount to a contract or anything like it: rather, it expresses the idea that a landowner can be required to recognise the rights of another over his land, however informally created, only when the landowner is, in some way, responsible for the situation.

Allied to the above point is the fact that the assurance given must be specific enough to justify the drastic effects of an estoppel. So, a statement that the defendant would welcome the claimant as his tenant is not an 'estoppel generating assurance' that a tenancy will be given (*Slater*), and an understanding between claimant and defendant that the former could be given an agricultural tenancy is not an 'estoppel-generating assurance' that he shall have one (*Orgee*). In the context of negotiations between parties intending to complete a fully binding contract, it will be rare for the court to find that an assurance has been made in those negotiations, especially if they are 'subject to contract' (*Edwin Shirley Productions v Workspace Mana Ltd* (2001)). So also, as is obvious, the assurance must be given to the person claiming the estoppel: in *Sledmore v Dalby* (1996), the assurance had been given to the claimant's wife (now deceased), and had been fulfilled, and so the claimant could not rely on it.

To conclude, then, the cases tell us that the assurance must be in the way of a loose understanding between claimant and defendant, be given to the claimant personally and amounting to the assurance of some specific right, either taking effect immediately or in the future. In *Orgee v Orgee* (1997), a further ground for dismissing the claim was that the assurance was silent as to the specific attributes of the right allegedly promised. The claim was for an agricultural tenancy and the court appeared to suggest that an estoppel would not be given because the terms of the tenancy (for example, the scope of the repairing obligations) were never the subject of a mutual understanding. This, it is respectfully submitted, is going too far. It should be enough that the claimant was assured of some clear right over the defendant's land: a lease, easement, licence, etc. It should not be necessary for the claimant to prove the terms of the lease, easement, etc. This would be to emasculate the doctrine of proprietary estoppel and is just as unjustified as the too generous approach typified by the *Lim* and *Quinn* cases.

9.5.2 The reliance

As we have seen, the 'assurance' may be entirely informal, but whatever form it takes, it is essential that it produces an effect on the claimant. The claimant must 'rely' on the assurance, in that it must be possible to show that he was induced to behave differently because the assurance had been given. Of course, in practice this can be very difficult to prove and a court may well be prepared to infer reliance if that is a plausible explanation of the claimant's conduct. Thus, in *Greasley v Cooke* (1980), the Court of Appeal held that if clear assurances have been made and detriment has been suffered, it is permissible to assume that reliance has occurred. Likewise, in *Wayling v Jones* (1993), the Court of Appeal looked only for a 'sufficient link' between the assurance made and the detriment incurred by the plaintiff, the existence of which would throw the burden of proof onto the defendant to show that there had, in fact, been no reliance. The crucial point seems to be that there will be no reliance *only* if it can be shown that the claimant would have done the detrimental acts irrespective of the defendant's conduct. In *Orgee v Orgee* (1997), for example, it was clear that much of the plaintiff's alleged detriment were ordinary expenses which would have been incurred normally. However, even this may be too restrictive. In *Campbell v Griffin* (2001), the claimant had been a lodger and over time had taken on the responsibility of caring for his 'landlords', an elderly couple. There was clear evidence of relevant assurances about the property. At trial, the claimant admitted that he would have assisted his landlords out of ordinary human compassion – rather than in clear reliance on their promises. Nevertheless, the Court of Appeal upheld the estoppel claim, noting that a dual motive for action (the assurance plus normal human compassion) does not thereby diminish the fact that reliance has occurred. This might seem overly generous, but it would be harsh indeed to dismiss a claim simply because the claimant was not, after all, a thoroughly selfish individual who was prepared to help only because of what was on offer. A further example of how reliance can be established is proved by *Chun v Ho* (2001) where Chun successfully established a claim in estoppel to a share in a business because her conduct in giving up her career and establishing a life with the property owner (to the disgust of her family: he was a convicted criminal) could not be solely because of love and pity. There must have been some reliance on his clear assurance about the business. Evidently then, reliance is critically dependant on the peculiar facts of each case and is not to be discounted merely because of family or emotional ties between claimant and landowner that might otherwise explain a course of action. Equally clear is the point made by the Court of Appeal when upholding the estoppel claim in *Gillet*: assurance, reliance and detriment are necessarily interwoven and the court should not approach them forensically as if they were entirely separate requirements. The case must be viewed in the round.

9.5.3 The detriment

Equity has always been wary of 'volunteers', that is, claimants who seek to enforce a promise even though they have given nothing in return. Similarly, proprietary estoppel cannot be established unless the claimant can prove that he has suffered some detriment in reliance on the assurance. Not surprisingly, so long as the detriment is not minimal or trivial, it may take any form. For example, it may be that the claimant has spent money on the land in reliance on the assurance, or has physically improved the land in some way or has devoted time and care to the needs of the landowner (*Campbell v Griffin* (2001) or has forsaken some other opportunity (*Lloyd v Dugdale* (2001))). Indeed, as this recent case shows, it is not necessary that the detriment be related to land at all, or the land in dispute (see also *Wayling v Jones* (1993)). It may be, for example, that the claimant has spent their money in other ways, on the faith of an assurance that they would have somewhere to live. The point is simply that an estoppel cannot be established unless there has been some detrimental reliance, for that is what makes a retraction of the assurance unconscionable (*Gillet v Holt* (2000)). Sufficient detriment is always a question of fact and, as indicated above, many claims fail because there was neither an assurance nor detriment. In other words, people do not usually act to their detriment unless that are certain they have been promised something concrete. In *Re Basham* (1986), the plaintiff had looked after the deceased without pay for many years and the implication of reliance and detriment was overpowering. Note, however, that detriment itself, however extensive, is not enough. In *Taylor v Dickens* (1997), the plaintiff worked for a number of years without pay in the expectation that he would inherit from the deceased. The deceased changed her will and left everything to another. Detriment was clear enough but, according to the trial judge, there was no assurance that the deceased would never change her will and so the claim failed. This case was settled before an appeal but now looks harsh in the light of the opposite decision of the Court of Appeal in *Gillet*. Even so, it remains the case that an unencouraged detriment is not sufficient to found an estoppel. Finally, in case there is doubt, *Lloyd v Dugdale* (2001) makes it clear that the detriment must be incurred by the person to whom the assurance is made. There is no concept of 'derivative detriment' and so Mr Dugdale had to prove (as he did) that the detriment was incurred by him personally and not his company (a separate legal entity).

9.5.4 Unconscionability

It is clear that Oliver J in *Taylor Fashions* regarded unconscionability as the very essence of a claim of proprietary estoppel. Indeed, in the great majority of cases, the simple fact that the landowner is seeking to retract an assurance given and relied upon will be unconscionable. In *Gillet*, at first instance Carnwath J put the matter succinctly by noting that '[n]ormally it is the promisor's knowledge of the detriment being suffered in reliance on his promise which makes it "unconscionable" for him to go back on it' and this was reiterated by the Court of Appeal in the same case. As noted above, it is this unconscionability that frees the court from the strictures of the formality requirements imposed by statute (for example, the LP (Misc Prov) A 1989; the Wills Act 1837) and allows the claimant to succeed. So, an oral agreement deliberately made 'subject to contract', as in *Canty v Broad* (1995) (and see *AG for Hong Kong v Humphreys* (1987)), or a void executory contract (that is, one which might never be binding as to substance) (*Ravenocean v Gardner* (2001)) cannot be enforced via estoppel, because there is no unconscionability in relying on the absence of formality requirements in these circumstances, even if there has been reliance and detriment. So also, the common understanding that a person is free to change their will makes it difficult to plead unconscionability when a will is changed: *Taylor v Dickens* (1997), although unconscionability may exist if the assurance is withdrawn after such a repeated and clear level of assurance that no one could doubt that the land owner meant what they said about the destination of their property on death, as in *Gillet v Holt* (2000). In *Gillet* itself, Mr Holt had promised Mr Gillet over a 40 year period that he (Gillet) would be the beneficiary of Holt's will. When Holt changed his will to exclude Gillet, a claim based on estoppel was successful, the Court of Appeal noting that the mere withdrawal of the assurance after such detriment (that is, 40 years of work at less than the market wage) was sufficient to establish unconscionability. This was part of the court's general approach that estoppel claims should not be dissected too closely by analysis of the three 'ingredients' but should be looked at in total to see if the denial of the claimant's right is unconscionable. Of itself, this formula presents certain difficulties for it appears to define unconscionability purely in terms of assurance, reliance and detriment (that is, unconscionability exists when the assurance is withdrawn after detrimental reliance) and so the 'all important' criterion of unconscionability, the *raison d'être* of estoppel (*Taylor Fashions* (1982)), becomes a mere shadow of the other three components. The case itself can be justified on the ground that (as noted above) the repeated assurances implied that Mr Holt would not exclude Gillet from the will and hence the unconscionability lay in the attempt to plead the formality of the new will in defiance of Gillet's claim. Clearly, the law must be astute to protect a claimant when there is genuine estoppel, but should not permit estoppel to be an easy way of avoiding the formalities normally required for conducting dealings with land. Thus, the common understanding that there is no contract for the sale of a house until formalised in writing explains why a house owner may accept and reject offers for the house at any point up to exchange of (written) contracts without behaving unconscionably. In the final analysis, unconscionability is, by its nature, a fluid concept and much depends on the facts of each case. It does not mean that the claimant must prove 'fraud' by the defendant, although there are elements of fraud in the concept (*Orgee v Orgee* (1997)). It means, simply (and unhelpfully!), whether, in all the circumstances, the landowner can resile from the assurance he has given and on which the claimant has relied to detriment. Crucially, even if the claimant has relied to detriment on an assurance, there can be no proprietary estoppel without unconscionability.

9.6 What is the result of a successful plea of proprietary estoppel?

The myriad circumstances in which proprietary estoppel can be established necessarily means that the remedy for each successful claimant will vary. Broadly speaking, however, two possibilities are available.

If the proprietary estoppel is established by a defendant in an action by the landowner, the landowner's claim will be dismissed and the defendant will be left to enjoy the right which the landowner was seeking to deny. This is estoppel as a shield, and is illustrated by *Gafford v Graham* (1998) where the landowner entitled to the benefit of a restrictive covenant was estopped from enforcing it due to his acquiescence in conduct contrary to the covenant by his neighbour.

More importantly for our purposes, if the estoppel is established by a claimant seeking to enforce a right against a landowner in consequence of an assurance, the court can award the claimant the remedy it deems appropriate, save only that *Orgee v Orgee* (1997) suggests that the court cannot award more than the claimant was ever assured. As explained in *Crabb v Arun DC* (1976), this means that the court can 'satisfy' the equity in any manner that is appropriate to the case before it, provided it does the minimum to achieve justice between the parties. The remedy may be 'expectation based' (the claimant gets that which was promised), 'reliance based' (the claimant gets a remedy commensurate with extent of their reliance) or a mixture (*Jennings v Rice* (2002)). Crucially, therefore, a court can award the claimant any proprietary *or* personal right over the defendant's land. For example, in *Dillwyn v Llewellyn* (1862) and *Pascoe v Turner* (1979), the claimant was actually awarded the fee simple in the land, in *Celsteel v Alton* (1987) and *Bibby v Stirling* (1998), there appears to have been an easement, in *Re Basham* (1986), a right under a testamentary disposition, and in *Voyce v Voyce* (1991) there was a complete readjustment of the parties' rights over the property. Yet although in all of these cases the claimant was awarded a proprietary right in the land, it is possible that he will be given only a personal right (a licence) to use the land. On one view, this occurred in *Inwards v Baker* (1965) where a father had encouraged his son to build a bungalow on his (the father's) land, and when the son, in reliance on this, went ahead, the court appeared to grant the son a licence to use the land for life. Likewise, in *Matharu v Matharu* (1994), the claimant's claim for a share of beneficial ownership was rejected, but she was awarded a licence to occupy for life. Again, there is no reason why any right over land – proprietary or personal – should be awarded at all. For example, in *Wayling v Jones* (1993), the claimant was awarded compensation in lieu of a proprietary interest, because the relevant land had been disposed of previously and in *Campbell v Griffin* (2001), the claimant was given a charge to the value of £35,000 over the property and was not permitted to remain in possession. The house was to be sold and the claimant paid out of the proceeds (see also *Jennings*: an award of £200,000).

As one can see, the range of remedies available to the court is open ended, and, importantly, does not necessarily have to result in the grant of a proprietary interest at all (as where a licence is granted or a money award made). Of course, this flexibility does produce a measure of uncertainty, both for the claimant and any potential purchaser of the land over which the estoppel is asserted. In fact, the most difficult problems in practice occur when the 'burdened' land is sold to a purchaser *before* the estoppel has been crystallised by decision of the court (as in *Bibby v Stirling* (1998); *Lloyd v Dugdale* (2001)). Naturally, the purchaser then attempts to deny the claimant any right over the land. In those circumstances, the court is faced with two issues:

(a) does the claimant have an estoppel in their favour?; and

(b) if they do, does that estoppel bind the purchaser?

In turn, this second question will depend on:

(a) the nature of proprietary estoppel itself; and

(b) whether the appropriate rules of registered and unregistered land have been observed, if relevant.

9.7 The nature of proprietary estoppel and its effect on third parties

The nature of proprietary estoppel is not easy to determine. There are two major strands of thought, but each has its own subtle nuances. Unfortunately, the question is of some importance, not least because it may determine how, if at all, the estoppel affects a transferee of the land over which it already exists.

9.7.1 Proprietary estoppel as an interest in land

One view of proprietary estoppel is that it is, itself, an interest in land, although necessarily an equitable interest because of the informal way it arises. In other words, it is irrelevant how the court satisfies the equity (for example, by easement, fee simple or licence), because the estoppel itself is proprietary in nature and itself is capable of binding a purchaser of the land. Thus, a purchaser buying land over which there is a potential estoppel claim could find the land subject to an adverse right if the claimant can prove that the original owner had 'created' an estoppel in his favour. Support for this view is derived from the claim that 'estoppel licences' are interests in land. As we know, licences *per se* are not interests in land, so if 'estoppel licences' are so regarded, it must be because the 'estoppel' element is proprietary. Further support may derive from *Ives v High* (1967) and *Inwards v Baker* (1965). In the latter case, the court indicated that the claimant should be awarded a licence to occupy the land, which could then bind third parties. The same solution was adopted in *Greasley v Cooke* (1980), and in *Re Sharpe* (1980) the court accepted that the estoppel (the 'equity') could bind a trustee in bankruptcy. In *Habermann v Koehler* (1997) and *Birmingham Midshires v Saberhawal* (1999), the Court of Appeal intimated, without deciding, that if the claimant could establish an estoppel, it (rather than the right it generated) might be an overriding interest under s 70(1) of the LRA 1925, thus indicating its proprietary status. The same could be said of *Bibby v Stirling* (1998), where the estoppel generated by the previous owner of the burdened land was said (without explanation) to bind the current owner. However, it is also true that both *Inwards* and *Cooke* can be justified on other grounds (that the claimant should have had a life interest under a settlement, see *Dodsworth v Dodsworth* (1973)), and *Bibby v Stirling* (1998) is probably an example of an existing easement (albeit generated by estoppel) binding the burdened land. Likewise, in *Williams v Staite* (1979) (another case often cited in support of this view), the matter was assumed, rather than argued. Finally, in the context of licences, the later decision in *Ashburn Anstalt v Arnold* (1989), that contractual licences are most definitely not interests in land, does raise further doubts, although, of course, there is no necessary connection between the status of licences and the status of proprietary estoppel. In other words, the case law has to now be ambiguous. Significantly however, perhaps the matter is now close to resolution because in *Lloyd v Dugdale* (2001), the Court of Appeal confirmed that contractual licences were not interests in land, but also that if the claimant had been in actual occupation of the property, his right arising by estoppel would have bound the purchaser (Lloyd) as an overriding interest under s 70(1)(g) of the LRA 1925. This is to date the clearest acceptance of the view that an estoppel is itself an interest in land: if it were not, it could not override under s 70(1)(g). As the judge says in *Dugdale*, were it not for the unfortunate circumstance that Mr Dugdale's company was in actual occupation rather than he personally, he would have succeeded in his claim against the purchaser because his estoppel would have bound. In fact, the decision in *Dugdale* anticipates the entry into force of s 116 of the Land Registration Act (LRA) 2002 which provides for registered land that an estoppel interest is to be treated as a proprietary right from the moment the equity arises, rather than the later date that the court crystallises it by giving an appropriate remedy. When this becomes law the matter will be beyond argument for registered land, and *Dugdale* may well produce the same result for land of unregistered title.

Assuming then that this is the correct approach, the 'estoppel interest' will bind a purchaser of the 'burdened' land according to the normal rules of registered and unregistered conveyancing, as follows:

- **In registered land**

   The most likely way in which 'an estoppel' will bind a purchaser in registered land is that it would amount to an 'overriding interest'. For example, many successful claimants will be in 'actual occupation' of the land and so fall within s 70(1)(g) of the LRA 1925, as suggested in *Habermann* and confirmed in *Dugdale*. Note also that, although the estoppel is equitable, and could in theory be protected by registration as a minor interest, this is most unlikely. It will be rare that the claimant will not know whether they actually have anything to register until the court adjudicates on their claim. The position will be similar under the LRA 2002, within the patent 'actual occupation' criteria of Scheds 1 and 3.

- **In unregistered land**

  As noted, estoppel interests are necessarily equitable. Equitable interests in unregistered land usually must be registered as land charges under the Land Charges Act (LCA) 1972. However, 'estoppels' are not within any of the statutorily defined classes of land charge. Consequently, whether an estoppel binds a purchaser of the 'burdened' land will depend on the old 'doctrine of notice'. For example, in *Ives v High* (1967), the Court of Appeal held that an estoppel easement was binding on a third party through notice.

9.7.2   Proprietary estoppel as a method of creating rights

The alternative view of proprietary estoppel does not see the estoppel as a right in itself but, rather, as a method of creating rights: a means to an end, not the end itself. If such a view is taken, estoppel can be regarded as a process whereby rights in, or over, land are created, rather like a contract or a deed, but, of course, much less formal. For such a view, it is not the fact of estoppel that is relevant, but the right that is created by the court when it satisfies the estoppel. So, for example, if the estoppel gives rise to a lease, a freehold, an easement or any other proprietary right, then there is no doubt that a third person buying the land over which the right takes effect may be bound by it: they are bound in the same way that any lease, freehold or easement would bind them. The essence of the matter is that the estoppel has generated a proprietary right and it is the *right* that is binding, not the estoppel. The obvious consequence of this is, however, that if the estoppel generates a personal right (that is, a licence), that licence is incapable of binding a purchaser, simply because it is personal (not proprietary) and the method of its creation (estoppel) is irrelevant. This alternative view of proprietary estoppel has much to commend it, not least that it maintains a clear distinction between proprietary and personal rights. Neither does it fetter a court in its discretion, for if the court wishes to ensure that a purchaser of the 'burdened' land is, in fact, bound, it can award the claimant a proprietary right. If it wishes to ensure that the remedy is effective *only* against the maker of the assurance, it awards a personal remedy. This flexibility is necessarily lost if *all* estoppels can bind a third party irrespective of the particular remedy. Of course, if we adopt the view that estoppel is merely a method of creating rights (albeit that case law is against this approach), then we must be clear about how a property right (created by estoppel) would *actually* bind a third party:

- **In registered land**

  Any proprietary rights generated by estoppel will, necessarily, be equitable. Again, they are unlikely to be protected by an entry in the minor interests register. Therefore, under current law equitable estoppel easements are likely to be overriding interests under s 70(1)(a) (*Celsteel v Alton* (1987)), and equitable estoppel leases and fee simples will be protected by actual occupation under s 70(1)(g) of the LRA 1925, at least until the register of titles can be rectified in their favour.

  The position would be different under the LRA 2002. Protection as a right that overrides through patent actual occupation will be similar to the current law (see Scheds 1 and 3), but equitable easements (if not supported by actual occupation) will have to be noted on the register.

- **In unregistered land**

  Theoretically, because rights generated by estoppel are equitable, they may be registrable as land charges under the LCA 1972. However, it is most unlikely that the 'owner' of the estoppel generated right will be aware of the need to register (even if their right is crystallised before a sale to a purchaser) and, clearly, it would be inequitable to allow a right that arose out of equity to be defeated by the procedural requirements of registration under the LCA 1972. Therefore, a court will strive to explain why an estoppel generated right does *not* fit in to one of the recognised classes of land charge defined in the LCA 1972. In consequence, the doctrine of notice will be used to determine the effect of any estoppel generated right on a third party. Clearly, this was the case in *Ives v High* (1967), where the equitable estoppel easement was not regarded as a Class D(iii) land charge, even though that category included 'equitable easements'.

9.7.3   Estoppel and the reform of registered land

It has been noted above that the Land Registration Act 2002 has confirmed that estoppel rights are proprietary from the moment the equity arises. It is a moot point whether this merely confirms the law as it is now (as s 116 of the Act implies, and see *Dugdale*) or whether it involves a substantive change in the nature of estoppel. For practical purposes of course it hardly matters (at least for registered land), for the Act will enter into force and s 116 settles the matter. There is, however, another way that the LRA 2002 may affect proprietary estoppel.

As discussed in Chapter 2, one element in the move to electronic conveyancing is to ensure that the creation of rights in registered land occurs simultaneously with their entry on the register. In essence, the right will not exist at all until it is on the register (see s 93 of the LRA 2002). In addition, it is clear that many rights in or over registered land will be capable of creation only electronically: that is, only by an electronic contract or deed that takes effect when a register entry is made (s 91 of the LRA 2002 and the intended s 2A of the LP (Misc Prov) A 1989). The necessary consequence is that paper deeds and written contracts will be a nullity. They will create nothing at all. Of course, this system will not bounce in over night, but when it does operate (perhaps within the next five years), it is a fair bet that people will still attempt to create rights by deed or written contract believing that they are doing all that the law requires. If the land is registered land, they will fail: creation will be by electronic entry on the register. Given then that proprietary estoppel is a way to create a property right without the required formality, it takes no foresight at all to realise that claims in estoppel are likely to boom when the mandatory electronic formality rules take effect.

9.7.4 Note: a similar, but very different, situation

In the above sections, we have been considering the situation where A's actions are such that they generate an estoppel interest in favour of B over A's land, and then A sells that land to a purchaser, P. The issue then is, clearly, whether the right existing between A and B can be binding on P, a third party. However, another possibility exists which appears to be very similar, but which is logically and legally different. Thus, A may so act so as to generate an estoppel in favour of B over A's land, and A again may sell the land to P. Yet this time, after the sale, P may confirm by words or conduct the continuance of B's right and so a new estoppel between P and B comes into existence. This is not a case of a pre-existing right binding P, but the generation of a new right by P's own conduct in favour of B. Indeed, one explanation of *Ives v High* (1967) is that A and B had, by their action, created an easement binding on A's land, and, when the land was sold to P, P so acted as to be estopped from denying the continuance of the right. In effect, this has nothing to do with the transfer of existing rights to a third party, because the alleged 'third party' is bound by estoppel due to their own actions: P is bound by his own estoppel, not that which existed between A and B.

9.8 Proprietary estoppel and constructive trusts

It will be apparent from the above analysis of the principles of proprietary estoppel that the doctrine has much in common with that branch of constructive trusts considered in Chapter 4 – that is, constructive trusts concerning the acquisition of an equitable interest in another person's land. As we know, an estoppel is triggered by an assurance, relied on to detriment where it would be unconscionable for the assurance to be withdrawn, and a 'common intention' constructive trust is triggered by an express promise or assurance as to ownership which is relied on to detriment. The similarities are obvious and in some cases (for example, *Re Basham* (1986)), it is clear that the court is content to rely on either (or both) doctrines in pursuit of a just outcome. More recently, in *Yaxley v Gotts* (1999), the claimant originally alleged an estoppel against Mr Gotts because of an agreement between them concerning ownership of land. The Court of Appeal allowed the claim, but on the basis that Mr Yaxley was the beneficiary under a common intention constructive trust. This case clearly raised questions concerning the relationship between the doctrines – questions that on the current state of the case law it is difficult to answer. The following is thus a very tentative attempt to compare and contrast the two doctrines. However, it should be noted at the outset that some of these comparisons and contrasts are not certain, not logical and not necessarily justifiable. They are a template for discussion:

(a) Both the constructive trust and proprietary estoppel are triggered by an assurance (express promise), reliance and detriment. In consequence, there are many cases where a claimant could plead either doctrine. It is generally thought, however, that estoppel is available in a wider range of circumstances because of the reference to common intention in constructive trusts and the use of estoppel in claims between persons who stand in no emotional relationship (see below, (b) and (c)).

(b) The constructive trust is often said to arise from a 'common intention' between the parties, whereas an estoppel might be thought to arise from a 'unilateral' promise. However, it is not at all clear that constructive trusts really result from a shared intention relating to the land and that estoppels always do not. The suggestion that constructive trusts are 'mutual' whereas estoppel is 'unilateral' is not proven.

(c) The constructive trust tends to be relied on in matrimonial or quasi-matrimonial disputes concerning the family home. Proprietary estoppel tends to be used for all other cases, both as between strangers and between persons in other family or friendship arrangements. This may be merely historical or traditional and without any logical base. Or it may not.

(d) Both the constructive trust and proprietary estoppel are a means of enforcing an 'informal' promise by a landowner made in favour of a claimant. They are methods by which a person may acquire an interest in land without having been granted that interest in writing or by deed and hence are exceptions to the need for 'formality' in land transactions.

(e) The constructive trust is statutorily exempt from the normal formality requirements for transactions involving land – s 53(2) exempts it from the requirements of s 53 of the LPA and s 2(5) exempts it from the requirements of s 2 of the LP (Misc Prov) A 1989. There is no statutory exemption for proprietary estoppel. In consequence, courts may feel on safer ground when relying on constructive trust (for example, *Yaxley*). Likewise, there is a need to explain why claims of proprietary estoppel are exempt from these formality requirements (there is no statutory approval) and this is usually done by reference to the criterion of 'unconscionability'. This may explain why 'unconscionability' is more overtly central in estoppel claims.

(f) A successful plea of constructive trust results in an equitable share of ownership for the claimant with the legal owner holding the land under a 'trust of land' governed by the TOLATA 1996. A successful proprietary estoppel may be 'satisfied' by the award of any proprietary right, any personal right (including a money award) or no right at all. In this sense, proprietary estoppel is more flexible.

(g) A constructive trust is certainly proprietary (it gives an equitable interest behind a trust of land), and now, following *Lloyd v Dugdale* (2001) and s 116 of the LRA 2002, so is proprietary estoppel irrespective of how the court crystallises it.

(h) It is sometimes said that a successful claim to a constructive trust is akin to a claim of right (that is, an interest will be awarded), whereas a successful claim of estoppel is more discretionary (that is, an interest may be awarded). However, such a distinction may be more apparent than real. Both are equitable doctrines and a court may refuse to grant relief (or will modify the quantum) where it is not 'deserved'. It may be simply that courts are more open about their discretion in estoppel cases.

(i) It has been said that the evidentiary requirements for the two concepts are different, in that a constructive trust can be more difficult to prove. Rarely is this acknowledged but it may be a sensible deduction from the results in cases. On the other hand, it could be (merely) a reflection of the fact that a constructive trust usually leads to the award of a proprietary right whereas estoppel does not always have this outcome ((f), above) and courts always require more proof where a claim to a proprietary right is concerned.

Clearly, it is dangerous to draw firm conclusions from these arguments. Many academics see the concepts as virtually indistinguishable as concepts while recognising that in practice they are used in different types of case. Other academics maintain that the concepts are inherently different, albeit that in some cases they overlap. The latter view appears to have been adopted by the court in *Yaxley v Gotts* (1999), but only just and certainly the case is not meant to be definitive.

LICENCES AND PROPRIETARY ESTOPPEL

The essential nature of a licence

There are no formal requirements for the creation of a 'licence' as such. A licence is given by the owner of land (the licensor) to some other person (the licensee), permitting them to do something on the owner's land. Without such permission, the activity would amount to a trespass. A licence may be given for any lawful purpose and not only to someone who also owns land. Crucially, the traditional view of licences is that they are not proprietary in nature.

Types of licence

A bare licence is a permission to enter upon the land given voluntarily by the owner who receives nothing in return. A bare licence lasts only for so long as the licensor wishes, terminable on reasonable notice:

- a 'licence coupled with a grant' is a permission that enables a person to exercise some other right connected with the land, usually a *profit à prendre*;

- a contractual licence is granted to the licensee in return for valuable consideration. It is founded in contract and the normal remedies for breach are available in the event of a failure to carry out its terms. The effect of these remedies can be to make the licence *de facto* irrevocable between the parties throughout the contractual period of the licence. Contractual licences are not interests in land. Notwithstanding this, a contractual licence can take effect against a purchaser of land by means of a *personal* constructive trust;

- an estoppel licence may arise out of a successful plea of proprietary estoppel. It is an interest in land *only* if 'the estoppel' itself is now to be regarded as a new species of property right. This appears to be the predominant view and is given effect to in s 116 of the LRA 2002.

The role of proprietary estoppel

Proprietary estoppel can provide a defence to an action by a landowner who seeks to enforce his strict rights against someone who has been informally promised some right or liberty over the land. Secondly, proprietary estoppel can generate new property interests in favour of a claimant. It can be a shield or a sword.

Conditions for the operation of proprietary estoppel

The modern doctrine of *Taylor Fashions v Liverpool Victoria Trustees* (1982) is that there must be:

- an assurance. The form of the assurance is irrelevant and it may be implied from conduct so long as the landowner is aware, or ought to have been aware, that the claimant is relying on the assurance;

- reliance on the assurance. This can be assumed from the fact that the claimant acted to his detriment. The assumption can be rebutted by evidence that the claimant would have behaved the same way irrespective of the landowner's assurance;

- detriment. This may take many forms, providing it is not minimal. It may involve expenditure on the land, work undertaken in connection with the land or work undertaken for the landowner without pay or at less than market pay;

- such circumstances that it would be unconscionable to allow the landowner to escape from his promise. Unconscionability is the reason why oral assurances can be enforced despite non-compliance with normal formality requirements. If the facts do not reveal unconscionability, then a simple assurance, reliance and detriment on their own cannot generate an estoppel.

What is the result of a successful plea of proprietary estoppel?

If a defendant establishes the proprietary estoppel in an action by the landowner, the landowner's claim will be dismissed and the defendant will be left to enjoy the right that the landowner was seeking to deny. If the estoppel is established by a claimant seeking to enforce a right against a landowner in consequence of an assurance, the court can award the claimant any remedy it deems appropriate, though probably not in excess of that which was actually promised.

The nature of proprietary estoppel and its effect on third parties

One view of proprietary estoppel is that 'the estoppel' is itself an interest in land, although necessarily an equitable interest because of the informal way it arises. Thus, to bind a third party:

- currently in registered land, the estoppel must amount to either an overriding interest (for example, by virtue of 'actual occupation' of the land within s 70(1)(g) or under s 70(1)(a)) or because of registration as a minor interest. The position will be different under the LRA 2002 when it comes into force;

- in unregistered land, the estoppel interest does not fall within the classes of registrable charges under the LCA 1972 and, in consequence, will bind a purchaser (if at all) through the doctrine of notice.

The alternative (and less supportable) view regards proprietary estoppel as a method of creating rights: a means to an end, not the end itself. So, the estoppel may give rise to a lease, a freehold, an easement or any other proprietary right. Likewise, the estoppel may generate a licence (a personal right). If (but only if) the estoppel gives rise to a proprietary right, it is capable of binding a third party in the following way:

- in registered land, the proprietary right will necessarily be equitable. It is unlikely to be protected by an entry in the minor interests register. Equitable estoppel easements are likely to be overriding interests under s 70(1)(a) and other estoppel rights can fall within s 70(1)(g) of the LRA 1925 as overriding interests;

- in unregistered land, estoppel proprietary rights are not registrable under the LCA 1972 and, in consequence, will bind a purchaser (if at all) through the doctrine of notice.

CHAPTER 10

THE LAW OF MORTGAGES

A mortgage is an extremely versatile concept in the law of real property. For most people, the mortgage signifies a method by which they may raise enough capital to purchase a house or other property. However, the use of a mortgage to finance the purchase of property is a relatively recent phenomenon, and mortgages have been used as security for the repayment of a debt owed by the landowner, or for the performance of some other obligation, for much longer.

10.1 The essential nature of a mortgage

There are several different aspects to a mortgage, the most important of which are discussed below.

10.1.1 A contract between borrower and lender

Like many other concepts in the law of real property, a mortgage is also a contract, this time between the borrower and the lender. Often, this contract is express – as where the parties negotiate and execute a mortgage by deed – and sometimes it is implied, as where the court decides that the conduct of the parties in relation to an asset (that is, land) amounts to a mortgage (or 'charge'), whether or not this was the intention of the parties. In the typical mortgage of land, with which this chapter is concerned, the borrower of money (the mortgagor) will enter into a binding contract with the mortgagee (the lender, often a bank or building society), whereby a capital sum will be lent on the security of property owned by the mortgagor. Moreover, as a matter of contract, the mortgagor and mortgagee are free to stipulate whatever terms they wish for repayment of the loan, the rate of interest, and so forth. Consequently, one of the remedies available to a mortgagee, when faced with a mortgagor who will not repay the loan, is to sue the mortgagor personally on the contract for repayment of the sum borrowed, plus interest and costs (see, for example, the discussion in *Alliance & Leicester v Slayford* (2001)). On the other hand, and as we shall see, the contractual nature of a mortgage is not always consistent with its status as a proprietary right.

10.1.2 An interest in land in its own right

Although the mortgage is also a contract, and the parties to it are subject to contractual rights and obligations, it also constitutes a proprietary interest in the land. Thus, under the mortgage, the mortgagee obtains an estate in the land with all that this entails, and the borrower retains an 'equity of redemption' – itself a proprietary right – which encapsulates his residual rights in the property. In fact, both mortgagee and mortgagor may transfer their respective interests under the mortgage to third parties, and this often occurs when a bank transfers its 'mortgage book' to another lender. In addition, the proprietary nature of a mortgage brings with it the intervention and attention of equity and this can result in a conflict between the mortgage as an interest in land and the mortgage as a creation of a contract.

10.1.3 The classic definition of a mortgage

At its root, a mortgage is security for a loan. A mortgage of real property comprises a transfer (conveyance) of a legal or equitable estate in the borrower's land to the mortgagee, with a provision that the mortgagee's interest shall lapse upon repayment of the loan plus interest and costs (*Santley v Wilde* (1899)). As noted above, the lender obtains not only a right to have the money repaid, but also a proprietary interest in the land. However, it is a fundamental principle of the law of mortgages that 'once a mortgage, always a mortgage', even if this contradicts the terms of the contract between the parties. In other words, the borrower has the right to have their property returned in full once the loan secured on it has been repaid and any clause of the mortgage which destroys the right will be struck out as inconsistent with the right to redeem (*Jones v Morgan* (2001)). Consequently, the proprietary nature of the mortgage lasts only for so long as the debt remains outstanding, and the mortgagee's remedies (which can be proprietary or contractual in nature) endure only so long as the borrower owes money.

10.1.4 The mortgage as a device for the purchase of property

In recent years, the mortgage has come to the fore as the major device by which individuals may finance the purchase of property. Of course, the mortgage is still security for a loan, but now the purpose of the loan is to purchase the very property over which the security is to take effect. Necessarily, this has given rise to some conceptual problems, not least that the purchaser must actually own the property before he can create a mortgage over it, but, of course, he cannot own it until he has the money which the mortgage will provide! In formal terms, this problem is dealt with by the transfer of the estate in the land to the new owner, followed immediately thereafter by the execution of a mortgage over that property and a transfer of the purchase price to the vendor. This is simple enough, but it does mean that *logically* there is a 'time gap' between the purchaser acquiring the property and the execution of the mortgage over it. This is known as a *scintilla temporis*. In practice, this *scintilla temporis* may only be a matter of a few minutes or moments, but it has the potential to create problems in some circumstances. For example, if the new owner holds the land on trust for another person (for example, their husband or wife as equitable owner), the moment the new owner acquires title to it, the equitable owner's interest also springs into life. Such an equitable interest would, therefore, come into existence a few moments before the mortgage is made, and thus have the potential to take priority over the mortgagee's interest (because it arose first). The following diagram will make this clear.

Figure 1

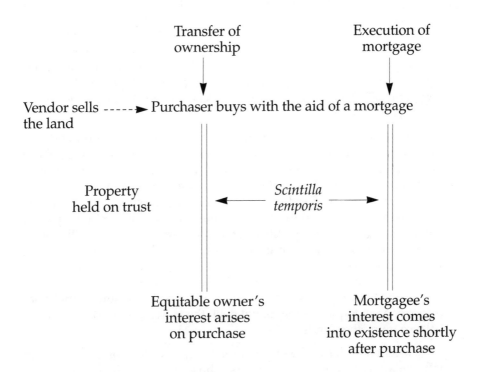

Fortunately, this logical problem has now been solved in a practical way. According to the House of Lords in *Abbey National Building Society v Cann* (1991) as a matter of *law*, there is no *scintilla temporis* between a purchaser's acquisition of title to a property and the subsequent creation of a mortgage over that property that has enabled the purchase to take place. Consequently, any potential equitable interest held by another person must always rank second in time to the mortgage, and cannot take priority over the mortgagee, as illustrated by in *Leeds Permanent Building Society v Famini* (1998). For all practical purposes this must be correct, for it is only a reflection in law of the real situation; viz, that the property would not have been purchased without the mortgage and, therefore, the interests of all the owners of the property (legal and equitable) should give way to the rights of the mortgagee.

10.1.5 Types of mortgage

The contractual nature of a mortgage means that each mortgage is potentially unique, depending on the needs of the particular mortgagor and mortgagee. The following is a non-exhaustive list of the different types of mortgage in general use, although it must be remembered that all are 'mortgages' within the Law of Property Act (LPA) 1925 and are governed by that Act:

(a) the 'repayment mortgage' is used most frequently for the purchase of residential property. The mortgagor borrows a capital sum and agrees to pay back that sum plus interest over a fixed period of time. The capital and interest are paid back in instalments, with the early instalments representing pure interest, and the later instalments comprising a greater and greater capital element. At the end of the period, the mortgage has been paid off, the property has been redeemed and the mortgagor owns the property absolutely;

(b) the 'endowment mortgage' is also used frequently for the purchase of residential property. The mortgagor borrows a capital sum for a fixed period (usually 25 years). This accumulates interest and the mortgagor repays that interest in regular monthly instalments. No part of the instalments goes towards repaying the capital sum. However, the mortgagor also enters into an 'endowment policy', whereby he pays a regular sum towards the purchase of an 'endowment', which will mature at the same time as the mortgage period ends. The endowment should realise a large enough capital sum to pay off the principal mortgage debt at the end of the period and, possibly, leave a sum of money for the mortgagor. However, if, when the endowment policy matures, it does not realise enough to pay off the capital debt, the mortgagor must provide the balance from other funds;

(c) the 'current account mortgage' is a relatively new type of mortgage that may be advantageous to borrowers whose only or principal debt is a mortgage. The lender will agree an overdraft facility on a current bank account to the value of the mortgage. The lender will provide these monies for the purchase of property (or other use) in the normal way and interest will be charged at the prevailing rate. The borrower will pay funds into the mortgage current account and some of these funds will pay the interest and/or capital repayments and be taken by the lender. Any surplus funds will go towards paying off the debt. This has the advantage that the mortgage debt decreases the more that surplus funds are paid into the account. Further, given that interest will be payable only on the actual mortgage debt, the borrower pays less interest over the period of the mortgage (assuming the capital debt is decreasing) than with a conventional repayment/endowment mortgage. Moreover, as the lender has promised an overdraft facility to the level of the original mortgage, the borrower can draw on the current account up to this limit (in effect recover any surplus paid) should the need arise;

(d) the secured overdraft is common where funds are required for commercial purposes, as where a businessman uses the family home to raise finance for his company. In essence, the lender promises to make an overdraft facility available and the borrower may draw monies up to this agreed overdraft limit as and when they are needed. No lump sum is paid, interest is charged on the amount of the actual debt and the total amount owed varies according to the level of current account indebtedness. Hence the value of the mortgage secured over the land fluctuates (or 'floats') in line with the indebtedness, as in *State Bank of India v Sood* (1997);

(e) the 'charge'. As we shall see, mortgages may be created in two distinct ways, one of which is the charge. A 'charge' does not refer to any specific type of mortgage, rather, to the manner in which any type of mortgage may be created. It is mentioned here because many cases refer to a mortgage of land as a 'charge over property', irrespective of whether the precise terms mean it is a repayment, endowment or other type of mortgage. Virtually all mortgages today take the form of the 'charge' (see below).

10.2 The creation of mortgages before 1925

Before 1 January 1926, if an owner of a legal or equitable estate in land wished to raise money on the security of that land, the borrower's entire interest in the property was usually conveyed in full to the lender. In other words, the borrower divested themselves entirely of their interest in return for the loan. Of course, the mortgagee promised to reconvey the land on repayment of the principal (that is, the capital sum), interest and costs but, importantly, the mortgage contract allowed the mortgagee to keep the borrower's land if he failed to repay the loan on the date stipulated in the mortgage contract. This date, known as the 'legal date of redemption', was crucial, and the consequences for the borrower of missing payment on that date were theoretically severe. To some extent, the position was mitigated by the intervention of equity. On the basis of the policy that 'once a mortgage, always a mortgage', an 'equity of redemption' was held to exist, whereby the borrower was entitled to a reconveyance of his property should he pay the full sums due under the mortgage, even though the 'legal date' for redemption had passed. This was simply an aspect of the rule that a mortgage really was security for a loan and did not represent an opportunity for the mortgagee to obtain the property of a solvent mortgagor if the debt could be repaid.

10.3 The creation of legal mortgages on or after 1 January 1926

The LPA 1925 made significant changes to the ways that mortgages could be created. The overall intent was to ensure that a mortgagor retained the fullest interest possible in their own property, even when seeking a mortgage of it, providing that the mortgagee had suitable remedies in the event of a failure to repay the loan. In general terms, as a consequence of the reforms of the LPA 1925, a mortgage of a legal estate does *not* occur through the transfer of the mortgagor's entire interest in the land to the mortgagee. However, the mortgagee is given some lesser proprietary right in the mortgagor's land appropriate to the type of mortgage created.

10.4 Legal mortgages of freehold property

Currently, under s 85(1) of the LPA 1925, there are two methods only of creating a legal mortgage of a freehold estate. Consequently, it is impossible to create a mortgage of a legal estate by a conveyance of the mortgagor's entire interest to the mortgagee (s 85(2) of the LPA 1925). Note also, that in respect of registered land, the Land Registration Act (LRA) 2002 provides that it shall not be possible to create a mortgage of registered land by long lease (demise or sub-demise) s 23(1)(a) of the LRA 2002. When this Act enters into force, it will mean that mortgages of registered land may be created only by using the 'charge' method (see below, 10.4.2.), and not the 'long lease' (see below, 10.4.1).

10.4.1 Long leases

The first current method is where the mortgagor grants the mortgagee a long lease over the land with a provision for the termination of the lease on repayment of all sums due under the loan: in technical terms, the mortgagor will 'demise a term of years absolute' to the mortgagee 'subject to a provision for cesser on redemption'. In the typical case, the mortgagee's lease is usually for 3,000 years, although the mortgage contract will fix an earlier contractual date for repayment and redemption. This earlier date comprises the legal right to redeem and often will be six months after the date of execution of the mortgage. However, as was the case before 1926, the mortgagor has an equitable right to redeem the mortgage, and terminate the lease, on the payment of all sums due at any time after this legal date has passed, and this may also be recognised by the inclusion of a right to pay by instalments (and hence postponement of the legal date for redemption). Of course, the grant of the exceptionally long lease to the mortgagee is something of a fiction, but it does have a number of important consequences:

(a) the mortgagor retains his legal fee simple throughout the term of the mortgage. In other words, the borrower always retains an estate in their own land and the mortgage is more accurately shown to be what it really is – the security for a loan;

(b) the mortgagee also acquires some proprietary interest in the land, being the leasehold granted to them. This preserves the efficacy of their remedies in the event of non-payment of the mortgage debt. It also means that, as a leaseholder, the mortgagee has a right to possession of the property although, in most cases, this will not be exercised and the mortgagor will be allowed to remain in occupation;

(c) perhaps the greatest advantage of the 1925 reforms is that it means that the mortgagor may create further legal mortgages of his land, in order to raise further sums. For example, because the mortgagor retains his legal fee simple, it is perfectly possible to obtain another mortgage from another mortgagee by granting a second leasehold over the property for a period longer than the first lease, say 3,001 years. The term granted to the second mortgagee will necessarily always be longer than that granted to the first, as this gives the second mortgagee a notional legal interest in the property distinct from that of the first mortgagee: in our example, one year more. Of course, the actual sum lent on the second mortgage will be calculated by reference to the value of the land, taking account of the debt owed under the first mortgage, but again the mortgagor retains the ultimate fee simple and the second mortgagee also receives a proprietary interest in the land. For example, if land is worth £100,000, the fee simple owner (Z) may seek a mortgage from A Bank plc in the sum of £45,000. A Bank will be granted a mortgage by way of a 3,000 year lease (with provisions for termination on repayment), and Z retains the fee simple. Z may then seek a second mortgage from B Bank plc, who may be willing to lend anything up to £55,000, taking a 3,001 year lease by way of mortgage (with provisions for termination on repayment), Z still retaining the fee simple.

10.4.2 The charge

Instead of the relative formality involved in granting the mortgagee a long lease over the land, the mortgagor may create a mortgage by executing 'a charge by deed expressed to be by way of legal mortgage' (ss 85(1) and 87 of the LPA 1925). This is a much simpler method of creating a mortgage than executing a long leasehold. It is, in effect, a statutory form of mortgage and is now the most common method of creating mortgages. Under s 87 of the LPA 1925, the charge must be made by deed, and it must be expressed to be by way of legal mortgage, that is, it must declare itself to be a 'legal mortgage made by charge'. However, that done, it is clear that a mortgagee under a legal charge will obtain the same powers and remedies as if they had been given a long lease of 3,000 years in the normal way (s 87 of the LPA 1925; *Regent Oil Co v Gregory* (1966)). For all practical purposes, the legal charge is as effective as a mortgage by way of demise of a term of years. It is, however, less complicated, and for that reason cheaper and easier to set up. As noted above, after the entry into force of the LRA 2002, this will become the *only* method of creating mortgages of registered land. Then it will not be possible to create a legal mortgage by demise or sub-demise.

10.5 Legal mortgages of leasehold property

There are also two current methods of creating mortgages of legal leaseholds, and these are substantially similar to that used for the freehold. Once again, before 1 January 1926, the leaseholder (the tenant) would assign his entire lease to the mortgagee (just as would the freeholder) but, once again, this is not now possible (s 86 of the LPA 1925). However, as above, the entry into force of the LRA 2002 will mean that mortgages of leaseholds of registered land may be created only by means of the 'charge'.

10.5.1 Long subleases

As with freeholds, the first current method of creating a legal mortgage of a leasehold is to grant the mortgagee a lease over the property. Of course, given that the mortgagor himself is a leaseholder, the 'mortgage-lease' will actually be a sublease (a 'sub-demise'). This sublease will necessarily be shorter than the lease that the leaseholder has, simply because the mortgagor cannot grant more than they have. In practice, the mortgagee's term will be 10 days shorter than that of the original leaseholder. For example, if the mortgagor has a lease of 100 days, a first mortgage will operate by the grant of a legal lease to the mortgagee of 90 days. In turn, this will ensure that the leaseholder can grant second and subsequent legal mortgages of the leasehold property by creating further subleases. These additional subleases will be longer than the first mortgagee's lease (so as to give the second mortgagee a separate interest in the property), but shorter than the mortgagor's own lease. Using the above example, the second mortgagee will be granted a legal lease of 91 days. Any mortgage which attempts to avoid these provisions, by providing that the leaseholder's entire term should be assigned to the mortgagee, will operate only as a sublease for a term shorter than that of the mortgagor (*Grangeside Properties v Collingwood Securities Ltd* (1964)).

10.5.2 The charge

The second method of creating a legal mortgage of a leasehold is to use the 'charge expressed to be by way of legal mortgage' under s 87 of the LPA 1925. This is substantially the same as for freeholds, and is the common form. Once again, it will become the only form for registered land once the LRA 2002 enters into force.

10.6 Registered land and the registration of legal mortgages

Strictly speaking, however, before the legal mortgage can take effect in registered land as a legal interest, it must be registered as a 'registered charge' against the registered title, showing the mortgagee as proprietor of the charge. In the language of land registration, the legal mortgage is not 'completed' until such registration (s 26(1) of the Land Registration Act (LRA) 1925). In fact, in the absence of such registration, it is clear that no legal mortgage exists and the mortgage (despite being created by deed, etc) will be treated as a minor interest requiring protection as such (s 106(2) of the LRA 1925). This is the natural consequence of the registration system: properly created legal mortgages need registration to ensure their existence as a legal interest.

Of course, in the normal course of events, the mortgagee will ensure that the mortgage is registered and this is normal practice among most institutional lenders. However, surprising though it may seem, some lenders feel it unnecessary to seek registration and are content to rely on possession of the land certificate (that is, the borrower's evidence of title) for protection. This is all well and good if the only concern is to prevent the borrower dealing with the title itself, but it offers little protection if the borrower is able to create another interest over his land after executing the mortgage that conflicts with the mortgage. For example, in *Barclays Bank v Zaroovabli* (1997), the mortgagee had not registered its mortgage and the borrower, after executing the mortgage and taking the money on the basis that the land was all his, created a legal lease in favour of the defendant. This lease was an overriding interest under s 70(1)(k) of the LRA 1925 and, even though coming after the mortgage, took priority over it. The bank, having failed initially to register its mortgage, was not then a purchaser of a legal estate and when it eventually sought registration some time later, the defendant's overriding interest already had come into existence. The bank's security was seriously diminished – if not destroyed. A very similar situation arose in *Leeds Permanent Building Society v Famini* (1998), the mortgagee failing to register and its interest taking effect only as an equitable mortgage, despite being created by deed, etc. Fortunately for the lender in that case, the tenancy created by the borrower after executing the mortgage was itself only equitable, and did not, on the facts, amount to an overriding interest. So, given that the mortgage and the tenancy were both equitable rights, the 'first in time' prevailed, and the mortgage took priority. Only with this smile from the gods did the Leeds Permanent not suffer for their failure to register.

The above principles of course apply in relation to the system of land registration as it is established by the LRA 1925. Indeed, this is the current law. However, the enactment of the LRA 2002 makes changes to the 'old' regime and these will be effective in due course when the relevant provisions of the LRA 2002 enter into force. Under the new system, and as we have seen already, mortgages of legal estates of freehold or registrable leaseholds (leases of over seven years) may be effected only by way of the 'charge' (s 23 of the LRA 2002). Furthermore, it is fundamental to the new system of land registration that the creation of interests in registered land eventually shall be coterminous with their registration. Consequently, when the full scheme of the Act is in play, the mortgage (the registered charge) will not exist *at all* until it is entered on the title of the registered land and it will be so entered electronically (s 93 of the LRA 2002). This necessarily has the consequence that there will eventually be no scope for the rule that a legal mortgage by charge takes effect in equity pending its registration, although this will be the case until full electronic conveyancing arrives (s 27 of the LRA 2002). Thus, under the new scheme, there will be no opportunity for the mortgagee to be bound by rights created later to its own (the old 'registration gap'): either the mortgage will exist and be fully protected, or it will not.

10.7 Equitable mortgages

The above sections have discussed the creation of mortgages where the borrower owns a legal estate in the land and it is this which is mortgaged formally in return for a loan. The result is a legal mortgage. By way of contrast, it is perfectly possible to create equitable mortgages of land and these may arise in a variety of circumstances. In simple terms, a mortgage may be 'equitable' either because the borrower originally has only an equitable interest in the land, or because the borrower has a legal interest, but the mortgage is not executed with sufficient formality for the creation of a 'legal' interest (that is, no lease by deed or charge by deed).

10.7.1 Mortgages of equitable interests

It may well be that the potential mortgagor only has an equitable interest in the land, as where they are an equitable owner behind a trust of land (see Chapter 4 and, for example, *Banker's Trust v Namdar* (1997)), or have only an equitable lease (see Chapter 6). Necessarily, it follows that any mortgage of that equitable interest will, itself, be equitable: the mortgagor can mortgage only that which they own. The LPA 1925 has not affected this matter to any great extent and mortgages of equitable interests are still carried into effect by a conveyance of the whole of the mortgagor's equitable interest to the mortgagee. This will, of course, be accompanied by a provision for retransfer of the equitable interest when the loan is repaid (*William Brandt v Dunlop Rubber* (1905)). Importantly, given that a mortgage of an equitable interest is achieved through a transfer (disposition) of it to the mortgagee, certain formalities must be met. There is no need to use a deed, but because the mortgage will amount to a 'disposition of a subsisting equitable interest' (that is, that of the mortgagor), it must comply with s 53(1)(c) of the LPA 1925. This requires the mortgage of the equitable interest to be in writing, on penalty of voidness. We might also note that, should it be possible for 'written' instruments to be created electronically (as is anticipated), an electronic 'written' instrument creating an equitable mortgage will be as effective as its paper counterpart.

10.7.2 'Informal' mortgages of legal interests

As we have noted above, currently a legal mortgage of a freehold or leasehold can be accomplished by either the grant of a legal lease/sublease, or the execution of a charge. In both cases, a deed will be used, and this is an essential element if the mortgage is to be legal in quality. It is perfectly possible, however, for the mortgagor and mortgagee to create a mortgage of a legal interest by 'informal' means, in other words, not using a deed. Such mortgages will necessarily be equitable in character as not complying with the formality necessary for the creation of legal interests.

As with many other equitable interests in land, an informal mortgage usually springs from a contract between the mortgagor and mortgagee, whereby each becomes committed by contract to proceed to create a legal mortgage. If this contract is not actually carried out (that is, the legal mortgage by deed is not executed), and the contract is capable of specific performance, the parties will be treated as having created an equitable mortgage in very similar fashion to the creation of equitable leases in *Walsh v Lonsdale* (1882). It is vital for the successful creation of this informal mortgage that the contract be in writing under s 2 of the Law of Property (Miscellaneous Provisions) Act (LP (Misc Prov) A) 1989 (or valid as an electronic contract when applicable (the intended s 2A of the LP (Misc Prov) A 1989)) and also be capable of specific performance. The latter condition is usually met in the case of contracts concerning land, given the inadequacy of damages for such a unique asset. If the requirements of a written contract and specific performance are met, the contract to grant the mortgage will be treated in itself as an equitable mortgage (*Parker v Housefield* (1834)), although, usually, the money will have to have been advanced already before equity will intervene in this manner.

10.7.3 Mortgages by deposit of title deeds

Prior to the 1989 Law of Property (Miscellaneous Provisions) Act, it was also possible to create an equitable mortgage by deposit of the title deeds of the property with the mortgagee. The deposit of the mortgagor's title deeds was treated as both evidence of a contract (as above) and 'part performance' of that contract under the then operative s 40 of the LPA 1925 (*Re Wallis* (1974)). This was, of course, a very informal but relatively efficient way of creating a mortgage, and the mortgagee was protected because it held the documents of title, so preventing the mortgagor from further dealing with the land. After

1989, however, contracts for the disposition of any interest in land (that is, to create a mortgage) must be in writing and this cannot be presumed to exist from the deposit of title deeds. Although there is evidence to suggest that the enactment of s 2 of the 1989 Act was not intended to do away with this informal method of creating equitable mortgages, the Court of Appeal in *United Bank of Kuwait v Sahib* (1996) has now confirmed that deposit of title deeds is an attempt to create a mortgage by unwritten contract and is, therefore, void. No such mortgage can be created. This is unfortunate and makes matters much less convenient for both borrower and lender – especially for short term loans – but at least it is consistent with the policy behind the 1989 Act of bringing more formality to dealings with interests in land. It is, perhaps, just possible that a court would be prepared to regard the deposit of title deeds *not* as an unwritten and void contract, but rather, as an assurance by the mortgagor to the mortgagee, which, if relied on by the mortgagor (say, by the payment of moneys by the mortgagee to the mortgagor) could generate an estoppel mortgage. As we know from *Taylor Fashions v Liverpool Victoria Trustees* (1982), if one person promises an interest in land to another, and that is relied upon to their detriment, equity will enforce the promise and give effect to the claim of the promisee (Chapter 9). So, if a lender has actually advanced money on the basis of a promise (represented by the deposit of title deeds), it is arguable that the mortgage will be enforced despite the absence of any formality. So far, this argument has not been tested in the courts and although it is unwise to make predictions, it may well be that the court would only enforce such a mortgage if there was real evidence of unconscionability on the part of one of the parties, rather than simply the absence of a written contract.

10.7.4 Equitable charges

Finally, mention must also be made of the equitable charge, a completely informal way of securing a loan over property. This requires no special form of words, only an intention to charge property with a debt (*National Provincial and Union Bank of England v Charnley* (1924)). Such a method is extremely precarious, and is rarely used for either commercial or residential mortgages.

10.7.5 A problem with equitable mortgages

An equitable mortgage suffers from the same vulnerability that affects all equitable rights in land, viz, it may be defeated by sale of the mortgaged land to a purchaser for value. Of course, if a valid mortgage has been created by a deposit of title deeds, the mortgagee is protected simply because no other dealings with the legal title can be made while the deeds are in the mortgagee's possession. If, however, the equitable mortgage is the second mortgage over property (the title documents being with the first mortgagee), or created differently (for example, by written contract), this *ad hoc* form of protection is not available. Therefore, in unregistered land, the equitable mortgage is registrable as a Class C(iii) land charge under the Land Charges Act 1972. If registered, it is binding on all subsequent transferees of the land over which the mortgage exists. In other words, the mortgagee will be able to exercise their rights against the land in priority to the new owner. If not so registered, the mortgage will be void against any purchaser for valuable consideration of a legal or equitable interest in the land. It will remain valid against someone who does not 'purchase' the land, such as the donee of a gift, devisee under a will or a squatter. Similarly, in registered land, the current position is that the land certificate is likely to be with the Registry, thus preventing any dealings with the registered title, and so protecting the second mortgage. In any event, the equitable mortgage may be registered against the title by means of a notice or caution and this is the surest form of protection. In those rare cases where an equitable mortgagee has entered into possession of registered land, they will be protected by means of an overriding interest within s 70(1)(g) of the LRA 1925.

Once again, however, the position in respect of registered land when the LRA 2002 comes into force is likely to be different. Pending operation of the full system of electronic conveyancing, equitable mortgages will still require substantive protection and may still amount to interests which override a registered proprietor if the equitable mortgagee is in actual occupation of the relevant land within the meaning of 'actual occupation' under Scheds 1 and 3 to the LRA 2002. Likewise, the equitable mortgage might be protected by an entry of a notice against the registered title in much the same way as minor interests are currently protected by notice or caution (this new 'notice' will replace notices and cautions for minor interests under the LRA 1925). However, when full electronic conveyancing is in force, the equitable mortgage of registered land is likely to be one of those interests specified under s 93(1)(b) of the LRA 2002 that will not exist at all unless it is entered electronically on the register of title. The equitable mortgages existence will thus coincide with its protection.

10.8 The rights of the mortgagor: the equity of redemption

The dual nature of a mortgage – as a contract and as an interest in land – means that the mortgagor has rights arising under the contract of loan as well as benefiting from the protection which a court of equity offers a mortgagor due to the proprietary interest they retain in their property.

10.8.1 The contractual right to redeem

As a matter of contract, the mortgagor has a contractual right to redeem the mortgage on the date specified in the mortgage contract. This is the legal date for redemption. This is often six months from the date of execution of the mortgage (or later, if instalment terms are agreed), although it may be any date specified by the parties (subject to the 'clogs and fetters' rules discussed below, 10.8.3). Obviously, it is rare for a mortgagor to redeem on this date, and due to the intervention of equity, he has the right to redeem on any later date on the payment of the principal debt, interest and costs. This right to redeem beyond the date fixed by the contract is known as the equitable right to redeem. The relevance of the passing of the contractual date for redemption is, however, that this can trigger the availability of the mortgagee's remedies under the mortgage.

10.8.2 The equitable right to redeem

At one time, if the mortgagor did not redeem on the legal date for redemption, the property was lost to the mortgagor. A few days, or even hours late, entitled the mortgagee to keep the property even if its value was far greater than the loan secured on it. Obviously, here was great opportunity for abuse and unfairness. In consequence, the court of equity, acting under the maxim 'once a mortgage, always a mortgage', would allow redemption of the mortgage after this date (*Thornborough v Baker* (1675)). This became known as the equitable right to redeem. The equitable right to redeem was the epitome of the property lawyer's approach to a mortgage: viz, that a mortgage was a security for a loan, not an opportunity for the mortgagee to obtain the mortgagor's property or impose any other burden upon him. It meant, in effect, that payment of principal, interest and costs even after the contractual date for redemption would free the land of the mortgage.

10.8.3 The equity of redemption

The equitable right to redeem the property at any time after the legal date for redemption has passed is certainly one of the most valuable rights which the mortgagor has. In fact, however, the intervention of equity is more robust than this. In this sense, the equitable right to redeem is just part of the wider rights that a mortgagor has under the mortgage, and these wider rights are collectively known as 'the equity of redemption'. The equity of redemption represents the sum total of the mortgagor's rights in the land which is subject to the mortgage: in essence, it comprises the residual rights of ownership that the mortgagor has, both in virtue of their paramount legal estate in the land, and the protection that equity affords them (*Re Sir Thomas Spencer Wells* (1933)). Indeed, the equity of redemption is itself valuable, and is a proprietary right which may be sold or transferred in the normal way. It represents the mortgagor's right to the property (or its monetary equivalent) when the mortgage is discharged (redeemed) or the property sold, and its existence is the reason why second and third lenders are willing to grant further loans.

As noted above, equity regards the mortgage as a device for the raising a loan, secured on property, which can be redeemed once the debt is repaid. Fundamentally, a mortgage is not seen as an opportunity for the lender to acquire the mortgagor's property. For this reason, a court of equity will intervene to protect the mortgagor and their equity of redemption against encroachment by the mortgagee. This protection manifests itself in various ways.

The rule against irredeemability

It is a general principle that a mortgage cannot be made irredeemable: it is a security for a loan, not a conveyance, and the right to redeem cannot be limited *pro tanto* to certain people or certain periods of time (*Re Wells* (1933)). Thus, any provision whereby the mortgagor is said to forfeit his property on the expiry of the legal right to redeem is void, and any undue postponement or limitation on the mortgagor's right to redeem thereafter will not be enforceable (*Jones v Morgan* (2001)). However, this does not mean that the parties' hands are always tied, especially in cases of mortgages negotiated between commercial corporations at arm's length. Consequently, a provision postponing the date of redemption may be valid where the mortgage is not otherwise harsh and unconscionable, so long as the right to redeem is not made illusory (*Knightsbridge Estates v Byrne* (1940); *Fairclough v Swan Breweries* (1912)). For example, a provision in a mortgage of residential property that the borrowers cannot redeem for 20 years unless they pay an additional percentage (say 35%) as a 'redemption fee', could be void as tending towards irredeemability. A similar provision in a mortgage between Powerful Industries plc and MegaBank plc may not.

The mortgagee and attempts to purchase the mortgaged property

A provision in a mortgage contract which provides that the property shall become the mortgagee's, or which gives the mortgagee an option to purchase the property, is void and it need not be shown that the mortgage or the offending term is also unconscionable (*Samuel v Jarrah Timber* (1904); *Jones v Morgan* (2001)). Such a term is repugnant to the very nature of a mortgage. The rationale is, of course, that the mortgagor needs protection when negotiating for a loan, often being in a vulnerable position. The mortgagor should not be forced into a conveyance when he requires only a loan. Again, this protects the mortgagor, despite the apparent terms of their contract with the mortgagee. However, an option to purchase the property given to the mortgagee in a separate and independent transaction can be valid, providing it does not *de facto* form part of the mortgage itself (*Reeve v Lisle* (1902); *Jones v Morgan* (2001)). A mortgage is a mortgage, but separate agreements will be enforced in the normal way. Of course, there may be some doubt as to whether the option to purchase is truly a separate transaction, and its artificial divorce from the mortgage is not enough. So, in *Jones v Morgan* (2001) a clause in a document executed in 1997 whereby the lender became entitled to a 50%

share of the borrower's land, after the borrower had redeemed the mortgage, was held void and this was so even though the document was executed some three years later than the mortgage itself. The 1997 document was treated as a variation of the original mortgage, and as part of it, and so the clause was unenforceable as being repugnant to the very nature of a mortgage. It should also be noted, for the sake of clarity, that the rule prohibiting the giving of a right to purchase the land as a term of the mortgage does not prevent the mortgagee exercising its normal rights over the land in the event of the mortgagor's default on the loan, for example, its power of sale.

Unfettered redeemability: collateral advantages

As a matter of principle, the mortgagor should be able to redeem the mortgage and have the mortgagee's rights extinguished on the payment of the principal, interest and costs. There should be no other conditions attached to the right of redemption because a mortgage is merely the security for a loan which ends when its reason – the money – has been repaid. Consequently, on several occasions, a court has struck down 'collateral advantages' made in favour of a mortgagee, as where the mortgage contract stipulates that the mortgagor should fulfil some other obligation as a condition of the redeemability or continuation of the mortgage. An example is where the mortgagor promises to buy all his supplies from the mortgagee, or to give the mortgagee some other preferential treatment. Typical cases would be brewery/mortgagees requiring pub landlords/mortgagors to take only the brewery's beer, or similar arrangements between oil companies and the owners of petrol stations. At one time, such collateral advantages were uniformly struck down as being a 'clog' or 'fetter' on the equity of redemption (*Bradley v Carrit* (1903)). They were seen as striking at the essence of the mortgage as only security for a loan. However, it is now clear that there is no objection to a collateral advantage which ceases when the mortgage is redeemed (*Santley v Wilde* (1899)). This is a matter of contract between the parties, and provided that the terms of the collateral advantage are not unconscionable, or do not, in fact, restrict the right to redeem, they will be valid (*Biggs v Hoddinot* (1898)). This is a fair outcome given the reality of many mortgage transactions which are more in the nature of a comprehensive tie up between mortgagor and mortgagee than simply about a loan. Indeed, with commercial mortgages made between equal parties at arm's length, *Kregliner v New Patagonia Meat Co* (1914) suggests that a collateral advantage which *does* continue after redemption (for example, a continuing obligation to take supplies from the mortgagee even though the mortgage has ended) may be acceptable, so long as the mortgagor's land returns to them in the same form that it was mortgaged. It seems that such commercial arrangements are acceptable, because they neither restrict the former mortgagor's use of the land as such, nor hinder the redeemability of the mortgage. They are truly 'collateral' and, therefore, not objectionable. Finally, it is obvious that this is one area where the 'contractual' nature of a mortgage may be in conflict with its 'proprietary' nature. As we have been discussing, the extent to which the parties to a mortgage should be able to modify the essential nature of a mortgage and provide additional benefits to the mortgagee is a matter for argument. Does it matter if the parties are commercial organisations, and should the same considerations apply to residential mortgages? How far may the parties to a mortgage – especially those with whole batteries of legal advisers and accountants – be permitted to change the essential nature of a mortgage from a security for a loan to something outside the realm of property law altogether?

Unconscionable terms and unreasonable interest rates

It is also clear that a court has the power to strike down any term of a mortgage – or indeed the whole mortgage – where it is the result of an unconscionable bargain and irrespective of whether it also amounts to a clog or fetter on the equity of redemption. The basic proposition is that found in the judgment of Browne-Wilkinson J in *Multiservice Bookbinding Ltd v Marden* (1979) to the effect that a term will be unconscionable (and hence unenforceable) where it is in substance objectionable and has been imposed by one party on the other in a morally reprehensible manner, being in a manner that affects his conscience. This means, in essence, that there must be some impropriety both in the substantive term and the conduct of the party imposing the term and which taken together 'shocks the conscience of the court'. An example is an interest rate at such a high level that it renders the equity of redemption valueless (*Cityland Properties v Dabrah* (1968)). However, in exercising this jurisdiction the court is not concerned with alleviating a mortgagor from the consequences of a bad bargain, especially if they have had the benefit of legal advice (*Jones v Morgan* (2001)). That is the mortgagor's own affair and a bad bargain, or hard terms, does not necessarily make an unconscionable mortgage.

In similar vein, it also seems from *Nash v Paragon Finance* (2001) that a mortgagee – at least a commercial mortgagee – is under an implied contractual obligation (a 'limited duty') not to set interest rates dishonestly, for an improper purpose, capriciously or arbitrarily and not in a manner that no reasonable mortgage lender would countenance (so called '*Wednesbury* unreasonableness'). However, with due respect to the Court of Appeal in *Nash*, it is not immediately clear where such a wide principle comes from, even though Paragon did not fall foul of it in this case. A commercial mortgagee is not in any sense a public authority (for *Wednesbury* unreasonableness) and the court gives little authority for the proposition that these implied terms can be imported into the mortgage contract. Consequently, it remains to be seen whether the courts run with this idea. If they do, the 'implied term' argument will add another string to the bow of the mortgagor in trouble.

10.8.4 Undue influence

In recent years, there have been many cases where a mortgagor has claimed that the mortgage is void (that is, unenforceable against them in whole or in part) because of 'undue influence'. In general terms, a mortgage may be struck down on the ground that it was obtained by the undue influence of the mortgagee directly, or by the undue influence of a third party dealing with the mortgagee (for example, a husband inducing his wife to sign a mortgage over the jointly owned matrimonial home: *Castle Phillips Finance v Pinnington* (1995)). In either case, the mortgagor or guarantor of the mortgagor who is released from the mortgage may be required to repay part of the sums lent if she derived some material benefit from it (*Allied Irish Bank v Byrne* (1995)). We should note, however, that the law in this area has undergone several transformations in recent years, not all of which are consistent with each other or earlier authority. However, the following is an attempt to highlight the basic principles of undue influence *after* the House of Lords' decisions in *Barclays Bank v O'Brien* (1992); *CIBC Mortgages plc v Pitt* (1993); and *Royal Bank of Scotland v Etridge (No 2)* (2001).

A mortgage will be set aside for undue influence when either there is 'actual undue influence' or 'presumed undue influence'. Actual undue influence arises where the claimant (that is, the mortgagor) proves affirmatively that undue influence has been exerted. This will be established from the facts of the case, ranging from a husband standing over his wife with a shotgun threatening her unless she consents to the mortgage, to a woman threatening to leave her lover unless he signs. The possibilities are endless. However, the influence must be both 'actual' and 'undue'. Persuasion after full explanation of what was involved is not undue, even though the influence may have been actual (in the sense of causative of the consent). Walking, eyes wide open, into a bad bargain, having made an informed choice, is unfortunate, but it is not the result of undue influence (a point strongly made by Scott VC, in the context of presumed undue influence, in *Banco Exterior Internacional v Thomas* (1997) and see also *Bank of Scotland v Bennett* (1998)). However, as *Steeples v Lea* (1998) illustrates, it is the *consent* of the claimant that must be given freely. So, being aware of the nature of a mortgage, after having received advice as to its effect, does not mean an absence of undue influence if the claimant can prove that she was not making a 'free' choice at the time. Note, however, that if 'actual' undue influence is proved, it is not necessary for the 'victim' (that is, the mortgagor or guarantor seeking to avoid the mortgage because they have been unduly influenced) to establish that the transaction was to their 'manifest disadvantage' (*O'Brien*), meaning a transaction obviously not to their benefit. It is enough in such cases that the victim was persuaded to enter into a transaction that they would not otherwise have entered into.

By way of contrast, presumed undue influence arises where the relationship between the mortgagee (or someone dealing with the mortgagee, for example, the claimant's husband) and the mortgagor is one of trust and confidence, so making it likely that unacceptable influence has been exerted. Following *Barclays Bank v O'Brien* (1992), presumed undue influence cases were subdivided into Class 2A and Class 2B type cases. Class 2A cases were where the relationship between persons was of such a nature that the presumption existed independently of the facts of the case. Typical examples are the relationships of doctor/patient, solicitor/client and parent/child (see, for example, *Langton v Langton* (1995)). These class A cases are rare in mortgage transactions, not least because doctors and solicitors do not normally lend money to patients or clients and rarely go into business with them. Note also, the relationship of bank/customer and husband/wife are not relationships where the presumption arises *pro tanto*. On the other hand, Class 2B cases of presumed undue influence were where, although the relationship *per se* was not one of the 'special' cases, nevertheless, the substance of the relationship between the parties was such that one person placed so much confidence in the other that the presumption of undue influence should arise. Clearly, husband/wife or lover/lover could fall within this class, as might employer/employee (*Steeples v Lea* (1997)).

In fact, the difference between Class 2A 'presumed' cases and Class 2B 'presumed' cases recently has been explored again by the House of Lords in *Royal Bank of Scotland v Etridge (No 2)* (1998) and this long and impressive judgment sheds much light on the issue. As is made clear in *Etridge*, if the case is not one of actual undue influence, it is true that undue influence may be 'presumed'. However, this presumption is properly to be regarded as an evidentiary presumption that simply shifts the burden of proof from the victim to the alleged wrongdoer (the influencer). Thus, successful reliance on the presumption of undue influence does not mean that undue influence exists, but rather that the burden of explaining why the impugned transaction was not caused by undue influence will pass to the alleged wrongdoer. The alleged wrongdoer may still dispel any whiff of undue influence by producing evidence as to the propriety of the transaction. Importantly, when viewed in this light, *Etridge* makes it clear that there is no real merit in adopting the *O'Brien* categories of 'Class 2A' and 'Class 2B' presumed undue influence. There are some relationships, such as parent/child and doctor/patient (the old 'Class 2A' cases), which necessarily and irrebuttably establish a relationship of trust and confidence and, if the transaction called for an explanation (was 'manifestly disadvantageous'), this shifts the burden of proof to the alleged wrongdoer to explain the transaction. Failure to do so necessarily leads to a finding of undue influence. There are other cases where the claimant can demonstrate on the evidence that a relationship was one of trust and confidence (the old 'Class 2B' cases) and, if the transaction called for an explanation (was 'manifestly disadvantageous'), this then shifts the burden of proof to the alleged wrongdoer to explain the transaction. Consequently, two things are now clear. First, that the 'presumption' of undue influence is no more than a tool to explain the shift of the evidentiary burden from the claimant and so 'manifest disadvantage' is necessary as it explains why the burden should shift. The 'presumption' is not that undue influence exists, but that it will exist if the wrongdoer cannot explain the transaction (that is, discharge the burden of proof). Thus, as noted above, manifest disadvantage (meaning a transaction which needs explaining) is not needed in 'actual undue influence' cases, because the claimant has already established undue influence on the facts. Secondly, the difference between the now defunct Class 2A and Class 2B cases is simply that in the former the fact of trust and confidence could not be disputed by the wrongdoer, whereas in the second it could. So, in the second type of case, the wrongdoer could adduce evidence to show that no such relationship existed and hence avoid even having to explain away the transaction. In the former case, a disadvantageous transaction always needs an explanation.

Although this seems complicated, *Etridge* has made the matter rather straightforward, and certainly more straightforward than was the case under the *O'Brien* approach. In cases of actual undue influence, any transaction (advantageous or not) can be attacked if the victim has shown by positive proof that they have been unfairly persuaded to enter a mortgage. In cases of a successful plea of presumed undue influence, only transactions which are 'manifestly disadvantageous' to the victim can be impugned (being transactions which on their face appear not to be for the benefit of the victim), because it is the existence of this disadvantage which, if not explained away, permits the court to infer that undue influence has occurred.

With this matter now clarified by *Etridge*, we must consider the circumstances in which a mortgage actually can be avoided as a result of proven actual or presumed undue influence. In reality, there are few cases where the mortgagee itself exerts the undue influence over the victim and the usual scenario (considered below) is that the victim claims first that they were unfairly induced to enter the mortgage by another person (usually the victim's domestic or business partner who co-owns the property and who is pressing for the mortgage) and secondly that this undue influence taints the mortgagee. According to *O'Brien*, there are two sets of circumstances where a mortgagee will not be able to enforce the mortgage against the victim, even though the mortgagee itself has not exercised undue influence:

(a) where the real inducer (the husband/wife, lover, etc) was acting, in a real sense, as agent of the mortgagee. This is quite unlikely in the majority of cases; or

(b) where the mortgagee has actual or constructive notice of the inducer's unfair conduct, and has not taken steps to ensure that the claimant has been independently advised. Moreover, a mortgagee will be deemed to have notice of the unfair conduct (and therefore risk losing the security unless they have offered independent advice) when the transaction is *prima facie* not to the advantage of the mortgagor, and the transaction itself is of such a kind that there is a substantial risk that undue influence may have been exerted. Such a risk, and therefore notice to the mortgagee, will be present when a person signs a mortgage as guarantor (surety) for the debts of their domestic partner (*O'Brien*), although such a risk may not be present, and therefore no notice to the mortgagee, when a person signs a mortgage as joint mortgagor for a loan made to the mortgagors jointly for their joint benefit (*Pitt*). In the end, however, as explained in *O'Brien*, the existence or absence of such notice very greatly depended on the particular facts and, following *Barclays Bank v Boulter* (1997), it was clear that the burden is on the mortgagee to prove that it is not tainted by the undue influence (or misrepresentation) of the actual inducer. So, the claimant may raise undue influence as a defence to an action on the mortgage instigated by the mortgagee, and the burden of proof then shifts to the lender.

As expected after *O'Brien* and *Pitt*, there was a wave of claims of 'undue influence' by mortgagors/guarantors/sureties facing repossession of their property or a demand for payment of moneys owed. Unfortunately, a consistent approach was not possible and two powerful difficulties emerged:

(a) if the mortgagee is to avoid being fixed with another person's undue influence (for example, that of the husband/wife, lover, etc), the mortgagee must ensure that the mortgagor is 'independently advised'. Does this mean advised independently from their partner (the undue influencer), independently of the mortgagee, or both? Some cases suggested that the mortgagee escaped liability by ensuring that the claimant was advised by someone other than its own staff (*Midland Bank v Massey* (1995); *Banco Exterior Internacional v Mann* (1995); *Scottish Equitable Life v Virdee* (1998)), and, conversely, did not escape when the adviser was closely linked with the mortgagee (*Byrne*), although the mortgagee did not seem to incur liability simply because the solicitor acted for both parties (*Bank of Scotland v Bennett* (1998)). Other cases, on the other hand, suggested that such advice must also be given independently from that given to the wrongdoer (*TSB v Camfield* (1995));

(b) if the mortgagee must take steps to see that the claimant has been independently advised, what steps are sufficient? Can the mortgagee avoid its potential liability by merely recommending the mortgagor to take independent advice? *Crédit Lyonnais Bank v Burch* (1997) (*contra* to the tenor of *Massey*) suggested that merely advising the claimant to seek advice may not be sufficient if the claimant did not then seek or receive such advice. Does this mean that the claimant must be led like a horse to water to a solicitor's office and be 'made' to listen? Again, *Dunbar* and *Midland Bank v*

Kidwai (1995) made it clear that, having received advice, the mortgagee is not tainted if the claimant then chose to ignore it. So why cannot a claimant legitimately choose to ignore the advice to seek advice?! May the mortgagee avoid liability by relying on a solicitor's certificate that the claimant has been given advice – even if this is not true? *Mann* suggests that reliance may be placed on a solicitor's certificate that independent advice has been given, even if this is not the case. *Camfield* suggests that the mortgagee may not avoid liability if, in fact, no proper advice has been given, even if the mortgagee was misled by a solicitor's certificate into believing that it had been. Again, in *Bank of Baroda v Rayarel* (1995), in a case of presumed undue influence, the mortgagee was held to be entitled to rely on a certificate that independent advice had been given by a solicitor who was independent of the bank and this appeared to be becoming the norm: *Virdee*.

Clearly, this was an unsatisfactory state of affairs and it became apparent that *O'Brien* had failed in its attempt to clarify the law. In fact, there was a litigation industry. Indeed, after *O'Brien* there were still many cases going to the Court of Appeal, not all taking a consistent approach to the problem, and in consequence, there was considerable uncertainty among lenders and borrowers alike. It was thus no real surprise when the House of Lords reconsidered the issue in *Etridge* (and seven other co-joined appeals). In that case, if any reminder was needed, Lord Bingham, leading the House, put the matter succinctly and his words bear repetition and need no elaboration:

> The transactions which give rise to these appeals are commonplace but of great social and economic importance. It is important that a wife (or anyone in a like position) should not charge her interest in the matrimonial home to secure the borrowing of her husband (or anyone in a like position) without fully understanding the nature and effect of the proposed transaction and that the decision is hers, to agree or not to agree. It is important that lenders should feel able to advance money ... on the security of the wife's interest in the matrimonial home in reasonable confidence that, if appropriate procedures have been followed in obtaining the security, it will be enforceable if the need for enforcement arises. The law must afford both parties a measure of protection ... The paramount need in this important field is that these minimum requirements should be clear, simple and practically operable.

Similarly, Lord Nicholls (in the pre-eminent judgment) noted that couples should not be restricted in using the matrimonial home to raise finance for business or any other purposes, and that over 95% of all business in the UK, responsible for nearly one third of all employment, were small businesses for whom this method of raising finance was essential. Consequently, the law should be as clear as possible and he then set out to state the law.

First, it is necessary to prove actual or presumed undue influence by the 'wrongdoer' over the claimant. This has been discussed above. Secondly, we must determine whether the mortgagee is put on inquiry as to the existence of the undue influence: in other words, assuming no agency, does the lender have notice of the undue influence so as to put its mortgage at risk? In this connection, the first point is that the House makes it crystal clear that 'notice' does not mean that the lender is in some way being bound by a proprietary right of the claimant. This is not property law notice of some equitable interest. Rather, it is a loose description of the idea that the lender can be affected by undue influence in certain circumstances and that, if so affected, it must take steps to prevent its mortgage being tainted (confirming *Barclays Bank v Boulter* (1997)). More importantly perhaps, the House then adopts a robust and blunt approach to the question of when such 'notice' exists. Recognising that there are difficulties, and that its approach is 'broad brush' rather than precisely analytical, the solution is that a lender will always be put on inquiry if a person is standing surety for another's debts, providing that such surety is not offered as a commercial service (that is, the guarantor is not charging for the service, as would a bank or other institution). This is both clear and an extension of existing law (that is, there is always 'notice' when one person is a non-commercial surety for another) and it has the great merit of ensuring that lenders do not have to probe the relationship of the parties in order to assess whether they are on notice. Thus, it is not the relationship between the parties that triggers the 'notice', but rather the very nature of the transaction irrespective of the relationship. The principle is thus not relationship specific and may apply equally to married and unmarried couples, same sex couples or persons in no emotional relationship at all. If, however, the loan is made to the parties jointly for their joint purposes (that is, the claimant is not merely guaranteeing the wrongdoer's borrowing but is also taking a benefit from the mortgages: for example, it is for a company jointly owned by the parties), then the lender is not put on inquiry unless it is aware that in reality the money is for the wrongdoer's purposes alone. One might add here, that possibly this should mean 'aware or ought to be aware' that it was in reality for the wrongdoer's purposes alone. Thirdly, there remains the question of what the mortgagee must do in order to avoid being tainted by the undue influence of which it has notice, for failure to take appropriate steps could result in the loss of its security.

Indeed, it is this aspect of the *Etridge* decision that is of the greatest practical importance. Lenders are not in the business of taking chances so, undue influence or not, they will adjust their lending practices just in case there is the possibility of the transaction being attacked. In fact, it seems that the judgment in *Etridge* is not principally concerned with preventing the occurrence of undue influence over a claimant at all, but rather identifying what a lender must do to avoid being tainted by it if such influence occurs. Fortunately (although it is not accidental) the steps which a lender must now take are such that the chances of undue influence occurring will be much reduced, but it is important to appreciate that the primary purpose of these steps is protect the bank, not to stop the undue influence. Thus, for past cases

– that is mortgages executed prior to the *Etridge* decision – the lender must take steps to ensure that the wife understands the risk she is running and should advise her to seek independent advice. For future cases – that is mortgages executed post-*Etridge* – the lender must insist that the wife attend a private meeting with the lender at which she is told of the extent of her liability, warned of the risk she is running and urged to take independent legal advice.

How this will operate in practice for 'past cases' will still be attended with some doubt, although it seems that it is not the lender's responsibility to see that no undue influence has been exercised, nor necessary that it seeks confirmation from a solicitor that no such influence exists (as opposed to confirmation that advice has been given). This is because the solicitor will be acting for the claimant and the lender can expect the solicitor to act properly for his or her client. Consequently, if a solicitor gives inadequate advice, the lender is not affected, provided the lender does not know (or ought to have known) that no advice was received or that it was inadequate. After all, the claimant can sue the solicitor. In reality then, the past practice of relying on solicitor's certificates will suffice, unless the lender knows or ought to have known that the claimant was not thereby properly warned of the nature of the transaction or of the risks it posed. In this sense, *National Westminster Bank v Breeds* (2001) is rightly decided as the lender should have known that the advice given to the claimant was defective despite receiving a certificate from the advising solicitor. Likewise, in *National Westminster Bank v Amin* (2002), a decision on a pre-*Etridge* claim, the House of Lords sent a case back for retrial on the basis that the Bank might have known that the solicitor had not given appropriate advice (for example, the Bank knew that the mortgagors could not speak English and the solicitor could not speak Urdu) and that it was not clear in any event whether the solicitor was acting for the mortgagors or for the Bank when giving advice.

For future transactions, the House in *Etridge* laid down what will almost certainly become a code of conduct for lenders. First, the lender should check directly with the claimant for the name of the solicitor who is acting for her or him, advising that it will seek written confirmation that advice about the proposed transaction has been given. The claimant should be told that this is because the lender does not intend that the claimant should be able to dispute the mortgage later. The claimant should also be told that she may (but not must) use a different solicitor from that which her partner uses. The lender must await a response from the claimant before it proceeds. Secondly, the lender should provide the advising solicitor with all the necessary financial information required for the solicitor to give proper advice: for example, level of total indebtedness of the husband, copy of the application form etc. This usually will require the consent of the other party failing which the mortgage is unlikely to go ahead. Thirdly, the lender must inform the solicitor of any concerns it has over the genuineness of the claimant's consent or understanding. Fourthly, the lender should obtain written confirmation that all these steps have been complied with and that appropriate advice has been given. If such steps are taken, the lender will be protected (as may well be the claimant) subject only to any defects in the role of the solicitor that the lender knew of, or ought to have known of.

We can but hope that *Etridge* will provide the certainty that the House of Lords anticipate. Undoubtedly, it will force a change in lending practices, but this will soon be absorbed into the administrative practices of the competent lending institutions. Of course, some lenders will fail to observe the new procedures and they are likely to get short shrift from the courts. After all, it is not that difficult to understand what must be done. As for the law, we now know or have had confirmed that the 'presumption' of undue influence is really a presumption that reverses the burden of proof and is not a presumption that such influence really exists. Hence it can be met with an explanation of why the transaction is undue influence free. We also know that 'manifest disadvantage' in the weak sense of a transaction which on its face needs explaining is still an element in 'presumed' cases because it (merely) helps prove the presumption to reverse the burden of proof; that the Class 2A and 2B dichotomy in presumed cases is not helpful; that 'notice' does not really mean property law notice; that a lender will always be on inquiry ('have notice') in non-commercial surety cases; that in other cases, the lender will be on inquiry only in exceptional cases because it is entitled to assume that a person knows what he or she is doing when the loan is for their own benefit; that for past cases, reliance on a solicitor's certificate will normally protect a lender; that for future cases, the steps a lender must take are greater than before, but not onerous and may both protect the lender and prevent any undue influence from arising in the first place; and finally, that a lender can never be protected when it knows, or ought to know, that the claimant has not received the guidance and counsel he or she needed to judge the appropriateness of the transaction. Of course, we also know that in reality *Etridge* has shifted the risk. The risk of being sued by a claimant because of undue influence can now be deflected by a bank on to the shoulders of the solicitor that advises the potential victim. Failure to give advice, or the giving of negligent advice, will no longer result in the mortgagee losing its security. However, it may well result in the solicitor being sued by the victim. Will this be a risk that solicitors are prepared to take and how much will they charge for the privilege?

Finally, we must consider the effect of a successful plea of undue influence on the mortgagee. For example, is the mortgagee's entire security voided (*Camfield*; *Pinnington*), or is it voided only to the extent that the undue influence was operative, as where the claimant genuinely agreed to a mortgage of £X, but in fact signed a mortgage for £X+Y. In *Barclays Bank v Caplan* (1998), the court held that, if a claimant could establish that only part of the mortgage transaction was void for undue influence, that void part could be severed, with the balance of the mortgage remaining valid. This might arise, for example, where the original mortgage was validly consented to, but a 'top up' sum was secured from the mortgagee only after undue influence. It is submitted that this is, indeed, the correct approach. The purpose of the undue influence rule is to ensure that mortgagors enter mortgages freely; it is not to give them a windfall by voiding an entire mortgage if only part is tainted by undue influence. Another way of apparently achieving the same result is to void the entire mortgage on condition that the claimant give credit to the mortgagee (that is, pay them) for any sums advanced that resulted in a benefit to that claimant (*Byrne*). However, although this seems attractive, in fact there is no necessary correlation between the extent of the undue influence and the benefit received by the victim. To put it differently, should the victim be made to account for a benefit they may not have wanted, and which was given in a transaction already held to have been procured by undue influence? Seen in this light, whether the claimant secured a benefit or not is *not* the real issue. The better view is that, either the entire mortgage is void for undue influence, or it remains valid in part to the extent of the borrowing to which the claimant really did consent.

10.8.5 Extortionate credit bargains

As noted above, mortgages are also contracts for the provision of credit. As such, they are subject to statutory controls similarly imposed on other types of credit relationships, that are designed to protect an impecunious borrower from the unfair practices of unscrupulous lenders. Thus a mortgage may fall within the provisions of the Consumer Credit Act 1974 as a regulated credit agreement. However, it is unusual for a mortgage to be regulated in this fashion, not least because the Consumer Credit Act 1974 applies only to those agreements where the credit offered by a company does not exceed £25,000. (There is no upper limit where the mortgagee is an individual, but this is rare for mortgages of land.) Again, mortgages offered by building societies fall within the category of 'exempt agreements', and are outside these provisions of the Act altogether, although mortgages by banks are within it. The practical effect of these provisions is that most mortgages caught by the main provisions of the Consumer Credit Act 1974 will be for small sums, usually with banks: a typical example being a second mortgage for, say, an extension or double glazing. Mortgages subject in this way to the Act may not be enforced without a court order. However, it is possible for any mortgage to be set aside, or its terms adjusted, if it is found to be an 'extortionate credit bargain' within the meaning of ss 137–40 of the Consumer Credit Act 1974, whether or not the mortgage is also a regulated credit agreement. Nevertheless, as *A Ketley Ltd v Scott* (1980) illustrates, the power to vary or void such mortgages under the Consumer Credit Act 1974 (that is, to interfere in the bargain struck by the parties) will be used sparingly, and only in the clearest cases of abuse of a dominant position by a lender. An example is *Equity Home Loans v Lewis* (1995), where the court held that the facts 'were extreme and the loan must have bordered on the extortionate'. Likewise, in *Falco Finance v Gough* (1999), the terms of the mortgage were so severe as to fall foul of s 138 of the Act. Although as *Nash v Paragon Finance* (2001) illustrates, whether a mortgage is extortionate within these provisions can be judged only by reference to the 'total charge for credit' as determined at the start of the mortgage. Consequently, a mortgage cannot become 'extortionate' merely because at some time after its commencement, the lender legitimately varies the interest rate so that the charge for credit becomes greater.

10.8.6 Restraint of trade

A mortgage which attempts to tie a mortgagor to a particular company or mortgagee may well fall foul of the contractual rules prohibiting contracts in restraint of trade. Typical examples include brewery mortgagees using the mortgage to tie the pub landlord to them as sole supplier of beer and oil company mortgagees using the mortgage to tie in the owner of a petrol station (see, for example, *Esso Petroleum v Harpers Garage* (1968)). However, once again, the unwillingness of the courts to interfere unduly with contractual relationships must be remembered, and in the same way that the courts have become more relaxed about collateral advantages, so these 'solus' agreements are less likely to be disturbed.

10.8.7 Powers of the mortgagor

As well as benefiting from the protective mechanisms outlined above, the mortgagor also has certain powers and rights under the mortgage or by statute. In outline, these are:

(a) the power to redeem the mortgage, which may be enforced by action in the courts (s 91 of the LPA 1925);

(b) the power to lease the property for certain limited purposes and the power to accept surrenders of existing leases (s 99 of the LPA 1925), but not contrary to the terms of the mortgage (*Leeds Permanent Building Society v Famini* (1998));

(c) the power to claim possession where this is not claimed by the mortgagee (s 98 of the LPA 1925);

(d) under s 91(1) and (2) of the LPA 1925, the mortgagor may apply to the court for an order for sale of the property, and this may be granted, even if the mortgagee disagrees. The court's discretion to order sale under this section is now thought to comprise a power to order sale even if the proceeds of sale will not pay off the mortgage debt (*Palk v Mortgage*

Services (1993)), and possibly even if the mortgagee is seeking possession of the property because of the mortgagor's inability to pay any sums due, although this is now doubted by *Cheltenham and Gloucester plc v Krausz* (1997) and *Scottish & Newcastle v Billy Row Working Men's Club* (2000) (and see below, 10.9.3). This right to ask the court for sale, and to have it granted against the wishes of the mortgagee, is particularly valuable to a mortgagor whose debt is increasing because of his inability to meet interest payments. Sale in such circumstances stops the debt increasing further, and the mortgagor remains liable only for outstanding sums. It is a power to be used sparingly, because of the effect on the mortgagee (*Cheltenham and Gloucester v Pearn* (1998)).

10.9 The rights of the mortgagee under a legal mortgage: remedies for default

A mortgage is as valuable to a mortgagee as it is to a mortgagor. Obviously, the main benefit is that a rate of interest can be charged for the money lent, and an income is generated for the mortgagee on the security of what is, in all but the most severe economic conditions, an asset that is going to appreciate in value. However, just as the property owner uses the mortgage to liquidate his assets, the mortgagee uses the mortgage to capitalise his income. As is apparent from all that has gone before, the essential characteristic of a mortgage is that it is security for money lent, and the ultimate goal of any mortgagee will be to recover payment of the principal debt, plus interest and related costs. As we shall see, this can be achieved in a number of ways, some of which spring from the nature of a mortgage as a contract, and some of which spring from the fact that the mortgagee has a proprietary interest in the land. Note, in this respect, a mortgagee under a mortgage created by 'a charge by deed expressed to be by way of legal mortgage', obtains the same powers and remedies as if the mortgage had been created by a long lease (*Regent Oil Co v Gregory* (1966); ss 85(1) and 87 of the LPA 1925). The particular remedy employed by the mortgagee will depend on the precise nature of the default of the mortgagor and the particular requirements of the mortgagee. So, some remedies are more suitable for the recovery of unpaid interest, while others are more suitable for recovery of the entire loan and the termination of the mortgage, or even the termination of the mortgagor's rights over the property.

10.9.1 An action on the contract for recovery of the debt

It is in the very nature of a mortgage as a contract of loan between the parties that the mortgagee has an action on the mortgagor's express contractual promise to repay the moneys owed. Such a contractual term forms part of every mortgage. In short, the mortgagor will promise to repay the sum due on a certain date plus accrued interest. This is the legal date of redemption (encapsulating the mortgagor's legal right to redeem) and as soon as this date has passed, the mortgagee has a personal action on the contract for repayment of the sum owed, unless the mortgagee has also promised to defer the remedy pending the payment of instalments. If the mortgagor fails to repay (or fails to pay a due instalment), the mortgagee can have the judgment debt satisfied in the normal way, including execution against the property of the mortgagor, whether comprised in the mortgage or not or by making the mortgagor bankrupt: *Alliance & Leicester v Slayford* (2001). It may seem surprising that the mortgagee has a remedy as soon as the legal date for redemption has passed, but this flows naturally from the mortgage as a contract, wherein each party has promised to fulfil certain obligations. Of course, in the normal course of events, the mortgagee will not sue for the money owed after such a short time, but will be happy to collect the outstanding interest. However, an action on the contract always remains a possibility, and may be used whenever the mortgagee wishes to recover the full amount of the debt, often in conjunction with other remedies. It is particularly useful if a sale of the mortgaged property (on which, see below, 10.9.2) fails to realise enough money to pay off the debt and the mortgagor has enough additional personal assets to meet their mortgage liability. Of course, being a personal remedy against the mortgagor (that is, not against the property), it is valueless if the mortgagor is bankrupt. On the other hand, being an action in debt (and not for breach of contract *per se*), the mortgagee is under *no* duty to mitigate its loss, and, therefore, cannot be compelled to exercise any of its other remedies (*Lloyds Bank v Bryant* (1996)). Moreover, it seems that the mortgagee has 12 years from the date of default in which to sue the mortgagor for this debt, rather than the usual six years on a 'normal' contract. This is because the right arises under a 'speciality' (that is, a deed) and so benefits from a longer limitation period than mere contractual debts. Although most lenders have voluntarily agreed that they will not enforce this claim beyond six years, it remains a valuable weapon and allows a mortgagee to return to a defaulting mortgagor many years after the property has been sold (assuming such sale did not pay off the entire debt).

10.9.2 The power of sale

Another remedy which is designed to recover the whole sum owed, and also thereby to terminate the mortgage, is the mortgagee's power of sale of the mortgaged property. In most cases, a mortgage will contain an express power of sale, but, if not, a power of sale will be implied into every mortgage made by deed by virtue of s 101(1)(i) of the LPA 1925, unless a contrary intention appears. Subject to any express provision in the mortgage itself, a mortgagee will be able to sell the mortgaged property and use the funds to satisfy the mortgage debt if two conditions are fulfilled.

The power of sale must have arisen

A mortgagee's power of sale will *arise* as soon as the legal (contractual) date for redemption has passed or, in the case of instalment mortgages, usually when one instalment is in arrears (*Twentieth Century Banking v Wilkinson* (1977)). Once again, this reflects the contractual nature of a mortgage and the liability of the mortgagor in debt when the stipulated date for redemption has passed.

The power of sale must have become exercisable

The mortgagee's power of sale becomes *exercisable* when the conditions specified in s 103 of the LPA 1925 are satisfied, either:

(a) notice requiring payment of the mortgage money has been served, and the mortgagor is three months in arrears with such payments since the notice was served; or

(b) the interest under the mortgage is in arrears, and unpaid for two months after becoming due; or

(c) the mortgagor has breached some provision of the mortgage deed (other than the covenant to pay the sum due), or a relevant provision of the LPA 1925.

The consequences of a sale

The point of the above provisions is that they give the mortgagee an effective power of sale of the mortgaged property should the mortgagor be in serious default, either because of a breach of the promise to repay the debt and interest, or breach of any other promise (for example, not to sublet the property). The consequences of a sale are that the proceeds of sale are applied to meet the mortgage debt and associated liabilities according to the provisions of s 105 of the LPA 1925: viz, first, in payment of the costs and charges incurred by the sale; secondly, in satisfaction of the principal debt, interest and costs, with the aim of discharging the mortgage; and thirdly, any remaining balance to the person entitled under the mortgage, usually being the mortgagor, as in *Halifax Building Society v Thomas* (1995).

Necessarily, a successful sale extinguishes the mortgagor's equity of redemption and transfers the land to the purchaser free of any claim of the mortgagor. Any equitable interests in the property are overreached (s 2(1)(iii) of the LPA 1925). In addition, the purchaser takes the land free of any *subsequent mortgages* (that is, those granted later than the mortgage under which the sale has taken place (ss 88 and 113 of the LPA 1925)), but subject to any previous mortgages. All subsequent mortgagees will be entitled to the balance of any money left after discharge of the mortgage under which sale has occurred, in the order in which those mortgages were made, but before payment of any balance to the mortgagor. In other words, subsequent mortgagees are 'persons entitled' to the proceeds of sale of the mortgaged property under s 105, above. Providing that property values have not fallen too far, and that subsequent mortgagees operated a sensible lending policy, there should be enough money to pay off the debt of the selling mortgagee and that arising under the later mortgages. For example, if a property worth £100,000 was subject to a first mortgage of £85,000, a second mortgage of £5,000 and a third mortgage of £7,000, a sale at £100,000 by the first mortgagee will enable payment of all three mortgagees plus some balance (if any, after costs) to the mortgagor. Similarly, if the second mortgagee was to exercise their power of sale, a purchaser would buy the land subject to the first mortgage, probably paying only £15,000 (£100,000 – the value – minus £85,000 – the first mortgage), and the second and third mortgagees would be paid.

Regulating the power of sale

It is clear that a sale of the mortgaged property is a calamitous event for the mortgagor. Essentially, it means forced loss of the land – often the home – with only the balance of the purchase price (if any) as a comfort. Not surprisingly, therefore, in addition to the limitations on the circumstances in which a sale by the mortgagee may be undertaken, the mortgagee is placed under common law and statutory obligations with respect to the conduct of the sale.

First, if a mortgagee sells the property *before* the power of sale has arisen, the purchaser obtains only the mortgagee's interest, and the mortgagor remains unaffected. It is as if the mortgagee had transferred only the mortgagee's rights to the purchaser.

Secondly, if a mortgagee sells after the power has arisen, but before it has become exercisable, the purchaser takes the land free of the mortgage, save that the mortgagor may be able to set the sale aside if the purchaser had notice of the mortgagee's fault (s 104 of the LPA 1925; *Cuckmere Brick Co v Mutual Finance* (1971)).

Thirdly, in cases where the power of sale has both arisen and become exercisable, the mortgagor must rely on the generosity of equity to protect their position. Consequently, the 'selling mortgagee' is under a duty of care to the mortgagor to obtain the best price reasonably obtainable (*Standard Chartered Bank v Walker* (1982)), although an open sale by auction, even when prices are low, satisfies this duty (*Cuckmere Brick Co v Mutual Finance* (1971); *Wilson v Halifax plc* (2002)). Moreover, this duty is not owed to any person other than the mortgagor – particularly, it is not owed to a person with an equitable interest in the property (*Parker-Tweedale v Dunbar* (1991)). It also seems that the mortgagors may agree specifically to a sale by a mortgagee at a price lower than the market price and, in that way, they become estopped from relying on the duty of care owed to them by the mortgagee. This appears to be the ratio of *Mercantile Credit Co v Clarke* (1997), although it does assume that the mortgagor's agreement to sale at a lower price was not tainted by undue influence or unconscionable action on the part of the mortgagee. Neither is the mortgagee a trustee of the power of sale and, therefore, his motives in choosing to exercise the power of sale are irrelevant so long as the conditions justifying a sale are established. However, if the mortgagee is negligent, and thereby obtains a lower price than they should otherwise have obtained, they are liable to the mortgagor for the difference (*Cuckmere*). Furthermore, if the mortgagee sells the property to himself or his agent, the sale may be set aside (*Williams v Wellingborough Council* (1975)), but a mortgagee may sell to a company in which he has an interest, providing that the best price was obtained, and may sell to himself with the sanction of the court (*Palk*).

Fourthly, although it is generally the mortgagee who will choose to sell the mortgaged property, a mortgagor may apply to the court under s 91 of the LPA 1925 for an order requiring a sale. As noted above, this is particularly beneficial to a mortgagor whose outstanding mortgage is greater than the value of the property, as a sale in these circumstances will terminate the mortgage and stop interest accruing (*Palk*). Of course, in such circumstances, the mortgagor will still be liable on their personal contractual promise to repay the whole sum borrowed, although insurance can be obtained for this eventuality.

10.9.3 The right to possession

The most effective way for the mortgagee to realise their security, in the event of default by the mortgagor, is to sell the property. However, for this to achieve its aim, the mortgagee will want the property to be put on the market with vacant possession, that is, after having ejected the mortgagor from the premises. In practice, therefore, before the mortgagee attempts to sell, he will exercise his right to possession of the mortgaged property. Moreover, although possession is often a prelude to sale, it can also be used as a method of securing recovery of the outstanding interest on a loan, for example, the mortgagee may take possession of the premises and manage them in such a way so as to generate income which can then be used to satisfy the mortgagor's obligations. Possession, then, does not necessarily mean the end of the mortgage, although termination through a sale may follow.

The mortgagee's right to possession is *exactly* what it says. By virtue of the way in which legal mortgages are created, the mortgagee will have an estate in the land (the long lease/sublease) and, in reality, the mortgagee has an immediate right to possession the moment the ink is dry on the mortgage (*Four Maids v Dudley Marshall* (1957); *Ropaigelach v Barclays Bank* (1999)). It is important to realise, then, that the mortgagee may take possession of the property at any time, *even if the mortgagor is not in default*, subject only to any provision to the contrary in the mortgage itself or in statute. Of course, in the normal course of events, the mortgagee will not exercise this right, and will be content to allow the mortgagor to remain in possession so long as the terms of the mortgage are observed and payments are made. Indeed, the mortgagee may have contractually promised not to seek possession unless the mortgagor defaults on the repayments or some other obligation, and, in this case, the mortgagor may claim possession under s 98 of the LPA 1925.

The consequences of the mortgagee taking possession

Another reason why the mortgagee may not choose to take possession is that it may be counterproductive. A mortgagee in possession of the mortgaged premises will be called to account strictly for any income generated by their possession (*White v City of London Brewery* (1889)). This means that the mortgagee will be taken to have received not only the actual income generated by their management of the property (which can go towards repayments), but also, any income that he should have received had they managed the property to the high standard required. Any shortfall between the actual income and the expected income will have to be made up by the mortgagee, who may find that he actually owes money to the mortgagor if the income that should have been received is greater than the money owed. This is why most commercial mortgagees desist from seeking possession, and why most residential mortgagees seek possession only as a prelude to sale. (For an exception, see *Palk*.)

Statutory restrictions on the right of possession

In the residential context, where the mortgage may well have been used to finance the purchase of the property in the first place, it is rare for the mortgagee to seek possession other than as a prelude to sale. The mortgagor will occupy the property unless there is a problem with the mortgage repayments and the mortgagee may well have contractually bound themselves not to seek possession unless this occurs. Moreover, if a mortgagee brings an action to recover possession of land, whether as a prelude to sale or not, 'which consists of, or includes, a dwelling house', the mortgagor may avail themselves of the protection afforded by s 36 of the Administration of Justice Act (AJA) 1970 (as amended by s 8 of the AJA 1973). Under s 36, as amended, an application by a mortgagee for possession of a dwelling house may be suspended, adjourned or postponed by the court, in its discretion, if it appears that the mortgagor would be able to pay within a reasonable period any sums due under the mortgage. Whether a property is a 'dwelling house' for the purpose of s 36 of the AJA 1973 is to be determined by reference to the state of the premises at the time the order for possession was sought. By virtue of the s 8 amendment (reversing *Halifax Building Society v Clark* (1973)), 'any sums due' may be treated only as those instalments that have not been paid by the mortgagor and not, as most mortgages provide, the whole mortgage debt once only one mortgage payment is missed. Likewise, the statutory relief is available for endowment mortgages, despite the elliptical wording of the statute (*Bank of Scotland v Grimes* (1985)), although there is some doubt whether the statutory discretion is available if the mortgagor is not actually in default under the mortgage (*Western Bank v Schindler* (1977)). The statutory discretion is not available once a warrant for possession has been executed, that is, if the mortgagee has actually recovered possession (*Mortgage Agency Services v Ball* (1998)). Moreover, while the 'reasonable period' which the mortgagor is given to repay his arrears might actually be the rest of the mortgage – so as to spread the debt evenly (*Middlesbrough Mortgage Corp v Cunningham* (1974); *Cheltenham and Gloucester Building Society v Norgan* (1996)) – the court has no discretion to make an order if there is no prospect of the mortgagor making a reasonable attempt actually to repay the accumulated arrears, let alone meet future repayments (*First National Bank v Syed* (1991); *Bristol & West Building Society v Dace* (1998)). An intended sale of the property by the mortgagor (even if not imminent) is a factor which could justify suspension of a possession order under s 36, as this might mean that the mortgagor is likely to be able to pay moneys due within a reasonable time (*National and Provincial Bank v Lloyd* (1996)). However, as that case and *Dace* show, there must be evidence to justify this conclusion, not mere hopes.

Prior to *Norgan*, the practice relating to a mortgagor's applications to suspend a mortgagee's possession order under s 36 had become somewhat rigid, with the courts (especially the county court where most of these applications are heard) generally suspending possession for an 'automatic' two years, so that the mortgagor had to make up the arrears in that time. As noted above, however, s 36 lays down no such time limit and *Norgan* itself contemplates a 'reasonable period' for repayment as being the whole of the remaining mortgage term, so spreading repayment of the arrears more thinly. Clearly, the thrust of *Norgan* is to use s 36 more effectively to protect mortgagors of residential property, and, to that end, the case established that a court should address a number of issues before deciding what is a 'reasonable period' for which to suspend possession. These considerations are designed to ensure that the particular circumstances of each mortgagor are given due weight: viz, how much can the mortgagor afford to pay? Is the mortgagor in temporary difficulty, or are his problems more enduring? What was the reason for the arrears? How long remains of the original mortgage period? What are the contractual terms relating to repayment of the capital sum; in particular, was this an instalment mortgage? Over what period is it reasonable to expect the mortgagee to wait for repayment of the arrears, bearing in mind that the mortgagee could be asked to wait even longer than the original mortgage term? How does the value of the land relate to the amount borrowed? Necessarily, this is a mixed bag, but the overall effect of *Norgan* is likely to be the adoption of a more generous approach to a mortgagor's application to suspend a mortgagee's possession order under s 36 of the AJA 1970.

Finally, it is important to note that a mortgagee does not actually need a court order to secure possession. The mortgagee's ability to possess arises *as of right* by virtue of the interest they have or are deemed to have in the land. Possession may then be taken peacefully through self-help without any application to the court. In most cases, of course, a lender will not pursue this option, not least because there is a real risk of committing criminal offences in the act of taking possession if there should be any person lawfully residing on the premises at the time. Moreover, the lender may well want the security that a court order brings and the assurance that the mortgagor is not trying to defeat the mortgage (and hence the right to possession) on other grounds (for example, undue influence). Importantly, however, if a lender does take possession of a property without a court order, the court then has no power to suspend the possession under s 36 of the AJA 1970. This is because that power – the power to suspend – arises when an application for a possession order is made to the court (see the terms of s 36) and not generally when possession is sought or taken. Clearly, this is an advantage to a lender, as exemplified by *Ropaigelach v Barclays Bank* (2000) where just such an event occurred and the Court of Appeal found itself without power to intervene on behalf of the borrower.

Other possible limitations on the right to possession

Even where it is available, the jurisdiction to suspend under s 36 of the AJA 1970 is not 'at large': it is restricted. So, suspension is possible only in respect of a 'dwelling house' (to be determined at the time the order is sought), and only when it is clear that suspension is 'likely' to enable the mortgagor to meet any sums due. In the absence of these conditions, the mortgagee cannot be denied possession under s 36 and may exercise their right to possession unhindered. However, there may be further limitations on the mortgagee's right to possession (note, these are in addition to the point made above, that a mortgagee may contract not to exercise their right until specified events occur):

(a) in *Quennell v Maltby* (1979), Lord Denning suggested that a court of equity could restrain a mortgagee from taking possession whenever there was no justifiable reason for that possession. His view was that possession could be sought only for a *bona fide* realisation of the mortgagee's security. Obviously, this directly contradicts the mortgagee's pure right of possession springing from their status as holder of estate in the land (or equivalent under the 'charge'). Consequently, it is doubtful whether the *dicta* in *Quennell* are correct and they have found little support in subsequent cases;

(b) following on from *Palk* in the Court of Appeal, it appears that a court may suspend a mortgagee's possession order if it concurrently orders sale of the property at the request of the mortgagor under s 91 of the LPA 1925. This presents no difficulty if the sale proceeds would pay off the entire sum owed – anyway, s 36 of the AJA 1970 could have been used, as the sale proceeds are 'likely' to pay the sum due (that is, the whole debt). However, if the sale proceeds would not pay off the whole debt – as in *Palk* itself – s 36 of the AJA 1970 is inapplicable and so the suspension of the mortgagee's possession in *Palk* seems to have derived from the wide discretionary power found in s 91 of the LPA 1925. This is a novel use of s 91, and in *Krausz*, the Court of Appeal appears to say that there is no power to suspend a mortgagee's possession unless s 36 could be used (that is, the proposed sale would, indeed, pay off the entire sums due). Yet, *Krausz* does not overrule *Palk* (which was followed in *Lloyds Bank v Polanski* (1999)), the latter being said to be limited to its 'special facts', being a case where the mortgagee wanted possession in order to lease the house, not to sell it. In fact, this distinction between *Palk* and *Krausz* as to the mortgagee's intentions is not convincing and, clearly, one case is not correct. So, for the present, if the mortgagor applies for sale under s 91 of the LPA 1925, there may – or may not – be an ancillary power to suspend a mortgagee's possession order while the sale takes place;

(c) *Albany Home Loans v Massey* (1997) establishes that a mortgagee cannot be granted possession of land mortgaged by joint mortgagors where, in fact, the mortgage turns out to be binding on only one of them. In that case, the mortgage of the house had been executed by the man and woman jointly and they were in default. However, the mortgage was held void as against the woman on the grounds of undue influence. In consequence, possession of the land could not be ordered, even though the man would remain living on the land with his partner;

(d) there are other statutory restrictions on the mortgagee's right to possession, which arise in very particular circumstances. These include attempts by the mortgagee to gain possession outside the time limit set by the Limitation Act 1980, or in contravention of the Consumer Credit Act 1974, Rent Act 1977 and Housing Acts 1985–96, or contrary to the dictates of the insolvency legislation;

(e) it remains to be seen whether a mortgagor can claim that the mortgagee's exercise of the right of possession contravenes the borrowers right to peaceful enjoyment of their property or their right to family life under the European Convention on Human Rights as enacted by the Human Rights Act 1998. Such an argument is tenable, though not likely to succeed given that such possession is in pursuit of the legitimate rights of the mortgagee, provided of course that such possessory rights are proportionate. On the other hand, the law of human rights is dynamic and still of uncertain scope in the English legal system and we cannot rule out a successful challenge to a possessory claim on human rights grounds.

10.9.4 Appointment of a receiver

The ability of a mortgagee to appoint a receiver to manage and administer the mortgaged property is another method by which it can recover the interest owed, and possibly sell the mortgaged property as a 'going concern' (see, for example, the *Billy Row* case (2000)). The right to appoint a receiver is often expressly included in the mortgage contract, but, in any event, such a power will be implied into every mortgage by deed (s 101 of the LPA 1925). The implied power becomes exercisable only in those circumstances in which the power of sale becomes exercisable, and it is often an alternative to that remedy. The great advantage of the appointment of a receiver is, however, that it avoids the dangers of the mortgagee taking possession of the property themselves. This is because the receiver is deemed to be the agent of the mortgagor, not of the mortgagee (*Chatsworth Properties v Effiom* (1971); *Lloyds Bank v Bryant* (1996)), with the consequence that any negligence in the administration of the property is not attributable to the mortgagee.

10.9.5 Foreclosure

The remedy of foreclosure is potentially the most powerful remedy in the armoury of the mortgagee, although it is now used only infrequently. If successful, foreclosure will extinguish the equity of redemption and result in the transfer of the mortgaged property to the mortgagee, free of any rights of the mortgagor. In other words, the effect of a foreclosure is to vest the mortgagor's estate in the mortgagee and to extinguish the mortgage and its terms (s 88 of the LPA 1925). So, if the property is freehold, the mortgagee will acquire that freehold, and similarly for a leasehold. The mortgagee's right of foreclosure arises as soon as the legal date for redemption is passed, although it is common for the mortgagee to promise not to foreclose without notice, and only in respect of specified breaches of covenant. Essentially, should the need arise, the mortgagee will begin an action in court asking for foreclosure unless the mortgagor repays the mortgage within a specified time. If repayment does not occur, the mortgagee will be given a foreclosure *nisi*, which, in effect, gives the mortgagor a further period (usually, six months) in which to raise the money to pay off the loan. Failing that, the order of foreclosure will be made 'absolute', and the mortgagor's interest in the property will be extinguished. This is usually the end of the matter, save that, in exceptional circumstances, the court may open a foreclosure absolute and allow the mortgagor to redeem the mortgage at a later date. This is very unlikely if the mortgagee has already sold the property to a purchaser who has no notice of the previous mortgage (*Campbell v Holyland* (1877)).

Statutory control of foreclosure

In view of the powerful nature of foreclosure, the court has power, under s 91(2) of the LPA 1925, to order sale in lieu of a foreclosure. If such a sale occurs, the proceeds will be distributed according to s 105 of the LPA 1925 (as above), and this may mean that the mortgagor receives any surplus funds after the mortgage is paid off. Obviously, such a solution is desirable from the mortgagor's point of view, especially where the mortgage debt is less than the value of the property. In fact, the ability of the court to order sale in lieu of foreclosure has meant a steep decline in the number of successful foreclosure actions. After all, it is a remedy which can destroy the mortgagor's entire interest in the property and for that reason alone should be viewed with some suspicion.

Effect of foreclosure on other mortgagees

If a mortgagee successfully forecloses, this necessarily has consequences for any other mortgagees who have also lent money to the mortgagor:

(a) the rights of mortgagees under mortgages that were created *before* the mortgage which triggers the foreclosure are unaffected. In other words, whoever obtains the land after the foreclosure takes it subject to all prior mortgages;

(b) the rights of mortgagees under mortgages that were created *after* the mortgage that triggers the foreclosure will be destroyed. This is because the foreclosure vests the mortgagor's estate in the 'foreclosing mortgagee' free of any subsequent interests. However, the subsequent mortgagees are given an opportunity to redeem any previous mortgages if foreclosure is likely. In effect, they are given the opportunity to take the place of previous mortgagees by paying them off.

10.10 The rights of a mortgagee under an equitable mortgage

The rights and remedies of a mortgagee under an equitable mortgage or charge are similar to that of the legal mortgagee, although modified, because the mortgagee does not have a legal estate in the land, viz:

(a) the equitable mortgagee or chargee has the right to sue for the money due in the same way as the legal mortgagee. This right is founded in the contract between the parties;

(b) in unregistered land, where the equitable mortgage is made by deed, the mortgagee has the power of sale, although no power to convey the legal estate to a purchaser. This defect can be overcome by conveyancing devices in appropriate cases. In registered land, a registered chargee under an equitable mortgage has the power of sale, although other equitable mortgagees do not. Where the power of sale does not exist, the equitable mortgagee may apply for sale at the court's discretion under s 91(2) of the LPA 1925;

(c) an equitable mortgagee under a mortgage created by an equitable lease/sublease probably has the right to possess the property (that is, as an equitable tenant), or may be given this expressly in the mortgage contract. An equitable chargee does not have a right of possession, as they have no estate in the land, unless possession is specifically given in the mortgage contract;

(d) the position in respect of the appointment of a receiver is the same as with the power of sale;

(e) an equitable mortgagee has a right of foreclosure in the same way as a legal mortgagee. An equitable chargee does not, as they have no estate in the land.

THE LAW OF MORTGAGES

The essential nature of a mortgage

A mortgage is a contract and the mortgagor and mortgagee are free to stipulate whatever terms they wish for repayment of the loan, the rate of interest and so forth. However, a mortgage also generates a proprietary interest in the land for both parties: both mortgagee and mortgagor have an estate in the land.

The classic definition of a mortgage

A mortgage is security for a loan. A mortgage of land comprises a transfer (conveyance) of a legal or equitable estate in the borrower's land to the mortgagee, with a provision that the mortgagee's interest shall lapse upon repayment of the loan plus interest and costs.

The creation of mortgages

For a legal mortgage, the mortgagor (having a legal estate) may grant the mortgagee a long lease or sublease over the land with a provision for its termination on repayment of all sums due under the loan. Alternatively, the mortgagor may create a mortgage by executing 'a charge by deed expressed to be by way of legal mortgage': ss 85(1) and 87 of the LPA 1925. Equitable mortgages may exist when there is a mortgage of an equitable interest; when there is an informal mortgage of a legal interest (that is, when writing but not a deed is used); under the rules for equitable charges; and, possibly, via the operation of proprietary estoppel.

The rights of the mortgagor: the equity of redemption

The mortgagor has a contractual right to redeem the mortgage on the date specified in the mortgage contract. Under the maxim 'once a mortgage always a mortgage', a court of equity would allow redemption after the legal date for redemption had passed. A mortgagor also enjoys the equity of redemption which represents the sum total of the mortgagor's rights in the property, including his paramount title out of which the mortgage is granted. The mortgagor's rights within the equity of redemption include: the rule against irredeemability; the invalidity of a mortgagee's option to purchase the property; the insistence on unfettered redeemability and the scrutiny of collateral advantages; the objection to unconscionable terms.

Undue influence

A mortgage (or a severable part of it) may be struck down if it was obtained by the undue influence of the mortgagee or a third party acting on behalf of the mortgagee. Undue influence may be 'actual' or 'presumed'. In cases of actual undue influence, it is *not* necessary to prove that the mortgage was to the 'manifest disadvantage' of the mortgagor. In cases of 'presumed' undue influence, this is necessary. In cases where the mortgagor is claiming that they were unfairly induced to enter the mortgage *not* by the mortgagee directly, but by another person, then the mortgagee will not be able to enforce the mortgage if either:

- the real inducer was acting as agent of the mortgagee (rare);

- or the mortgagee had actual or constructive notice of the inducer's unfair conduct and had not taken adequate steps to ensure that the claimant was independently advised.

Extortionate credit bargains

Mortgages are subject to statutory controls designed to protect an impecunious borrower from the unfair practices of unscrupulous lenders: ss 137–40 of the Consumer Credit Act 1974.

Restraint of trade

A mortgage which attempts to 'tie' a mortgagor to a particular company or mortgagee may fall foul of the contractual rules prohibiting contracts in restraint of trade.

The rights of the mortgagee under a legal mortgage: remedies for default

- An action on the contract for recovery of the debt. The mortgage is a contract and can be sued on in the normal way.

- The power of sale. If the power of sale has both arisen and become exercisable, the mortgagee may sell the property and apply the proceeds of sale to meet the mortgage debt and associated liabilities according to the provisions of s 105 of the LPA 1925.

- The right to possession. By virtue of the way in which legal mortgages are created, the mortgagee will have an estate in the land and an immediate right to possession, even if the mortgagor is not in default, subject only to any provision to the contrary in the mortgage itself or in statute. The consequences of taking possession are that the mortgagee will be called to account strictly for any income generated by their possession. If a mortgagee brings an action to recover possession of land 'which consists of or includes a dwelling house', the mortgagor may plead the protection of s 36 of the AJA 1970 (as amended by s 8 of the AJA 1973). Certain other limitations on the mortgagee's right to possession may exist.

- Appointment of a receiver. The right to appoint a receiver is often expressly included in the mortgage and such a power will be implied into every mortgage by deed: s 101 of the LPA 1925. The receiver is deemed to be the agent of the mortgagor, not of the mortgagee, and so the mortgagee can avoid the dangers of taking possession.

- Foreclosure. If successful, foreclosure will extinguish the equity of redemption and result in the transfer of the mortgaged property, to the mortgagee, free of any rights of the mortgagor: s 88 of the LPA 1925. The court has power under s 91(2) of the LPA to order sale in lieu of a foreclosure and the proceeds will be distributed according to s 105 of the LPA 1925. The rights of a mortgagee under a mortgage created before the mortgage which triggers the foreclosure are unaffected, but the rights of a mortgagee under a mortgage that was created after the mortgage that triggers the foreclosure will be destroyed.

The rights of a mortgagee under an equitable mortgage

The rights and remedies of a mortgagee under an equitable mortgage or charge are similar to those of a legal mortgagee, although modified because the equitable mortgagee does not have a legal estate in the land. The equitable mortgagee has the right to sue for the money due on the contract; in unregistered land, where the equitable mortgage is made by deed, the mortgagee has the power of sale, although no power to convey the legal estate to a purchaser. In registered land, a registered chargee under an equitable mortgage has the power of sale, although other equitable mortgagees do not. Where the power of sale does not exist, the equitable mortgagee may apply for sale at the court's discretion under s 91(2) of the LPA 1925; an equitable mortgagee under a mortgage created by an equitable lease/sublease probably has the right to possess the property or may be given this expressly in the mortgage contract. An equitable chargee does not have a right of possession as he has no estate in the land, unless possession is given specifically in the mortgage contract; the appointment of a receiver is as the power of sale; an equitable mortgagee has a right of foreclosure in the same way as a legal mortgagee. An equitable chargee does not, as he has no estate in the land.

CHAPTER 11

ADVERSE POSSESSION

The law of adverse possession is something of a peculiarity in English law. It is, in effect, a set of rules that allows a mere trespasser actually to acquire a better title to land than the person who 'legally' owns it and to whom it was once formally conveyed with all the solemnity of a deed or registered disposition. In fact, adverse possession is rooted in the feudal origins of English law for it is the most obvious modern example of the 'relativity of title' that lay at the heart of the doctrine of estates. For example, given that no person may own land itself (only an estate in it), it is in theory perfectly possible for someone other than the 'paper' or 'formal' owner to gain a better title without any formal transfer of 'ownership'. A person's title to land, including the paper owner's, is only as good as the absence of a person with a better title.

The fact that the common law should have developed a set of principles which can operate to deprive a 'paper' owner of his title to land is not as remarkable as might first appear. Historically, the common law always has been more concerned with the development of remedies for concrete situations rather than the formulation of abstract rights and so the apparent lack of regard for the 'rights' of the paper owner, expressed in terms of a denial of a remedy if the defendant can plead limitation (that is, adverse possession), is not particularly surprising or unique. That aside, it is also clear that a doctrine of adverse possession can be justified on substantive grounds. In terms of the legal process, adverse possession is an expression of a policy that denies legal assistance to those that sleep on their rights, as well as ensuring that there is an end to claims concerning ownership of land (*RB Policies v Butler* (1950)). Similarly, land is a finite resource, and the principles of adverse possession can help to ensure its full economic and/or social utilisation (*Hounslow v Minchinton* (1997)).

However, it would be a mistake to accept unquestionably the relevance of adverse possession in our modern system of land law, especially one that is moving towards electronic dealings with land. This is especially so in the context of land of registered title where entry of the 'paper owner' on the register of title – with a title guaranteed by the State – seems to preclude even the possibility that some interloper might acquire that ownership by mere possession of the land. Indeed, in so far as adverse possession had developed as a response to difficulties of proving title to land (for example, where deeds were lost or no 'root' could be shown), compulsory and widespread registration of title has removed its *raison d'être*. Indeed, there is a point of principle here. If being registered as proprietor of an estate in the land is supposed to be a guarantee of the validity of that title to the whole world (subject only to the court's power to rectify the register under the relevant Land Registration Act), should the registered owner ever be susceptible to the claim of a mere trespasser? Could the very existence of principles of adverse possession be seen as fundamentally opposed to a system of registration of title?

Such concerns have, in fact, proved decisive, and the Land Registration Act (LRA) 2002 establishes a new regime for adverse possession in registered land. When the relevant parts of this Act enter into force, it will effectively prevent very many successful claims to adverse possession of registered land. This means that, in time, there will be two sets of rules concerning adverse possession in operation. First, the 'traditional principles' applicable to land of unregistered title (and to land of registered title prior to the commencement of the LRA 2002) and, secondly, the statutory scheme applicable to land of registered title found in the LRA 2002 but which utilises some (but not all) of the 'traditional' concepts. Of course, instances of adverse possession of unregistered land will fade away (as most land becomes registered) and it may well be that the existence of a statutory scheme for registered land that is markedly less favourable to adverse possessors will encourage voluntary registration of title. Some might say this is one of the motivating factors behind the new system. For the present however, the student must be aware of both the traditional rules (unregistered land, pre-LRA 2002 registered land) and the way in which these will be modified when the LRA 2002 enters force.

11.1 The basic principle of adverse possession: the limitation of actions for unregistered land and pre-LRA 2002 registered land

The ability of an adverse possessor (a 'squatter' or 'trespasser') to acquire a better claim to the land than the paper owner is based on the principle of limitation of actions. In simple terms, 'limitation of actions' expresses the idea that a person must sue for an alleged wrong within a specified period of time from the moment the alleged wrong took place (see the Limitation Act 1980). In the context of adverse possession, this means that a person (for example, the paper owner of the land) may be 'statute barred' from bringing a claim against the adverse possessor to recover possession of their land after the period of limitation has passed. Thus, as against the adverse possessor, the paper owner has no means of recovering the land, and so the adverse possessor has 'acquired' a better right to the land. To look at it slightly differently, if an estate owner sleeps on his rights, those rights will be extinguished, in the sense that a court will not enforce them against the person actually in possession of the land. In this sense, therefore, adverse possession operates negatively: it prevents an estate owner from suing on his rights and operates to extinguish his title. Conventionally, this is taken to mean that adverse possession does not actually give a title to the squatter but, by virtue of the doctrine of relativity of title, the person now in actual possession may have the best claim to the land, and, thereby, become 'owner' of it to all intents and purposes. Importantly, however, this position (that is, no transfer of title to adverse possessor) is inaccurate in the context of registered land. Section 75 of the Land Registration Act (LRA) 1925 (that is, the 'old' registered land approach) declares that a registered proprietor of an estate (freehold or leasehold) holds that estate on trust for a successful squatter pending registration of the squatter as the new proprietor (see, for example, *Minchinton*). This suggests a parliamentary conveyance of the paper owner's title to the squatter, or, at the very least, the survival of the 'old' title until the new owner can be registered with a 'new', but identical, title. Indeed, in *Central London Commercial Estates Ltd v Kato Kagaku Ltd* (1998), Sedley J held that a registered proprietor's leasehold was held on trust for the successful squatter with the benefits and burdens of the lease intact (confirming the wider view of *Spectrum Investment Co v Holmes* (1981): see below, 11.5.3). A similar view is inherent in *Chung Ping Kwan v Lam Island Development Co* (1996), where the Privy Council held that on expiry of a lease under which the tenant had been ousted by a successful squatter, the squatter was able to take advantage of a right to renew the lease given to the tenant by the original lease: hence the landlord could not evict. Again, this implies that the adverse possessor has succeeded to the tenant's original interest.

In relation to adverse possession under the scheme established by the LRA 2002, it will be seen below that different considerations apply. Effectively, under this scheme – which will apply to all new claims to adverse possession of registered land after the Act enters into force – there is no limitation of action (s 96 of the LRA 2002). The registered owner is set no time limit in which to take action to evict the adverse possessor. Instead, it is up to the adverse possessor to apply to be registered with the title and, failing a successful application, the 'true' owner retains the title. Thus the 'true' owner may sleep on their rights until such time as the adverse possessor apples to be registered, even if this be 40 or 50 years. It is only after such an application that the 'true' owner must take some action to recover possession. There is no automatic barring of title.

11.2 The limitation period for unregistered land and pre-LRA 2002 registered land

If the essence of adverse possession is that a paper owner will be prevented from bringing an action to recover land against the person in actual possession of it, it is crucial to know exactly when this 'bar' will come into effect. In other words, how long must a squatter be in adverse possession before the paper owner is statute barred from bringing an action? How long is the limitation period for unregistered land and pre-LRA 2002 registered land? It should come as no surprise to learn, first of all, that the limitation period for actions concerning land depends on the circumstances of each particular case. Fortunately, there are some general rules:

(a) in the great majority of cases, the limitation period will be 12 years from the moment of adverse possession by the squatter (s 15 of the Limitation Act 1980). This is the normal period of limitation for actions concerning land;

(b) where the paper owner of the land is a 'sole' charitable corporation (such as a bishop), the period of limitation is 30 years from the moment of adverse possession (Sched 1, para 10 of the Limitation Act 1980);

(c) where the paper owner of the land is the Crown, the period of limitation is 30 years from the moment of adverse possession (Sched 1, para 11 of the Limitation Act 1980);

(d) if land is owned by someone for life, with remainder in fee simple to another person (for example, to A for life, remainder in fee simple to B), then the limitation period is either, adverse possession of six years from the date at which the interest in remainder falls into possession (that is, the death of the life tenant), assuming 12 years or more already have been completed against the life tenant, or adverse possession of 12 years from the time the life tenant was dispossessed, whichever is the longer (s 15 of the Limitation Act 1980). So, assuming land is held by A for life, remainder to B, adverse possession of 12 years or more against A will extinguish A's interest, and a further six years will be necessary on the death of A also to extinguish B's interest;

(e) if the current paper owner is a tenant of the land under a lease, the period of limitation against the tenant is 12 years (*Chung Ping Kwan v Lam Island Development Co* (1996)). Expiry of the period will, therefore, extinguish the tenant's title against the squatter. Importantly, however, extinguishment of the tenant's title has no immediate effect on the title of the reversioner (that is, usually the freehold landlord), simply because until the end of the lease, the landlord has no right to possess the land at all. Therefore, time does not begin to run against the landlord until the original term of the lease expires (or, possibly, is otherwise brought to an end: see below, 11.5.3). When the original term of the lease expires, and assuming 12 years' adverse possession against the tenant, the landlord will have a further 12 years to recover the land. Of course, after that period, the landlord's title is also extinguished (s 15 and Sched 1, para 4 of the Limitation Act 1980). Obviously, it is crucial for these rules to know when the lease has ended. This will usually be the expiry of the stated term (or statutory extension thereof), and, for a periodic tenancy, this is treated as the end of the last period for which rent was paid. Note, however, that although the normal rule is that the landlord's right of action against the squatter arises when the original term of the lease ends, there is an exception to this. So, if the lease itself gives the tenant an option to renew the lease when it expires, the squatter who has evicted that tenant also may rely on the right to renew to defeat the landlord's claim to possession (*Chung v Lam* (1996)). The landlord (and any person claiming through the landlord, such as an alleged new tenant) must, it seems, wait until the period given under the right to renew also has expired. The rationale is that, as the landlord could not have evicted the original tenant (because of the option to renew), so the landlord cannot evict the squatter who has displaced that tenant. This is logical, but it does give the lie to the idea that the squatter's title is completely unconnected to that of the paper owner he dispossesses.

Whatever period of limitation is applicable, it starts to run against the relevant paper owner from the first moment of adverse possession. Consequently, if the alleged adverse possessor never, in fact, has been in adverse possession, time cannot start against the owner, and he cannot lose title. For example, in *Smith v Lawson* (1997), the defendant had been given an occupation licence of the disputed land for life, and so her possession was not adverse. Although this meant that the claimant had no right to recover the land during the defendant's life, it also meant that the defendant had no claim in adverse possession. However, once time has started, it is sufficient to establish that the full period has been completed at any time before the paper owner seeks to enforce his title to the land. It is not necessary to establish that the squatter is in adverse possession at the moment the action for recovery is commenced, provided that the period has, by then, been completed (*Minchinton*). So, if S, the squatter, has adversely possessed A's land for 12 years, but has left possession before A commences an action to recover the land, A's title will be barred and he will be unable to recover the land from whomever now is in possession. A's title has been extinguished, and the person in possession has the best relative title. Of course, if S has left the land and nobody is in possession, then A may retake possession, but will, himself, have to wait a further 12 years before being confident of defeating a returning S. Note, however, that under the LRA 2002, the right of an adverse possessor who has not sought registration of title will only constitute an overriding interest against a new registered proprietor (so as to affect that proprietor) if the adverse possessor is in actual occupation of the land at the time of the registration of the new proprietor. This would mean that those going out of possession, even after completing the relevant period of adverse possession required to found a claim, will have no right against the new proprietor. This marks a change from the present law where the right of an adverse possessor is, without more, an overriding interest under s 70(1)(f) of the LRA 1925.

As noted above, generally under the LRA 2002 scheme, there is no concept of limitation of actions, and thus no limitation period. The adverse possessor is, in broad terms, given the right to apply for registration as proprietor at any time after 10 years' adverse possession (Sched 6 to the LRA 2002). Subject to some exceptional situations (see below, 11.8), this will give the 'true' registered proprietor a further two years to recover possession from the adverse possessor, failing which the adverse possessor may reapply and will be registered as the new owner. Importantly, the adverse possessor need not apply for a title after 10 years – or at all. The 10 years is the minimum period of 'adverse possession' which must be completed before an application to be registered can be made. The 'true' registered proprietor thus will have two years to act (exceptional cases aside) following an application by the adverse possessor irrespective of the time in which the adverse possessor has been in adverse possession – there is no limitation of action.

11.3   How is adverse possession established

Whether the claim for adverse possession is made in respect of land of unregistered title, registered land prior to entry into force of the LRA 2002 or registered land subject to the new regime of the LRA 2002, the crucial question still remains: when will possession be adverse so as to trigger a claim. Or, to put it another way, how is the reality of 'adverse possession' established? Fortunately, the rules about this are the same irrespective of whether the land is unregistered land, registered land subject to the LRA 1925 or registered land subject to the LRA 2002 (see Sched 6, para 11 of the LRA 2002).

The relevant principles are not found in statute, not even in the Limitation Act 1980 itself, but have been developed through case law over generations. As judge-made law, these are flexible, changeable, malleable and not always consistent. This has the advantage that they may respond to changing times, but the disadvantage of making it less easy to predict a court's decision. There is no doubt, for example, that recent decisions have been 'squatter friendly', in the sense that the courts no longer manifest an inbuilt hostility to the adverse possessor. That said, the Court of Appeal, in *Buckinghamshire CC v Moran* (1990), sought to codify the principles of adverse possession in an attempt to bring some certainty and clarity to the law. This case now is regarded as the definitive statement of the modern law (*Bolton MBC v Qasmi* (1998)), and its reasoning forms the basis of the following discussion.

In simple terms, adverse possession is established by demonstrating the required degree of exclusive physical possession of the land, coupled with an intention to possess to the exclusion of all others, including the paper owner. It is, therefore, the conjunction of acts of possession with an *animus possidendi* that establishes adverse possession.

11.3.1 An intention to possess

As recognised by the court in *Powell v McFarlane* (1979), to some extent, the requirement that the adverse possessor must 'intend' to possess the land adversely to the exclusion of all others is artificial. For example, some adverse possessors may appreciate fully that the land is not theirs and act deliberately to exclude the world; others may believe honestly that the land is theirs already, and so do not, for one moment, think they are excluding the 'true' owner; others still may have formulated no intention at all, but simply treat the land as their own because it is there. In other words, we are not looking here for 'intention' in the traditional legal sense of a *mens rea*, either objectively or subjectively established. What is required is evidence that the adverse possessor, for whatever reason, regarded the land as being his to do with as he chooses, whether or not he also knew that some other person had a claim. The key is a state of mind which regards the land as 'belonging to' the possessor: that is, in the language of *Moran*, an intention to possess rather to an intention to own *per se*. Consequently, although the adverse possessor's mere knowledge of another's claim to the land is no bar to adverse possession (although see the contrary and, it is submitted, incorrect view in *Batt v Adams* (2001)), a belief that the land is possessed with the permission of the paper owner is fatal. You cannot intend to treat the land as within your ultimate control if you believe that you are permitted to be there by the owner.

Likewise, as is demonstrated by *Pye v Graham* (2001) if the alleged adverse possessor once occupied the land with the permission of the paper owner, it takes clear evidence to show that continued occupation after the permission has ceased is done with the relevant *animus possidendi*, especially if (as in *Pye*), the adverse possessor would have accepted a new permission from the paper owner if one had been offered. It is not, however, that it is impossible to show an intention to possess in such cases, rather that there must be strong evidence that the intention now exists. So, in *Lambeth LBC v Blackburn* (2001), Blackburn was able to demonstrate an intention to possess the land – through clear acts of possession – even though he knew that the land was another's and would have accepted a permission (a lease) if one had been offered. Despite this, he did have a current intention to possess and, after 12 years, this barred the title of the paper owner.

It will be appreciated immediately that this intention to possess can be difficult to prove. There are few difficulties if the alleged squatter has acknowledged the true owner's title in some way (for example, *Archangel v Lambeth LBC* (2000)), or, conversely, if the squatter has placed a sign at the entrance to the land saying 'Keep Out: Private Property'. Most cases are, however, somewhere in between. *Moran* itself establishes that the actions of the squatter in seeking to assert physical possession of the land also may give a strong indication as to whether the necessary intention exists. This must be correct, for it is wrong to regard the question of intention and of physical possession as being separate and disconnected. They are part and parcel of the same inquiry: viz, does the claimant establish adverse possession? So, enclosing land by a fence may constitute both the act of possession and demonstrate the intention to possess (*Moran*) as might changing locks to a flat (*Blackburn*), and the burden of proving the intention may be lighter in cases where the true owner has, to the knowledge of the squatter, abandoned the land (*Minchinton*). It is clear, then, that unequivocal conduct in relation to acts of possession on the land are the best evidence of an intention to possess. Such acts may need to be more forceful where the land was once occupied with permission (contrast the forceful acts in *Blackburn* with the passive acts in *Pye*), but it will be a question of degree in each case. Importantly, awareness that the land belongs to another cannot prevent the existence of a current intention to possess (*Blackburn*), but an acknowledgement that the land belongs to another will (*Archangel* and *BRB (Residuary) v Cully* (2001)).

This brings us to the difficult question of how far the squatter can establish an intention to possess when he (the squatter) knows that the true owner has some future use for the land which is not made impossible by the squatter's current use. As above, if the squatter believes he is on the land with the permission of the owner, then the intention required to establish adverse possession is absent. Conversely, if the squatter knows of the intended future use of the land by the paper owner and himself uses the land in such a way to make that intended use impossible or impractical, the intention to possesses may be inferred readily. The difficult case is where the squatter knows of the owner's future intended plans and uses the land in a manner that does not prevent the accomplishment of those plans. In such cases, *Moran* suggests that it may be more difficult – but certainly not impossible – to prove an *animus possidendi*, because the squatter's actions may imply an awareness that the land belongs ultimately to another. However, it was also explained in *Moran* that the squatter's awareness of the paper owner's intended future use of the land did not, of itself, mean that the squatter's acts of possession were to be regarded as being with the permission of the owner (*Minchinton*). This might appear to be contradictory, but the point is that the court in *Moran* was attempting to highlight when an appropriate inference as to intention can be drawn, and when it cannot. Perhaps the position is that, if it can be shown positively that the squatter's actions on the land were organised deliberately not to compromise the paper owner's plans for the land, then the squatter can be taken as lacking the *animus possidendi*. If, however, there is no evidence that the squatter took account of those plans, there is equally no evidence that the squatter lacked the necessary intention.

11.3.2 Physical possession, adverse to the paper owner

As well as demonstrating an intention to possess the land, the adverse possessor must also demonstrate a physical assumption of possession in a manner that is adverse to the owner. Hidden in this simple statement of the law is the important qualification that not just any taking of possession will do: it must be 'adverse'. So, taking possession under a lease or licence from the owner is not adverse (*Smith v Lawson* (1997)), as the possession, even if exclusive, is by agreement of the title holder. This is perfectly straightforward in theory, but it can pose great difficulties in practice. For example, possession may start as non-adverse (for example, under a licence or lease (*Pye*; *Blackburn*)), but it may become adverse if the lease/licence ends and the person remains in occupation, or if the tenant ceases to pay rent (or otherwise breaches the terms of a lease) and this goes unchallenged (for example, *Hayward v Chaloner* (1968): non-payment of rent since 1942). Consequently, in many cases of adverse possession, the paper owner will claim that the squatter is on the land by virtue of some pre-existing entitlement (as in *Smith v Lawson* (1997)), so that even if the paper owner cannot recover immediately (because the alleged right is still in existence), at least his title is not extinguished.

A particular difficulty in this regard concerns the circumstances in which the squatter can be said to occupy the land by licence from the paper owner. Clearly, if the licence is express and provable, possession is not adverse, as where the paper owner and alleged squatter have agreed the terms of the latter's use. But what of so called implied licences, where the paper owner alleges that the facts of the case imply that the squatter is on the land by virtue of a licence? There are two general rules. First, as discussed above, if a squatter uses the land in a manner which does not contradict the owner's future use of the land, this should *not* be taken as implying a licence from the owner (*Moran*; *Minchinton*). At one time, when the law was less generous to squatters, a 'hypothetical licence' would be implied in favour of the squatter in such cases, simply because his current use did not obstruct the paper owner's future use, irrespective of whether any licence in fact existed (see *Leigh v Jack* (1879); *Wallis's Cayton Bay Holiday Camp v Shell-Mex and BP* (1975)). This doctrine was exploded in *Moran* on the rather obvious ground that it was pure fiction. Of course, as that case pointed out (and see *Minchinton*), a squatter's knowledge of the intended use might negative an *animus possidendi*, but this is a question of fact, not of implication, and it certainly did not deny the possession of its 'adverse' quality. Secondly, however, it is perfectly possible for a true licence to be implied from the facts. All this means is that the paper owner and squatter do not have to agree expressly that the latter is in possession by permission: it can be implied from their conduct if, but only if, this is a true interpretation of the facts. To put it another way, a hypothetical licence cannot exist, but a genuine implied licence can. What this means in a practical context is that a squatter will be able to prove the adverse quality of the possession much more readily and will be in danger only if a genuine permission has been given and accepted, either expressly or by necessary implication, from the conduct of the parties.

Already, we have seen that the concept of adverse possession is not one-dimensional: there must be an intention to possess, and the possession must be 'adverse'. Vitally, we must now consider what activities on the land might amount to physical possession. According to prevailing theories, claims of adverse possession fall into one of two categories. The squatter must demonstrate adverse physical possession in consequence of either a 'dispossession' of the paper owner, or following a 'discontinuance' of possession by him. It will be apparent immediately that, in fact, these labels are descriptive only: they do not identify the need for a different quality of possession by the squatter (in either case, it must be adverse and possessive), but they do describe a different factual context for that possession. So, 'dispossession' occurs where the paper owner is effectively driven out by another (for example, *Rains v Buxton* (1880)), although it is clear that this is not usually some dramatic event, but a gradual exclusion of the paper owner. Indeed, the paper owner does not need to know or realise that they have been dispossessed for adverse possession to operate (*Powell v Mcfarlane* (1979)). By way of contrast, 'discontinuance' occurs where the paper owner abandons the land, and, although this is not to be presumed from mere lack of use by the paper owner (*Techbild v Chamberlain* (1969)), it does arise where the paper owner has made it impossible for himself to use the land (*Minchinton*: land enclosed by fence built by paper owner and no access except from others' land). Necessarily, although in cases of 'discontinuance' the same quality of adverse possession is required of the adverse possessor as in 'dispossession' cases, this may be established by acts of a lesser magnitude and intensity than might be required for the latter (*Minchinton*). Again, this should come as no surprise, for all we are saying is that it takes more 'squatter activity' to possess land actively possessed by another (dispossession), than it does to possess land that has been abandoned.

In trying to discern what types of act may amount to physical possession, it is important to accept the unhelpful truth that everything turns on the facts of each case. Whether the squatter has succeeded in securing physical possession of the land will depend not only on whether it is a case of 'dispossession' or 'discontinuance', but also on the type of land involved, its location, its physical state and its relation to adjoining plots. This is not an exhaustive list of considerations. For example, it may be easier to establish physical possession over land which is not susceptible to developed use (*Red House Farms v Catchpole* (1977)), or which cannot be used by anyone except the adverse possessor (*Minchinton*). Further, there is no requirement that the acts of possession must inconvenience the paper owner (*Treloar v Nute* (1976): although they often do!), but possession will not be presumed lightly from acts which are equivocal in nature or temporary in purpose, such as growing vegetables, or clearing land to enable one's children to play (*Shell-Mex*; *Techbild v Chamberlain* (1969)). Enclosing the land is always strong evidence of physical possession (*Moran*), as is fitting new locks to doors (*Blackburn*) and, in this regard, the motives of the squatter are not relevant. For example, in *Minchinton*, the successful adverse possessor had fenced off part of the claimant's land, apparently to prevent the escape of her dogs which she exercised on the land. Not surprisingly, counsel for the paper owner submitted that the enclosure was not designed to exclude the world, but to confine the animals, and should not, therefore, be regarded as possession. The court, however, took the view that it was the effect of the squatter's actions that were important, not their motive (assuming, of course, an otherwise established *animus possidendi*). So, if the effect of the fence was to keep out the world as well as keep in the dogs, it amounted to physical possession. This is fairly generous to the squatter, although it does have the great advantage of rooting the requirement of physical possession in objective fact, rather than subjective motive. In this regard, it is similar to the court's approach to assessing whether 'exclusive possession' exists in the lease/licence debate and whether 'actual occupation' exists under s 70(1)(g) of the LRA 1925 – *Malory Enterprises Ltd v Cheshire Homes and Chief Land Registrar* (2002). In *Minchinton* itself, the squatter had demonstrated an assumption of possession by other means in addition to enclosure and this really illustrates the heart of the matter. In answering the question 'has the squatter demonstrated physical possession of the land', it is the whole of his activity on the land that is relevant, as in the successful claim in *Burns v Anthony* (1997). The individual activities may seem equivocal or trivial, but if, taken together, they paint a picture of a person in control of land, they will amount to possession.

11.4 Stopping the clock of limitation for unregistered land and pre-LRA 2002 registered land

Assuming that the land is unregistered land, or registered land not yet subject to the new scheme under the LRA 2002, if the squatter is in adverse possession of the land, this means that the paper owner has the limitation period (usually, 12 years) to assert their paramount title and recover possession. Of course, a successful action for possession by the paper owner before expiry of the period will necessarily 'stop the clock' and any claim of adverse possession will have to begin afresh. There are, in addition, other matters which may effectively bring an uncompleted period of adverse possession to an end. The most obvious is where the squatter acknowledges the paper owner's title in writing, either expressly, or by some other act, such as accepting a lease. Likewise, the payment of rent by the squatter is an acknowledgment of the owner's title (ss 29 and 30 of the Limitation Act 1980). However, apart from these examples, it is not clear what other actions by the paper owner will be sufficient to 'stop the clock', and every case falls to be determined on its own facts. In *Moran*, for example, a letter sent by the paper owner asserting title was not sufficient, although a letter evincing a definite intention to sue may well be (*Shell-Mex*). The clearest advice to an estate owner faced with an adverse possessor is to bring proceedings for possession, or an action for a declaration as to title, as soon as possible. It may be sufficient for the paper owner to retake physical possession of the land himself, but such self-help is not always successful, and may attract the attention of the criminal law.

If the registered land is subject to the new scheme under the LRA 2002 (that is, the Act is in force and the claim arises after this date), there is no 'clock' of limitation to stop as there is no limitation period. However, it is clear that the adverse possessor must have completed a minimum of 10 years adverse possession before being able to apply to be registered as the new proprietor and so it is perfectly possible for the true owner to prevent this 10 years from accruing by taking such action as would 'stop the clock' under the traditional principles.

11.5 The effect of a successful claim of adverse possession in unregistered land and pre-LRA 2002 registered land

This section deals with the effects of a successful claim of adverse possession on land of unregistered title and as is currently the case with registered land under the LRA 1925. (The position under the new scheme of the LRA 2002 is discussed below.) In these cases, it should come as no surprise to learn that the effects of a successful claim of adverse possession vary according to the perspectives of the parties. In particular, the effect on tenants has attracted much interest in recent years.

11.5.1 Effect on the paper owner

It is settled law that, once the limitation period has run its course, both the paper owner's right to sue and their title are extinguished by operation of statute (s 17 of the Limitation Act 1980). After this date, the conventional wisdom is that no acknowledgment of the paper owner's title, written or otherwise, and no payment, or rent, or other sum, can revive the title (*Nicholson v England* (1962)). This should be uncontroversial, as it is simply the consequence of the application of the Limitation Act 1980 and an expression of its underlying policy. However, the Court of Appeal has held, in *Colchester BC v Smith* (1992), that, in some circumstances, a written acknowledgment of the paper owner's title by the squatter, given *after* the period of limitation has ended, can be enough to prevent the squatter relying on adverse possession in the face of an action for possession by the owner. This remarkable decision appears to be based on an application of the estoppel doctrine, in that the squatter is estopped from denying the paper owner's title by the written acknowledgment, freely given. Surprisingly, the court offers no convincing reason why the Limitation Act 1980 should be ignored in this fashion, or even why the paper owner deserves to benefit from an estoppel: after all, the paper owner has slept on his rights, and why should a court of equity now come running to his aid? Neither does the court consider *Nicholson v England* (1962) and, in this sense, the decision in *Smith* can be regarded as *per incuriam*. However, at present, the *Colchester* decision may be authority for the proposition that a *bona fide* compromise of a dispute between two persons (that is, paper owner and squatter), both of whom had legal advice, should be upheld on public policy grounds, even if the 12 year period of limitation has run. In other words, a man will be bound by his contract. Unfortunately, this seemingly unobjectionable principle does not, in the context of adverse possession, recognise that there is also a policy consideration – recognised and effected by Act of Parliament no less – to the effect that sleeping on one's rights deprives a person of those rights. In short, the judgment in *Smith* fails to explain why a contract between the parties can override the express provisions of an Act of Parliament. Although some commentators accept that, in principle, contracting out of the Limitation Act 1980 should be possible, it is submitted that this should not be permitted, save in the most exceptional circumstances.

11.5.2 Effect on the squatter – generally

As noted at the outset of this chapter, the traditional doctrinal position is that a successful plea of adverse possession does not transfer the paper owner's title to the squatter. It operates negatively, to prevent the paper owner from suing the squatter (or person now in possession: for example, a purchaser from the squatter) and extinguishes the title (s 17 of the Limitation Act 1980). There is no conveyance of the land from paper owner to squatter. Moreover, because the squatter is not a purchaser from (or even transferee of) the paper owner, the squatter takes the land subject to all proprietary obligations, whether these are registered or not. So, a squatter will be bound by the burden of unregistered equitable easements and unregistered restrictive covenants in both registered and unregistered land. The squatter can never be 'equity's darling' or the 'Registrar's darling', as the case may be. Yet, it is also true that a squatter does acquire something as a result of a successful adverse possession, because the squatter may go on to deal with the land as if it were his own. He may sell it, lease it, devise it (that is, by will), give it away, grant easements over it, etc. In other words, a successful adverse possessor does acquire a valuable asset. How, in practice, does this work?

In unregistered land, as noted above, the squatter does not take, and is not treated as taking, a conveyance from the paper owner. Consequently, the paper owner has a bundle of worthless title documents and the squatter has no proof of title at all. Yet, in practice, a squatter with proof of established adverse possession usually can find a willing purchaser and will convey the land by deed to that purchaser. This new deed will be the first evidence of the squatter's title and first evidence of the new purchaser's. Necessarily, of course, the squatter will not be able to make out a good 'root of title' (see Chapter 3), but the purchaser may be happy with a statutory declaration of good title, supported, perhaps, by 'title insurance', being an insurance policy, paid for by the squatter, guaranteeing compensation if the squatter's title should prove to be defective. In effect, then, a 'new' title is generated by the conveyancing process.

In registered land under the LRA 1925, the position is strikingly different. As we have seen in Chapter 2, registration as proprietor is a solid guarantee of title, and the paper owner is not deprived of that registration simply because adverse possession has run against them. However, according to s 75 of the LRA 1925, the registered proprietor (that is, paper owner) is deemed to hold his estate on trust for the adverse possessor until such time as the squatter can apply for rectification of the register and the registration of himself as proprietor. This will occur in due course (that is, on proof of adverse possession), and pending such rectification, the squatter's interest is protected as an overriding interest under s 70(1)(f) and 70(1)(g) of the LRA 1925. So, should the paper owner seek to dispose of the land prior to rectification, the purchaser from the paper owner will find himself bound by the rights of the successful adverse possessor and himself be subject to rectification. To all intents and purposes, then, the mechanics of the LRA 1925 operate to ensure that the successful adverse possessor is protected and duly becomes registered proprietor, although usually, at first, with possessory title only. Interestingly, however, the fact that s 75 of the LRA 1925 says that the paper owner holds the estate on trust for the adverse possessor suggests that the estate acquired by the adverse possessor is equivalent to the estate formerly held by the paper owner. It may be true that registration of the squatter creates a 'new' title, but the fact that this title springs from that held on trust by the former paper owner illustrates that, in registered land, it is not necessarily accurate to say that nothing has been transferred from paper owner to squatter. In effect, there does appear to be a 'parliamentary conveyance'. In the context of freehold land, this has little significance, but it becomes vital when considering leaseholds.

11.5.3 Effect on the squatter – leaseholds

The traditional doctrinal position that there is no conveyance of the paper owner's estate to the squatter has some unusual consequences in the context of leaseholds, although recent decisions have suggested changing attitudes. It will be remembered that a successful 12 years' adverse possession against a tenant extinguishes only the tenant's estate, and the landlord has a further period after the end of the original period of the lease in which to eject the squatter before he, also, loses his title. This is all well and good because, as noted above, time can only run against a person when he has a right to recover land, and a landlord only has such a right when the lease expires.

However, while it is true that the tenant has lost his estate by adverse possession vis à vis the squatter, it is also true that the tenant remains as tenant vis à vis the landlord for the entire duration of the original lease period. Once again, title is relative. So, during the lease, the landlord can bring forfeiture proceedings against the tenant for, say, non-payment of rent, even though the squatter is in possession of the land under a successful adverse possession. The effect of such forfeiture (in which the squatter has no right to apply for relief: *Tickner v Buzzacott* (1965)) is to terminate the lease and bring forward the landlord's right to eject the squatter. Note, however, that the converse of the rule, that the ejected tenant remains 'tenant' vis à vis the landlord, is that the squatter is not the tenant, nor an assignee of the tenant, so cannot be liable on any leasehold covenants save those enforceable as restrictive covenants under *Tulk v Moxhay* (1848) (which run against any occupier: see Chapters 6 and 8).

Although apparently complicated, the picture painted above is quite simple: the squatter has extinguished the tenant's title as far as the squatter is concerned, but the tenant remains the tenant of the landlord. The difficulties arise when the ejected tenant seeks to manipulate his continuing relationship with the landlord to defeat the adverse possessor. For example, we have just noted that the landlord may forfeit the lease in an action against the ejected tenant, thereby bringing forward the landlord's right of action against the squatter: the landlord does not have to wait until the lease term has expired. What, however, if the tenant surrenders his lease to the landlord, despite having 'lost' title vis à vis the squatter? Does this also terminate the lease, and bring forward the landlord's right of action?

In unregistered land, the case of *Fairweather v St Marylebone Property Co Ltd* (1963) appears to provide a clear answer. In that case, a tenant against whom adverse possession had been completed successfully surrendered the lease to the landlord, and the House of Lords held that this was equivalent to the case of forfeiture. The lease was brought to an end by a person (the ejected tenant) who still had an estate vis à vis the landlord. The squatter had no remedy against the subsequent early termination of the lease by the landlord because the squatter is not the assignee of the tenant. The squatter does not occupy under the original lease, and is not entitled to remain for its full period if that lease is lawfully terminated. Logically this is difficult to fault, although, on a common sense view, it is difficult to see why the ejected tenant should have the power to surrender a lease which, to all intents and purposes, is an empty shell. The inequity to the squatter is even more apparent if the landlord, having then evicted the squatter, regrants a new lease to the ejected tenant.

In registered land subject to the LRA 1925, that is, where the lease is substantively registered with its own title number, the position is different. In *Spectrum Investment Co v Holmes* (1981), the ejected tenant again tried to surrender the lease to the freeholder, and so cause an early termination of the squatter's rights, but the attempt was thwarted by the court. The narrow ground for the decision was that, by the time the ejected tenant attempted to surrender, she was no longer the registered proprietor of the lease, the register having been rectified in the squatter's favour and the squatter given a new title. In other words, the ejected tenant had nothing to surrender, and the squatter could enjoy the remainder of the term. Obviously, such an outcome is different from *Fairweather*, although the principle of *Fairweather* was sidestepped, rather than departed from because of the registration issue. However, the case of *Central London Commercial Estates Ltd v Kato Kagaku Ltd* has tackled the matter head on. In that case, the ejected tenant surrendered its lease to the freeholder, and the registered title to that lease was closed. The squatter had not sought rectification in time, and the freeholder sought to evict the squatter before the period of the lease had expired. However, the court held that the effect of s 75 of the LRA 1925 was to ensure that the tenant's interest was held on trust for the squatter, and that the tenant could not surrender after the period of limitation had run. In effect, the court held that the tenant's interest in the lease did pass to the squatter, and the squatter could remain on the land for the remainder of the term. In fact, Sedley J goes so far as to say that there was, in reality, a statutory conveyance of the original lease with benefits and burdens intact. This has three important consequences. First, there is now a confirmed difference between unregistered and registered land: the ejected tenant may surrender to the landlord before the lease expires in the former case, but not in the latter. Secondly, in registered land, it seems as if there is a conveyance of the tenant's interest to the squatter, along with all benefits and burdens of the lease. This is undoubtedly the sensible approach and it is confirmed obliquely by the Privy Council in *Chung v Lam* (1996), where the squatter was able to take advantage of a provision in the original lease and enforce it against the landlord. If correct, it has important consequences, and gives both landlords and squatters more rights and obligations than they might have thought (for example, under the leasehold covenants). Moreover, although this ignores traditional doctrine, it is interesting that the Privy Council, in *Chung*, refused to comment on *Fairweather*, save only to point out the 'powerful critique' by one academic commentator. This must be a hint that *Fairweather* would, today, be overruled. Thirdly, if a tenant cannot surrender before the lease expires (at least in registered land), can the landlord still forfeit the lease against that tenant? The logic of *Spectrum*, *Central* and *Chung* would suggest not, again on the simple ground that the tenant holds the lease on trust for the squatter and has ceased to have a meaningful interest. The lease has passed to the squatter. So, this might mean that the landlord must attempt to forfeit against the squatter and, if so, it must also mean that the squatter can apply for relief or avoid forfeiture by performing the covenants. Perhaps also *Tickner v Buzzacott* (1965) is now wrong.

11.6 The substantive nature of the squatter's rights prior to completing the period of limitation in unregistered land and pre-LRA 2002 registered land

Finally, it should be noted that, pending completion of the period of limitation under the unmodified rules, the adverse possessor is taken to have certain rights in the land, even though these can be completely defeated by the paper owner within the period. Thus, an adverse possessor awaiting completion of the period may transfer such rights as they do have (for example, two years' worth of possession, 10 years' worth, etc) to another person either by will or *inter vivos* (*Asher v Whitlock* (1865)). The period so transferred may then be added to any period successfully completed by the legatee/assignee of the squatter's rights in order to make up a total of 12 years' worth of adverse possession. Such part-completion of the limitation period is also protected against a purchaser of registered land from the paper owner by s 70(1)(f) of the LRA 1925, being an overriding interest. So, if S has achieved six years' adverse possession against A, and A sells the land to P, S's six years' worth of adverse possession is binding on P. Yet, although the squatter carries forward the part completion against the new paper owner, the new paper owner can bring immediate proceedings to recover the land before 12 years are completed. It should be noted, however, that under the LRA 2002, 'squatters rights' *per se* will not be overriding interests. Instead, such rights will only override the estate of a registered proprietor if the adverse possessor is in actual occupation of the land (the old s 70(1)(g) of the LRA 1925) within the meaning of Scheds 1 and 3 to the LRA 2002. Of course, most adverse possessors will meet this criterion, but it does mean that those that quit the land will effectively lose their accumulated possession in the face of a new registered proprietor.

11.7 Adverse possession and Human Rights

It is clear from the preceding analysis that the rules of adverse possession – be they in relation to unregistered land, pre-LRA 2002 registered land or under the scheme of the LRA 2002 – can result in the destruction of the title of a duly certified 'owner'. On a simple view, this might be thought to contradict a person's right to peaceful enjoyment of their property under Art 1, Protocol 1 of the European Convention on Human Rights, as enacted in to English law by the Human Rights Act 1998. Not surprisingly, this argument has been raised already and took up much of the time of the Court of Appeal in *Pye v Graham* (2001). In that case, the Court of Appeal was faced with a barrage of arguments concerning adverse possession and its relation to the right to property guaranteed by Art 1 of Protocol 1. As it turned out, the discussion was *obiter* as the court denied that any case of adverse possession was made out and hence the alleged violation of the paper owner's right of property was not in issue. However, Mummery LJ for the court gave a robust response to the human rights argument. In his view, it was clear that rules imposing a time limit on when persons could bring claims was not itself a contravention of any convention right. More importantly, the English rules on adverse possession (that is, no claims after 12 years' adverse possession) were a lawful and proportionate application of the limitation rules and so title defeated by adverse possession was not title denied in violation of Art 12 of Protocol 1. Put simply, the rules on adverse possession were consistent with human rights law on the right to property. This is convincing reasoning as the right in Art 1 of Protocol 1 is not absolute and must yield in the face of public policy, as exemplified by rules limiting legal claims. Necessarily, given that the scheme of the LRA 2002 generally makes it more difficult to 'take' a registered proprietor's land, it also must conform to the Convention and as much was certified during the passage of the Act through Parliament. Finally, we should note that the reasoning of the Court of Appeal in *Pye* (albeit *obiter*) is much more persuasive that that of the High Court in *Family Housing Association v Donellan* (2001) when considering the same issue. In *Donellan*, Park J suggests that 'adverse possession' is not contrary to Art 1 of Protocol 1 because this Article is designed to prevent State (that is, governmental) interference with property rights. It was not meant, apparently, to interfere with 'private law' issues like adverse possession, the latter being one individual 'denying' the property right of another and having nothing to do with the State. Two things only need be said about this. First, in *Pye* the Court of Appeal, decided that in substance the law of adverse possession was not contrary to human rights law. The identity of the person asserting adverse possession (State or individual) was irrelevant and the court proceeded on the basis that human rights law is relevant in 'private' law actions. Secondly, Park J's formulation revisits the argument about whether the Human Rights Act 1998 is 'vertically' effective (applicable only where a public authority is one of the parties) or 'horizontally' effective (applicable where the parties are private litigants). The answer to that question really revolves around the meaning of the Human Rights Act 1998, particularly ss 3 and 6. It is not to be found in a restrictive interpretation of the very rights themselves.

11.8 Adverse possession under the Land Registration Act 2002

As has been indicated above, when the relevant sections of the Land Registration Act 2002 enter force (which may be as early as 2003), a new scheme for dealing with claims of adverse possession of registered land will come into existence. Until that time, the 'old rules' will operate in the manner discussed in this chapter.

Under the new scheme, there will be no period of limitation and no sense in which a registered proprietor loses title merely because another person has adversely possessed the land for a fixed period of time (s 96 of the LRA 2002).

The onus shifts from the true owner to the adverse possessor. Thus, where a person claims to have completed at least 10 years' adverse possession (and this is to be assessed by the traditional rules: Sched 6, para 11 of the LRA 2002), that person may apply to the Registrar to be registered as proprietor. This application will trigger notice to the current registered proprietor (and certain other persons, Sched 6, para 2 of the LRA 2002) and, if there is objection from such person, the adverse possessor cannot be entered as new registered proprietor unless either of three exceptional grounds are established. These are where (Sched 6, para 5 of the LRA 2002):

> ... it would be unconscionable for the current proprietor to dispossess the adverse possessor because of an estoppel and the circumstances are such that the adverse possessor ought to be registered; or
>
> where the adverse possessor is 'for some other reason' entitled to be registered as proprietor; or
>
> where there is a boundary dispute concerning adjoining land and for at least 10 years the applicant reasonably believed the disputed land to be his, provided that the disputed land had been registered land for more than one year prior to the application.

However, assuming none of these grounds to be made out (and we must await litigation for their meaning to be elucidated), the 'true' registered proprietor will then have two further years following the application by the adverse possessor to recover possession of the land. If he does not so recover, then the adverse possessor may reapply at the expiry of the two year period and he will be entered as proprietor. If then registered as proprietor, the adverse possessor takes the land subject to any interests affecting the estate, except any registered charge (unless registration is because of the exceptional situations outlined above in para 5): Sched 6, para 9 of the LRA 2002.

Clearly, this new scheme will have a dramatic effect on the frequency and success of claims of adverse possession. In essence, a registered proprietor will receive notice of any application by an adverse possessor and, unless one of the three exceptional grounds is made out, will have two years to recover possession. This is the case whether the adverse possessor applies for registration after 10 years or 110 years: there is no period of limitation. So, if the adverse possessor makes no application for registration, or does so and is evicted (assuming the exceptions do not apply), the registered proprietor is safe. For sure, this will do much to encourage the voluntary registration of titles, especially by those owners of large landholdings who find it difficult to monitor the state of their land: for example, large farms, local authorities. It will effectively reduce adverse possession of registered land to a trickle unless one of the 'justice' exceptions applies. Of course, we may well see 'sympathetic' interpretations of these exceptions, so as to permit adverse possession of registered land in a wider range of circumstances than is really intended by the Act. Then again, we may not. What is clear, however, is that this scheme means the end of one of the last operative feudal elements of English land law. Possibly, we should not lament it. On the other hand, we must also ask whether the LRA 2002 scheme will do anything to encourage negligent or inefficient landowners to make the most of their precious resource called 'land'. Prior to entry into force of the LRA 2002, a landowner had to be attentive to his estate and failure to use land meant others could acquire it and use it more beneficially (see the *Lambeth LBC* cases, especially *Lambeth LBC v Ellis* (2000)). After the entry into force of the LRA 2002, a landowner with registered title can sit back and wait for the Registrar to inform him that his land is subject to another's claim and then he can evict at any time within the next two years. Then he can sink back into slumber.

ADVERSE POSSESSION

The traditional principle of adverse possession: the limitation of actions

The ability of an adverse possessor (a 'squatter' or 'trespasser') to acquire a better right to the land than the paper owner is based on the principle of limitation of actions. This means that a person (for example, the paper owner of the land) may be 'statute barred' from bringing a claim against the adverse possessor to recover possession of the land after the period of limitation has passed. In this sense, adverse possession operates negatively: it prevents an estate owner from suing on his rights and operates to extinguish his title. This will continue to govern cases in relation to unregistered land and registered land pending the entry into force of the LRA 2002.

The limitation period

In most cases, where a limited period is applicable (that is, not under the LRA 2002) that period will be 12 years from the moment of adverse possession by the claimant: s 15 of the Limitation Act 1980. If land is owned by someone for life, with remainder in fee simple to another person, the limitation period is either: adverse possession of six years from the date at which the interest in remainder falls into possession (assuming 12 years or more against the life tenant), or adverse possession of 12 years from when the life tenant was dispossessed, whichever is the longer (s 15 of the Limitation Act 1980). If the current paper owner is a tenant of the land under a lease, the period of limitation against the tenant is 12 years. The period for the landlord is also 12 years, but does not start to run until the original term of the tenancy has ended: Sched 1, para 4 of the Limitation Act 1980.

An intention to possess

In order to mount a successful claim, the adverse possessor must have an intention to possess the land adversely to the exclusion of the whole world, including the paper owner.

Physical possession, adverse to the paper owner

The claimant must take adverse possession of the land as a matter of fact, either in consequence of the 'dispossession' of the paper owner or following 'discontinuance' of possession by him.

Dispossession occurs where the paper owner is effectively driven out by another, although it is clear that the paper owner does not need to know that they have been dispossessed. Discontinuance occurs where the paper owner abandons the land, but this is not to be presumed from mere lack of use by the paper owner. The degree of physical possession required will vary with the type of land involved. There is no requirement that the adverse possession must actually inconvenience the paper owner, but possession will not be taken to be established from acts that are equivocal in nature or temporary in purpose. Following *Buckinghamshire CC v Moran* (1990), there is no presumption of a licence in favour of an adverse possessor (so destroying adverse possession) *just because* his possession is consistent with the paper owner's planned use of the land.

Stopping the clock of limitation

A successful action for possession will necessarily 'stop the clock', as will an acknowledgment of the paper owner's title in writing and the payment of rent: ss 29 and 30 of the Limitation Act 1980. Once the limitation period has expired (where applicable), both the paper owner's right to sue and his title are extinguished by operation of statute: s 17 of the Limitation Act 1980. After this date, the conventional wisdom is that no acknowledgment, written or otherwise, and no payment or rent or other sum, can revive the paper owner's title: *Nicholson v England* (1962), but see *Colchester BC v Smith* (1992). The same principles can stop the 10 year period under the LRA 2002.

The effect of a successful claim of adverse possession of unregistered land and registered land pre-LRA 2002

On the paper owner generally

Successful adverse possession prevents the paper owner suing and effectively extinguishes his title (s 17 of the Limitation Act 1980).

On the adverse possessor in unregistered land under the LRA 1925

Conventional wisdom is that a successful adverse possession does not transfer title to the claimant. The adverse possessor will not be a purchaser for value of a legal or equitable interest for the purpose of the LCA 1972 or the doctrine of notice. The claimant may sell or otherwise deal with the land because the absence of title deeds is dealt with by appropriate conveyancing devices (for example, statutory declaration, title insurance).

On the adverse possessor in registered land

The paper owner will be the registered proprietor but is deemed to hold his estate in the land on trust for the claimant until such time as the adverse possessor can apply for rectification of the register and registration as proprietor (s 75 of the LRA 1925). In the meantime, the possessor's rights will be protected as an overriding interest under s 70(1)(f) of the LRA 1925. Recent authority suggests that the effect is similar to, if not equivalent to, a transfer of title from paper owner to claimant (a statutory conveyance). Again, however, the squatter cannot be regarded as a purchaser of land for the purposes of the LRA 1925.

On the adverse possessor claiming against a tenant

In unregistered land, it seems the displaced tenant remains in a relationship with his landlord and can surrender his lease, so allowing the landlord to take early action against the claimant to evict. In registered land, recent authority suggests that the adverse possessor steps into the shoes of the tenant (s 75 of the LRA 1925; *Kato*), so allowing the claimant to remain in possession for the remainder of the tenant's full term and even to enjoy rights granted to the tenant – such as the right to extend the lease.

The substantive nature of the squatter's rights

Pending completion of the period of limitation, the adverse possessor has certain rights in the land, even though these can be completely defeated by the paper owner within the period. An adverse possessor awaiting completion of the period may transfer such rights as they do have to another person either by will or *inter vivos*. The period so transferred may then be added to any period successfully completed by the legatee/assignee in order to make 12 years' adverse possession in total.

Adverse possession under the Land Registration Act 2002

Under the new scheme, there will be no period of limitation and no sense in which a registered proprietor loses title merely because another person has adversely possessed the land for a fixed period of time (s 96 of the LRA 2002). The onus shifts from the true owner to the adverse possessor. Thus, where a person claims to have completed at least 10 years' adverse possession (and this is to be assessed by the traditional rules: Sched 6, para 11 of the LRA 2002), that person may apply to the Registrar to be registered as proprietor. This application will trigger notice to the current registered proprietor (and certain other persons, Sched 6, para 2 of the LRA 2002) and, if there is objection from such person, the adverse possessor cannot be entered as new registered proprietor unless either of three exceptional grounds are established. These are where (Sched 6, para 5 of the LRA 2002):

> ... it would be unconscionable for the current proprietor to dispossess the adverse possessor because of an estoppel and the circumstances are such that the adverse possessor ought to be registered; or

> where the adverse possessor is 'for some other reason' entitled to be registered as proprietor; or

> where there is a boundary dispute concerning adjoining land and for at least 10 years the applicant reasonably believed the disputed land to be his, provided that the disputed land had been registered land for more than one year prior to the application.

However, assuming none of these grounds to be made out (and we must await litigation for their meaning to be elucidated), the 'true' registered proprietor will then have two further years following the application by the adverse possessor to recover possession of the land. If he does not so recover, then the adverse possessor may reapply at the expiry of the two year period and he will be entered as proprietor. If then registered as proprietor, the adverse possessor takes the land subject to any interests affecting the estate, except any registered charge (unless registration is because of the exceptional situations outlined above in para 5): Sched 6, para 9 of the LRA 2002.

FURTHER READING

General Matters

Battersby, G, 'Informally created interests in land', in Bright, S and Dewar, J (eds), *Land Law: Themes and Perspectives*, 1998, Oxford: OUP

Jackson, P and Wilde, D (eds), *The Reform of Property Law*, 1997, Aldershot: Dartmouth

Dixon, M, 'Proprietary and non-proprietary rights in modern land law', in Tee, L (ed), *Essays in Land Law*, 2002, Devon: Willan

Chapter 2: Registered Land

Cooke, E, 'The Land Registration Bill' [2002] Conv 11

Law Commission, *Land Registration for the 21st Century: A Conveyancing Revolution*, Report No 271, 2001, London: HMSO

Chapter 3: Unregistered Land

Harpum, C, '*Midland Bank Trust Co Ltd v Green*' [1981] CLJ 213

Wade, HWR, '*Land charge registration revisited*' [1956] CLJ 216

Chapter 4: Co-ownership

Dixon, M, '*Midland Bank v Cooke*' [1997] Conv 67

Ferris, G and Battersby, G, 'The impact of the Trusts of Land and Appointment of Trustees Act 1996 on purchasers of registered land' [1998] Conv 168; and see the reply of Dixon, M [2000] Conv 267

Glover, N and Todd, P, 'The myth of common intention' (1996) 16 LS 325

Hopkins, N, 'The Trusts of Land and Appointment of Trustees Act 1996' [1996] Conv 411

Kenny, P, *The Trusts of Land and Appointment of Trustees Act 1996*, 1997, London: Sweet & Maxwell

Law Commission Working Paper on the Rights of Homesharers (expected June 2002)

Lawson, A, 'The things we do for love: detrimental reliance and the family home' (1996) 16 LS 218

Ross-Martyn, JG, 'Co-owners and their rights of occupation' [1996] Conv 87

Tee, L, 'Severance revisited' [1995] Conv 105

Chapter 6: Leases

Bridge, S, 'Former tenants, future liabilities and the privity of contract principle: the Landlord and Tenant (Covenants) Act 1995' [1996] 55 CLJ 313

Bridge, S, 'Landlord and tenant law', in Tee, L (ed), *Essays in Land Law,* 2002, Devon: Willan

Bridge, S, 'Putting it right: the Law Commission and the condition of tenanted property' [1996] Conv 342

Hill, J, 'Intention and the creation of proprietary rights: are leases different?' (1996) 16 LS 200

Law Commission, *Termination of Tenancies by Physical Re-entry: A Consultative Document*, 1998, London: HMSO

Smith, PF, '*Billson v Residential Apartments Ltd*' [1992] Conv 273

Sparkes, P, '*Prudential Assurance Co Ltd v London Residuary Body*' (1993) 108 LQR 93

Thornton, R, 'Enforceability of leasehold covenants: more questions than answers' (1991) 11 LS 47

Walter, P, 'The Landlord and Tenant (Covenants) Act 1995: a legislative folly' [1996] Conv 432

Bruton v London and Quadrant Housing Trust [1999] 3 WLR 150; [2000] CLJ 22

Chapter 7: The Law of Easements

Barnsley, DG, 'Equitable easements 60 years on' (1999) 115 LQR 89

Luther, P, 'Easements and exclusive possession' (1996) 16 LS 51

Tee, L, 'Metamorphoses and s 62 of the Law of Property Act 1925' [1998] Conv 115

Chapter 8: Freehold Covenants

Martin, J, 'Remedies for breach of restrictive covenants' [1996] Conv 329

Scamell, EH, *Land Covenants*, 1996, London: Butterworths

Chapter 9: Licences and Proprietary Estoppel

Battersby, G, 'Contractual and estoppel licences as proprietary interests in land' [1991] Conv 36

Battersby, G, 'Informal transactions in land: estoppel and registration' (1995) 58 MLR 637

Bright, S, 'Bright: the third party's conscience in land law' [2000] Conv 388

Baughten, S, 'Estoppels over land and third parties: an open question?' (1994) 14 LS 147

Cooke, E, 'Estoppel and the protection of expectations' (1997) 17 LS 258

Howard, M and Hill, J, 'The informal creation of interests in land' (1995) 15 LS 356

Chapter 10: The Law of Mortgages

Bamforth, N, 'Lord Macnaughten's puzzle: the mortgage of real property in English law' [1996] CLP 207

Capper, D, 'Undue influence and unconscionability' (1998) 114 LQR 479

Dixon, M, 'Combating the mortgagee's right to possession: new hope for the mortgagor in chains?' (1998) 18 LS 279

Dixon, M and Harpum, C, 'Fraud, undue influence and mortgages of registered land' [1994] Conv 421

Haley, M, 'Mortgage default: possession, relief and judicial discretion' (1997) 16 LS 483

Law Commission, *Land Mortgages*, Report No 204, 1991, London: HMSO

Roplaigeach v Barclays Bank [1999] 3 WLR 17; [1999] CLJ 281

Chapter 11: Adverse Possession

Cooke, E, 'Adverse possession, problems of title in registered land' (1994) 14 LS 1

Dockray, M, 'Why do we need adverse possession?' [1985] Conv 272

Harpum, C, *'Buckinghamshire County Council v Moran'* [1990] CLJ 23

Tee, L, 'Adverse possession and the intention to possess' [2000] Conv 113

Harpum, C and Radley-Gardner, O, 'Adverse possession and the intention to possess – a reply' [2001] Conv 155

See reforming provisions of the Land Registration Act 2002

Human rights and Property Law

Howell, J, 'The Human Rights Act 1998', in Cooke, E (ed), *Modern Studies in Property Law*, 2001, London: Hart

Halstead, P, 'Human property rights' [2002] Conv 153

INDEX